Free and open source software and technology for sustainable development

Free and open source software and technology for sustainable development

Edited by Sulayman K. Sowe, Govindan Parayil and Atsushi Sunami

United Nations University Press

TOKYO · NEW YORK · PARIS

© United Nations University, 2012

The views expressed in this publication are those of the authors and do not necessarily reflect the views of the United Nations University.

United Nations University Press
United Nations University, 53-70, Jingumae 5-chome,
Shibuya-ku, Tokyo 150-8925, Japan
Tel: +81-3-5467-1212   Fax: +81-3-3406-7345
E-mail: sales@unu.edu   General enquiries: press@unu.edu
http://www.unu.edu

United Nations University Office at the United Nations, New York
2 United Nations Plaza, Room DC2-2062, New York, NY 10017, USA
Tel: +1-212-963-6387   Fax: +1-212-371-9454
E-mail: unuony@unu.edu

United Nations University Press is the publishing division of the United Nations University.

Cover design by Ian Youngs

Printed in the United States of America for the Americas and Asia
Printed in the United Kingdom for Europe, Africa and the Middle East

ISBN 978-92-808-1217-6
e-ISBN 978-92-808-7186-9

Library of Congress Cataloging-in-Publication Data

Free and open source software and technology for sustainable development /
edited by Sulayman K. Sowe, Govindan Parayil and Atsushi Sunami.
    p. cm.
 Includes bibliographical references and index.
 ISBN 978-9280812176 (pbk.)
  1. Information technology—Economic aspects—Developing countries. 2. Open source software—Developing countries. 3. Sustainable development—
Developing countries. 4. Economic development—Developing countries.
I. Sowe, Sulayman K. II. Parayil, Govindan, 1955- III. Sunami, Atsushi, 1965–
HC59.72.I55F74   2012
338.9'2702855—dc23   2012024270

Contents

List of figures and tables viii

Contributors xi

Abbreviations xxii

Acknowledgements xxv

Introduction 1
    Sulayman K. Sowe, Govindan Parayil and Atsushi Sunami

Part I: FOSS research, theory, technology adoption and practice .. 5

1 Making sustainable open source software infrastructures by federating and learning in the global context 7
    Gianluca Miscione

2 Innovative tools for sustainable agriculture in developing countries: The impact of open source biotechnology 24
    Ademola A. Adenle and Obijiofor Aginam

3 FOSS as a driver: Perspectives from the ICT development agenda 48
    Tomonari Takeuchi

4 A participatory service learning process for FOSS-based
  solidarity projects 74
  *David Franquesa, David López, Leandro Navarro and
  Fermín Sánchez*

5 Open source software migration: Capturing best practices
  using process reference models 96
  Onkgopotse Molefe and Thomas Fogwill

6 Exploring FOSS opportunities in natural hazard risk
  assessment and disaster management 122
  Coley Zephenia

7 Open source software adoption best practices: Myths,
  realities, processes and economic growth 141
  Carlo Daffara

8 Language data as a foundation for developing countries:
  The ANLoc 100 African Locales Initiative 164
  Martin Benjamin

**Part II: FOSS case studies, surveys, policy development and
experience reports** 183

9 The open source ecosystem in Tunisia: An empirical study 185
  Imed Hammouda

10 Adoption and diffusion patterns of FOSS in Jamaican SMEs:
   A study of perceptions, attitudes and barriers 212
   Maurice McNaughton, Sheryl Thompson and Evan W. Duggan

11 Development NGOs as potential groups for expansion of
   FOSS: The case of Iran 243
   *Saeid Nouri Neshat, Parvin Pakzadmanesh, Mehdi Almasi
   and Mohammad Amin Ameri*

12 Improving public healthcare systems in developing countries
   using FOSS: The EHAS Foundation case 262
   *Carlos Rey-Moreno, Inés Bebea-González, Ignacio Prieto-
   Egido, Seth Cochran, Ignacio Foche-Pérez, Jose García-
   Múñoz, Andrés Martínez-Fernández and Javier
   Simó-Reigadas*

13 FOSS in school communities: An experience report from Peace Corps volunteers in Ghana 286
Caroline Hardin

Part III: Conclusion 313

14 Conclusion 315
Sulayman K. Sowe

Glossary of terms 321

Index 325

List of figures and tables

Figures

3.1	Gap between FOSS rationale and reality	53
3.2	Current FOSS advocacy	57
3.3	Extent of influence of FOSS advocacy	58
3.4	FOSS-enabled new development paradigm	59
3.5	Sustainable FOSS4D model	69
5.1	Approach to project Vula	106
5.2	High-level process model diagram	109
5.3	Generic process models	114
6.1	Natural disaster hotspots and vulnerable countries	124
6.2	Disaster management life cycle	128
6.3	Disaster management components	129
8.1	Sample of required data in Amharic locale, using Afrigen software	166
8.2	Some of the 294 locales configured for Afrigen users to complete	171
8.3	Kenyan languages completed by the University of Nairobi	175
9.1	Familiarity with the concept of FOSS	192
9.2	Stakeholders in the Tunisian FOSS ecosystem	193
9.3	An empirical FOSS adoption model in Tunisian software industry	196
9.4	Role of company participation in FOSS	198
9.5	Type of company participation in FOSS	199

9.6	Central management for software purchase and licences ...	199
9.7	Consequences of using FOSS in an organization	200
9.8	FOSS business models in Tunisian companies.............	201
9.9	Inhibiting factors for FOSS adoption	202
10.1	MSME landscape in Jamaica	218
10.2	Research phases using design science research methodology...	221
10.3	Sample characteristics	224
10.4	Use of ICT and the internet	226
10.5	Business applications and key influences	227
10.6	Main determinants of ICT adoption	228
10.7	Awareness and perceptions of FOSS	229
10.8	Hosted information system service option...............	230
10.9	SME FOSS business solutions	233
11.1	Fields of respondent NGOs' activities	251
11.2	Knowledge of respondents about FOSS..................	252
11.3	Preference for Firefox over Internet Explorer	252
11.4	Percentage use of FOSS	254
11.5	FOSS applications for NGOs...........................	255
11.6	Advantages of FOSS for NGOs	256
11.7	NGOs' willingness to attend a FOSS training workshop....	256
12.1	Health post in a rural area of Peru.....................	264
12.2	Health centre in a rural area of Peru	264
12.3	EHAS model for sustainable improvement of public healthcare services....................................	269
12.4	EHAS VHF station	271
12.5	EHAS WiFi router	273
12.6	Management framework for operation and maintenance of rural e-healthcare	275
12.7	Workflow for incident escalation in management framework	276
12.8	EHAS tele-stethoscope................................	277
13.1	How much do you like Ubuntu, Microsoft Windows?	301
13.2	How much do you like OpenOffice, Microsoft Office?	305
13.3	How much do you like Mavis, Tux?	306

Tables

3.1	General merits of FOSS	52
4.1	Assessment of TxT projects according to real access/real impact framework	91
5.1	Steps	108
5.2	High-level processes: Input and output resources and goals..	110

5.3	Extraction of process reference models from the high-level processes	116
6.1	Sample comparison of per capita GDP and Windows XP licence fees	137
7.1	Fixed and mobile subscribers per head of population	144
7.2	Positive variables	145
7.3	Negative variables	145
7.4	Ecosystem revenues compared with Microsoft revenues by partner type	149
9.1	Open source action plan for Tunisia	207
10.1	Design science research guidelines – Activity mapping	220
10.2	Summary of ICT artefacts to support SME FOSS business implementation	235
10.3	Sample of SME business case studies	236
11.1	Six reasons for not using Linux operating system among NGOs in Iran	253

Contributors

Ademola A. Adenle holds an MSc and PhD in genetics and molecular toxicology from the University of Sussex and University of Nottingham, UK, respectively. He has published in *Toxicology Journal* and won the best student prize in 2008 for his PhD research presentation at the British Toxicology Society's Annual Congress. He wrote a paper on space flight which attracted interest from UK and US media. His current research at the United Nations University Institute of Advanced Studies is based on the role of biotechnology in sustainable agriculture and climate change mitigation in developing countries, and he coordinates the project in five African countries (Ghana, Nigeria, South Africa, Swaziland and Kenya). He is also a visiting scholar at the National Graduate Institute for Policy Studies, Tokyo, Japan.

Obijiofor Aginam was educated in Nigeria and Canada. He holds a bachelor of law *magna cum laude* from the University of Nigeria, a master of law from Queen's University, Kingston, Canada, and a PhD from the University of British Columbia, Canada. Before joining United Nations University he held a tenured academic position as associate professor of law at Carleton University, Ottawa, Canada, where he taught and researched emerging global issues that cut across globalization, global governance of health and environmental issues, South-North relations, international organizations and third world approaches to international law.

Mehdi Almasi is the manager of an active environmental NGO, Boompajuhan Society, involved in training and capacity building in Iran; he is also a PhD student in environmental management at the

University of Malaya. Between 2004 and 2010 he acted as coordinator, project manager and volunteer in different programmes at local level in Iran to conserve endangered species within the framework of GEF/SGP/UNDP, Malaysian Department of Environment, the Conservation of Asiatic Cheetah Project and Siberian Carne Wetland Project. He has contributed to various publications: *Game Guard Guide*, *Experiences from Community-based Activities to Protect Environment and Natural Resources*, *Lessons Learnt: Community Empowerment and Awareness Raising for Conservation of Asiatic Cheetah in Touran Biosphere Reserve* and *Trainers' Manual for Conservation of Asiatic Cheetah*.

Mohammad Amin Ameri gained his first degree in electrical and computer engineering in Iran in 2004, and his MSc in business IT from Manchester Business School in 2007. He worked for two years as a software developer and information system manager in the United Kingdom, and cooperated with charity projects in Sri Lanka, United Arab Emirates and Cameroon. He also has experience as a teacher assistant in computer education. Amin is currently studying for a master's in technology of environmental management at the University of Malaya; he is interested in environmental management systems, waste minimization, solid waste management and wastewater treatment.

Inés Bebea-González received a postgraduate degree in telecommunication networks for developing countries from Universidad Rey Juan Carlos (2010) and her master's in telecommunication engineering from Carlos III University (2008), including a research period at Heinz Nixdorf Institute (Germany). In 2004 she volunteered for non-profit organizations such as Engineers without Borders, and in 2007 joined the UN Volunteers UNITeS Programme for fighting the digital divide under the Millennium Development Goals in Cape Verde. In 2008 she worked as a design and optimization engineer for Ericsson Network & Services in urban/rural cellular networks, and for Intecdom in domotics. She is currently project coordinator at EHAS Foundation managing e-health projects in rural areas of Peru and Ecuador, and is an Ashoka Chair of Research on Entrepreneurship on ICT4D member. Her research interests focus on sustainability and impact assessment in ICT4D. She presented "Management Framework for Sustainable Rural E-Healthcare Provision" at the IADIS International Conference e-Society 2011.

Martin Benjamin is founder and executive director of the Kamusi Project, an NGO based jointly in the United States and Switzerland that is dedicated to producing free dictionary and terminology resources for African languages. He received his PhD in anthropology from Yale University in 2000, with a research focus on poverty, health and development in Tanzania. After teaching Swahili and anthropology at university level, in 2007 he turned full time to developing learning and information technology resources for African languages. He is the editor of the *Internet Living Swahili Dictionary*, which is used around the world more than a million times a month, and author of the popular *Lonely Planet Swahili Phrasebook* and an unpublished dissertation, "Development Consumers: An Ethnography of the 'Poorest of the Poor' and International Aid in Rural Tanzania". He currently lives in Lausanne, Switzerland.

Seth Cochran is a social entrepreneur with extensive experience developing new business and social cause initiatives in private sector and non-profit environments spanning the globe. He started several health service delivery organizations, including OperationOF, for which he was named an Ashoka Young Champion of Maternal Health. Cochran has bachelor's and master's degrees in operations research from the College of Engineering at Cornell University, where he currently serves on the board of the Engineering Alumni Association. He also holds a joint degree in financial engineering from the S.C. Johnson Graduate School of Management at Cornell. Seth is originally from Texas, and currently resides in London.

Carlo Daffara is head of research and development at Conecta Research, a consulting firm specializing in open source systems. He is the Italian representative at the European Working Group on Libre Software, the first EU initiative in support of open source and free software, and chairs the SME working group of the EU Task Force on Competitiveness and the IEEE open source middleware working group of the Technical Committee on Scalable Computing. He is on the editorial review board of the *International Journal of Open Source Software & Processes*, and is a member of the FSFE European Legal Network and two regional open source competence centres. He worked as part of SC34 and JTC1 committees in the Italian branch of ISO, UNINFO, and participated in the Internet Society Public Software working group and many other standardization-related initiatives. Since 1998 he has acted as a project reviewer for the European Commission in the field of international collaboration and open source software.

Evan W. Duggan is executive director and professor of MIS at Mona School of Business, University of the West Indies (UWI). He obtained PhD and MBA degrees from Georgia State University with majors in decision sciences and computer information systems, and a BSc from the UWI, Mona. He has several years of industrial experience, has published in IS and allied journals, edited books and major conference proceedings and is co-editor of the book *Measuring Information Systems Delivery Quality*. Professor Duggan is a section editor for *African Journal of Information Systems*, associate editor of *Communications of the Association for Information Systems* and on the editorial boards of several international journals, scholarly publishers and book series.

He has taught MIS and decision sciences courses in several US institutions and at the UWI.

Thomas Fogwill is a research group leader at the CSIR Meraka Institute, focusing on R&D in next-generation software and mobile systems. Thomas has many years of experience in the software industry, primarily in leading the development of complex software systems. His research interests include computational logic, description logics and semantic web technologies, software engineering, next-generation mobile systems and future internet. He is also a keen advocate and user of open source software and led the technology track of the CSIR's Vula OSS migration project.

David Franquesa graduated from Barcelona in 1979, received an MSc from the Universitat Politècnica de Catalunya (UPC) in 2006 and is a doctoral candidate in the UPC programme in technology, humanism and sustainability at the UNESCO Chair on Sustainability. His thesis deals with the use of business intelligence technologies for adaptive management of organizations to a sustainability model. Other topics of interest are ICT4D and service learning, on which he has published 12 papers in the last two years. He is secretary and founder of the association TxT, where for eight years he has conducted and supervised projects in Guatemala, Peru, Morocco and Bolivia.

Jose García-Muñoz obtained bachelor's and master's degrees in computer science at Oviedo University in 2001 and 2005 respectively. In the last four years he has worked in international cooperation project management with a technological focus on water supply and ICT for development with the NGO Engineers without Borders. He has finished his master's studies at Rey Juan Carlos University (Madrid) on telecommunication networks to rural areas for developing countries. At the same time he is working as a researcher with Rey Juan Carlos University and EHAS Foundation on issues related to medical databases and electronic medical records for health facilities in developing countries.

Imed Hammouda is currently an adjunct professor at Tampere University of Technology (TUT), Finland, where he heads the international masters programme in the Department of Software Systems. He got his PhD in software engineering from TUT in 2005. Dr Hammouda's research interests include open source software, community-driven software development and software architecture. He is leading the TUTOpen research group on open source software, and has been the principal investigator in several research projects related to open initiatives. He is the author of more than 40 scientific works. In addition to his academic career he has worked as a software development manager at Suvisoft Oy, a Finnish service provider specializing in online event management solutions.

Caroline Hardin earned her BSc in computer science at the University of Wisconsin – Madison. She served as a Peace Corps volunteer in Ghana (2007–2010), where she taught and administered high school, college and library computer labs. She was distinguished as a volunteer trainer, nominated for the Ghana Education Service "Best Teacher" awards and invited to speak at many conferences, including the 2010 FOSSFA FOSS Day and the 2010 TEDx Ghana conference. She also served as the coordinator of the Peace Corps Ghana ICT Think-Tank, which organizes FOSS in development projects. She now lives in Madison, Wisconsin, where she is the educational technology coordinator at Sector67 Center for Prototyping, Technology, and Advanced Manufacturing, and the IT committee chair for Grassroots Leadership College. Caroline publishes and researches in FOSS educational resources and community organizing tools.

David López graduated from Barcelona in 1967 and holds an MSc (1991) and a PhD (1998) from the Universitat Politècnica de Catalunya, both in computer science. He also received an MA in Asian studies, majoring in East Asia arts and societies (Universitat Oberta de Catalunya, 2008). His research interest covers the areas of computer architecture and the relationship of sustainability, education and ethics with computing and services, having published about 30 papers on this topic in the last five years. Since 1991 he has been lecturing on computer organization, storage, input/output devices and operating systems. Since 2001 he has been associate professor of the Computer Architecture Department at UPC-BarcelonaTech, teaching at the Barcelona School of Infomatics. Dr López is editor of *ReVisión Magazine* and one of the founders of the TxT organization, where he advises several cooperation projects.

Andrés Martínez-Fernández is a professor of signal theory and communications and former coordinator of the masters in telecommunication networks for developing countries at Universidad Rey Juan Carlos, Spain. He holds a PhD in telecommunications engineering from the Polytechnic University of Madrid (Spain), and has extensive experience in the field of information technology and communications in isolated areas of developing countries. He has participated in numerous research projects, most related to rural telemedicine, worked on projects and consultancies for various institutions and published several scientific papers included in the Science Citation Index and several books. He is a director at EHAS Foundation and held an Ashoka Fellowship in 2009.

Maurice McNaughton is director of the Centre of Excellence for IT Innovation at the Mona School of Business, University of the West Indies (UWI). He obtained a PhD from Georgia State University with a focus on decision sciences, and gained BSc and MSc degrees in engineering at the UWI and the Phillips International Institute of Technology in Eindhoven, Netherlands, respectively. Dr McNaughton has over 15 years' senior management and leadership experience in the planning and direction of enterprise-level information technology in organizations. His current research agenda emphasizes the use of ICTs to enable business innovation in the small/medium enterprise sector in Jamaica, and includes applications of free and open source software, cloud computing and open data initiatives. He teaches graduate-level courses in software engineering, software economics and IT governance in the MIS and MBA programmes at the UWI.

Gianluca Miscione is at University College Dublin Business School, having previously worked at its Department of Urban and Regional Planning and Geo-Information Management as assistant professor of geo-information and organization. After gaining his PhD from the Sociology Department of the University of Trento, with research on information technologies and healthcare organizations in the Amazon, he joined the Department of Informatics of the University of Oslo, where he developed his research on information infrastructures on a broader scale. He has conducted and contributed to research in Latin America, Europe, India and East Africa and on the internet, with a focus on the interplay between technologies and organizing processes. His works are published on several peer-reviewed journals and books on information science and management.

Onkgopotse Molefe is a researcher at CSIR Meraka, pursuing a path in business processes and business analysis. In 2009 she gained an MTech degree in information technology from the University of South Africa, with a dissertation focusing on open source software and process reference models – she has written five publications in these areas. She also holds a BTech degree in information technology acquired in 2006 at Tshwane University of Technology, where she specialized in software development. Onkgopotse has worked for organizations such as the UN Development Programme, and was a network administrator at South African Rail Commuter Corporation (now Passenger Rail Agency of South Africa) before moving to CSIR in 2006.

Leandro Navarro joined the Computer Architecture Department of the Universitat Politècnica de Catalunya as an associate professor in 1988, after receiving his degree in telecommunication engineering from UPC. He received his PhD from UPC in 1992. Leandro's research interests include the design of scalable and cooperative internet services and applications. He is a member of the Association for Computing Machinery (SIGOPS, SIGCOMM), Association for Progressive Communications (council member), International Federation of Information Processing (TC6-WG6.4 member), Centre de Cooperació per al Desenvolupament-UPC (council member) and Institute for Electrical and Electronic Engineers (Computer Society). He was a founding member of Pangea, an NGO providing internet services to not-for-profit organizations and social movements, and founding member of two spin-off companies, Espais Telemàtics and Rededia. He has many publications in conferences and journals and has been author of the national report on Spain for the Global Information Society Watch since 2007.

Saeid Nouri Neshat is a PhD candidate at the Faculty of Economics and Administration, University of Malaya, and has a master's degree in public law. He has been active in the NGO community in Iran for years as a fundraiser, planner, activist, workshop trainer and facilitator, and has contributed to, translated and edited various books. His major contribution is a three-volume training manual on human rights for all in Persian: *Human Rights Education*. He has also edited a book on community work based on his experience: *Action Research and Planning for Conservation of Environment and Natural Resources*. He is very interested in sustainable development and empowerment approaches and patterns at local level.

Parvin Pakzadmanesh is a PhD student in social anthropology at the University of Malaya Faculty of Art and Social Sciences gender studies programme. She received a master's in social welfare management at the University of Social Welfare and Rehabilitation Sciences and a bachelor degree in psychology at Shahid Beheshti University, Tehran. Her main field of study and work is women's empowerment through community-based practices in rural areas. As a trainer in workshops and facilitator in community-based projects, she has experience and knowledge in helping people to shape self-help groups and do teamwork. During her activities in the last five years she has worked on empowering many NGOs and local groups. She has also written books and booklets on community-based initiatives in cooperation with Saeid Nouri Neshat and Mehdi Almasi.

Govindan Parayil, an Indian national, joined the United Nations University as vice-rector in August 2008 and became director of the UNU Institute of Advanced Studies in January 2009; he currently serves in both posts. Prior to joining UNU he had served as full professor at the Centre for Technology, Innovation and Culture, University of Oslo (Norway) since 2004, where his research focus was on science, technology, innovation and sustainability. He served concurrently as director of research and leader of the Innovation Group for two years. Prior to that he was head of the Information and Communications Management Programme and member of the Faculty of Arts & Social Sciences at the National University of Singapore (2001–2004), and on the faculty of the Division of Social Sciences of the Hong Kong University of Science and Technology (1994–2001). His previous academic affiliations include Cornell University, Illinois Institute of Technology and Rensselaer Polytechnic Institute (USA), and the University of Sulaimaniyah (Iraq).

Professor Parayil holds a BSc degree (electrical engineering) from the University of Calicut (India), an MSc (science, technology and values) from Rensselaer Polytechnic Institute, an MA (development economics) from American University (USA) and a PhD in science and technology studies from Virginia Polytechnic Institute and State University (USA). He authored *Conceptualizing Technological Change* (1999), edited *Kerala: The Development Experience* (2000) and *Political Economy and Information Capitalism in India* (2006) and has written numerous book chapters and articles in international journals. His latest book (co-edited with A. P. D'Costa) on *The New Asian Innovation Dynamics: China and India in Perspective* was published in 2009. He is active in research and advocacy work in science, technology and innovation for sustainable societies.

Ignacio Foche Pérez is a researcher in the Signal Theory and Communications Department at Universidad Rey Juan Carlos (Madrid). He studied telematics at Universidad Carlos III (Madrid). He joined the EHAS Foundation IT team in 2007, where he worked as system administrator and telemedicine services in charge for three years. In 2010 he gained an MSc in telecommunication networks for developing countries at Universidad Rey Juan Carlos, with a thesis on the development by the EHAS-Fundatel team of the tele-stethoscope software described in this book. He works in the areas of telemedicine, embedded systems and energy-saving systems for wireless networks.

Ignacio Prieto-Egido received his degree in telecommunication engineering at Carlos III University in Madrid. He worked for Albentia Systems as a field applications engineer and later participated in the UNV University Volunteers Programme providing ICT support and working on capacity building for UNV and FAO representations in Cambodia. He is now a researcher at ICAM, Castilla-La Mancha University, studying the impact of climate change on Spanish crops. He also collaborates with EHAS Foundation researching applications of broadband wireless technologies to connect rural and remote areas of developing countries.

Carlos Rey-Moreno is a telecommunications engineer graduate of the Universidad Carlos III, Madrid, and gained a master's in development cooperation and international relations at the University of Aalborg (Denmark) and a master's in telecommunications networks for developing countries at Universidad Rey Juan Carlos (Spain). He has been a member of EHAS Foundation since 2007, carrying out research and innovation work in the field of broadband wireless infrastructure to connect rural and remote areas of developing countries – he participated in the deployment of networks the foundation has implemented in Peru and Malawi. Currently he is employed by the Department of Signal Theory and Communications at the Universidad Rey Juan Carlos, and is part of the ICT Group for Human Development, within which he is conducting his doctoral thesis.

Fermín Sánchez received a degree in industrial electronics from the E. A. SEAT in 1981, and a degree in computer science (1987) and a PhD in computer science (1996) from the Universitat Politècnica de Catalunya. His current research is focused on new multithreaded VLIW (very long instruction word) architectures and the development and introduction of new educational strategies for adapting Spanish university studies to the European Higher Education Area. He was an associate professor in the UPC Computer Architecture Department from 1997, and member of the teaching staff since 1987. He became a consultant at the Universitat Oberta de Catalunya in 1997. Dr Sánchez has been coordinator in the Barcelona Supercomputing Center of the European mobility programme HPC-Europa since 2004. He has held the position of vice-dean of innovation at the Facultat d'Informàtica de Barcelona since 2007, and has several research publications.

Javier Simó-Reigadas is professor at the Department of Signal Theory and Communications and current coordinator of the masters in telecommunication networks for developing countries and the masters in networks and mobile communication services at the Universidad Rey Juan Carlos, Spain. He has a PhD in telecommunications from the Polytechnic University of Madrid. His research interests include wireless networks, applied broadband to rural areas of developing countries, support for quality of service in mesh networks and optimization of protocols in WiFi and WiMax networks. He is technical director at EHAS Foundation, has participated in various R&D projects and is a reviewer for several publications.

Sulayman K. Sowe is a Japan Society for the Promotion of Science research fellow at the United Nations University Institute of Advanced Studies in Yokohama, Japan, and a visiting scholar at the National Graduate Institute for Policy Studies, Tokyo, Japan. He holds a PhD, MSc and advanced diploma in computer science, BEd in science education and a higher teachers' certificate. He has worked as a senior researcher at the UNU Maastricht Economic and Social Research institute on Innovation and Technology, Netherlands; as a research fellow with the Software Engineering Group, PLaSE Lab in Greece; as a teacher, head of science department and an administrator with the Ministry of Education in Gambia; as an assistant registrar and system administrator for the West African Examinations Council; and as a database manager for the Medical Research Council in Gambia. He has extensive teaching experience in computer science, software engineering and information systems in Europe, Asia and Africa. His research interests include free and open source software development, knowledge management and sharing, information systems evaluation, human-computer interaction, social and collaborative networks, software engineering education, the digital divide and ICT for sustainable development. He has published in various scientific journals, conferences, book chapters and international workshops, and is a co-editor of *Emerging Free and Open Source Software Practices* (IGI Global, 2008).

Atsushi Sunami holds a BSFS from Georgetown University, and obtained an MIA and PhD in political science from Columbia University. From 2001 to 2003 he was a fellow at the Research Institute of Economy, Trade and Industry established by the Ministry of Economy, Trade and Industry, Japan. He worked as a researcher in the Department of Policy Research at Nomura Research Institute from 1989 to 1991, and was a visiting researcher at the Science Policy Research Unit, University of Sussex, UK, and Tsinghua University, China. Atsushi Sunami is currently an associate professor at the National Graduate Institute for Policy Studies, Japan; he is also an affiliated fellow of the National Institute of Science and Technology Policy, deputy director of the China Research Center, Japan Science and Technology Agency, and affiliated professor at the United Nations University. His current research concentrates on a comparative analysis of national innovation systems and an evolutionary approach in science and technology policy and public policy analysis in general.

Tomonari Takeuchi is an information and communication technology for development (ICT4D) advocate with a strong interest in ICT for education, ICT-related social business, social media and free/open source software. He began working in the international development field as a voluntary computer teacher in Ethiopia in 2003. After teaching in rural high schools for two years, he worked as a consultant for grant assistance for grassroots projects at the Japanese embassy in Ethiopia. In 2007 he gained an MSc in ICT for development at the University of Manchester, UK, with a thesis on ICT for education projects in Ethiopia. After graduation he joined the Japan International Cooperation Agency (JICA). He is currently engaged in ICT4D projects as assistant director of the Planning and Coordination Division and Transportation and ICT Division, JICA Economic Infrastructure Department.

Sheryl Thompson received her PhD from Lancaster University in 2007; prior to this she worked as an IT professional in Jamaica. Currently she is a lecturer at the University of the West Indies Western Jamaica Campus, where she is the programme coordinator for the BSc (management information systems) degree programme. Her work has been disseminated via book chapters, journals and premier information systems conferences.

Coley Zephenia is an established solutions consultant with over eight years' diverse experience in the IT, financial and other industry sectors. He has been involved in the development of value-adding IT systems and business solutions for different clients and organizations, working in information management, project management, enterprise architecture, business analysis, computer networking, IT training and research. Coley has worked with and is a member of a number of international NGOs, including the International Council for Science Regional Office for Africa (Young Scientist), Young Earth Scientists, Centre for Community Networks and Research, International Development Informatics Association and FOSSFA.

Abbreviations

ABET	Accreditation Board for Engineering and Technology
ANLoc	African Network for Localization
BOP	base of the pyramid
Cambia	Centre for the Application of Molecular Biology to International Agriculture
CBD	Convention on Biological Diversity
CBSE	component-based software engineering
CCD	Cooperation for Development Centre (Spain)
CEO	chief executive officer
CGIAR	Consultative Group on International Agricultural Research
CLDR	Common Locales Data Repository
COSPA	Consortium for Open Source Software in the Public Administration
CRM	customer relationship management
CSIR	Council for Scientific and Industrial Research (South Africa)
CSR	corporate social responsibility
DFSA	Digital & Free Software Association (Tunisia)
DM	disaster management
DMIS	disaster management information system
EHAS	Enlace Hispano Americano de Salud – Hispano American Health Link
ERP	enterprise resource planning
EST	expressed sequence tag
EU	European Union
FOSS	free and open source software
FOSS4D	free and open source software for development
FOSSFA	Free Software and Open Source Foundation for Africa

FSF	Free Software Foundation
GDP	gross domestic product
GES	Ghana Education Service
GIS	geographic information system
GM	genetically modified
GPL	General Public License
GPLPG	General Public License for Plant Germplasm
GTZ	Deutsche Gesellschaft für Technische Zusammenarbeit
GURT	genetic use restriction technology
HC	health centre
HF	high frequency
HIS	health information system
HP	health post
ICSU	International Council for Science
ICT	information and communication technologies
ICT4D	information and communication technologies for development
IDRC	International Development Research Centre
IFOSUC	Iran Free/Open Source Software Users Community
IICD	International Institute for Communication and Development
IOSN	International Open Source Network
IP	intellectual property
IPR	intellectual property rights
IT	information technology
L10n	localization
LTSP	Linux Terminal Service Project
MDG	Millennium Development Goal
MIS	management information system
mSMEs	micro, small and medium-sized enterprises
MTCE	Mampong Technical College of Education (Ghana)
NASS	Nalerigu Senior Secondary School (Ghana)
NGO	non-governmental organization
NMS	network management system
ODF	Open Document Format
OpenUP	Open Unified Process
OS	operating system
OSI	Open Source Initiative
OSS	open source software
PCV	Peace Corps volunteer
PHI	Programme on Health Information
PIPRA	Public Intellectual Property Resource for Agriculture
PRM	process reference model
QSOS	Qualification and Selection of Open Source
R&D	research and development
RUP	Rational Unified Process
SBAJ	Small Business Association of Jamaica
Sida	Swedish International Development Cooperation

SL	service learning
SMEs	small and medium-sized enterprises
TAM	technology acceptance model
TCO	total cost of ownership
T-GURT	trait-specific genetic use restriction technology
TRIPS	Agreement on Trade-Related Aspects of Intellectual Property Rights
TxT	Technology for Everyone
UN	United Nations
UNCTAD	UN Conference on Trade and Development
UNDP	UN Development Programme
UNICEF	UN Children's Fund
UPOV	International Union for the Protection of New Varieties of Plants
UTAUT	unified theory of acceptance and use of technology
V-GURT	variety-level genetic use restriction technology
VHF	very high frequency
VoIP	voice over IP
WHO	World Health Organization
WiLD	WiFi over long distances
WTO	World Trade Organization

Acknowledgements

This book is a partial fulfilment of my postdoctoral FOSSINA research fellowship. I wish to extend special thanks to the Japan Society for the Promotion of Science for awarding me the unique opportunity to pursue this fellowship with my host institution, the National Graduate Institute for Policy Studies (GRIPS) in Tokyo, and the United Nations University Institute of Advanced Studies (UNU-IAS) in Yokohama, Japan, which coordinated, supported and supervised my research.

I wish to extend warm gratitude to my fellow researchers and the entire staff at UNU-IAS. They have been my family and offered moral and academic support during my tenure. I am indebted to my research team colleagues at the Science and Technology for Sustainable Societies unit of UNU-IAS for providing a conducive and enabling environment to support my research and this book project.

The book would not have been possible without the dedication, fortitude and expert advice of the UNU vice-rector and director of UNU-IAS, Professor Govindan Parayil, who is both a co-editor of the book and my adviser. Professor Atsushi Sunami of GRIPS, also a co-editor of this book and my host researcher, has been inspirational. His guidance and encouragement and that of the GRIPS staff helped me simplify my research life in Japan.

The editors would sincerely like to acknowledge the unflinching support of all the individuals involved in the book's compilation and review process. Without their support this project would not have been satisfactorily completed. Thanks go to the manuscript reviewers for their constructive and comprehensive comments, which helped us improve the quality of some of the chapters. Special thanks also go to all the staff at UNU Press, whose contribution throughout the editorial process has been invaluable.

Our thanks go to the software and technology developers and users, researchers, policy-makers, ICT4D experts and all participants, including the authors, in the technology for sustainable development debate for highlighting the development flux in developing countries and at the same time proposing the way forward.

Last but not least, I would not have had the peace of mind to accomplish this research project without the dedicated support of my family and relatives. They continue to give me all the love, support and hope I need away from home – in particular Yasmin Thies, Mame Yacine Sowe, Awa Ba and Amadou Sowe, and all my relatives at home and abroad, too numerous to list here, but certainly not forgotten.

Sulayman K. Sowe
UNU-IAS, Yokohama, Japan
March 2012

Introduction

Sulayman K. Sowe, Govindan Parayil and Atsushi Sunami

In formulating a global agenda for change and reflection to bring about a fair and sustainable world, the 1987 Brundtland Report broadly defined sustainable development as "development that meets the needs of the present without compromising the ability of future generations to meet their own needs" (World Commission on Environment and Development, 1987). Since then, documents such as the UN Agenda 21 have complemented the key concepts contained in this definition. Chapter 23 of the agenda stressed that one of the fundamental prerequisites for achieving sustainable development is broad public participation in decision-making. There is an urgency to understand and act to ensure that the essential (technological) needs of the world are prioritized and being met – especially those technologies that support public participation and openness. Developing countries continue to make substantial strides in information and communication technologies for development (ICT4D); adopting and using technologies in all sectors of life including education, agriculture, health, government, and infrastructure and social development. This has far-reaching implications for understanding current technology transfer issues as well as the creation, deployment and usage of technologies to boost the ICT (information and communication technologies) infrastructure and bring about sustainable progress in developing countries. More importantly, perhaps, experts and practitioners involved in ICT initiatives in these countries need to rethink the best way to leverage and support their ICT potentials and expertise.

Free and open source software and technology for sustainable development, Sowe, Parayil and Sunami (eds), United Nations University Press, 2012, ISBN 978-92-808-1217-6

We are experiencing a significant shift away from the use of technologies and services based on proprietary software and towards free and open source software (FOSS) solutions and services. A plethora of FOSS technologies is increasingly playing an essential role in the sustainability agenda. As some of the early myths (difficult to use, unreliable, insecure, inadequate support, etc.) are being debunked, FOSS is influencing all aspects of ICT, from supporting core ICT infrastructure to areas such as e-learning, e-government, e-health and much more.

The general concept behind FOSS is making the human-readable source code of software accessible to anyone who wants to obtain it. Users can freely share, customize and adapt the software to their local needs. As such, it can be argued that FOSS technologies support the broadest public participation, limited not by copyright restrictions but by one's ability to learn and modify the technology to meet present needs while laying the foundation for future generations to meet their own needs. However, if FOSS and technologies are to have an impact and contribute to sustainable development, they must not only be accessible in a format that allows present and future users to modify them in any way to suit their needs, but there must also be a strategic plan for training and learning to ensure that the present generation can archive, share and transfer the technology to future generations.

FOSS transcends geographical and cultural boundaries to usher in a new software development paradigm where volunteers collaboratively create software for the commons. The FOSS phenomenon has come of age and is redefining the way we develop, distribute, use, maintain and support software. The political economy of FOSS technologies has far-reaching implications for world development because of the centrality of information and communications technologies for development (ICT4D). The global trend in the diffusion and adoption of FOSS technologies is a testimony to the socio-economic and technological impact the software has for both developed and developing economies. While FOSS development, education and business potentials may appear as a phenomenon for the developed world, a sizeable number of developing countries have undertaken bold measures – implementing FOSS policies, supporting R&D, initiating projects – all with the ultimate aim of bringing about innovation, sustainable ICT development and technology independence. Amid the debate about what sort of technology is appropriate for achieving sustainable development, FOSS offers some solutions to today's and tomorrow's technology challenges for developing countries. Empirical and anecdotal evidence continues to demonstrate the potential FOSS technologies have in empowering individuals and communities, giving technology users ownership rights and enabling countries and regional institutions to collaborate with technology partners of their choice at an unprecedented rate. These characteristics have the intrinsic value of giving people the opportunity to participate actively in the development and shaping of their own technology, stimulating the growth of indigenous software industries, creating local jobs and lowering technology acquisition and deployment costs.

There is thus an urgent need to compile and develop a framework that can help us better understand how FOSS and other technologies can bring about sustainable development. This book is a compilation which highlights technology adoption and use in various sectors, lessons to be learnt and how best to use this understanding to support regional and international technology cooperation.

The *key ideas* in this book come from diverse and interrelated topics covering qualitative and quantitative research. The chapters deal with implications for understanding FOSS and technology diffusion and adoption, bring to the fore theories and best practices on FOSS for sustainable development and introduce scientifically grounded models to explain the complex relationships between FOSS technologies and sustainable development. There are discussions pertaining to the subject of FOSS technologies and intellectual property rights (IPR), case studies and surveys with an emphasis on lessons to be learnt and experience reports on FOSS, technology policy formulation and obstacles to policy implementation in developing countries.

The book is a compendium of scholarly chapters that will give the reader a synergetic overview of the status and projected trends of FOSS technologies. Contributions come from a wide range of knowledge experts who are able to combine their technology experiences from developing countries with their informed knowledge from developed countries to provide a comprehensive outlook on the themes in this book. The volume benefits from 33 contributors from 14 countries, spread throughout Africa, Asia, Europe and North and South America.

The *overall objective* of the book is to raise awareness, increase deployment and capture the socio-economic, technical and educational impact of FOSS technologies for sustainable development. To achieve this aim, the book integrates chapters covering both theoretical and practical implications of FOSS technologies. The authors include experts from social, natural and human sciences, with contributions coming from researchers and practitioners in both developing and developed countries.

The *target audience* of the book are ICT4D and sustainable development experts in both the developed and developing worlds, FOSS developers and users, policy-makers, ICT-based small and medium-sized companies leveraging benefits inherent in FOSS technologies to support and sustain their business practices, non-governmental organizations working in ICT and sustainable development in developing countries, international organizations with technology transfer initiatives, information systems practitioners and research institutions. The book also targets curriculum designers, universities, colleges and training institutions interested in the pedagogical aspects of FOSS technologies.

Organization of the book

Initially the editors received 48 abstract submissions. These were screened by an expert panel of reviewers to gauge their relevance to the aim and overall objective of the book. Thirty-one abstracts made it through this process, and these authors were invited to contribute full chapters. From this cohort, 28 chapters were submitted and subjected to a blind peer review. Using the results, we selected 13 high-quality chapters for inclusion in this book, plus a concluding chapter. The chapters are broadly organized into two main sections.

- *Part I: FOSS research, theory, technology adoption and practice.* In the first eight chapters of the book, the authors discuss themes related to qualitative and quantitative research that have implications for the diffusion and adoption of FOSS technologies in the public and private sectors of developing countries. These include theories of information society, learning in ICT4D projects and best practices on FOSS technology sustainability and innovation. This section also covers the use of FOSS technologies and services as tools to achieve sustainable development, their relationship with IPR and lessons to be learnt from FOSS research and cooperation projects between developing and developed countries.
- *Part II: FOSS case studies, surveys, policy development and experience reports.* Five chapters in the second part of the book document case studies and surveys which demonstrate practical implementation of FOSS technologies in the public and private sectors of developing countries, with emphasis on relevance and lessons to be learnt. The section also addresses the development, formulation, evaluation and review of appropriate policies that are responsive to technological trends, what works and what does not work in existing ICT policies in developing countries and obstacles to policy implementation.

REFERENCE

World Commission on Environment and Development (1987) *Our Common Future*, Oxford: Oxford University Press.

Part I

FOSS research, theory, technology adoption and practice

1
Making sustainable open source software infrastructures by federating and learning in the global context

Gianluca Miscione

> I think that if the developing country is serious about not just seeing ICT as a cost center, but as a requirement for national development, the real advantage of open source ends up being able to build up your own knowledge base. And that is not cheap in itself – you'll likely pay as much for that as you'd pay for a proprietary software solution. The difference being that with the proprietary solution, you'll never catch up, and you'll have to pay forever, without ever learning anything yourself. (Linus Torvalds, quoted in Weerawarana and Weeratunge, 2004)

Introduction

The idea of the "network society" has highlighted how the logic of networks has shaped the contemporary world, with a specific emphasis on the role of information technology (IT). More than a decade ago Castells (1998), engaged by the UN Research Institute for Social Development Conference on Information Technologies and Social Development, wrote: "The most critical distinction in this organizational logic is to be or not to be – in the network. Be in the network, and you can share and, over time, increase your chances. Be out of the network, or become switched off, and your chances vanish, since everything that counts is organized around a worldwide web of interacting networks." Such networks do not emerge and sustain themselves autonomously; they are in interplay, shaping and shaped by large IT systems, here referred to as "information infrastructures", comprising practices, institutions and organizing

Free and open source software and technology for sustainable development, Sowe, Parayil and Sunami (eds), United Nations University Press, 2012, ISBN 978-92-808-1217-6

processes. Information infrastructures are unevenly distributed and evolving. Organizational contexts have a central role in such unevenness. Such unbalanced situations are mostly evident in developing contexts; it is widely known that many approaches to implementing IT in developing countries have been tried, with some succeeding and many failing to be sustainable. This chapter proposes that successful ongoing projects can be hubs of a broader infrastructure possibly constituted by federating them, rather than as best practices to be replicated, as commonly suggested. In such a process, it is argued here that learning is crucial.

Often there is a mismatch between skills implied and required by IT and those available. This reproduces the marginalization and exclusion that Castells warned about. IT projects in developing contexts suffer from both horizontal (local versus global) and vertical (across initiatives) fragmentation. From a vertical view, IT projects are run by different organizations, like local ministries, the United Nations, the World Health Organization (WHO), the Organisation for Economic Co-operation and Development, donors, national public agencies, non-governmental organizations (NGOs) and consulting firms. The coordination across these efforts is often insufficient to create sustainability. Horizontally, the introduction of IT is expected to change processes and management across levels. In public administrations (and not least in developing contexts), bureaucratic procedures and decision-making tend to be top-down. This goes for most mainstream software engineering approaches as well. On the other side, the actual processes of development and implementation of IT are not linear due to the variety of contexts with multiple rationalities (Avgerou, 2002; Chilundo and Aanestad, 2004). The mismatch between formal bureaucracies' functioning, mainstream top-down software development schemes and actual trajectories of development initiatives provides a promising field for research and, in turn, relevance for practice. This chapter intends to approach such issues by looking at the connections between free and open source software (FOSS) and learning. The focus on organizational aspects complements existing studies on the economical and technological relevance of FOSS.

FOSS has been attracting the interest of organizations involved in development and implementation of IT in developing countries for years. But the usual assumptions on which FOSS relies cannot be taken for granted in contexts of actual use. For instance, dispersed and mobilizable IT capabilities may not be widely available in developing contexts, and copyright and other FOSS-related rules may not be present, or not enforced. This environmental complexity is exacerbated by lack of coordination across efforts, resulting in local organizations spending inordinate amounts of time and resources in dealing with separate – and sometimes conflicting – initiatives and actors.

The importance of considering the actual consequences of FOSS has already been highlighted (for instance by Miscione and Johnston, 2010). This chapter uses a step-deductive argument: by selectively discussing existing concepts and approaches it aims to draw a line connecting emerging infrastructures as federations, FOSS and learning. In doing so, it scrutinizes the usual assumption that FOSS is "good" because it is based on "good" principles.

Due to the deductive structure of the argument proposed here, the methodology – the approach and techniques for data collection and analysis – is not given the same centrality as in empirical papers and data-driven research. Indeed, relevant empirical cases are selected for illustrative purposes, rather than being the ground from which the theoretical proposal emerged. In spite of these premises, it is important to state how the empirical part of this chapter has been produced. For about two years the author has taken part, at different levels and with different tasks, in a global long-term action research initiative to develop and implement health information systems in developing countries. This involvement, initially framed by action research, progressively became more informed by participant observation, which implies less direct responsibility for action on the researcher's side. Action research provided direct access to globally dispersed activities and accountability lines. Participant observation reduced bias and provided an accurate understanding of infrastructure development phenomena. Interviews and documentary study enriched data throughout the research process.

The argument is structured as follows:
- Infrastructures are central for providing services, especially those in which economy of scale plays a determinant role.
- Federations hold a pivotal role in establishing wide infrastructures (for example Edwards, 2010; Miscione, Staring and Georgiadou, 2009), and require particular strategies and ability to learn.
- Learning in turn can be facilitated by FOSS.

Federations for infrastructures

The term "federation" has been borrowed from political science because it expresses metaphorically my proposal for agreements and shared power without constituting a unitary organization, as a unitary state form would. Federalism combines autonomy for sub-central units with a central authority, whose power and constraints are constitutionally defined. This understanding of federalism resonates with the view of infrastructures as federations of existing information systems. Through this chapter, it is argued that federations of socio-technical systems can help in reducing the design/reality gap by linking locally rooted information systems with globally distributed information infrastructures, which do not depend on single transnational authorities.

From a historical perspective, we can note that many infrastructures (like telephony, internet, even railways) emerged through the integration of existing systems, with incremental standardization being a key element in their establishment. But the scalability of infrastructures is not simply the outcome of interoperability and standards. Without considering organizational and political aspects of the actual contexts of implementation, integration of systems and scaling up of information infrastructures do not happen. This is the reason for calling this process "federation", to avoid both technological reductionism and the tight technical coupling implied by "integration". Facilitation of interoperability among existing projects, as well as with new ones, is my proposal for a first step in such direction (Hanseth, 2002).

An information infrastructure has been described as a "shared, evolving, heterogeneous, open and standardized installed base of IT-capabilities" (Hanseth and Lyytinen, 2004). Another widely accepted concept of such infrastructures comes from Bowker and Star (1999), who studied classification systems. Both address the heterogeneity of what constitutes infrastructures and their unfolding nature. As discussed by Miscione, Staring and Georgiadou (2009), establishing coordination across IT programmes, thus across organizations, requires inscribing co-operative features and revising lines of accountability. This is not a linear process because technology tends to inscribe the contexts from which it originates, which may impede its "transfer". The dialectic of local and global, flexibility and standardization (Hanseth and Monteiro, 1997; Braa et al., 2007) is pervasive in building information infrastructures. To identify working balances between diverse forces – depending on local specificity, interoperability and standardization – Rolland and Monteiro (2002) refer to open processes of continuous and long-term negotiation.

Lanzara (2009), echoing Latour and actor-network theory, terms "assemblage" the interweaving of IT with institutional forms. The assemblage is a heterogeneous collection of technical and organizational components with their specificities, not reducible to a single logic. An assemblage may comprise "a plethora of actors like political authorities, technical agencies, bureaucratic organizations, IT providers, professional service firms, regulatory bodies, software engineering companies, research centers, together with the technical, functional and normative components by which they run their transactions" (ibid.). These constellations are loosely structured and can be evolving and changing. Lanzara (ibid.) further argues that technology performs in the same way that institutions do by producing regulatory constraints in organizations and societies. I find this concept useful to account for the entanglement of IT and organizations when, in both industrialized and developing contexts, disparate inter-organizational arrangements emerge in relation to IT.

The stance embraced here is empirically inspired by the activities of an international network devoted to development and implementation of reporting software for aggregated data from primary healthcare facilities in developing countries. The Programme on Health Information (PHI – a disguised name) started in South Africa in the mid-1990s to support the reorganization of the post-apartheid healthcare system. Its software and approach were subsequently introduced in several other African and Asian countries. PHI is now an assemblage of various actors and partnerships involving universities, public health authorities, NGOs, donors, international organizations and consultants. PHI operates at both the global level (participating in a broad and heterogeneous network of organizations like universities and research centres, international donors and ministries of different countries) and local levels (where systems are piloted and implemented, capacity building is carried out and requirements for further developments are collected).

Two prominent characteristics of this project are interesting here: its adoption of FOSS and its reliance on participatory design principles, which promote learning processes. Participatory design and action research – in line with the Scandinavian tradition from which PHI originated – provided guiding principles of PHI activities. Indeed, it relies explicitly on participatory design as an action research method to understand and empower peripheral levels of public healthcare systems. This goal is pursued by supporting the use of health-related information for action (monitoring, planning, management, etc.). PHI emphasized that centralized information systems hinder the local use of information, and hence change in organizational behaviour. A key issue was to inscribe health personnel's practices into customized information systems, which would be based on the information actually needed. Under the slogan "information for action", the general goal was "to provide useful information for management at each level of the health services", as proposed by Sauerborn, Bodart and Lippeveld (2000). On the government and funding agency side, PHI promises an improvement of healthcare delivery through supporting the use of reliable information for decision-making. It is important to stress the characteristic of the assemblages of not being locally confined. Case studies of PHI implementations in Indian states and several African countries have to be considered as hubs in the broader PHI assemblage.

Over several years of activity, PHI developed a standard approach for health information system (HIS) roll-out within healthcare systems:

- initial contacts with healthcare authorities
- situational analysis and assessment of HIS
- participatory customization of HIS
- start of a pilot implementation
- training
- scaling up of HIS and aiming at institutionalization.

This pattern of activity inscribes the participatory principles of PHI. In most places of implementation, PHI followed those stages.

Learning for federations

Avgerou (2008), in her critical review of the contemporary literature on information systems in developing contexts, addresses three discourses: transfer and diffusion, social embeddedness and transformation. The latter, rooted in the second, is different from the first as it is conscious of its reductionism. This chapter situates FOSS in the transformational discourse, between globally accepted emancipatory discourses (for example Thompson, 2004) and emphasis on implementations and social embeddedness in general, strongly advocated by Escobar (1998) in development efforts. Analytically, FOSS assemblages can be seen as "transformative" as far as learning allows bridging the (usually wide) gaps between global trends and local dynamics. Then the question is "Where does learning happen?" Assemblages span global and local levels. Such "dispersed local" patterns needs to be identified for situating FOSS. A micro-sociology of global IT is being tried by scholars like Pinch (2010) and Knorr-Cetina (2009), and is promising in framing some issues discussed in this chapter. Empirically, this level is between the two usual poles of decision-makers (public administrators and software developers, both oriented by a top-down approach to systems design) and actual developments and implementations (usually sensitive to the variety of contexts). Here there is scope for FOSS and learning.

The "organizing" aspect of infrastructures is usually understudied, although crucial in understanding and managing the entangling of organizations and technology (Orlikowski and Scott, 2008). Bowker (2000) argues that the establishment of an information infrastructure operates simultaneously at the concrete level of participatory design and implementation (e.g. fields in a database, capacity building, integration of datasets and organizational practice) and at a theoretical one (dealing with the relationships between information science, organization and global software development, among others). Furthermore, though it is useful to separate these issues analytically, they are closely intertwined from a practitioner's point of view. For example, research on databases, human resource management and IT governance involves different disciplines, but these topics are hardly distinguishable in what people do on a daily basis, and in how technology changes and can be changed. Thus these different sides have to be tackled holistically by considering the continuous redefinition of socio-technical arrangements.

An empirical vignette from a PHI implementation in Kerala state in India is presented here for illustrative purposes. The case is described on one side from the principles of the supporting network and local politics. The other side looks at the implementation dynamic, which is underestimated in the common approach to IT for development (Avgerou, 2008). The empirical data from Kerala, as other sites, are not intended to be a self-contained case, but a perspective on a constituting globally dispersed infrastructure.

Among PHI nodes, Kerala is an interesting case because of emphatic expectations for FOSS-related emancipation in the "knowledge society" on the part of the public administration:

> ICT has opened up the possibility of radically different information exchange patterns by facilitating faster and more efficient dissemination of information. It can play a vital role in sustaining the democratic ethos of the Indian society and ensuring a high level of transparency and accountability in governance ... The Government has a comprehensive view of ICT as a vehicle for transforming Kerala into a knowledge-based, economically vibrant, democratic and inclusive society ... The Government realizes that Free Software presents a unique opportunity in building a truly egalitarian knowledge society. The Government will take all efforts to develop Free Software and Free Knowledge and shall encourage and mandate the appropriate use of Free Software in all ICT initiatives. (Government of Kerala, 2007)

In May 2007 the Kerala health secretary gave a presentation at the PHI coordinating university, pinpointing the main issues that an HIS can help in improving:
- ineffective referral system
- escalating health expenditure
- ineffective manpower
- poor recording, reporting and documentation
- lack of supervision of transfer of institutions to local bodies.

To cope with these matters the HIS was expected to streamline information flow to and from the top administrative level. This centralization of information flow contrasts with what PHI advocates and supports: decentralization of action through local use of information. In spite of the substantial divergence of final scopes, reliance on FOSS narrative from both sides facilitated the establishment of cooperation with the state of

Kerala, whose positive orientation towards FOSS is clearly expressed by official documents.

On this basis, choosing FOSS was desirable for both practical and ideological reasons. Practically, the software can be "massaged" more by local stakeholders and a globally dispersed developers' team. This has been crucial when the suite of programs must be made available on many terminals. Ideologically, the Kerala government believed that FOSS could be used to enact and guarantee cooperation and communal property, which was more consistent with its own ideological dispositions. So FOSS indigenization processes cannot be understood only on the local or global levels: the organizational ability to "assemble" the very different actors is key for understanding and implementing FOSS, possibly not only in so-called "developing contexts".

Free and open source software for learning

As infrastructures are fundamental in service provision, and federating is a convenient strategy in building them, learning to develop and implement IT accordingly is the consequent step forward. The point proposed here is that the role of FOSS stays in making organizations become more able to "assemble". Besides the technological and economic relevance, the relevance of FOSS (and potentially of open technologies more broadly) is in allowing learning within public administrations and across different kinds of organizations in dispersed settings. Building on the concept of assemblage, there is a need to account for how such configurations tend towards some patterns rather than others. The implications and consequences of "assemblages" need to be specified in respect to the dynamics of such hybrid and open-ended arrangements. For instance, when data flowing from different vertical health programmes have to be interconnected, different information systems and datasets are brought into contact. New information flows are likely to affect the activities related to those data. So different organizational settings, with their own specific dynamics and constraints, will interplay. The outcome of such interweaving is hardly predictable, as it does not depend entirely on the design of the federative efforts. Indeed, distributed coordinated actions rely on many issues which are often out of the control and view of those who design and develop information systems. In identifying a balance between unpredictable dynamics and tendencies towards accepted configurations, the role of learning is highlighted, in the sense of achieving the ability to arrange and align distributed socio-technical networks (Czarniawska, 2004).

More empirically, software developed by PHI has always been free, but it was initially based on a proprietary platform which was well established by the mid-1990s. Within a few years the diffusion of the internet and related technologies made this solution seem outdated. As the project evolved, it became apparent that the tools required for continuous updating and customization of the software had to be freely available. So purely FOSS version development was started, with the intention of making it web-based and platform-independent. Some underlying concerns about the switch are spelled out in this message between PHI coordinators on the PHI mailing list:

Just two generic comments to this discussion:
1 A fundamental challenge with the DHIS is that it *must* be able to address the needs and information infrastructures of different developing countries (at least), which *in practice* vary far more than the information infrastructure in any single country (and in general vary more than the current information infrastructure in rich countries). In practice this means for instance that it should:
- Run on any "platform" from a standalone PC to a thin-client based WAN (whether internet or intra-net based)
- Be able to communicate with other HIS instances using any standard medium (diskettes, low bandwidth dial-ups, broadband connections). These will often have to be mixed in any specific environment – if the network goes down, you need to use diskettes etc.

Even if we don't cater for *all* such scenarios in the beta version, it must be catered for in the system analysis.

2 Be careful about limiting your "systems thinking" to what is currently addressed by AccessMD. There are some obvious extensions of this that we have already done development work for or at least have been discussing extensively in South Africa:
- Staff and patient based surveys (Client Satisfaction Survey, Waiting time survey)
- Human Resource Development (HRD module)
- Patient-based data for specific purposes (Special Patient Data module etc)
- Web based reporting and data mining (web pivot reporter, web portal)
- GIS
- Management modelling (Equity Gauge)

I also know there's been significant development work done in e.g. Ethiopia and India to cater for additional needs (disease surveillance etc).

Some of the above would be unknown to most of you (and I don't have time now to write up stuff – I'm on holiday!!), but my point is just that you must *not* limit your scope of version 2 to only address monthly routine data.

Finally, also don't forget to consider the issue of multi-language support – as the DHIS grows, ensuring efficient multi-language support mechanisms will be crucial.

The centrality of learning and FOSS is now exemplified through short cases from the implementation side. The actual roll-out of the PHI effort in Kerala had to cope with a different set of issues than those perceived at the policy-making level. For example, many problems were encountered when installing and using the health data reporting software in peripheral clinics. Here computer skills were rare, with regard to both use and maintenance of terminals. The lack of reliable internet connections (and in many cases of continuous electricity supply) did not allow for on-line access to the HIS from a central server. Installing and maintaining locally all the needed components turned out to be a hard, and sometimes unmanageable, task for health personnel, and the limited number of PHI facilitators could not cope with all the problems in geographically dispersed facilities. Computer viruses spread through USB memory sticks after each formatting, with anti-virus updates not easily accessible, and the configuration of machines proved difficult for most users. The initial solution drew on the possibilities offered by the FOSS programs and tools used. This allowed the redesign of the whole set of required programs. Bootable CDs with a stripped-down version of GNU/Linux as well as the PHI programs would have allowed users to solve these problems of viruses and configurations. Because of concerns about the little RAM available on computers in the clinics, this solution had not really been tried out on a large scale. Another less "radical" solution was the development of a single installer, including a "wizard" to guide users through the installation of all programs. The installer reduced the burden of maintaining and updating the tools on both technical and health personnel. Such solutions would have been impossible if the program was not based on FOSS, technically, legally and also in terms of the distributed organizational ability to create it. This illustrates how FOSS allows assemblages to address and solve problems which do not have a pure local or global solution. The assemblage, composed of FOSS programmers from different countries, graduate students from the coordinating university, primary health facilities with their needs and health system officers among others, is an example of an agency which is globally dispersed but not amorphous, as the term assemblage may suggest.

A first counterexample, in which non-open policy obstructed learning and produced a failure, comes from an integration module to be implemented between different applications used by the healthcare system. One system was proprietary, the other was developed by PHI. As healthcare officers could not provide the source code to the proprietary system, the PHI software developer team had to proceed with a trial-and-error heuristic to understand how exported data were formatted (this would provide the basis for integration). Such "reverse engineering" efforts were resource consuming, and had to be carried out by a graduate computer science student from the coordinating European university, as the local workers did not have the required skills to do it. A second counterexample on a similar line is sketched through an empirical vignette of the tentative development of a geographical information system (GIS) in Gujarat, another Indian state in which PHI was involved. Geo-Info (an imaginary alias) is a quasi-government organization with the official mandate to develop GIS and related applications. Cooperation between PHI and Geo-Info began, since in abstract terms it had great potential to provide a GIS solution to the state health department. The linkage was pursued through two key strategies. Firstly, a clear separation of the HIS and GIS applications had to be made, with PHI and Geo-Info independently responsible for their respective applications. Secondly, a "loose integration" would have been made by establishing a module at the database level, where software routines were created so that the routine data being collected through the HIS would be made available in the appropriate format to the GIS application, which could then use these data and display them on the maps. Despite these positive premises, the collaboration did not really produce the expected results. Among the causes, one is of salient interest here: the Geo-Info software code was not available, therefore the software adaptations had to be done internally. In spite of assurance that necessary human resources would be available, it proved not to be the case. Also, code writers were located within different organizations, and no shared practice was established.

The example and the two counterexamples substantiate the claim that without FOSS, federating a system to develop larger ones, and possibly infrastructures, is difficult if not impossible.

Discussion

Rottenburg (2000) highlights the paradox between predictability and accountability in development projects: a development vision has to be translated into procedures, to which actors are held accountable, rather than to unpredictable results. The multiple logics of the assemblage do not necessarily follow such a distinction so linearly. The example of the installer shows how an *ad hoc* assemblage – as response to unforeseen conditions – can cope with unpredictability in an accountable way. When assemblages include target organizations and final beneficiaries, they act following a mix of procedures and improvised arrangements accountable to local needs (like reducing exposure to scarce technical skills and computer viruses) or visions (like FOSS to link Kerala to the knowledge society).

The interactions around local technical skills improvement and the increased ability for organizations to formulate, express, negotiate and inscribe their needs in technology are proposed as a chance for organizational learning. In contexts of multiple accountabilities (Suchman, 2002), the claim is that the relevance of FOSS emerges from negotiating alliances and does not inhere in FOSS itself. FOSS facilitates learning as far as its openness is allowed by software development processes and enacted by brokering activities to relate dispersed practices (Gherardi and Nicolini, 2002). Along this line, organizational learning is a theoretical posture alternative to technical and rationalistic views and approaches to organizational change (Dierkes et al., 2001). One fundamental of organizational learning is that knowing is situated: learning takes place in different contexts, and produces different capabilities. *Rather than a transmission of knowledge, learning "happens" through tuning in sets of activities.* How can organizational learning take place or be facilitated in relation to FOSS-based information systems development and implementation? As it is unusual in developing contexts to have spontaneous voluntary participation, software development needs to be designed and carried on in a way that allows local organizations to assemble with others, and to cooperate to "indigenize" FOSS.

Camara and Fonseca (2007) relate modalities of participation to code writing and software modularity. They propose a two-dimensional model to categorize FOSS projects, with one axis representing shared conceptualization among the people involved and the other modularization of the software. Well-established FOSS projects like Linux score high on both counts. In the low/high quadrant are pieces of software whose community is well defined, but in which the architecture does not allow for easy subdivision of parts of work (e.g. OpenOffice). In high/low you find highly modular projects in which a large number of communities and individuals work without even knowing about each other (i.e. Apache). Finally, low/low is where most projects start, and where mortality is high. This scheme can be used to frame some of the relations between technological choices and assemblage "dispersion". Indeed, the authors conceptualize a strong relation between software design and possibilities for division of labour. A coherent attitude can be found in a message from one of the PHI coordinators on the PHI mailing list:

> A modularized system enables the projects to assign complete parts of the system to distributed nodes. Such modularization can greatly benefit from having well-defined interfaces for the modules to interact with each other. If the system is in rapid development, and the developers are unable to keep from changing these interfaces frequently, the effort involved to keep this modularization increases dramatically. Additionally, I have observed that changes in the

interfaces results in additional need for coordination. This also seems to be the case when modularity in general is suffering. In a project like [PHI], with its problem of integrating the distributed nodes with the global development network, lessons suggest that design choices that increase the need for coordination, have direct impact on the distributed nodes' ability to carry out their assigned tasks.

This excerpt provides an example of focusing on modularization, while not considering shared conceptualization nor local contexts' concrete needs and intentions. In that view, nodes of the network have "assigned tasks", rather than being part of an assemblage within which the logic is not merely of outsourcing, command and control. Indeed, that approach created a paradoxical lock-in situation for the leading university. Hustad (2008), who worked on capacity building in PHI India, argues that open standards and technologies aimed at opening and decentralizing software development (Raymond, 1999) ended up concentrating the burden of development on the coordinating department of computer sciences, because the skills to write code using state-of-the-art frameworks and following application programming interfaces requirements were not available at low salaries in target organizations in India and Viet Nam. Only if software development is carried out in an open and supportive fashion can FOSS fluidity inscribe a variety of context-bound socio-technical arrangements (De Laet and Mol, 2000), and also avoid path dependencies and vendor lock-ins (Weerawarana and Weeratunge, 2004).

As mentioned earlier, Avgerou (2008) highlights the transformative role of IT. It does not conceive target contexts as passive recipients of IT, but as parties in the evolution of innovations. In Avgerou's view, social embeddedness of information systems is not only locally constructed, "transformative discourse is explicitly concerned with the way IT is implicated in the dynamic of their change" of social, economic and political relations in a developing country or the world at large. The transformative view introduces new elements beyond organizations and inter-organizational links: institutions (intended as broad social models), implying power relations beyond specific organizational settings. Thus the transformative discourse intercepts an empirical area situated at the meso level, between global initiatives and discourses and emphasis on individual implementations.

Conclusions and recommendations

Fragmentation of IT projects can be tackled, it is suggested here, by supporting coordination through the establishment of "federations", in which technology has to be considered as a relevant actor. The consequent recommendation is the revision of IT development strategies to conceive of them as potential parts of larger networks, possibly included in or converging towards a broader infrastructure. Design and implementations have to be organized accordingly: by thinking about ongoing information systems as dots to be connected for future information infrastructure. Hanseth and Lyytinen (2010) distilled a set of principles to design infrastructures in their (typical) complex environment. The basis for this view lies in recognizing the importance of the "installed base" of what is already in place and being done.

Understanding which infrastructural elements can be translated into the heterogeneous public and private sector contexts in the global South is a matter of development strategies. As it is a matter of federating existing and successful IT projects, the possible nodes of an emerging infrastructure cannot be identified a priori. To deliver sustainable benefits over their lifetime, infrastructures need to enable processes of experimentation, discovery and invention through trial and error. In coherence with the theoretical framework delineated before, technical and organizational aspects have to be considered at the same time for the establishment and maintenance of new networked and collaborative courses of activities.

On this basis, besides the emphasis on technical skills and economic aspects, learning has to be considered in the light of the actual and possible role of FOSS.

- FOSS can be relevant in developing contexts not so much because of open and dispersed participation of an indefinite number of people over the net (crowdsourcing – Benkler, 2006), but for different organizations to learn how to create and maintain dispersed local assemblages able to "indigenize" FOSS.
- FOSS "discourse" is an increasingly accepted source of legitimization. FOSS narrative and expectations can make a heterogeneous set of actors (like ministries, research and healthcare institutions, consultants, NGOs, WHO and European Union personnel) perform distributed and coordinated activities. Myths and narratives are discussed by Czarniawska (1997) in neo-institutional terms; Czarniawska and Sevón (2005) look at the travel of ideas at the global level. The legitimizing role of myth is clearly presented by Noir and Walsham (2007) through a case from India.
- Organizational learning is a suitable paradigm for understanding explicit and tacit knowledge in the entanglements of technology and organizations (Orlikowski and Scott, 2008).

A crucial challenge for FOSS in developing contexts concerns functioning and sustainable implementation. Scaling up information systems has been described as a strategy to achieve sustainability and more relevance (Braa, Monteiro and Sahay, 2004). Given the novelty of organizational forms required and implied by FOSS, the local elaboration and eventual consolidation of FOSS-based systems cannot avoid considering socio-technical fragmentation, which is often the main obstacle to successful implementation. The recommendation for a federative attitude as constitutive in designing and implementing FOSS-based information systems contrasts with a conceptualization of sustainability as an add-on to undertake at later stages of IT development. The proposed federative *modus operandi* has to be viewed in contrast to the assumptions of both grassroots spontaneity and one-size-fits-all approaches, which fail in addressing scalability/sustainability and context variety, respectively.

REFERENCES

Avgerou, C. (2002) *Information Systems and Global Diversity*, Oxford: Oxford University Press.
—— (2008) "Information Systems in Developing Countries: A Critical Research Review", *Journal of Information Technology* 23(3), pp. 133–146.
Benkler, Y. (2006) *The Wealth of Networks: How Social Production Transforms Markets and Freedom*, New Haven, CT: Yale University Press.
Bowker, G. (2000) "Biodiversity Datadiversity", *Social Studies of Science* 30(5), pp. 643–683.
Bowker, G. and Star, S. L. (1999) *Sorting Things Out: Classification and Its Consequences*, Cambridge, MA: MIT Press.
Braa, J., E. Monteiro and S. Sahay (2004) "Networks of Action: Sustainable Health Information Systems across Developing Countries", *MIS Quarterly* 28(3), pp. 337–362.
Braa, J., O. Hanseth, A. Heywood, W. Mohammed and V. Shaw (2007) "Developing Health Information Systems in Developing Countries: The Flexible Standards Strategy", *MIS Quarterly* 31(2), pp. 381–402.
Camara, G. and F. Fonseca (2007) "Information Policies and Open Source Software in Developing Countries", *Journal of the American Society for Information Science and Technology* 58(1), pp. 121–132.
Castells, M. (1998) "Information Technology, Globalization and Social Development", paper prepared for UNRISD Conference on Information Technologies and Social Development, Geneva, 22–24 June; available at www.komm.ruc.dk/mcmc/extdocs/castells.html (accessed 5 April 2012).
Chilundo, B. and M. Aanestad (2004) "Negotiating Multiple Rationalities in the Process of Integrating the Information Systems of Disease Specific Health Programmes", *Electronic Journal of Information Systems in Developing Countries* 20(2), pp. 1–28.
Czarniawska, B. (1997) *Narrating the Organization: Dramas of Institutional Identity*, Chicago, IL: University of Chicago Press.

—— (2004) "On Time, Space, and Action Nets", *Organization* 11(6), pp. 773–791.
Czarniawska, B. and G. Sevón (2005) *Global Ideas. How Ideas, Objects and Practices Travel in the Global Economy*, Copenhagen: Liber/Copenhagen Business School Press.
De Laet, M. and A. Mol (2000) "The Zimbabwe Bush Pump: Mechanics of a Fluid Technology", *Social Studies of Science* 30(2), pp. 225–263.
Dierkes, M., A. Berthoin Antal, J. Child and I. Nonaka (eds) (2001) *Handbook of Organizational Learning and Knowledge*, Oxford: Oxford University Press.
Edwards, P. N. (2010) *A Vast Machine: Computer Models, Climate Data, and the Politics of Global Warming*, Cambridge, MA: MIT Press.
Escobar, A. (1998) "Whose Nature, Whose Knowledge?", *Journal of Political Ecology* 5, pp. 53–82.
Gherardi, S. and D. Nicolini (2002) "Learning in a Constellation of Interconnected Practices: Canon or Dissonance", *Journal of Management Studies* 39(4), pp. 419–436.
Government of Kerala (2007) "Information Technology Policy – Towards an Inclusive Knowledge Society", Department of Information Technology, Thiruvananthapuram Kerala; available at www.keralaitmission.org/web/main/ITPolicy-2007.pdf (accessed 22 February 2012).
Hanseth, O. (2002) "Gateways – Just as Important as Standards. How the Internet Won the 'Religious War' about Standards in Scandinavia", *Knowledge, Technology and Policy* 14(3), pp. 71–89.
Hanseth, O. and K. Lyytinen (2004) "Theorizing about Design of Information Infrastructures: Design Kernel Theories and Principles", Sprouts Working Papers on Information, Environment Systems and Organizations, Article 12; available at http://sprouts.aisnet.org/124/1/040412.pdf (accessed 5 April 2012).
—— (2010) "Design Theory for Dynamic Complexity in Information Infrastructures: The Case of Building Internet", *Journal of Information Technology* 25(1), pp. 1–19.
Hanseth, O. and E. Monteiro (1997) "Understanding Information Infrastructure", Manuscript 27; available at http://heim.ifi.uio.no/oleha/Publications/bok.pdf (accessed 22 February 2012).
Hustad, O. K. (2008) "Challenges of Open Source Software Capacity Building among DHIS2 Developers in India", master's thesis, Department of Informatics, University of Oslo (unpublished).
Knorr-Cetina, K. (2009) "The Synthetic Situation: Interactionism for a Global World", *Symbolic Interaction* 32(1), pp. 61–87.
Lanzara, G. F. (2009) "Building Digital Institutions: ICT and the Rise of Assemblages in Government", in F. Contini and G. F. Lanzara (eds) *ICT and Innovation in the Public Sector*, Basingstoke: Palgrave Macmillan, pp. 9–48.
Miscione, G. and K. Johnston (2010) "Free and Open Source Software in Developing Contexts from Open in Principle to Open in the Consequences", *Journal of Information, Communication and Ethics in Society* 8(1), pp. 42–56.
Miscione, G., K. Staring and Y. Georgiadou (2009) "A Federative View for Information Infrastructures in Developing Contexts", in E. Byrne, B. Nicholson and

F. Salem (eds) *Proceedings of the 10th International Conference on Social Implications of Computers in Developing Countries: Assessing the Contribution of ICT to Development Goals*, Dubai: Dubai School of Government, pp. 209–221.

Noir, C. and G. Walsham (2007) "The Great Legitimizer: ICT as Myth and Ceremony in the Indian Healthcare Sector", *Information Technology & People* 20(4), pp. 313–333.

Orlikowski, W. and S. Scott (2008) "The Entangling of Technology and Work in Organizations", Innovation Group Working Papers No. 168, February, London School of Economics and Political Science, London.

Pinch, T. (2010) "The Invisible Technologies of Goffman's Sociology – From the Merry-Go-Round to the Internet", *Technology and Culture* 51(2), pp. 409–424.

Raymond, E. (1999) "The Cathedral and the Bazaar", *Knowledge, Technology & Policy* 12(3), pp. 23–49.

Rolland, K. H. and E. Monteiro (2002) "Balancing the Local and the Global in Infrastructural Information Systems", *Information Society* 18(2), pp. 87–100.

Rottenburg, R. (2000) "Accountability for Development Aid", in H. Richard Kalthoff and Hans Jürgen Wagener (eds) *Facts and Figures. Economic Representations and Practices*, Marburg: Metropolis, pp. 143–173.

Sauerborn, R., C. Bodart and T. Lippeveld (2000) *Design and Implementation of Health Information Systems*, Geneva: World Health Organization.

Suchman, L. (2002) "Located Accountabilities in Technology Production", *Scandinavian Journal of Information Systems* 14(2), pp. 91–105.

Thompson, M. (2004) "ICT, Power, and Developmental Discourse: A Critical Analysis", *Electronic Journal of Information Systems in Developing Countries* 20(4), pp. 1–25.

Weerawarana, S. and J. Weeratunge (2004) "Open Source in Developing Countries", SIDA; available at www.eldis.org/fulltext/opensource.pdf (accessed 22 February 2012).

2
Innovative tools for sustainable agriculture in developing countries: The impact of open source biotechnology

Ademola A. Adenle and Obijiofor Aginam

Introduction

Sustainable agriculture is widely acknowledged as a fundamental component of any strategy to fight poverty and food insecurity in developing countries. Agricultural practices – the source of livelihood for more than 86 per cent of poor people living in developing countries (World Bank, 2005) – can only be sustained if the right facilities and measures are put in place. As a research tool, agricultural biotechnology has potentials to contribute to sustainable agriculture. Recent reports have shown that such biotechnology (especially biotech crops) made significant impacts in terms of increase in yields and income and improving the quality of life in developing countries (James, 2009). Drought-tolerant, herbicide-tolerant and insect/pest-resistant crop varieties have been developed using agricultural biotechnology. However, sustainable agricultural development is still far from being accomplished in developing countries due to a variety of problems, particularly the introduction and diffusion of new technologies.

One notable problem in the area of biotechnology research and development (R&D) is increased intellectual property (IP) protection, which often impedes the adoption of agricultural biotechnology in developing countries. Biotechnology R&D, dominated by multinational corporations, is very expensive and investment oriented with a huge capital base; but by placing strong IP protection on agricultural inventions, including research tools, the multinationals have contributed considerably to little or

---

Free and open source software and technology for sustainable development, Sowe, Parayil and Sunami (eds), United Nations University Press, 2012, ISBN 978-92-808-1217-6

no innovation in developing countries. Because research tools needed for the development of subsistence crops are not readily available, open source biotechnology for agricultural practices is now increasingly advocated in developing countries.

The application of open source in software development led to the concept of applying it in agricultural biotechnology (Srinivas, 2002). It is believed this will create an opportunity through which life science inventions could become available to the public and the broad research community (BiOS, 2005; Thorisson et al., 2005), particularly where IP protection impedes innovation. Open source as an alternative to proprietary technologies is gradually becoming popular in developing countries, especially in the area of information and communication technologies (ICT). Free accessibility and low cost as characteristics of open source make it an attractive proposition to poorer communities (Hoe, 2006). Developing countries are taking advantage of using open source in solving problems in agriculture, health, environment and education to improve livelihoods in rural areas.

This chapter is structured as follows. The first section introduces the issue linkages of IP protection, agricultural biotechnology and food security in developing countries, and the second focuses on how the concept of open source software is similar to traditional farming practices that are built on free access, sharing and exchange. The third section discusses the tools used by the IP protection system in agricultural biotechnology, while the fourth discusses the potential impacts of open source based on different examples, including the famous Cambia initiative and PIPRA. The next section examines the constraints associated with the adoption of open source biotechnology and assesses policy implications that can help towards the development of open source in developing countries. In conclusion, the chapter argues that open source biotechnology can contribute to sustainable agriculture if all the necessary resources are made available in addition to the implementation of policies that favour open source development in agricultural practices.

Open source and agricultural innovation

The term "open source" was first used in free software development (Stallman, 2002). Many licences used by free software and open source are covered under the auspices of free and open source software (FOSS). For example, the Free Software Foundation General Public License (GPL) uses a free software licence and the Open Source Initiative uses an open source licence. Other FOSS movements include FOSS Bazaar, Creative Commons and the Debian Linux Community (Raymond, 1999;

Stallman, 2002; Weber, 2004). The FOSS development project has been remarkably successful, with many open source programs available; some of the best known are Linux, Apache and BIND. This success can largely be attributed to flexible licences such as the GPL, which allow copying, distribution and preparation of derivative work (Rosenberg, 2000). The open source concept is based on freedom to use, copy, study, modify and distribute the software programs without payment, and this gives the opportunity to modify the software or technology to the desired taste or for different purposes with full access to the source code (Hope, 2004). With regards to modification, the author must state the changes made, when the code was written and by whom, and the derivative work must be published under the GPL – "copylefted" (Cassier, 2006; FSF, 1991). For example, open source technology can be made available under a copyleft licence that prevents any individual or organization from modifying or reproducing the technology for proprietary purposes since the initial access to the technology is open and free. The idea of a copyleft licence is to ensure that everyone has free access to the innovation without further restrictions. The principle of "viral effect" is applied, in that software incorporating other GPL software must also be licensed under a GPL-compatible licence.

Open source technologies can be freely used and modified. Users can derive economic benefit from the modified technology, but cannot prevent others from using the technology or modifying further for their own economic gain.

Over the past decade awareness of open source has grown worldwide. The concept holds enormous promise for developing countries, particularly in the area of biotechnology (e.g. agriculture, health). Due to the open source mode of operation and the benefits associated with the concept, different initiatives are being deployed across various fields to promote its use for the good of society. Examples of initiatives using the open source and copyleft approach for their research tools are the International HapMap Project for mapping haplotypes of the human genome (Thorisson et al., 2005), computational drug discovery and development by the Tropical Disease Initiative (Wake and Ridley, 2003), biological information and bioinformatics on drug discovery by the Indian Council of Scientific and Industrial Research, and advanced genetics for improving agriculture and sharing biological innovations in poor communities by Biological Innovation for Open Society (BiOS, 2005), founded by the Centre for the Application of Molecular Biology to International Agriculture (Cambia).

Agricultural innovations are widely recognized as the key driving force of rural development in developing countries. Farmers play a vital role in the process of innovation, but they face problems of insects and pests, low income, small yields and lack of communication. Some of these problems are partly due to multiple intellectual property claims on key inputs and tools used in agricultural biotechnologies. Because of these factors, and the need for innovation to be more affordable and become more decentralized, open source presents an alternative distributive model in technological development for agricultural innovation. Authors have pointed out that some versions of open source may be directly relevant to agricultural research and development.

As an example, Douthwaite (2002) and Srinivas (2002) refer to the case of the seed industry and computer software in the 1970s. They noted that it was a traditional practice for computer programmers to exchange code freely among themselves, similar to farmers sharing seed freely with others to grow, improve, save and reproduce it. These days it is a different ball game: private companies in software and agriculture seek gains and benefits through private appropriation, in direct contrast to old practices of free sharing. As discussed above, the copyleft open source mechanism was developed so that any innovation born out of this approach is not protected or barred from copying or modification either by the original licensor or licensees under the open source licence (Hope, 2004). The same copyleft approach can be applied in agriculture to enable innovations to be developed and shared freely among the innovators as bound by the rules and agreement of open source licences, allowing further improvements and distribution without any obstacles. Open source technology can thus play a significant role in future agricultural development, especially in light of the domination of the seed industries by multinational corporate interests that restrict access to the distribution of seeds through various forms of IP protection.

Implications of intellectual property rights for agricultural biotechnology

The roles of patent in agricultural biotechnology

The existing IP protection relevant to agricultural biotechnology is complex and mostly serves corporate interests, despite some international regulatory bodies. Most international agreements focus on different aspects of agricultural IP that are governed by different sets of rules, guidelines and policies. For example, the International Union for the Protection of New Varieties of Plants (UPOV) focuses on protecting the rights of seed producers (e.g. commercial plant breeders), the Convention on Biological Diversity (CBD) focuses on protecting the right of farmers using landraces and the Agreement on Traded-Related Aspects of Intellectual

Property Rights (TRIPS) enforced by the World Trade Organization (WTO) works specifically on strengthening the rights of inventors.

These international regulatory mechanisms and regimes do not often work in harmony towards a unified common goal. For example, UPOV was established by six European nations in 1961, and subsequently revised in 1972, 1978 and 1991. Its emergence in 1961 triggered the enactment of the Plant Variety Protection Act in the United States in 1970. Differences in regulatory and legislative policies between North America and Europe (Bocci, 2009) largely impeded access to informal exchanging, saving and replanting of seeds between farmers. This is in sharp contrast to the original UPOV, which allowed breeders to exchange or sell their seeds within member countries (Pardey et al., 2004).

The current international environment, with several entities representing different interests, contributes to the complexity of the IP regime. The lack of coherence across international IP agreements and regimes has created loopholes in the agricultural biotechnology sector that are now being exploited by multinational corporate interests in most developing countries. The CBD, for instance, has been criticized for not recognizing IP protection within the context of TRIPS (Safrin, 2002). This undermines the CBD's role in conserving biodiversity and managing genetic resources. As IP protection increasingly becomes transnational, developing countries that are members of the WTO are obligated under the TRIPS agreement to offer IP protection to plant varieties. As critical IP discourses have revealed, most WTO agreements, including TRIPS, were pushed by the industrialized countries based on corporate lobbying and without sufficient input from developing countries (Jawara and Kwa, 2003; Bello, 2009). However, the UN Food and Agriculture Organization has played an important role in concluding the International Treaty on Plant Genetic Resources for Food and Agriculture, which is beneficial to developing countries (Cooper, 2002).

IP protection emerged as the driving force of innovation in life sciences following two events in the United States in 1980: the legislative approval and implementation of the Bayh-Dole Act, and a Supreme Court decision in favour of patent protection for genetically modified (GM) organisms in the landmark case of *Diamond v. Chakrabarty* (Rai and Eisenberg, 2003). After these remarkable developments, huge investments were made in agricultural technology in the private sector in collaboration with universities in most industrialized countries, especially the United States. Modern IP regimes (notably patents) have been heavily criticized because of non-disclosure of most innovations that can benefit the public. The private sector is mainly involved in biotech industries where strong IP protection is used to maximize profit. Multinationals such as Mosanto, DuPont, Syngenta and Dow are famous for acquiring large numbers of patents, holding more than 70 per cent of the patents in agricultural biotechnology in 1994. In 1999 six integrated companies held 67 per cent of biotech patents, of which 77 per cent were obtained by smaller biotech and seed firms (de Janvry et al., 2000). Some of these biotech companies have large markets in developed countries, with strong IP protection on cash crops (corn, cotton and soybean) through patents. The lack of free access to innovative tools was largely responsible for the development of biotech crops for herbicide tolerance, as claimed by American Cyanamid (Pray and Naseem, 2005). In addition, the multinationals mainly concentrate on crops with huge commercial benefit, neglecting the innovation needed to develop orphan crops that are simple and cost-effective for poorer countries.

However, when large companies come together with the sole aim of acquiring innovation for profit, there is a problem of research costs increasing as proprietary protection increases, and this may adversely affect the volume and efficiency of R&D. As Rai (2004) observed, "large pharmaceutical firms, once vertically integrated engines of innovation, must negotiate a complex array of university and small firm proprietary claims on research inputs". This scenario constrains innovation, as it may result in "patent thickets" due to numerous negotiations that involve high transaction costs and uncertainty with different patent holders.

A famous example of a patent thicket is "golden rice", which experienced many delays before it was brought to market. Given the importance of a biotech innovation like golden rice, which can potentially solve vitamin A deficiency problems in developing countries where millions of children are dying of malnutrition, it perhaps should not have become a contentious issue among more than 20 biotech companies claiming patents for the innovation. The golden rice saga clearly demonstrated that multiple owners holding overlapping and fragmented IP rights to different components of a large innovation can be an impediment to innovation, making it inaccessible to the public. Academic researchers are affected when there is high transaction cost on a wide range of innovations, and it becomes more difficult when academics are not sure whether they can do research that might infringe company patents, sometimes regarded as "research exemption", without seeking licence (Heller and Eisenberg, 1998). This has led to questions of whether enforcement of patents stands in the way of basic research in universities and research institutes. Genetech argued that open science was being encouraged without enforcing patent rights on research tools. This is in contrast to the argument presented by Heller and Eisenberg, which was based on high transaction costs for acquiring proprietary research tools that involved many different institutions. Two cases cited by Heller and Eisenberg are patents on research tools of rDNA and polymerase chain reaction by

Cohen Boyer and Hoffman La Roche respectively. Heller and Eisenberg further argue that strong IP protection on research tools leads to reduced innovations and underused knowledge, creating rights of exclusion (anti-commons) by IP holders. An example of expressed sequence tag (EST) was given, where some groups attempted to patent EST but reneged due to resistance from competitors.

While Heller and Eisenberg and others argued that patents create less innovation and adversely affect R&D, another school of thought argues that patents may enable collaborations and facilitate negotiations between research tool users and producers, leading to development (Arora and Merges, 2004; Bureth, Penin and Wolff, 2006; David, 2004). But little empirical work has been done on adverse effects of patents on innovation, thus lack of empirical evidence may undermine the effect of IP regimes on innovation.

In summary, the use of patent rights over research tools could hinder aspects of R&D. Once there is patent lock on innovative tools it creates a logjam in health, agriculture, environment and energy development worldwide (Jefferson, 2007a). In agricultural biotechnology that requires innovative tools to improve pest/disease-resistant and drought-tolerant crop varieties, a strong IP regime might impede innovative developments that are critical to sustainable solutions to food security, malnutrition and low agricultural productivity in developing countries. Given the likely adverse effect of IP regimes on innovative tools, as demonstrated here, and a potential patent thicket or anti-commons IP protection in the future, open source technology should be encouraged for free access to research tools.

What role can "terminator" technology play?

One of the primary purposes of IP protection in biotech industries is to gain profit through the application of patents, especially in agricultural biotechnology. This is obvious in most of the plant patents held by private firms situated in developed countries. These patents generate revenue from the poorest to the richest countries. With the development of new plant varieties by these companies, a different strategy is devised where IP protection is ineffective. The use of terminator technology has the potential to serve this kind of purpose. The word "terminator" was coined by activist groups in an attempt to ban the use of sterile seed technology (ETC Group, 2002); the original name is genetic use restriction technologies (GURTs). GURTs were granted a US patent (5,723,765) in 1998 to a joint partnership between the US Department of Agriculture and Delta & Pine Land Company (the biggest US cotton supplier) for two types: trait-specific (T-GURT) and variety level (V-GURT) (Jefferson, 2001). While T-GURT is designed for GM trait specifics (e.g. disease resistance), V-GURT is designed for GM crop varieties through seed sterility.

The mode of action of T-GURT is to induce the disease-resistant expression of a protected trait through the application of an activator. For example, when a chemical (activator) is added, an expression of a desired trait specific to resist a targeted disease is produced (ibid.). Shoemaker (2001) suggests that spraying a standing crop with a highly specific and proprietary compound may activate T-GURT. The V-GURT mechanism is based on application of a sensitive chemical compound (e.g. antibiotic tetracycline) that switches on the gene for an enzyme to activate a toxin that prevents germination (Odell, Hoopes and Vermerris, 1994). Alternatively, it can be defined as a genetic switch that either suppresses or activates the enzyme and toxin, switching germination either on or off. Terminator technology (V-GURTs) applies genetic engineering techniques to modify a plant's DNA by killing its own embryo to render the seed sterile. In other words, the seeds containing the gene can only be used for one generation of plant production, preventing farmers from saving harvested seed to grow next season. This means farmers must purchase further expensive seed, usually accompanied by heavy GM seed technology licensing fees from biotech industries.

Terminator technology is mostly targeted at developing countries where IP protections are either very weak or largely non-existent, and it may not have much effect in developed nations as other technologies can be used to unravel and relocate innovative characteristics for plant breeding. Moreover, terminator technology will only be developed for certain crops that may not be available in developing countries, and the crops may be forced on these countries through the introduction of one regulation or another by patent holders, thus reducing the chance of making innovations in developing countries. In the light of the fact that terminator technology may force farmers to buy seeds annually, it could lead to cross-pollination with other non-GM crops, gene silencing during seed production, toxicity to plants and other gene containment problems (Daniell, 2002).

Contrary to biotech industries, the idea of introducing terminator technology is to prevent the flow of unwanted genes from GM crops, thereby protecting biodiversity, and also to increase continuous access to new and improved crops.

Although it is possible that the T-GURT form of terminator technology could serve a good purpose in terms of disease resistance (Shoemaker, 2001), saving the seeds (excluding transgenic traits) (Thies and Devare, 2007), there is as yet no clear scientific evidence to support this argument. This suggests that more evidence-based research will need to be done, but opportunities may not exist in the future as terminator kinds of approach in agricultural biotechnology are widely opposed. For example, as a result of wide criticism of terminator technology (V-GURT in particular), application of V-GURTs for different varieties was disqualified in India (Pedleton, 2004) and rejected by the Rockefeller Foundation (1999) and the Consultative Group on International Agricultural Research (CGIAR, 1998).

In this regard, it may be difficult for GURT to replace IP and serve the same purpose in most developing countries without a well-functioning IP system. Clearly, the approach used by multinationals is less innovative and may hinder the development of agricultural biotechnology in developing countries. Given the ambiguity of introducing transgenic traits within the context of GURT varieties so as to make a profit, open source biotechnology can be important in making innovative traits freely available.

Freedom to operate innovative technology

The role of IP protection in accessibility of innovative technology is questionable, especially in agricultural biotechnology. Concerns over access to research tools are based on the belief that IP protection is still having adverse effects on important innovations. Open source has thus become an important mechanism in the attempt to provide global free access to innovative technology. Alternative means are being proposed, but none of these has been institutionally effective enough to preserve the innovations that are important to humanity. In agricultural biotechnology, the emergence of the patent as the dominant intellectual property right has been heavily criticized due to its failure to protect public interests. Most multinationals with a strong IP protection on research tools stand in the way of innovation. And when a monopoly right is conferred on innovation, it becomes a potential threat to freedom to operate. For example, in one case a Canadian farmer was sued by Monsanto for planting glyphosate-tolerant canola patented by Monsanto. Even though the origin of the seed was unclear, the court ruled that the farmer had infringed a valid patent held by Monsanto by cultivating the seeds.

Research is an integral part of innovation, and most breakthroughs in science and technology today are a result of work at either universities or research institutions. However, IP-related problems can become an impediment when a research activity leads to commercialization. Use of a patented technology is allowed under particular licences for research purposes, but the result may not be commercialized. Many universities using a patented technology for research do not carry out an early-stage assessment of IP protection, as would normally be done by commercial firms. This becomes a big problem for the universities when heading towards commercialization, as any innovations achieved under the research licence may be blocked from commercial use. In one case researchers using biotechnological tools were stopped from further application of innovative technology (Wright, 1998). In this case and that of golden rice, described above, IP was an impediment to the commercialization of research within academic institutions. Academics thus find it difficult to advance in their research work by using tools that could lead to more innovations due to these associated risks.

Moreover, anecdotal evidence suggests that researchers are experiencing difficulty, delay and redirecting of work due to high costs or problems of accessing permission to use patented technology that can benefit research for commercial purposes (Erbisch and Maredia, 2004; Wright, 1998). Even though this kind of problem often happens in developed countries, without doubt it becomes a spillover problem in developing countries as most technologies are transferred from the developed world. And when this occurs, freedom to operate becomes difficult due to lack of easy and quick access to material held by others. IP as a constraint to innovation is not peculiar to academia or developing countries: it could also pose a serious threat to the supply of food and fibre to the poor in the global South due to the problem of access to patents in the North found by the international research and donor communities (Pardey and Wright, 2003).

While the potential of agricultural biotechnology (e.g. biotech crops) to contribute to the solution to food security and poverty crises in developing countries is recognized, there remain serious problems in growing biotech crops partly due to IP protection issues. Also, GM technology is currently applied in commercial agriculture but it is still difficult to access this technology in developing countries, as biotech companies are often reluctant to invest in its development. Most developing countries do not have a strong and effective legal and regulatory framework for IP protection and enforcement. Getting access to innovative technologies that have potential benefits for orphan crops (e.g. millet, cassava, potato, sweet potato, banana, cowpea and sorghum) production in developing countries will thus take a long time. Findings on trade data suggest that problems of freedom to operate are more likely to occur in most orphan crops grown in developing countries due to IP protection (Binenbaum et al., 2000).

The open source approach that was originally employed in agricultural practices could be a potential solution to freedom to operate in agricultural biotechnology. The famous plant biotechnologist Richard Jefferson, through his BiOS project, is already taking the lead by encouraging scientists, academic and non-academic institutions, governments and the public to adopt open source as an alternative to the proprietary technology that has dominated multinational corporations. Of all approaches, the BiOS open source initiative is arguably the most outstanding in countering restrictions imposed by IP on innovative technologies due to its openness and transparency, particularly regarding freedom to operate.

Although international regulatory frameworks such as TRIPS, UPOV, the CBD and CGIAR are in place, they are not adequate to align the current IP system with the interests of the public, particularly in developing countries. CGIAR, for example, coordinates 40 major staple crops (with the exception of soybean) for exchange of materials through a common material transfer agreement (Evenson and Pingali, 2007). This is aimed at addressing equity concerns among different contributing parties, including farmers, while benefiting access and sharing in developing countries. Despite the database and legal structures put in place, the longer-term task of creating a tracking system for materials remains a significant challenge. As a result of this challenge and IP-related problems in plant germplasm, a BioLinux/GPLPG-MTA approach could be a potential solution (Desmarais, 2007).

Impact of FOSS and technological innovation for sustainable agriculture

Open source can be an alternative to ensure that innovative technology (e.g. biotechnology) is provided and made available to farmers for sustainable agricultural practices. Innovative technology is critical to the development of sustainable agriculture around the world. As noted, innovations are often impeded by either patents or licences, making free access difficult. A lack of relevant innovations can be a big problem in supporting or promoting agricultural practices. Innovative technologies can facilitate access to sustainable practices by agriculture professionals working with smallholder farmers and other stakeholders for rural development in developing countries. For example, the AgriBazaar initiative is a collaborative effort between the Agriculture Department of Malaysia and the Malaysian Institute of Microelectronic Systems to promote and develop their agro industries. As stated by the Malaysian government, open source was chosen for the AgriBazaar project due to its free accessibility, low maintenance and cost-effectiveness. It will provide an opportunity to increase usage of ICT and the internet, increase income and improve livelihoods for people in rural areas, particularly farmers.

The efforts of individuals or groups of organizations to ensure that innovations are freely made available through open source initiatives can make a great impact on sustainable agricultural development in developing countries. This has led to various innovations in terms of operating systems and products. The free open source GNU/Linux operating system first initiated by Linus Torvalds (Hope, 2008; Weber, 2004) had a significant impact in advocating open source development, and many others have followed this example. The Cambia BiOS initiative under the leadership of Richard Jefferson has been at the forefront of promoting open source for sharing biological innovation. Sustainable agricultural development in developing countries is one of the prominent BiOS activities through which open source development is being promoted (Cambia, 2009; *Nature*, 2004). The idea is to ensure that biotechnological tools are made available to poor people to practise innovative agriculture. For example, biotechnological innovation through open source development has led to the emergence of the β-glucuronidase (GUS) reporter gene system and *Rhizobium* strains (TransBacter system), which are provided and shared freely by Cambia BiOS (Jefferson, 2007b). Their development has created an opportunity to operate freely where critical restrictions are placed on agricultural biotechnology (e.g. plant genetics) through the *Agrobacterium tumefaciens* gene transfer patent thicket (Dennis, 2004).

BioForge is another innovation developed by BiOS, and primarily targets agriculture, public health and environment through cooperative open access technology development (BiOS, 2005). For example, a BioForge project called BiOsentinels is an agricultural diagnostic portfolio developed to incorporate sensor components for local challenges in farming and signalling components for detecting crop species that grow in particular regions in developing countries. There is also a free full-text searchable database for intellectual property informatics and analysis, Patent Lens, containing over 1.6 million patents in the life sciences. Where IP protection or patents restrict free access to diagnostic technology, these BioForge open source innovations can be a useful tool to solve farming problems.

BiOS has also launched a campaign to provide communication systems that allow dispersed individuals to participate in and benefit from decentralized innovative research. But the BiOS initiative is not just about campaigns or creating awareness, but practical examples in donating free technologies through open source licence. When a company or institution invents a technology, a patent is usually filed to protect it from free use and regain any investment made in the invention. In most cases the company retains exclusive use of the technology for about 20 years, until the patent runs out. Placing restrictions on a scarce technology kills innovation. But while company-owned technology is protective, open source technology is free. Free access to innovative technology has contributed to R&D around the world, especially in developing countries with limited resources. For example, the GUS reporter system arguably remains the most widely used staining technique in plant science, with over 4,000 literature citations (Boetigger and Wright, 2006). Various academic institutions have benefited from using open source tools to carry out experimental research in agriculture (Thomas, 2005). Scientists at Cornell University in collaboration with a small group of farmers from the Hawaiian Papaya Growers Co-operative used Cambia open source research tools to find a solution to a virus problem in papaya; and at Huazhong University more than 20,000 unique lines were created by Zhang Qifa, a leading Chinese plant biotechnologist.

The Public Intellectual Property Resource for Agriculture (PIPRA) involves a group of non-profit institutions from more than 15 countries around the world. It focuses on intellectual property issues (e.g. patents) by providing free access to patented technology, particularly agricultural biotechnology, under a set of shared principles. A concerted effort has been made to develop a database of 6,600 agricultural patents involving 45 different countries. PIPRA's goal is to ensure farmers, researchers and other organizations are provided with the right resources for clarity and analysis of patented technology through effective implementations. One goal is to mobilize and encourage innovative technologies among various institutions for the development and distribution of subsistence crops for humanitarian purposes in developing countries.

However, PIPRA can be distinguished from open source, as the two movements have different approaches to sharing innovations. PIPRA offers services in terms of collaborations with institutional members on IP policy analysis, biotechnology resources and commercialization strategy to improve and develop shared technology packages (Atkinson et al., 2003; PIPRA, 2006). In open source, service is focused on cumulative improvement which requires downstream transfer of the materials under a copyleft-style "grant-back mechanism" whereby licensees must agree to share and allow the right to reuse improvements made to research tools under open source licence (Penin and Wack, 2008). But while the initiatives differ, they serve the research community well and achieve their purpose of encouraging and sharing innovation by creating more free access to research tools that can benefit institutions across different countries.

To show that open source technology is gradually gaining ground in agricultural practices, the General Public License for Plant Germplasm (GPLPG) for the seed sector was proposed by Tom Michaels in 1999. The GPLPG mechanism can contribute to strategies of impeding dispossession and enabling possession when implemented under open source licence (Kloppenburg, 2010). Michaels (1999) reported that the GPLPG could be an effective, simple way to promote the continued free exchange of germplasm, thereby resisting enclosure and restricted access to vital information on the gene-scape (Deibel, 2006; Hope, 2008). It can be useful among breeding communities, farmers, plant scientists, universities, non-governmental organizations and government agencies. In addition, the mechanism could be a means of sharing and distributing freely a pool of plant germplasm in "bazaar" fashion among peers, based on protected commons (Michaels, 1999; Raymond, 1999). It shares similar ideas with the CGIAR General Challenge Program in providing a common pool of genomic knowledge and research tools where IP restrictions are placed on agricultural innovation (Ruivenkamp and Jongerden, 2010).

Moreover, application of open source innovation can promote and share the benefit derived from growing orphan crops on a large scale by resource-poor farmers and wider communities in future. Orphan crops that are grown mostly in developing countries may attract BioLinux open source when a variety of improved seeds becomes available for sharing among the farmers. For example, farmers in countries such as Mali, India, Indonesia and Colombia have been adversely affected by seed industry sectors, so these countries are likely to welcome the BioLinux approach (Aoki, 2008; Desmarais, 2007; Douthwaite, 2002; Kloppenburg, 2010). The opportunities offered by open source go a long way in contributing to sustainable agricultural development through free access to modern biotechnology techniques and advances.

Apart from its potential roles in sustainable agricultural development, the use of open source in genetically engineered products, particularly in drug discovery for improving health, can be very important in developing countries. Although agricultural and pharmaceutical projects and their designs vary, there is a common goal to ensure that biotechnology advances (e.g. proteomics, genomics) important to both fields become available to a broad research community and have continuous open access. Availability of open source in drug discovery may play a big role for pharmaceutical companies in the future, hence the need to expand this area. An effort has been made in proposing the Tropical Disease Initiative with a view to developing drugs to fight tropical diseases (Wake and Ridley, 2003) – the project will focus on different tasks of identifying new drug targets. For example, a gene or protein can be identified from human molecular structure that plays a particular role in the mechanism of a disease (e.g. malaria). Similar efforts using open source drug discovery to achieve research goals include the International HapMap Project that specializes in mapping the human genome (Thorisson et al., 2005) and the Council of Scientific and Industrial Research focusing on identification of non-toxic drug targets for *in vitro* and *in vivo* validation (Brahmachari, 2010). All these projects are designed such that universities, research institutions and corporations can work together to achieve a common goal in solving complex problems associated with discovering novel therapies. For example, the complete sequence of *Mycobacterium tuberculosis* genome in 2008 was made available to the scientific community through open source. In addition, the initiatives are aimed at providing affordable and cost-effective healthcare services to the developing world.

Challenges in FOSS biotechnology adoption and proposed solutions

Constraints in adopting open source biotechnology

Although open source biotechnology has several potentials to benefit human development, there are fundamental challenges that must be properly addressed to ensure these potentials are fully maximized. Challenges will vary from country to country, but the developing world will likely face the most, largely due to high levels of poverty, illiteracy, political crisis and economic instability. However, open source adoption will remain a global problem as long as the majority of world populations have little or no access to it. The challenge in using open source biotechnology will not only be in the area of agricultural practices but in every aspect of biological innovation.

Introducing open source biotechnology in developing countries will require a considerable amount of capacity building in terms of ICT infrastructure development and human training. In Malaysia, for example, using FOSS tools in AgriBazaar was difficult due to a lack of familiarity among software developers. Some of the engineers were used to proprietary software products, and it can take some time to get used to a new product. Coupled with interoperability problems, this may cause reluctance among users and organizations to change to open source. In many developing countries, lack of basic infrastructure such as telecommunications and electricity may delay the application or adoption of open source biotechnology. Other factors such as shortage of IT professionals and absence of IT industries in developing countries can delay open source development. Each of these requires enormous capital to tackle.

The challenge of IP protection is arguably the most complex issue due to the high costs involved. This is especially the case for farmers with limited financial resources to protect their farm products. Beck (2011) suggested an open source consortium may be able to act on behalf of farmers to secure IP to protect their resources. Although general open source licence policy is based on the promise to keep source code free and allow free access to copyright-protected aspects of the code, challenges still remain in biotechnology, including the translation of the open source software model to biotechnology due to the different requirements of patent laws. To achieve protected commons in open source, copyright as the dominant IP licence is the key legal right of access in open source software, whereas patent (not copyright) is the dominant form of IP protection in open source biotechnology (Hope, 2008). In terms of standard, patentability is much higher than copyrightability (Lemley and O'Brien, 1997). And the cost of getting patents for innovations in biotechnology can be exorbitant and time-consuming, compared to open source software that costs little or nothing and takes less time. Thus patenting can cause a setback in research and limit experimentation by a scientist or individual farmer. In addition, the research culture in open source software is different from that in open source biotechnology. For example, the equipment used in biotechnology is very expensive, while software creation requires just a computer and a desk. Considering these factors, the open source approach could be slower to take root in biology than in software.

Several disputes involving open source and proprietary software could pose a big threat to future development and adoption of open source technology, particularly in code ownership (IP) and licence enforcement issues (copyright licence and contract) in developing countries. FOSS licensing models can be unreasonable by exploiting IP rights designed to exclude people from copying software, as opposed to a proprietary licence dictating what can be done to software by a licensee. Code ownership in the IP system will remain a complex issue in global markets due to the international nature of FOSS. Licensing laws and IP systems (between licensees and licensors) vary from country to country. For example, patent protection for data and computer programs is robust in the United States but intensely debated in Europe and other parts of the world. In a lawsuit involving Sitecom/Netfilter, a German court stopped Dutch company Sitecom from distributing code licensed under GPL as Sitecom did not include the source code (Shankland, 2004). In a similar scenario the SCO Group of Utah sued IBM for $5 billion, claiming that SCO's proprietary code was included in a Linux distribution by IBM (Shankland, 2005). These are just two examples of dispute over copyright licences; other legal cases involve big companies, and this can potentially affect adoption of open source. Although a number of organizations have an extensive interest in FOSS viability and widespread adoption, they nonetheless have to deal with many legal uncertainties.

Patent misuse through a grant-back mechanism is another challenge in open source biotechnology. As the technology advances, it may be difficult to keep research tools and inventions within the confines of the open source arena as they become available to a wider research community. For example, an attempt to seek reward or compensation for an improvement made to the technology may result in litigation if the innovator involved feels that the improvement should attract greater reward notwithstanding the original open source licence. Under normal principles of patent law, people making novel improvements to the core technology are entitled to apply for patents so long as the requirements of patentability are met and the right procedures are followed. This can sometimes lead to shrouded overlapping rights on research tools among multiple parties (Feldman, 2004), thereby keeping the innovation out of reach for poor communities. The issue of the grant-back mechanism in open source licences may discourage collaborations that facilitate increased creativity and better innovations among young generations of scientists. For example, the grant-back mechanism and BiOS viral licence have led to PIPRA's rejection of BiOS licensing terms (PIPRA, 2006). Moreover, in the context of the grant-back approach, researchers who are interested in commercializing their work can decide not to participate when confronted with such a policy.

As mostly practised in developed countries, the governance structures of academic communities are built around commercial purposes; as a result, privacy and confidentiality of research work tend to affect the sharing of data. This may limit the free flow of scientific knowledge and innovations to the public through an open source model. Commercial relationships between many universities and biotech industries could mean that some data may not be shared with the public to protect the patentability of research work in progress. In this case, access to innovations through open source biotechnology becomes difficult in developing countries.

Policy implication for open source development

Provision of adequate training

Training is the hallmark of effective and good management. Open source development requires adequate training in various aspects of FOSS to facilitate the introduction and growth of open source biotechnology in developing countries. It is necessary to establish technical support and a training policy for open source development, particularly in ICT. ICT policies should be part of the process to promote open source in developing countries, and should support education and training at different levels. Due to the low level of ICT literacy in these countries, training strategies or policies should reflect basic skills (e.g. basic understanding of IT) and user-friendly methodology in the language of choice of the rural poor. In Malaysia, the FOSS software used to connect farmers and buyers in AgriBazaar was designed to serve these communities in various local languages. This contributes to acceptance and participation among the targeted group at grassroots level. Moreover, training should be given regularly in the course of evaluation and adaptation processes, and where necessary retraining should be provided for sustainability and continuity.

Provision of adequate resources and facilities

Given the importance of open source biotechnology for the benefit of society, adequate resources must be committed to support open source development in developing countries. Apart from education and training, basic facilities such as telecommunications and electricity to facilitate the application of open source should be provided. In all these, open source technology will require huge financial investment from governments. Nonetheless, providing FOSS can be cheaper relative to proprietary software. For example, the Ugandan University's migration to open source was as a result of cost reduction (Bruggink, 2003). This is one example among many showing that FOSS is cheap and easily adaptable to local needs for various purposes. In sharp contrast, proprietary vendors are globally profit-oriented with little or no attention on local needs (Ghosh and Schmidt, 2006). Thus government policy should recognize the importance of FOSS and address the provision of the right resources and allocation of budgets for the development of open source.

Collaboration and network expansion

Collaborative data sharing should be encouraged among academic communities, particularly in developed countries, as this will provide opportunities for researchers in developing countries to benefit. Most researchers in developing countries depend on scientific data and publications from developed countries to advance their work. For example, developing countries have created successful science policies through two-way contributions in international scientific exchange (Forero-Pineda, 1997). Collaborative data sharing through open source is one of the best approaches to encourage networking between scientists in developed and developing countries. Moreover, collaboration based on common pools where individual sharing of discoveries in biological innovation is possible should be encouraged between universities and multinationals, thereby paving the way for open source biotechnology.

Effective policy and legislation

The success of open source depends on an effective policy and legislative framework in developing countries. Governments should formulate policies that encourage open source development, focusing on supporting ICT in education and government at all levels; creating an enabling environment for access to ICT by citizens, business and government; providing local professionals with adequate training and skills in relevant software development to compete in the market; identifying and prioritizing areas of need, such as local software and IT industries; and adopting open standards for data storage and preservation. Further, governments should work within the framework of relevant international regimes such as the CBD, TRIPS and UPOV to create a friendly IP system that encourages open source for innovative technologies in developing countries. This will decentralize patented technologies and make them freely accessible to researchers in these countries, particularly in agriculture biotechnology.

Flexible licensing policies

Open source licence policy should be flexible enough to allow interested parties to use innovation with freedom of choice. For example, the availability of genomic databases through bioinformatics gives flexibility in the terms chosen by users. By contrast, biotechnology research does not usually provide an avenue for freedom of choice. Also, the current BiOS licensing policy does not encourage freedom of choice due to the grant-back mechanism. Encouraging flexible licensing policy under the open source approach could lead to rapid development of research tools and increased economic benefits for users in developing countries.

Conclusion

In the field of agriculture, open source biotechnology is being adopted rapidly but several challenges still constitute barriers to its use in developing countries. Given the rate of adoption of commercial biotech crops between 1996 and 2009 around the world, particularly in developing countries (80-fold increase – James, 2009), open source will have an important role to play in sustainable agriculture in the near future. Furthermore, the open source regime will provide means and ways to compensate farmers for contributing to the growth of plant resources, and may serve as an information resource for farming communities (Beck, 2011). But if open source biotechnology is to contribute to sustainable agriculture in developing countries, some of the issues facing its adoption must be properly addressed.

Adequate provision of basic infrastructures and financial resources will play a vital role in the adoption of open source technology. After these necessary facilities, education forms the basis through which open source development can be promoted among citizens, thus quality education on ICT should be provided to encourage wide grassroots participation. Lack of political support due to low levels of awareness among government officials in developing countries can slow down open source development, so a concerted effort should be made to educate and encourage officials at all levels.

IP is another serious challenge in the field of agricultural biotechnology. Because IP protection restricts research tools, this stifles innovation that can benefit developing countries. The IP system affects collaboration and scientific networking between developed and developing countries, resulting in little or no data sharing. Without doubt, the current IP system is not in good shape, particularly in the crop biotechnology that has great potential for improving food security and the quality of life of resource-poor farmers in developing countries. The profusion of patents in agricultural biotechnology creates problems for future downstream research. The IP system must be redesigned in a research-friendly way to suit all the parties involved in biotechnology R&D of crops that are important to poor people in developing countries. Functional and transparent international regulatory frameworks that support and protect plant resources of farmers in developing countries should be provided. In as much as biotechnology is applied in agriculture practices, the issue of IP remains central. For agricultural biotechnology to fulfil its great promise, an effective open source IP management plan is required. Open source offers a promising solution to the problems plaguing scientists and farmers only if the IP system is fair, friendly and supportive of the interests of all stakeholders.

This chapter has explored emerging challenges in the adoption of open source biotechnology in agricultural practices. Given the IP-related constraints on access to innovations in agricultural biotech, more efforts are required from organizations, individuals, governments and international agencies to support and promote open source biotechnology for sustainable agricultural development in poorer countries. Moreover, a lot of work still needs to be done in terms of case studies to assess fully the major areas where open source is being adopted, and the benefits and constraints associated with its adoption in developing countries.

Finally, if the introduction of open source biotechnology is to contribute to sustainable agriculture in developing countries, enabling environments in terms of policy formulation and implementation for establishing, supporting and providing the capacity building and resources required to develop open source must be put in place. Most importantly, the attention and focus of open source development should not be restricted to one area, but should address every need that will benefit humanity, including health and environment.

REFERENCES

Aoki, K. (2008) *Seed Wars: Controversies and Cases on Plant Genetic Resources and Intellectual Property*, Durham, NC: Carolina Academic Press.

Arora, A. and P. Merges (2004) "Specialised Supply Firms, Property Rights and Firm Boundaries", *Industrial and Corporate Change* 13(3), pp. 451–475.

Atkinson, R. C., R. N. Beachy, G. Conway, F. A. Cordova, M. A. Fox, K. A. Holbrook, D. F. Klessig, R. L. McCormick, P. M. McPherson, H. R. Rawlings III, R. Rapson, L. N. Vanderhoef, J. D. Wiley and C. E. Young (2003) "Intellectual Property Rights. Public Sector Collaboration for Agricultural IP Management", *Science* 301(5630), pp. 174–175.

Beck, R. (2011) "Farmers' Rights and Open Source Licencing", *Arizona Journal of Environmental Law and Policy* 1(2), pp. 10–28.

Bello, W. (2009) *The Food Wars*, London and New York: Verso.

Binenbaum, E., C. Nottenburg, P. G. Pardey and B. D. Wright (2000) "South-North Trade, Intellectual Property Jurisdictions, and Freedom to Operate in Agricultural Research on Staple Crops", Environment and Production Technology Division Discussion Paper No. 70, International Food Policy Research Institute, Washington, DC.

BiOS (2005) "Biological Innovation for Open Society"; available at www.bios.net/daisy/bios/home.html (accessed 8 April 2012).

Bocci, R. (2009) "Seed Legislation and Agrobiodiversity: Conservation Varieties", *Journal of Agriculture and Environment for International Development* 103(2), pp. 31–49.

Boetigger, S. and B. D. Wright (2006) "Open Source in Biotechnology: Open Questions", Cambia-BiOS Innovations Case Discussion; available at http://are.berkeley.edu/~wright/INNOV0104__boettiger-wright.pdf (accessed 11 September 2011).

Brahmachari, S. K. (2010) "The Open Source Drug Discovery (OSDD) Update"; available at www.osdd.org/ (accessed 11 September 2011).

Bruggink, M. (2003) "Open Source in Africa: Towards Informed Decision-Making", International Institute for Communication and Development Research Brief No. 7; available at www.iicd.org/files/Brief7.pdf (accessed 11 September 2011).

Bureth, A., J. Penin and S. Wolff (2006) "Entrepreneurship in Biotechnology: The Case of Four Start-ups in the Upper-Rhine Biovalley", BETA Working Paper No. 2006-21, Göteborg; available at http://portale.unibocconi.it/wps/allegatiCTP/August2006_WP2a_17.pdf (accessed 11 September 2011).

Cambia (2009) "BiOS: A Framework to Collaboratively Solve Our Shared Challenges", available at www.bios.net/daisy/bios/mta.html (accessed 8 April 2012).

Cassier, M. (2006) "New 'Enclosures' and the Creation of New 'Common Rights in the Genome and in Software'", *Contemporary European History* 15(2), pp. 255–271.

CGIAR (1998) "Shaping the CGIAR's Future: Summary of Proceedings and Decisions", Consultative Group on International Agricultural Research International Center Week, 26–30 October, CGIAR Secretariat, Washington, DC.

Cooper, H. D. (2002) "The International Treaty on Plant Genetic Resources for Food and Agriculture", *Review of European Community & International Environmental Law* 11, p. 116.
Daniell, H. (2002) "Molecular Strategies for Gene Containments in Transgenic Crops", *Nature Biotechnology* 20(6), pp. 581–586.
David, P. A. (2004) "Can 'Open Science' Be Protected from the Evolving Regime of Intellectual Property Rights Protections", *Journal of Theoretical and Institutional Economics* 160(1), pp. 1–26.
de Janvry, A., G. Graff, E. Sadoulet and D. Zilberman (2000) "Technological Change in Agriculture and Poverty Reduction", concept paper, University of California, Berkeley.
Deibel, E. (2006) "Common Genomes: Open Source in Biotechnology and the Return of the Commons", *Tailoring Biotechnology* 2(2), pp. 49–84.
Dennis, C. (2004) "Biologists Launch Open-Source Movement", *Nature* 431(7008), p. 494.
Desmarais, A. (2007) *La Via Campesina: Globalization and Power of Peasants*, Halifax, NS: Fernwood Publishing.
Douthwaite, B. (2002) *Enabling Innovation: A Practical Guide to Understanding and Fostering Technical Change*, Boston, MA: Zed Books.
Erbisch, F. H. and K. M. Maredia (2004) *Intellectual Property Rights in Agricultural Biotechnology*, Wallingford: CAB Publishing International.
ETC Group (2002) "Ban Terminator Before It's Too Late", *ETC News*, 5 April.
Evenson, R. and P. Pingali (2007) "Agricultural Innovation: Investment and Incentives", in *Handbook of Agricultural Economics*, Vol. 3, Amsterdam: Elsevier, pp. 25–81.
Feldman, R. (2004) "The Open Source Biotechnology Movements: Is It Patent Misuse?", *Minnesota Journal of Law, Science and Technology* 6(1), pp. 118–167.
Forero-Pineda, C. (1997) "Convergence of Research Processes, Big and Small Scientific Communities", paper presented at IIASA Workshop on Global Science System in Transition, Laxenburg, May.
FSF (1991) "The GNU General Public License (GPL) Version 2", Free Software Foundation; available at www.gnu.org/copyleft/gpl.html (accessed 11 September 2011).
Ghosh, R. A. and P. Schmidt (2006) "Open Source and Open Standards: A New Frontier for Economic Development?", UNU-MERIT Policy Brief No. 1, Maastricht.
Heller, M. A. and R. S. Eisenberg (1998) "Can Patents Deter Innovation? The Anticommons in Biomedical Research", *Science* 280(5364), pp. 698–701.
Hoe, N. S. (2006) "Breaking Barriers: The Potential of Free and Open Source Software for Sustainable Human Development – A Compilation of Case Studies from Across the World", UNDP Asia-Pacific Development Information Programme, Bangkok; available at www.apdip.net/publications/ict4d/BreakingBarriers.pdf (accessed 20 January 2011).
Hope, J. (2004) "Open Source Biotechnology", PhD thesis, Australian National University, Canberra; available at http://rsss.anu.edu.au/~janeth/OpenSourceBiotechnology27July2005.pdf (accessed 11 September 2011).

—— (2008) *The Open Source Revolution and Biotechnology*, Cambridge, MA: Harvard University Press.

James, C. (2009) "Global Status of Commercialized Biotech/GM Crops: 2009", Brief No. 41, International Service for the Acquisition of Agri-biotech Applications, Ithaca, NY.

Jawara, F. and A. Kwa (2003) *Behind the Scenes at the WTO: The Real World of International Trade Negotiations*, London and New York: Zed Books.

Jefferson, R. (2001) "Transcending Transgenics – Are There 'Babies' in the Bathwater, or Is That a Dorsal Fin?", in P. G. Pardey (ed.) *The Future of Food: Biotechnology Markets and Policies in an International Setting*, Washington, DC: IFPRI, pp. 75–98.

—— (2007a) "Freely Sharing Innovation Is the Only Way to Face the Future", *The Australian*, 31 August, p. 12.

—— (2007b) "Science as Social Enterprise: The Cambia BiOS Initiative", *Innovations: Technology, Governance, Globalization* 1(4), pp. 13–44.

Kloppenburg, J. (2010) "Impeding Dispossession, Enabling Repossession: Biological Open Source and the Recovery of Seed Sovereignty", *Agrarian* 10(3), pp. 367–388.

Lemley, M. A. and D. W. O'Brien (1997) "Encouraging Software Reuse", *Stanford Law Review* 49(3), pp. 225–305.

Michaels, T. (1999) "General Public License for Plant Germplasm: A Proposal by Tom Michaels", paper presented at Bean Improvement Cooperative Conference, Calgary, 18–20 March.

Nature (2004) "Open-Source Biology", *Nature* 431(7008), p. 491.

Odell, J. T., J. L. Hoopes and W. Vermerris (1994) "Seed-specific Gene Activation Mediated by the Cre/lox Site-specific Recombination System", *Plant Physiology* 104(2) pp. 447–458.

Pardey, P. G. and B. D. Wright (eds) (2003) "Intellectual Property and Developing Countries: Freedom to Operate in Agricultural Biotechnology", IFPRI Biotechnology and Genetics Resource Policies Brief 3, January, Washington, DC.

Pardey, P. G., J. M. Alston, C. Chan-Kang, E. Castello Magalhaes and S. A. Vosti (eds) (2004) "Assessing and Attributing the Benefits from Varietal Improvement Research in Brazil", IFPRI Research Report No. 136, Washington, DC.

Pedleton, C. N. (2004) "The Peculiar Case of Terminator Technology: Agricultural and Intellectual Property Protection at the Crossroads of the Third Green Revolution", *Biotechnology Law Report* 23(1), pp. 1–29.

Penin, J. and J. Wack (2008) "Research Tool Patents and Free-Libre Biotechnology: A Suggested Unified Framework", *Research Policy* 37(10), pp. 1909–1921.

PIPRA (2006) "PIPRA's Evaluation of the BIOS License", *PIPRA Newsletter* 5; available at www.pipra.org/en/documents/PIPRA-Newsletter-Issue5.pdf (accessed 11 September 2011).

Pray, C. E. and A. Naseem (2005) "Intellectual Property Rights on Research Tools: Incentive or Barriers to Innovation? Case Studies of Rice Genomics and Plant Transformation Technologies", *AgBioForum* 8(2/3), pp. 108–117.

Rai, A. K. (2004) *Open and Collaborative Research: A New Model for Biomedicine*, Durham, NC: Duke University School of Law.

Rai, A. K. and R. S. Eisenberg (2003) "Bayh-Dole Reform and the Progress of Biomedicine", *Law & Contemporary Problems* 66(1/2), pp. 289–300.
Raymond, E. (1999) *The Cathedral and the Bazaar: Musings on Linux and Open Source by an Accidental Revolutionary*, Sebastopol, CA: O'Reilly Media.
Rockefeller Foundation (1999) "Food Gains for the World's Poor Are Being Threatened by Furor Over Genetically Modified (GM)", press release, Rockefeller Foundation, Washington, DC.
Rosenberg, D. (2000) *Open Source: The Unauthorized White Papers*, Foster City, CA: M&T Books.
Ruivenkamp, G. and J. Jongerden (2010) "Open Source and Commons in Development", paper presented at ISDA Conference, Montpellier, 28 June–2 July; available at www.isda2010.net/var/isda2010/storage/fckeditor/file/posters/ISDA_Ruivenkamp.pdf (accessed 22 February 2012).
Safrin, S. (2002) "Treaties in Collision? The Biosafety Protocol and the World Trade Organization Agreements", *American Journal of International Law* 96(22), pp. 607–628.
Shankland, S. (2004) "GPL Gains Clout in German Legal Case", *CNET News*, 22 April; available at http://news.com.com/2100-7344_3-5198117.html?part=business2-cnet (accessed 11 September 2011).
—— (2005) "Judge Slams SCO's Lack of Evidence against IBM", *CNET News*, February; available at http://news.com.com/Judge+slams+SCOs+lack+of+evidence+against+IBM/2100-7344_3-5570265.html?tag=nl (accessed 11 September 2011).
Shoemaker, R. (2001) "Economics Issues in Agricultural Biotechnology", US Department of Agriculture Economic Research Service Agricultural Information Bulletin No. 762, Washington, DC.
Srinivas, K. (2002) "The Case for BioLinuxes and Other Pro-Commons Innovations", in *The Cities of Everyday Life*, New Delhi: Center for the Study of Developing Societies.
Stallman, R. (2002) *Free Software, Free Society*, Boston, MA: GNU Press.
Thies, J. E. and M. Devare (2007) "An Ecological Assessment of Transgenic Crops", *Journal of Development Study* 43(1), pp. 97–129.
Thomas, Z. (2005) "Open Source Agricultural Biotechnology", *Current Science* 88(8), pp. 1212–1213.
Thorisson, G. A., A. V. Smith, L. Krishnan and L. D. Stein (2005) "The International HapMap Project Website", *Genome Research* 15(11), pp. 1591–1593.
Wake, S. and R. G. Ridley (2003) "Virtual Drug Discovery and Development for Neglected Diseases through Public-Private Partnerships", *Nature Review* 2(11), pp. 919–928.
Weber, S. (2004) *The Success of Open Source*, Cambridge, MA: Harvard University Press.
World Bank (2005) *Agricultural Growth for the Poor: An Agenda for Development*, Washington, DC: World Bank.
Wright, B. D. (1998) "Public Germplasm Development at a Crossroad: Biotechnology and Intellectual Property", *California Agriculture* 56(6), pp. 8–13.

3

FOSS as a driver: Perspectives from the ICT development agenda

Tomonari Takeuchi

Introduction

Information and communication technology (ICT) is regarded as a powerful tool for development. In particular, free and open source software (FOSS) can help developing countries to solve the financial and technical problems involved in utilizing ICT. There are many advantages of FOSS, including free use, reasonable total cost of ownership (TCO), reduced copyright infringements and achievement of vendor independence. However, despite the efforts of governments and international organizations to diffuse it in the developing world, few of the poorer countries are successfully utilizing FOSS for their development.

Why is the diffusion of FOSS not occurring? The reason is that its recognized strengths are not attractive to local people. Though it is common to stress the advantages of FOSS by comparing it to proprietary software, this method may not be adequate. The purpose of FOSS for development (FOSS4D) is not to contest proprietary software but to help the poor to improve their lives. When advocating FOSS4D, FOSS should not merely be compared to proprietary software; rather, it is necessary to focus on its unique nature, namely the paradigm in which volunteers collaboratively create software for the common good. This unique feature brings positive effects beyond the FOSS4D field, and leads to a new paradigm for development.

The objective of this chapter is to inspire more attention on a new role for FOSS in development. Thus far, arguments about FOSS tend to focus

Free and open source software and technology for sustainable development, Sowe, Parayil and Sunami (eds), United Nations University Press, 2012, ISBN 978-92-808-1217-6

on its economic and technical advantages. However, it has the potential to bring more actors into the development field and change the paradigm of traditional development activities. This chapter tries to illustrate this aspect of FOSS by rethinking its merits beyond economic and technical aspects.

To accomplish this, this chapter attempts to discover a new role for FOSS by recognizing the current trends of three related fields: international development in general, the ICT for development (ICT4D) area and technology innovation. Among all these fields, the common keyword is "participation". The FOSS-driven new scheme for development work is derived from this word. Participation – among not only local users and local engineers but also new actors from developed countries – delivers more resources for development projects and realizes the new paradigm for development.

The discussion in this chapter begins by introducing the generally recognized advantages of FOSS as a background for the argument, and pointing out the weaknesses of these conventional advantages. A new and more important role for FOSS is then suggested. The future trend of FOSS as a driver for the new development scheme is explained, and challenging issues such as sustainability are addressed. The concluding section summarizes the overall discussion.

Background

Definitions

In general, FOSS refers to software that provides free access to source code and can be freely modified, distributed and used. Free does not mean free of charge, but rather refers to "freedom". The abbreviation "FOSS" actually contains two terms: "free software" and "open source software". There is an organization representing each term: the Free Software Foundation and the Open Source Initiative. Thus FOSS can be defined as "software that is distributed under a license that is recognized either as free software by the Free Software Foundation (FSF) or as Open Source Software (OSS) by the Open Source Initiative (OSI)" (Hoe, 2006: 4).

The two organizations seem to have the same purpose, but they have their own philosophies about commonly used software. The free software movement directed by FSF is a social movement with the objective of making all software in the world free to run, copy, distribute, study, change and improve – all based on the idea that information should be free for society. The open source movement directed by OSI pursues better development methodology to realize free access to source code (Elliott and Scacchi, 2008). However, in general their positions are similar. For example, OSI defines OSS according to 10 criteria, but these include FSF's definition of free software. Thus, in practice, both terms are used without a clear distinction, though there is a philosophical difference between FSF and OSI. The term "FOSS" is typically used in such a way that it expresses the combined meaning of both terms. This chapter uses "FOSS" in accordance with this general definition.

Merits of FOSS

Most developing countries have been utilizing ICT for development. For example, among 29 countries that have poverty reduction strategy papers, 12 treated ICT as a tool for poverty alleviation and/or as an independent item, and the other 17 countries underlined rural telecommunications as a key component of infrastructure development (Duncombe, 2006). Regarding software, many developing countries (e.g. South Africa, India, Pakistan, Thailand, Brazil and Malawi) pay attention to FOSS (Dravis, 2003; Reijswoud and Jager, 2008), not only for its software implementation but its background philosophy (ibid.). In 2003 African countries established the Free Software and Open Source Foundation for Africa (FOSSFA), an offspring the ICT Policy and Civil Society Workshop at the UN Economic Commission for Africa in 2002, to disseminate FOSS in Africa (FOSSFA, 2008). Wong (2004) insists that FOSS application can play a crucial role in achieving the Millennium Development Goals because it possesses a variety of merits when used in developing countries. International organizations and governments of developed countries have been advocating the advantages of FOSS (Wheeler, 2007). For example, in 2003 the International Open Source Network (IOSN) was initiated by the UN Development Programme (UNDP) with support by the International Development Research Centre (IDRC), aiming at treating FOSS-related issues in the Asia-Pacific region (IOSN, 2007). Similarly, bilateral aid agencies such as the IDRC, Deutsche Gesellschaft für Technische Zusammenarbeit (GTZ) and Swedish International Development Cooperation (Sida) have supported FOSS-related projects in developing countries (IDRC, 2007; ict@innovation, n.d.; Weerawarana and Weeratunge, 2004). The rationale behind this is that there are advantages to FOSS. The primary merits of FOSS mentioned by several authors are clarified in Table 3.1.

These merits are repeatedly cited by international organizations and donors such as UNDP and the IDRC. The governments of developing countries have also made efforts to disseminate FOSS by establishing a related policy (Dravis, 2003). For example, Malawi's 2005 National ICT for Development policy document advocates the use of FOSS as an alternative to commercial software (Reijswoud and Jager, 2008). Similarly, the second Thailand ICT master plan (2009–2013) contains strategies to utilize FOSS in education as well as to promote FOSS business (MICT, 2009). In this context, several FOSS4D projects are being conducted with various objectives, such as "ICT awareness and bridging the digital divide", "FOSS advocacy and capacity building", "better government–citizen communication and interaction", "assisting specific communities" and "solving specific problems" (Hoe, 2006).

Research questions

At this point, however, a simple question must be asked: are the merits of FOSS really attractive to people in developing countries? Reviewing FOSS penetration provides a hint in seeking the answer. This penetration can be grasped by two aspects: "user" and "area". Firstly, according to research, the world penetration of server-related FOSS such as Linux, Apache and My SQL is higher than proprietary software; on the other hand, client software such as OpenOffice and Firefox is very limited compared to proprietary software (Wheeler, 2007). This means FOSS is more commonly used by computer engineers (server users) than ordinary people (client users). Secondly, regarding area, research by the International Institute for Communication and Development (IICD) reveals that actual use of FOSS in least developed countries is very limited compared to more developed countries such as South Africa and Brazil (Reijswoud and Jager, 2008). These facts indicate that the merits of FOSS are attractive to system engineers and to more developed countries. In other words, despite the advantages of FOSS, it may not be attractive to ordinary users and its adoption does not spread out easily in least developed countries. If FOSS provides the various merits mentioned above, why is its use so limited? Furthermore, why are ordinary people at the user level in least developed countries not benefiting from the merits of FOSS despite the fact that they should be the target of development attempts? It could be true that there is a gap between the rationale and the reality of FOSS use (Figure 3.1). In the next section, the reason behind this situation is examined from the perspective of the reality of local people in developing countries.

The gap between traditional FOSS advantages and the reality

As shown above, several advantages of FOSS are frequently mentioned by international organizations and donor countries in their initiatives (e.g. UNDP supported the IOSN and GTZ supported ict@innovation).

Table 3.1 General merits of FOSS

Merit	Description	Reference
Low cost	FOSS does not mean free of cost, but most software is free of charge since it can be copied and distributed freely. It is difficult for developing countries to use ICT due to high costs of software and hardware. Software users must pay a licence fee; some software also requires expenses related to upgrades and support. FOSS does not involve software fees and related costs.	Hoe (2006); Paudel, Harlalka and Shrestha (2010); Reijswoud and Jager (2008); Wong (2004)
Localization	Since FOSS can be modified freely, users can improve software to fit their environment and requirements. It is possible for users to apply local languages and unique interfaces, which may not be available in propriety software.	Hoe (2006); Paudel, Harlalka and Shrestha (2010); Reijswoud and Jager (2008); Thomas (2010); Wong (2004)
Prevents vendor lock-in	Using proprietary software forces users to follow standards established by corresponding vendors; following such a standard is advantageous only for specific vendors, and users cannot choose new vendors or software because they must ensure compatibility in ongoing systems. Using FOSS can prevent vendor lock-in since source code is accessible.	Office of Government Commerce (2002); Paudel, Harlalka and Shrestha (2010); Wong (2004)
Reduces copyright violations	In developing countries pirated software is commonly used, regardless of users' intentions. Copyright violations could be reduced by making FOSS pervasive in the public sphere.	May (2006); Wong (2004)
Learning opportunity	FOSS can be modified and improved freely. Access to source code provides opportunities for engineers in developing countries to learn software development.	Hoe (2006); Reijswoud and Jager (2008); Paudel, Harlalka and Shrestha (2010); Wong (2004)

Table 3.1 (cont.)

Merit	Description	Reference
More security	Source code for proprietary software is not open to users, so they must use a system as if it is a black box; there is a security risk involved in this, especially in such important systems as are found in governmental or financial applications. FOSS does provide information about mechanisms inside software: users are able to interact with a system about which they know everything.	Fuggetta (2002); Hansen, Köhntopp and Pfitzmann (2002); Wong (2004)
Fosters ICT industry	FOSS enables entrepreneurs to start software businesses easily because it eliminates much of the time and expense of producing software from scratch. As more FOSS businesses are created, more competition is brought into the market, the price of proprietary software decreases and functionality improves.	Hoe (2006); Reijswoud and Jager (2008); Wong (2004)

Figure 3.1 Gap between FOSS rationale and reality

Such advantages generally involve comparing FOSS to proprietary software, and the advocacy seems aimed at system engineers and government officials in technical and economic aspects rather than non-technical ordinary users who are actually the majority. However, does the use of FOSS in developing countries aim to eliminate proprietary software? Is the aim of FOSS4D to provide benefits for computer engineers and government officials? Why is FOSS not so common in less developed countries as in more developed countries? In this section the stated advantages of FOSS are examined to determine if they are actually beneficial for people in developing countries, especially ordinary people at the user level in least developed countries.

Does FOSS really provide economic advantages?

The most emphasized advantage of FOSS is the economic benefit of the free software licence. However, in reality it is easy to obtain proprietary software almost free, although it is pirated copy version. According to research by the Business Software Alliance (BSA/IDC, 2010), there are 25 countries with greater than 85 per cent software piracy rate; all are from the developing world, including newly industrializing economies. The same research shows that the average worldwide PC (client) software piracy rate increased to 49 per cent in 2009 from 47 per cent in 2008 as a result of PC market growth in Brazil, India and China. Moreover, the IICD research reported that people pay too little attention to copyright issues in most least developed countries (Reijswoud and Jager, 2008). This indicates that the economic benefit itself is not necessarily a crucial reason for selecting FOSS, especially in least developed countries. It may even be the case that downloading a FOSS application from the internet is more costly than buying a pirated version of proprietary software sold in markets for much less than the cost of using an internet service for the download (ibid.). In this regard, realistically the free licence offers minimal advantage for people in less developed countries.

Though some researchers insist that the TCO of FOSS is lower than that of proprietary software (Wheeler, 2007), others indicate that the opposite is true (Paudel, Harlalka and Shrestha, 2010). For example, research conducted by the International Data Corporation shows that the TCO of a Windows server system is lower than that of a Linux system because the Linux management tools bundled by vendors are not free (Shankland, 2002). There is as yet no clear answer to this issue, because the findings vary according to who (e.g. Microsoft or Linux vendors) conducts the research.

Additionally, recently it has become increasingly difficult to determine which TCO is lower because the share of the software licence fee in the TCO has been shrinking. Private software companies tend to offer software at a low price to gain future market share, then sell valuable services such as customization and system integration for a higher price. Microsoft offering Windows OS for the One Laptop Per Child project seems to illustrate a strategy that many software companies may pursue. The traditional business model based simply on selling software licences is changing, and consequently the licence fee is becoming a small part of the TCO. Regarding the cost for service products, such as software development and technical support, there is no significant difference between FOSS and proprietary software since the required manpower is similar for the two types. Thus the benefit of the free licence is becoming less meaningful than in the past.

What about a user's skill?

The economic merit of FOSS is related to a user's skill. Access to source code is an important advantage of FOSS, but the source code is of little value without software engineering skills (Blake and Tucker, 2006). Some aspects of FOSS are truly valuable when users have adequate technical skill. If a user (or someone who works with a user) can read source code, understand system structure and customize/localize software, adopting FOSS is cheaper than purchasing commercial software. In developing countries, however, especially least developed countries, a limited number of engineers have sufficient technical skill and most organizations, except government entities and large corporations, do not have such skilled computer experts on hand. Consequently, it is necessary for most organizations to hire FOSS experts or computer firms to localize software or improve system security. Unfortunately, the cost of such work may not be significantly different from the cost of customizing proprietary software. In this regard, the benefit of FOSS goes to skilled engineers and government entities and large corporations. In the case of small and medium-sized enterprises (SMEs) without an IT section, openness of source code does not matter. Furthermore, in some least developed countries finding experienced FOSS engineers may be difficult: there are not many FOSS developers compared to commercial software ones since FOSS is less common than proprietary software, and also the lack of fast and reliable internet connections makes it difficult to train skilled engineers because knowledge about FOSS is stored and shared primarily on the internet (Reijswoud and Jager, 2008).

Are the advantages of FOSS truly relevant to local people at the user level?

Most of the stated benefits of FOSS are presented as advantages over proprietary software. However, in developing countries these advantages are relevant only to specific groups. It seems that most FOSS merits are applicable to the rich and not to the poor. For example, it provides learning opportunities for software engineers in developing countries, as they can participate in the FOSS forum on the web and access source code written by skilled engineers all over the world. Through communication with mature experts, they can learn software engineering skills and develop the ability to work effectively and efficiently with others. However, to benefit from such opportunities people must be rich enough to access an environment where PCs and stable internet connection are available, educated enough to have good communication and presentation skill (i.e. internet literacy) and already have a certain knowledge of software engineering. In contrast, the poor who cannot afford to use the internet for long periods or do not understand English well cannot take advantage of such learning opportunities. Thus this benefit is available only to wealthy people. Nowadays, most people in developing countries are able to use mobile phones, regardless of economic, social and educational level, but it is too difficult to receive the benefits of FOSS. It requires the above-mentioned resources and skills.

Similarly, "vendor lock-in" is prevented only in the case of organizations that can employ computer experts. Since SMEs do not have such technical staff, they must pay a vendor for system development. Even if FOSS is selected by user organizations, the vendor tries to hold on to customers by concealing its knowledge and technical methods used in system development. Consider Linux, for instance, which is a commonly used FOSS. There are numerous companies that provide Linux-related services, and they have their own unique knowledge and skills. Unless users possess highly developed technical skills, they must rely on vendors to maintain and renovate the system. SMEs that lack highly skilled software engineers cannot prevent "vendor lock-in" – only large organizations with an IT section and SMEs with skilled FOSS engineers can do so.

Regarding copyright violations, it is true that the use of FOSS will reduce their frequency, making it of great value to government officials and corporations. However, this merit of FOSS does not necessarily drive ordinary users to prefer it. According to BSA/IDC (2010), more than 90 per cent of the software in Bangladesh, Georgia, Moldova and Zimbabwe was illegally obtained. Moreover, the report states that the commercial value of pirated software in the Middle East/Africa (US$2,887 million) is much lower than in North America (US$9,379 million). This reality shows that regardless of a country's development status, there are many people who do not care about copyright violation. In this situation, FOSS does not help much in solving the copyright infringement issue because unless the moral perspective changes, the issue will remain. Fundamentally, this issue should be solved by advocacy and awareness campaigns and development of legal systems at international level. Since it is necessary to minimize copyright violations, this merit of FOSS is attractive to governments and large corporations but not to ordinary people at the user level, not only in developing countries but also developed countries.

Finally, though it is said that FOSS fosters the local ICT industry, one is tempted to ask whether FOSS-related business is actually attractive to ICT companies in developing countries. Reijswoud and Jager (2008) point out that the absence of role models and the lack of large projects hinder the growth of FOSS businesses in these countries. In commercial software there are role models, such as Bill Gates and Larry Allison, who inspire young entrepreneurs to start successful software companies; but in the case of FOSS there are no such wealthy role models. Though there are some successful FOSS business models, as the ict@innovation (n.d.) project has reported, most are relatively small. Without good examples, why would entrepreneurs want to start FOSS businesses in an environment where proprietary software is used more than FOSS? In fact, some large FOSS projects – such as African Virtual Open Initiatives and Resources in South Africa – attract academics but do not encourage the local business community (Reijswoud and Jager, 2008).

What is the purpose of current FOSS4D advocacy?

The doubts and shortcomings regarding the FOSS hype are explained above. Two characteristics are found in current FOSS advocacy: firstly, the accent on technical and economic superiority compared to proprietary software, and secondly a tendency to focus on specific groups (i.e. skilled engineers, governments and large organizations). It is reasonable to think that the first characteristic leads to the second. Economic advantages attract government officials and technical ones attract engineers. It is not accurate to claim that all the advantages of FOSS are invalid, but it is true that FOSS4D advocacy should incorporate an alternative direction since the current approach lacks relevancy to the majority group (i.e. ordinary users), despite the fact that they, rather than the specialist group, are supposed to benefit from FOSS4D (Figure 3.2).

Let us reconsider the purpose of FOSS4D advocacy. It is obvious that its aim is to disseminate FOSS in developing countries with the intention of improving the lives of these countries' inhabitants. Repeating FOSS hype against proprietary software, however, is not an effective way to achieve this goal, because the advantages are limited mainly to system

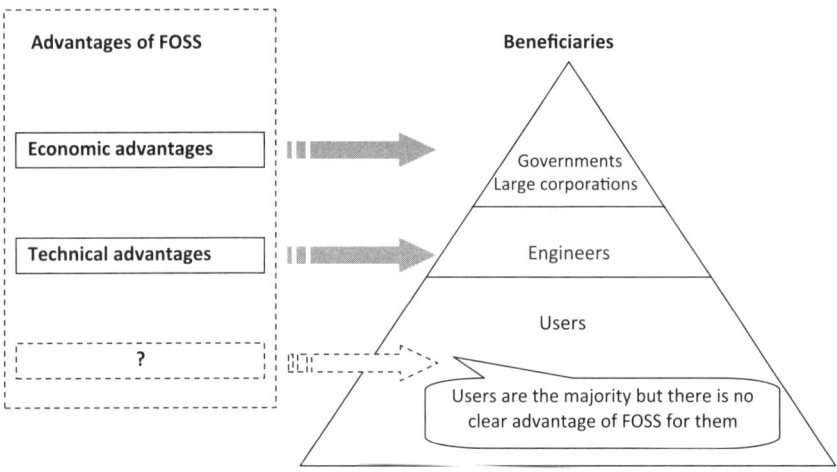

Figure 3.2 Current FOSS advocacy

engineers and large organizations like government entities, and do not directly benefit local users who are the majority. It is time to consider changing the traditional method of FOSS4D advocacy.

What is the new role of FOSS?

As discussed, current FOSS4D advocacy tends to target system engineers, governments and large corporations rather than non-technical ordinary people. Of course, such advocacy is important, but FOSS has more potential to influence a wider range of people. Beyond the current targets, the benefits of FOSS4D projects can be received by more people, including those in developed countries, and the impact can be felt not only economically and technically but also socially (Figure 3.3).

FOSS can make more meaningful impacts than competing proprietary software. To realize this future, FOSS4D advocacy must be approached in a new way. Two questions must be addressed: what is the new role of FOSS in development, and what is an alternative method of advocating FOSS for development?

To discover a new role for FOSS, it makes sense to focus on its unique ideology and methodology. Sound development in the developing world requires active participation by local people, and in this context there is similarity, in terms of ideology and methodology, between FOSS development and international development. In particular, the FOSS philosophy and participatory development have much in common. Thomas (2010)

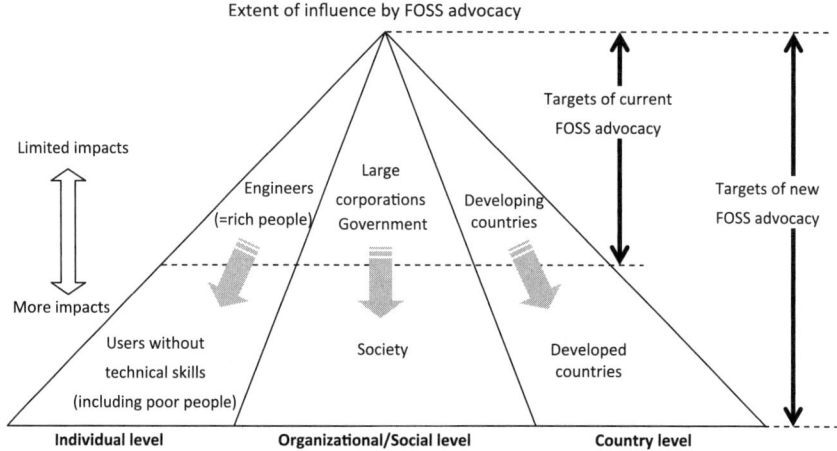

Figure 3.3 Extent of influence of FOSS advocacy

points out three elements, "democratism", "collectivism" and "contextualism", that are present in both the FOSS movement and the participatory development approach. The FOSS and participatory development philosophies are based on democratic principles, both methodologies are collaborative and both prioritize locality (ibid.). In other words, FOSS has two dimensions: its ability to gather computer engineers in the Western world and its ability to involve locals in the third world, as in participatory development. These characteristics lead to the opinion that FOSS can generate a paradigm in which various actors voluntarily work towards collaborative production – such as of software, services or websites – for the common good. FOSS can encourage more actors, from both developed and developing countries, to participate in development activities. A greater number of actors generates increased funding and greater contributions are provided for development projects. This means that the amount of resources (people and money) available for development activities will increase, and hence the impact will exceed that of current FOSS4D. In addition, collaborative work among people from the developed North and the developing South will lead to better relationships between developed and developing countries at the grassroots level.

Seeking an alternative direction for FOSS4D advocacy, it is suggested that FOSS is able to act as a driver in bringing about this new paradigm for development. This new role for FOSS can be derived by considering the current trends of three related fields (Figure 3.4).

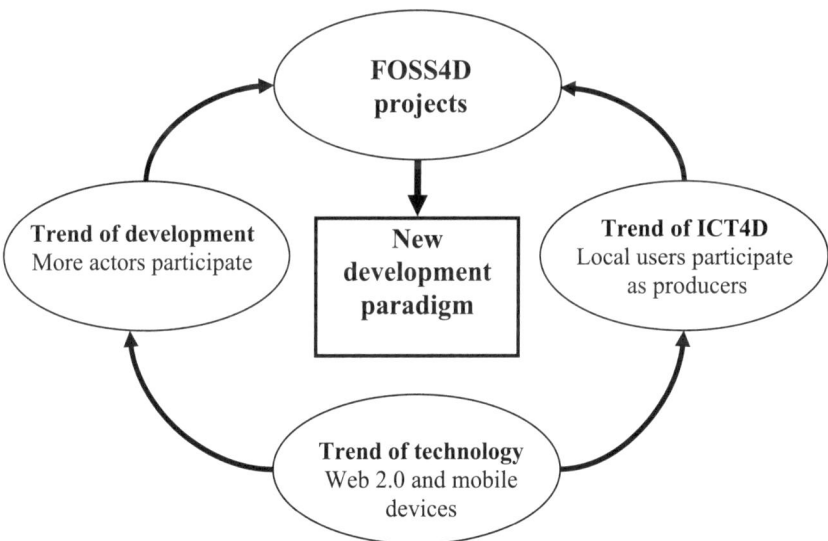

Figure 3.4 FOSS-enabled new development paradigm

Firstly, as a general trend, more actors are now joining international development, as represented by BOP (base of the pyramid) business and CSR (corporate social responsibility) activities. Secondly, in the ICT4D field there is a move to consider local people in developing countries as producers instead of consumers (Heeks, 2009, 2010). Such user participation is key to successful ICT4D projects, and this is true for FOSS4D projects as well. Finally, in the technology field, along with the diffusion of Web 2.0 tools and mobile phones, a new platform is emerging for many purposes, and finding ways to use such a platform has become increasingly important for businesses. Why not for development? Utilizing the platform for FOSS4D projects will trigger a new FOSS-enabled development paradigm. The trends in each field lead to the new role for FOSS.

Trend of international development

Recently, new types of actors have become engaged in the development field. As Prahalad (2010) mentions, there are 4 billion people in less developed countries who are potential consumers of commercial products. Many private companies are now interested in BOP business. For example, Unilever has implemented several activities in developing markets – such as India, Pakistan and Bangladesh – in collaboration with aid agencies such as the US Agency for International Development and the UN Children's Fund (UNICEF). Unilever sells small pieces of soap that low-income families can afford, and provides information about hand-washing which contributes to improved hygiene and health conditions (Unilever, 2010). In addition, some BOP businesses are becoming major actors in development. A typical example is a mobile phone business. Mobile companies from the Western world have been expanding their markets in developing countries, and their business activity results in a better life for people in these countries. M-PESA and M-KESHO in Kenya enable poor people to access financial services through mobile phones. CSR is another way for corporations to become involved in international development. As with BOP business, CSR activity has been expanding. In this context, the impact of the participation of private companies is becoming increasingly significant in the international development field.

Moreover, not only companies but also individuals are contributing to international development through ICT. There are several websites that enable individuals to help people in developing countries. For instance, Kiva is a website where people in the developed world can lend a small amount of money as capital to poor people who are ready to start a small business. Through Kiva, over $220 million in loans (as of June 2011) have helped poor people to start businesses and thus pursue better lives (Kiva,

2011). Such schemes, known as "peer-to-peer funding", are becoming more common. There are similar websites where ordinary individuals can lend or donate money directly to beneficiaries by way of microfinance (e.g. MYC4), scholarships (e.g. Vittana) or venture capital (e.g. Venture Capital for Africa).

There is now a trend whereby new kinds of actors – besides traditional aid workers, international organizations and governments – are entering the development field. Experience indicates that with more actors, more development is realized. In this context, collaboration is important in achieving better development.

FOSS4D projects allow new actors to participate in development activities, including IT companies and software engineers. FOSS4D projects are opportunities for IT-related companies to explore BOP business and CSR activities. Assisting with software development in developing countries enables these companies to find new markets and advertise their social contributions.

Trend of ICT for development

When it comes to ICT4D, there is a trend of moving from "ICT4D 1.0" to "ICT4D 2.0", as Heeks (2009) insists. In the early stages of using ICT for development, ICT was brought from developed countries to developing ones. In this technology-driven and technology transfer phase, referred to as ICT4D 1.0, the owners of ICT are people from the West, while people in the third world are passive recipients or mere consumers of information. There is no chance for poor people to control and gain ownership of ICT. However, in the current era, known as ICT4D 2.0, people in the developing world are becoming producers of ICT and of information. They are able to participate in producing information and creating new ways of applying ICT. For example, projects using community radio and/or video enable them to broadcast and share important information that is not brought from the Western world, but rather generated by local people (ibid.). In addition, they can act as innovators to create unique ways of using ICT in their environments (Heeks, 2010). For instance, they use mobile phones for communication by simply recognizing ring tones (without talking), and reduce expenses by sharing one mobile phone among several people (ibid.). Such ways of using these phones are not taught by aid agencies or governments of economically developed countries. The inhabitants of developing countries learn to use ICT within their particular restrictions, such as limited financial resources or unreliable electricity service. These examples should inspire international organizations and donor countries to consider people in developing countries as producers and innovators rather than passive recipients and consumers. Such a perspective is a key feature of the ICT4D 2.0 era, and it is essential in making ICT4D projects successful.

Similarly, "participation" is the basis of FOSS development. Based on the FOSS philosophy, projects have been conducted collaboratively by numerous contributors from around the world (Okoli, 2008). FOSS is a suitable tool for promoting participation because its development methodology is participatory, open, sharing and collaborative, and it has elements similar to those of the participatory development approach, namely democratism, collectivism and contextualism (Thomas, 2010). Thus FOSS4D projects have the potential to enable local people to participate in development as positive producers.

But local people do not constitute a homogeneous group. There are essentially two social groups: the rich (e.g. educated engineers, government officials, large corporation workers) and the poor (e.g. ordinary users, but not necessarily all – there are rich users, too). Wealthy people can easily take part in FOSS4D projects because they have the knowledge and motivation to improve their skills. The participation of the poor is more important – and also more difficult to achieve, because they do not have resources (e.g. money and time), adequate skills or knowledge. Poor people are the targeted beneficiaries of development, and they tend to be the local "users" of the systems that are established. Thus they should be included in FOSS4D projects – the local users know the requirements that are most important for system development. It sometimes happens in ICT projects that a project is started without recognizing the real needs, and after it is completed no one wants to use the system because it does not address the real requirements (Curtis and Cobham, 2005). To avoid such failures, the development process must involve not only local engineers but also "users" as producers.

Trend of technology

As mentioned, user participation is very important, but it is also easily ignored because the users are the "have-nots" who do not have enough resources, skill or knowledge. However, technology improvement provides possible solutions, namely Web 2.0 and mobile devices. The big Web 2.0 wave is one of the most significant trends occurring today. The definition of Web 2.0 varies; according to O'Reilly (2005), it can be phrased concisely as follows:

> Web 2.0 is the network as platform, spanning all connected devices; Web 2.0 applications are those that make the most of the intrinsic advantages of that platform: delivering software as a continually-updated service that gets better the more people use it, consuming and remixing data from multiple sources,

including individual users, while providing their own data and services in a form that allows remixing by others, creating network effects through an "architecture of participation," and going beyond the page metaphor of Web 1.0 to deliver rich user experiences.

As the definition indicates, Web 2.0 is a platform, and this platform could be used for FOSS4D projects. There are many Web 2.0 services, including social networking, social bookmarking, blogging, wikis, map mashups, social news and media sharing. According to Hitwise (2010), on 13 March 2010 Facebook outranked Google as the most visited website in the United States. In many African countries Facebook is the first or second most commonly accessed website, and the number of African users doubled from August 2010 to April 2011 (*Balancing Act*, 2011). Presently, many people are seeking a strategy involving Web 2.0 tools that will provide business opportunities, advertisement or national services.

In international development there are also many attempts to use Web 2.0 tools to create better lives for people in developing countries. For example, Kiva collaborates with Twitter to obtain investments for small business owners in poor countries, while a website named Refugee United is like a Facebook that helps refugees to find their families.

Along with the software innovation represented by Web 2.0, there is also innovation in hardware technology: the mobile phone. Access to Web 2.0 tools may be problematic in developing countries, where internet connections are often unreliable, but mobile phones can improve this situation (Addison, 2009). Improvements in technology have made mobile phones more functional and less expensive in terms of both hardware and communication fees. Mobile phones enable more people to access the internet. There are significant changes in penetration: in 1998 only 2 per cent of people in developing countries were mobile subscribers, but this figure had increased to 55 per cent by 2008 (Heeks, 2010). There are more mobiles phones in less developed countries than in developed countries. According to International Telecommunication Union statistics, the developing world's share of mobile subscriptions increased from 53 per cent in 2005 to 73 per cent in 2010 (ITU, 2010). This means that more than two-thirds of the world's mobile phones are in developing countries. This mobile penetration enables people, including the poor, to access information and services. There are many examples of "mobile for development" projects. Farmers in rural areas of Africa use mobile phones to determine the current crop price and thus maximize their profits. People in Kenya can transfer and save money through mobile banking services, such as M-PESA and M-KESHO, even if they do not have a bank account. The mobile phone is now recognized as a powerful development tool that allows local people to get involved in the information society (Donner, 2010). People can enter the interactive Web 2.0 information world via mobile phones, even from rural areas in African countries.

Given the trends of international development and ICT4D, these technology innovations – Web 2.0 tools and mobile phones – can provide a platform for collaboration between actors from developed countries and people in developing countries. The new actors can join development activities through this platform, and local people in developing countries can also be involved using the same platform. For non-technical locals, using a mobile phone makes the barrier to the internet much lower than using a computer. Since FOSS development is based on communities on the internet, there is a possibility of conducting FOSS4D projects based on new communities and new actors on the new platform. Such projects have two positive impacts: first, a product can be developed to meet real user requirements, and second the new actors are encouraged and empowered through the software development processes. These FOSS4D projects will bring about a new development paradigm.

FOSS as a driver for a new development paradigm

Using FOSS is not important in itself, but what is achieved by using it is very important. If the purpose of utilizing FOSS is merely to produce application software or achieve system integration, there is no significant difference between FOSS and proprietary software. Either one can achieve the user's goals. So why select FOSS? For developing countries, the reasonable cost is considered to be a strong factor. However, as mentioned earlier, there is minimal economic difference between FOSS and commercial software, and this advantage is not attractive to a wide range of people in developing contexts. So why do Western donor countries – where most people use proprietary software – recommend FOSS for developing countries? How can aid agencies using Microsoft Word and Excel persuade people in developing countries to choose OpenOffice? The rationale behind using FOSS for development should be based on what is delivered through the process of FOSS4D projects: "encouragement" and "empowerment" of new actors through this new platform.

Firstly, FOSS4D projects can encourage newcomers from the Western world to take action. Private IT companies can join the development effort by allowing their workers to participate in FOSS4D projects. Since working on the platform via the internet does not require them to go to another country, the impediments to participation are much smaller than those associated with traditional development activities. There are additional ways of contributing, such as offering server hosting services or providing technical knowledge. Apart from businesses, it is also possible for individuals to participate in FOSS4D projects if the platform is accessible. Many individuals already support the poor in the developing world through peer-to-peer web schemes, as mentioned, thus there are many potential individual supporters of FOSS4D projects. There will be someone in Japan helping with programming, someone in the United States offering language translation services, someone in Korea acting as a test user and so on. Anyone can contribute to FOSS4D with their speciality, because development projects involve a wide variety of information, skills and knowledge.

Secondly, FOSS4D projects can empower local people – not only engineers but also users. Web-community-based FOSS development processes involve engineers in developing countries who can benefit from working with experienced engineers. This is a clear merit included in the traditional FOSS4D advocacy. However, a new merit is the involvement of very ordinary local people at the user level. The Web 2.0 platform enables non-technical locals to voice their needs, from which system requirements are derived. Their voice could be expressed through blog comments or a vote function, similar to Facebook's "like" button. Another option is using voice messages or SMS via mobile phones. This does not require complicated operation, and mobile access allows people to participate casually yet honestly. Since the first step in system development is properly understanding users' demands, their contribution is crucial for success. Simultaneously, this empowers ordinary local users who do not obtain clear benefit from the current FOSS4D advocacy. They are directly involved in the development process; thus they are treated as producers even if they do not have technical skills. If they are treated as producers and if engineers take account of their input, local users will be able to exercise their autonomy. This empowerment is actually more important than the application software, which is developed through fruitful collaboration.

In sum, FOSS4D projects can enable more people to become active participants in international development. The ideology of FOSS, which involves "free" and "open", is relevant to social movements. Thus far, however, this movement has stayed within groups of highly skilled engineers. If it becomes open to more people in the form of FOSS4D projects, a new development paradigm will emerge in which more actors and more support from developed countries are mobilized, and local users are empowered through their active participation. Additionally, through the interactive and participatory FOSS development process, an unprecedented grassroots relationship may emerge between people in the developed world and people in the developing world. The FOSS4D process may extend and enhance development activities – from traditional governmental schemes to open, flexible contributions and activities. These advantages –

rather than the benefits of FOSS as compared to proprietary software – should be considered as the merits of using FOSS for development.

Emerging and future trends

Recent activities indicate that FOSS can act as a driver for the new development paradigm. Cases involving the use of FOSS in developing countries demonstrate the feasibility of realizing this FOSS-enabled paradigm, but examples of FOSS4D projects also reveal challenges associated with achieving the paradigm and potential solutions.

FOSS4D projects as a sign of the new development paradigm

A fruitful area for Web 2.0-enabled FOSS4D projects is in the disaster management field. Ushahidi – which means "testimony" in Swahili, the local language of Kenya – is a website that collects and shares information about real situations when exact or reliable information is unavailable as a result of disasters or riots. It was designed using FOSS with mobile text message functionality and Google Maps. The story of Ushahidi's development exemplifies the desirable aspects of future FOSS4D.

In Kenya a serious dispute associated with the presidential election occurred in December 2007. Ory Okolloh (2009: 59–60), a Kenyan activist and lawyer (not an engineer), created Ushahidi to help citizens to avoid accidents during this crisis. She describes the birth of Ushahidi as follows:

> On 3rd January 2008, I shared my thoughts on my blog and encouraged Kenyan "techies" who were interested in building such a website to get in touch. The response was lightning fast. Within a day or two a group of volunteers had coalesced and domain was registered. That was the genesis of Ushahidi, which means "testimony" in Kiswahili.

Following this blog, the website was developed using FOSS. Fifteen to 20 software developers, most of whom were from Africa, participated with various contributions. Surprisingly, the website was released within one week (ibid.). Because it is a FOSS application, it was possible for Ushahidi to be customized and used for several purposes in other countries. For instance, it was used in Haiti for sharing information about the 2010 earthquake disaster, in Israel for distributing information about conflicts in Gaza and in Uganda for election monitoring. Software developers from several countries, including Kenya, the United States, Holland, Uganda and Ghana, participated in the development of Ushahidi (Phillips, 2011).

This process provides an example of the new development paradigm. Engineers and non-technical people meet on a Web 2.0-enabled platform, and the system is established according to the real needs of local people. The process is implemented by actors from both developed and developing countries. A similar example is the FOSS disaster management system named Sahana. When Sri Lanka was damaged by tsunamis in 2004, Sahana was initially built by volunteers from the Sri Lanka IT industry; subsequently, international contributors, including programmers and disaster management experts, became involved (Treadgold, 2006). Through collaboration among Sida, IBM and the US National Science Foundation, it eventually became a generic disaster management tool and is currently utilized by some governments and non-governmental organizations (NGOs). These two examples clearly confirm the feasibility of the new development paradigm proposed in this chapter, which aims to enable more creators and users to participate in FOSS4D projects.

In the near future there will be many websites that allow people without technical skill, including the poor, to upload their needs and requests using such tools as SMS, blogs, Facebook or Twitter, and voluntary supporters, including companies, organizations and individuals from around the world, will determine which projects they can contribute to and how they can help – such as by writing code, sharing knowledge, performing translation services, providing server space or offering grant money. When needs and resources correspond, a project will be initiated. This is similar to a FOSS4D version of Kiva. Considering the FOSS philosophy and the context, in which Web 2.0 tools lead to new forms of contribution and mobile phones remove the impediments to internet access, such platforms will prove successful in the near future. This facilitates support for and participation in development activities, and more resources will be used for development. Development activities will become the work not only of aid agencies but of individuals of all kinds. The new role of FOSS is to facilitate this shift from traditional development to the new development paradigm.

Challenges facing the new development paradigm

There are several challenges involved in implementing the new role of FOSS. First of all, accessibility is a serious difficulty in most ICT4D attempts, as many scholars (Addison, 2009; Duncombe, 2006; Ndou, 2004) point out. It is difficult to secure accessibility in the vulnerable environment present in some developing countries, especially in least developed countries, which have an unreliable electric power supply and limited internet bandwidth. There is no simple or comprehensive solution to this problem. It is necessary to improve infrastructures consistently.

However, mobile phones can be a potential solution to improve accessibility (Addison, 2009; Kleine and Unwin, 2009). Mobile networks now cover 90 per cent of the world population; even in rural areas, mobile access is available to 80 per cent of the population (ITU, 2010). Despite their cost, mobile phones are dramatically changing the current situation. The decreasing cost of mobile usage and the rapid penetration of mobile access indicate that the accessibility challenge will be at least partially overcome in the near future.

Secondly, the low level of (ICT) literacy is also a serious problem (Roman and Colle, 2002; Warschauer, 2003). Even if access to the internet is secured, people will not be able to present their opinions if they cannot read and write. Or if they can read and write but are not accustomed to using the internet, they still cannot make their voices heard. Of course, improving education is the long-term solution. However, the story of the earthquake in Haiti demonstrates other potential solutions. When Haiti was devastated by an earthquake in 2010, a hotline was set up by an American aid agency to accept SMS from victims of the disaster. Unfortunately, American NGO workers could not read the messages, which were written in the local language. The solution was crowdsourcing. As soon as the text messages arrived, they were forwarded to Haitians living around the world, who translated them into English and returned them to the NGO workers in Haiti. This crowdsourcing proved immensely helpful (Heinzelman and Waters, 2010; Nelson, Sigal and Zambrano, 2010). The case shows that there is an alternative method that does not require users to do something they cannot do. In the future, technology and innovation, as in this crowdsourcing example, will further lower ICT literacy barriers.

Finally, the issue of sustainability presents the most serious difficulty. There is a hope that technological improvements and innovation will overcome the first two challenges, but the issue of sustainability cannot be resolved through technological progress. Hoe (2006) suggests that it is crucial to secure funding in order to pay people who are working to sustain FOSS4D projects. Voluntarism can initiate a project, but it cannot make it sustainable. Without a realistic approach (e.g. payments), it is difficult to continue a project. Based on research about Sahana, Treadgold (2006) claims that at least core members of a project should be paid to ensure sustainability, since it is risky to depend entirely on volunteers – every project requires uninteresting yet necessary work. On the other hand, some researchers insist that the motivation to contribute to FOSS projects is not strictly related to money. Elliott and Scacchi (2008) assert that the motivation for participation is based on the ideology of the free software movement, which, as Richard M. Stallman (2002) claims, is a belief in the "freedom" of information for society. Additionally, Lakhani

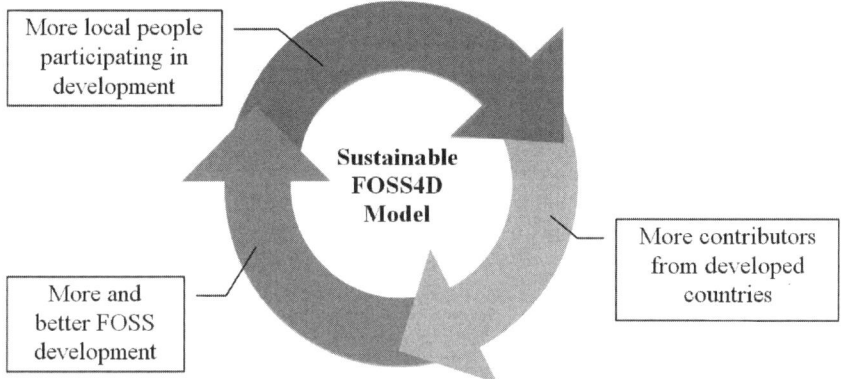

Figure 3.5 Sustainable FOSS4D model

and Wolf (2003: 2) conclude that "enjoyment-based intrinsic motivation, namely how creative a person feels when working on the project, is the strongest and most pervasive driver".

As indicated by these contrasting research results, there is no clear answer to this issue – motivation varies from individual to individual. In general, motivation is not based on a single factor: most people are motivated by a mixture of different factors. Thus to attract as many actors as possible, it is important both to secure funds and to emphasize the value and meaning of participation. For sustainable FOSS4D projects, it is important to work in a virtuous cycle (Figure 3.5): as more participants become involved, more development will be achieved. As a result of this greater achievement, more people become involved. Therefore, any possible ways should be used to involve as many actors as possible.

Conclusion

Summary of the discussion

This chapter attempts to describe FOSS merits from a different perspective to that of traditional FOSS4D advocacy. For this purpose, current FOSS4D advocacy is reviewed. International organizations, donors and governments in developing countries tend to think that FOSS is an alternative to proprietary software. They advocate FOSS4D by presenting FOSS in comparison to commercial software and discussing such merits as cost-effectiveness, reduction of copyright violations and prevention of vendor lock-in. However, there is a need to modify this advocacy given the gap between it and the local reality. The merits of FOSS currently emphasized are not attractive to ordinary people at the user level in developing countries. New advantages of FOSS are suggested: it can act as a driver for a new development paradigm which encourages the participation of more actors from developed countries and involves local people, not only engineers but also users. The rationale behind the new role of FOSS is explained in reference to current trends in three related fields, namely the emergence of more actors in international development, the necessity of the participation of local users as producers in ICT4D and the penetration of Web 2.0 tools and mobile phones. This new development paradigm is emerging in the context of FOSS4D projects. Two examples, Ushahidi and Sahana, are introduced and future trends are discussed, including the challenges of bringing about the FOSS-enabled new development paradigm and potential solutions.

Concluding remarks

Vision must be shifted according to the trend of the times, since ICT is always changing, as symbolized by the term "dog years". What is impossible today will be possible tomorrow. Thus the role FOSS plays in international development should be modified in accordance with current technological innovation. It is not reasonable to continue advocating the merits of FOSS in the traditional way. FOSS has the potential to bring new actors into the traditional development field. It is beneficial not only for engineers but also users, likewise not only for developing countries but also developed countries. In the developed world there are many people who would like to do something to help the poor or improve society, but not everyone is able to travel to Africa to work as a volunteer for a few years. Consequently, easier ways to contribute – such as peer-to-peer funding – are becoming more common. Since FOSS development is web community based, many actors from all over the world can participate in the process. The new paradigm encourages people in developed countries to take action on their own, and the participatory process of FOSS development allows people in the developing world to join in with a degree of autonomy. Technological innovation enables them to act as producers of new systems. Furthermore, such FOSS4D projects can bring about a better grassroots relationship between developing and developed countries through collaboration between ordinary people from both Northern and Southern worlds.

Finally, it is necessary to recall that ICT – including FOSS, Web 2.0 tools and mobile phones – is only a tool, not a solution. The action of human beings is what is truly important. If more people are determined to support and work for less developed countries, more and better development will be achieved. After all, whether or not FOSS can bring about the desirable development paradigm depends on ordinary people, who can work together to achieve extraordinary things.

REFERENCES

Addison, C. (2009) "The Two Hands of Web2forDev: A Conference Summary", *Participatory Learning and Action* 59(1), pp. 21–26.

Balancing Act (2011) "Africa's Facebook Explosion – User Numbers Double in Many Countries in Just Seven Months", *Balancing Act* No. 551, 21 April; available at www.balancingact-africa.com/news/en/issue-no-551/top-story/africa-s-facebook-ex/en (accessed 1 April 2011).

Blake, E. and W. Tucker (2006) "Socially Aware Software Engineering for the Developing World", paper presented at Proceeding IST – Africa 2006, Pretoria, 3–5 May.

BSA/IDC (2010) "Seventh Annual BSA/IDC Global Software 09 Piracy Study", Business Software Alliance; available at http://portal.bsa.org/globalpiracy2009/index.html (accessed 6 February 2011).

Curtis, G. and D. Cobham (2005) *Business Information Systems: Analysis, Design, and Practice*, 5th edn, Edinburgh: Prentice Hall.

Donner, J. (2010) "Framing M4D: The Utility of Country and the Dual Heritage of 'Mobiles and Development'", *Electronic Journal on Information Systems in Developing Countries* 44(3), pp. 1–16.

Dravis, P. (2003) *Open Source Software: Perspectives for Development*, Washington, DC: World Bank.

Duncombe, R. (2006) "Analyzing ICT Applications for Poverty Reduction via Micro-enterprise Using the Livelihoods Framework", Development Informatics Working Paper No. 27, IDPM, University of Manchester.

Elliott, M. S. and W. Scacchi (2008) "Mobilization of Software Developers: The Free Software Movement", *Information Technology & People* 21(1), pp. 4–33.

FOSSFA (2008) "History of FOSSFA"; available at www.fossfa.net/node/5 (accessed 3 September 2011).

Fuggetta, A. (2002) "Open Source Software – An Evaluation", *Journal of Systems and Software* 66, pp. 77–90.

Hansen, M., K. Köhntopp and A. Pfitzmann (2002) "The Open Source Approach – Opportunities and Limitations with Respect to Security and Privacy", *Computers & Security* 21(5), pp. 461–471.

Heeks, R. (2009) "The ICT4D 2.0 Manifesto: Where Next for ICTs and International Development?", Development Informatics Working Paper No. 42, IDPM, University of Manchester.

—— (2010) "Development 2.0: Transformative ICT-Enabled Development Models and Impacts", Development Informatics Short Paper No. 11, IDPM, University of Manchester.

Heinzelman, J. and C. Waters (2010) "Crowdsourcing Crisis Information in Disaster-Affected Haiti", Special Report 252, US Institute of Peace; available at www.usip.org/files/resources/SR252%20-%20Crowdsourcing%20Crisis%

20Information%20in%20Disaster-Affected%20Haiti.pdf (accessed 6 February 2011).
Hitwise (2010) "Facebook Reaches Top Ranking in US"; available at http://weblogs.hitwise.com/heather-dougherty/2010/03/facebook_reaches_top_ranking_i.html (accessed 6 February 2011).
Hoe, N. S. (2006) "Breaking Barriers: The Potential of Free and Open Source Software for Sustainable Human Development – A Compilation of Case Studies from Across the World", UNDP Asia-Pacific Development Information Programme, Bangkok; available at www.apdip.net/publications/ict4d/BreakingBarriers.pdf (accessed 20 January 2011).
ict@innovation (n.d.) "About the ict@innovation Project"; available at www.ict-innovation.fossfa.net/ (accessed 4 September 2011).
IDRC (2007) "Africa Source II: Free and Open Source Software for Local Communities"; available at http://idrc.org/en/ev-121430-201-1-DO_TOPIC.html (accessed 4 September 2001).
IOSN (2007) "The International Open Source Network (IOSN)", UNDP Regional Centre Bangkok, Asia-Pacific Development Information Programme; available at www.iosn.net/ (accessed 3 September 2011).
ITU (2010) "The World in 2010: ICT Facts and Figures", International Telecommunication Union; available at www.itu.int/ITU-D/ict/ (accessed 5 February 2011).
Kiva (2011) "About Us"; available at www.kiva.org/about (accessed 14 June 2011).
Kleine, D. and Unwin, T. (2009) "Technical Revolution, Evolution and New Dependencies: What's New about ICT4D?", *Third World Quarterly* 30(5), pp. 1045–1067.
Lakhani, K. R. and R. G. Wolf (2003) "Why Hackers Do What They Do: Understanding Motivation and Effort in Free/Open Source Software Projects", MIT Sloan Working Paper No. 4425-03, September, Cambridge, MA.
May, C. (2006) "Escaping the TRIPs' Trap: The Political Economy of Free and Open Source Software in Africa", *Political Studies* 54(1), pp. 123–146.
MICT (2009) "The Second Information and Communication Technology (ICT) Master Plan (2009–2013)", Ministry of Information and Communication Technology, Thailand; available at www.mict.go.th/download/Master_Plan.pdf (accessed 3 September 2011).
Ndou, V. (2004) "E-Government for Developing Countries: Opportunities and Challenges", *Electric Journal on Information Systems in Developing Countries* 18(1), pp. 1–24.
Nelson, A., I. Sigal and D. Zambrano (2010) "Media, Information Systems and Communities: Lessons from HAITI", InterNews, Communications with Disaster Affected Communities, Knight Foundation; available at www.knightfoundation.org/research_publications/detail.dot?id=377092 (accessed 6 February 2011).
Office of Government Commerce (2002) *Guidance on Implementing UK Government Policy on Open Source Software*, Norwich: OGC.
Okoli, C. (2008) "A Brief Review of Studies on Open Source Software in Developing Countries in Peer-Reviewed Journals", Sprouts: Working Papers on

Information Systems 8(45); available at sprouts.aisnet.org/860/1/Okoli_2008_OSS_dev_lit_review.pdf (accessed 13 June 2012).

Okolloh, O. (2009) "Ushahidi or 'Testimony': Web 2.0 Tools for Crowdsourcing Crisis Information", *Participatory Learning and Action* 59(1), pp. 65–70.

O'Reilly, T. (2005) "Web 2.0: Compact Definition?"; available at http://radar.oreilly.com/archives/2005/10/web-20-compact-definition.html (accessed 6 February 2011).

Paudel, B., J. Harlalka and J. Shrestha (2010) "Open Technologies and Developing Economies", Open Technologies Resource Center; available at www.otrc.gov.np/sites/default/files/OpenTechnologiesAndDevelopingEconomies_OTRC_2010_paper.pdf (accessed 6 February 2011).

Phillips, S. B. V. D. (2011) "Human Rights Resources Profile", Center for Research Libraries; available at www.crl.edu/sites/default/files/attachments/pages/Ushahidi_Profile_6%2012%2011_FINAL_0.pdf (accessed 21 February 2012).

Prahalad, C. K. (2010) *The Fortune at the Bottom of the Pyramid: Eradicating Poverty Through Profits*, Upper Saddle River, NJ: Wharton School Publishing.

Reijswoud, V. V. and A. D. Jager (2008) *Free and Open Source Software for Development: Exploring Expectations, Achievements and the Future*, Milan: Polimetrica.

Roman, R. and R. D. Colle (2002) "Themes and Issues in Telecentre Sustainability", Development Informatics Working Paper No. 10. IDPM, University of Manchester.

Shankland, S. (2002) "IDC: Windows Cheaper than Linux", CNET News, 3 December; available at http://news.cnet.com/IDC-Windows-cheaper-than-linux/2100-1012_3-975938.html (accessed 6 February 2011).

Stallman, R. (2002) *Free Software, Free Society*, Boston, MA: GNU Press.

Thomas, B. K. (2010) "Participation in the Knowledge Society: The Free and Open Source Software (FOSS) Movement Compared with Participatory Development", *Development in Practice* 20(2), pp. 270–276.

Treadgold, G. (2006) "Sahana – Engineering a Sustainable ICT Solution for Disaster Management", paper presented at Digital Earth '06 – Summit on Sustainability, Auckland, 27–30 August.

Unilever (2010) "Lifebuoy Way of Life, Toward Universal Handwashing with Soap: Annual Review 2008/09"; available at www.unilever.com/images/sd_WayofLifeJan2010_for_web1_tcm13-212739.pdf (accessed 6 February 2011).

Warschauer, M. (2003) *Technology and Social Inclusion: Rethinking the Digital Divide*, Cambridge, MA: MIT Press.

Weerawarana, S. and J. Weeratunge (2004) "Open Source in Developing Countries", Sida; available at www.eldis.org/fulltext/opensource.pdf (accessed 4 September 2011).

Wheeler, D. A. (2007) "Why Open Source Software/Free Software (OSS/FS, FOSS, or FOSS)? Look at the Numbers!"; available at www.osepa.eu/site_pages/News/43/WhyOSS_Look_at_the_numbers_Wheeler_2007.pdf (accessed 4 September 2011).

Wong, K. (2004) *Free/Open Source Software: Government Policy*, New Delhi: Elsevier.

4

A participatory service learning process for FOSS-based solidarity projects

David Franquesa, David López, Leandro Navarro and Fermín Sánchez

Introduction

Software and information and communication technologies (ICT) can be key elements for social development, especially in developing countries. Projects on ICT for development (ICT4D) are an important tool to incorporate positive changes in these communities. However, as with other technologies, ICT and particularly software supporting social processes have a huge potential for change, and for replication to many of these communities, but also a huge potential for disruption. From experience in over 50 ICT4D projects, we have learned how important it is to design and implement an open and participatory process based on the service learning (SL) concept, where different forms of learning, service and free and open source software (FOSS) become natural and interdependent parts of social development. The lessons learned help us in designing sustainable processes for positive change supported by FOSS that can be appropriated by indigenous communities, contributing to their social development and social justice.

ICT4D processes are characterized by the design of intertwined processes in coordination with multiple stakeholders. These processes include understanding the social and technological environment, learning about diverse technical and social aspects, software development, decision-making and introduction, adoption and redesign of social processes and software. The stakeholders are students and teachers at a university, a partner local organization and members of the target community.

Free and open source software and technology for sustainable development, Sowe, Parayil and Sunami (eds), United Nations University Press, 2012, ISBN 978-92-808-1217-6

Software systems and ICT infrastructures can be key elements to foster the social development of communities, as computer support enables or facilitates certain processes, empowering people to learn, coordinate, work effectively and reshape their own communities in social and economic terms. The openness in FOSS is a natural part of promoting social development where local and external actors work together to bring in knowledge or resources, but sustainability can only be ensured by supporting a process designed and run in the long term by the target communities. This long-term sustainability implies a long-lasting learning process.

This chapter describes the usefulness of open and participatory SL processes in software engineering education that complements FOSS development. Service learning is a method that integrates meaningful community service with instruction and reflection to enrich the learning experience. It supports the organizational learning and change that occur when FOSS is introduced in a developing community. Thus it has a key role in the sustainability of ICT4D projects on social development in poorer countries, and also in creating awareness in developed countries.

The lessons learned from projects we have carried out show how a carefully designed open and participatory process, combining FOSS development and service learning as key elements, reduces dramatically both barriers to participation and cost, and stimulates the indigenous socio-economic system, opening opportunities for wider collaboration between many actors in developing and developed countries. Furthermore, scenarios for ICT4D tend to be fragile and risks should be carefully avoided, as the effects can amplify in less developed areas.

This chapter first establishes the theoretical framework for our work, where FOSS and SL get combined for successful ICT4D projects. It then focuses on selected projects, presenting empirical and anecdotal evidence and specific lessons learned. We derive the generic lessons learned based on our experience of 15–20 years in ICT4D projects, and the quality factors that we apply in successive projects, which can also be generalized. Finally, results and conclusions are presented.

Theoretical framework

We are university academics developing ICT4D projects in collaboration with our students. So we first describe the service learning educational methodology we follow in our projects. We then analyse different ways of assessing the impact of ICT4D projects in the target community, with a stress on their resilience – the capacity to adapt and learn from change. Finally, the real access/real impact framework we use is described.

Service learning in ICT4D projects

Our work is based on the principles of service learning. Service learning (Jacoby, 1996; Duffy, Tsang and Lord, 2000) is a method of teaching and learning that combines an academic classroom curriculum with meaningful service in the community. As a learning methodology it falls within the philosophy of experiential education. More specifically, it integrates community service with instruction and reflection to enrich the learning experience, encourage civic responsibility and lifelong civic engagement and strengthen communities for the common good.

Service learning has been widely studied in relation to engineering (Tsang, 2000) and applied in some programmes, such as those at Purdue University (Coyle, Jamieson and Oakes, 2005). Real-world problems presented through service learning help students to engage in active learning and problem solving, which can develop knowledge on sustainability, create new perspectives and give them exposure to real techniques in the practice of engineering. In the Barcelona School of Informatics of Universitat Politècnica de Catalunya (BarcelonaTech) we use FOSS for solidarity and development projects because we believe that it holds the potential to provide a rich education experience for students. Hislop, Ellis and Morelli (2009) give a more detailed account of the impact on students' attitudes of using FOSS in solidarity projects.

ICT4D project life-cycle tasks and responsibilities

The development of an ICT4D project requires at least two partners: one local and one international. To facilitate the assignment of responsibilities and tasks according to the project stage, several teams are created.
- The *management team* is responsible for overall management and financing issues. It must include people from both local and international partners.
- The *requirements team* must define the needs involved and how they will be covered. This takes local and international expertise. Local experts have knowledge of the real problems and constraints of the target communities. International experts provide technical expertise, and also a holistic knowledge of how other communities are dealing with similar problems.
- The *development team* is responsible for finding hardware (when needed) and adapting or developing new software, validating and implementing the requirements previously defined. It is a task for the international partner.

- The *operation team* is responsible for operating the system once it is installed. This team consists of local participants, although the international team can be "on the ground" for installing and training the operation team.
- In projects developed using service learning, another group is required: the *training team*, responsible for introducing concepts of human development and ICT4D to students.

Once the project has been developed, there is one important question to answer: do these projects have a real impact on developing communities? To respond to this, an evaluation in the field of sustainable development has to be performed.

Real impact of ICT4D projects

Sustainable development requires a process of dialogue and ultimately consensus building of all stakeholders as partners who define the problems together, design possible solutions and collaborate in implementing them and monitoring and evaluating the outcome (Hemmati, 2002).

There are two key properties to navigate towards sustainability: resilience and adaptive capacity. Resilience (Folke et al., 2002) is defined as the capacity of a system to absorb disturbance and reorganize while undergoing change, so it still retains essentially the same function, structure, identity and feedbacks. Adaptive capacity is the general ability of institutions, systems and individuals to adjust to potential damage, take advantage of opportunities or cope with the consequences.

It is fundamental for ICT4D projects to help people in the target communities to adapt to the new tools, but without breaking resilience. In other words, the project must be useful, appropriate, affordable and relevant for their progress, but also must integrate in the target society, because this society must retain its identity. ICT4D projects must empower the community, offering the opportunity to develop, but without the loss of the community particularities. Thus the impact of ICT4D projects on the target community must be evaluated.

Evaluation is a tool for learning and steering interventions, and can be used for controlling and legitimizing political decisions and priorities. In evaluation practice a huge number of tools have been developed to conduct assessments, including indicators, models, surveys, cost-benefit analyses and cost-effectiveness studies, but it is difficult to know how and when to combine these in carrying out sustainability assessments (Herwijnen, 2008). Assessment approaches also differ in their application – whether to policies, programmes or agreements; to the national, regional or international level; or to particular discipline-specific, issue-specific or application-specific sectors. In addition to the methodology itself, the procedures for conducting assessments are important to sustainable development – particularly transparency and the involvement of all stakeholders.

Several impact assessment frameworks on ICT4D projects can be found in the literature on FOSS (Hoe, 2006) and more generally. For instance, Heeks and Molla (2009) build on a model to create a sequence (value chain) of linked ICT4D resources and processes. It is divided into four main targets for assessment.

- *Readiness:* "e-readiness" assessment typically measures the systemic prerequisites for any ICT4D initiative, e.g. presence of ICT infrastructure, skills, policies and so on.
- *Availability:* implementation of the ICT4D project turns the inputs into a set of tangible ICT deliverables.
- *Uptake:* assessment typically measures the extent to which the project's ICT deliverables are being used by its target population.
- *Impact:* assesses the impact of the project.

Another well-known way to evaluate technology adoption is the technology acceptance model (TAM – Venkatesh and Davis, 2000). TAM assumes that beliefs about usefulness and ease of use are always the primary determinants of IT adoption in organizations. According to TAM, these two determinants serve as the basis for attitudes towards using a particular system, which in turn determines the intention to use and then generates the actual usage behaviour. Perceived usefulness is defined as the extent to which a person believes that using a system would enhance his or her job performance. Perceived ease of use refers to the extent to which a person believes that using a system would be free of mental efforts. Venkatesh et al. (2003) developed the unified theory of acceptance and use of technology (UTAUT) model to consolidate previous TAM-related studies. In the UTAUT model, performance expectancy and effort expectancy were used to incorporate the constructs of perceived usefulness and ease of use in the original TAM study. A TAM 3 model has also been proposed (Venkatesh and Bala, 2008).

In this chapter we use the real access/real impact model developed by the Bridges organization (Bridges, 2010). In this model, 12 criteria frame the analysis of all issues surrounding ICT access and use, including the "soft" aspects that are often overlooked. They are designed to anticipate or detect the reasons why ICT development initiatives, government e-strategies or grassroots projects fail to achieve their goals, or highlight how and why these projects succeed.

- *Physical access to technology:* basic infrastructure requirements, such as electricity, can be barriers to technology access. People with disabilities have particular needs.

- *Appropriateness of technology:* the developed projects must be appropriate to local needs and requirements in terms of power supply, security, environment conditions, usefulness, etc.
- *Affordability of technology and technology use:* we must be sure that the target communities can afford to obtain, or access, the proposed technology.
- *Human capacity and training:* technology is useless if the members of the target community are not trained to use it, or cannot imagine its possibilities. Users must be empowered to innovate for themselves in the use of technology in their environment.
- *Locally relevant content, applications and services:* if ICT provides few or no benefits in the short term, it will not be relevant for local communities.
- *Integration into daily routines:* life in developing countries can be hard. If ICT is not perfectly integrated into daily routines, it can be seen as another burden in already overburdened lives. The benefits of incorporating ICT must reward the effort.
- *Socio-cultural factors:* across the globe, people are held back from full participation in their societies or economies on the basis of race, gender, class, age, etc. Development initiatives need to be aware of these socio-cultural factors in the target community, in order not to increase the digital divide.
- *Trust in technology:* the level of confidence in ICT is fundamental in its acceptance. It is important to inform people about the advantages, but also about the risks involved in ICT use to help new users guard against them.
- *Local economic environment:* ICT programmes must be useful to create local opportunities. Failed projects can lead communities to reject future technology projects, where they feel that funds might have been used for other things.
- Points 10 (*macro-economic environment*), 11 (*legal and regulatory framework*) and 12 (*political will and public support*) are related, and refer to national and regional economics, legal regulations and mid- and long-term visions of technology that can benefit or hinder ICT projects.

The relationship between service learning, ICT4D and FOSS

Service learning allows us, teachers in developed countries, to offer a real experience to our software and computer engineering students. Participating in ICT4D projects forces students to work under real constraints in terms of time, resources and a target community with some real and specific requirements. Moreover, it offers a new perspective of life, values and the real impact of technical solutions, beyond our well-known and comfortable environment.

Engineering students offer time and knowledge to develop these projects. In return, they receive new skills such as a knowledge of contemporary issues and work in multidisciplinary teams, the broad education necessary to understand the impact of engineering solutions in a global, economic, environmental and societal context, or the ability to design a system, component or process to meet desired needs within realistic economic, environmental, social, political, ethical, health and safety, manufacturability and sustainability constraints. All these skills are part of the Accreditation Board for Engineering and Technology (ABET) criteria, a set of 11 skills which are extremely important to achieve the US curricula quality accreditation (Shuman, Besterfield-Sacre and McGourty, 2005).

To use ICT4D projects to implement service learning, a university must be a part of the international partnership in the project's management team. Without the support of the university, these projects cannot be implemented. It is obvious that our students must be part of the development team, but must also participate in the requirements team discussions as part of their learning process. Finally, it completes the process if students can travel to the target community to install the software and train the operation team. To deal directly with final users and know their needs and daily life, and how will they use the software, can be one of the most rewarding experiences of student life.

This process cannot be achieved without working with FOSS. One reason – not the most important but sometimes basic – is that target communities very often cannot afford the cost of a proprietary software licence, and even if they can, they could not adapt the software to their own needs and bounds, especially the cultural ones. FOSS offers free licences, documented software, a community of experts around the world who can help and many other advantages (see other chapters of this book). But from the point of view of service learning, FOSS is fundamental: our students have learnt operating systems, networks or software engineering concepts just by understanding and modifying existing code, and we can only train them in the requirements for ICT4D projects by using FOSS, because students can analyse and modify the software with absolute freedom. Without this previous training and knowledge, ICT4D projects would be unaffordable.

Case studies

Our experience

In the Barcelona School of Informatics we have been introducing sustainability and social commitment concepts in our daily teaching activity

(López et al., 2011). As part of this objective, we have developed several ICT4D projects to implement service learning. Most of these help local communities and non-governmental organizations (NGOs), but about one-third (the more complex projects) are oriented to support communities in developing countries with ICT access and use to contribute to their sustainable development. In these international projects, the receptors receive hardware, when required; software, mainly tailored to receptor needs; training in ICT; and our students' time and dedication with the guidance of faculty. All four elements are necessary to develop this kind of project.

Hardware is provided through a "reuse workshop" that is held twice at year at our school. In this workshop, students and teachers donate their time to refurbish and repair second-hand PCs and install free software for use in solidarity projects (Franquesa et al., 2010). Sometimes the software requirements are quite simple, so no new software is needed. In this case, FOSS is installed in the computers, adapted to the final users. For instance, in 2007 we donated several computers to a school in Morocco and installed Ubuntu and FOSS educational software for children under 14, in Arabic and French. If the project is more complex and requires new or adapted software, some of our students develop it as part of their bachelor or master theses.

There are two essential factors for the success of these projects that we as teachers cannot control: volunteers and institutional support. Without volunteers, almost nothing can be done. We need academic staff to integrate these ideas into their subjects and advise on projects. Students are required to implement the projects. Administration staff are needed to help maintain the system. And institutional support is required: the university and the school should facilitate and motivate these initiatives.

A growing movement in solidarity exists in our university and enjoys strong support from the institutional framework. Our Institute for Sustainability (http://is.upc.edu) encourages the reduction, reuse and recycling of various materials, in particular electronic equipment. Another institution, the Cooperation for Development Centre (CCD; www.upc.es/ccd/), coordinates this movement. This centre has as its aim the centralization of all the university's solidarity initiatives. CCD's support is absolutely vital for the success of the projects, because they involve travelling to the destination community to implement the project in the field and train final users. This fundamental part of the project cannot be done without CCD's legal, logistic and financial support.

However, the most important resource is people. The Barcelona School of Informatics supports an internal NGO named Technology for Everyone (TxT; http://txt.upc.edu). TxT consists of students, academics and administration staff, and coordinates participation in these solidarity projects around the world (Farreras, Franquesa and López, 2009). Volunteer training is carried out by the requirements team, and part of the training process is done via an online platform (based on Moodle) that enables students and final users to interact before starting the project – in some cases the target community select the students who better fit their requirements.

The benefits of ICT4D projects as a tool for service learning

These activities are aimed at reinvigorating the civic mission of higher education and instilling in students a sense of social responsibility and civic awareness through the development of teaching and learning opportunities.

First, from the educational point of view, opportunities for integrating and relating theory to practice are created: academic theory is experienced in a real-world context, and new education techniques are promoted. The university finds a teaching environment in the community, and the academic and professional capacity of students is increased. Furthermore, since the European Higher Education Area first drew attention to the learning process from the student perspective, evolving from "teaching" to "learning how to learn", the practical aspect in education has increased in importance (Alonso et al., 2008). Secondly, the community benefits from the service: issues vital to social, civic and political society are explored, and the civic and personal capacity of students is enriched. Finally, the university receives feedback from the community: real-world problems learned from active participation in the community can influence the university to adapt its programme so that it can teach what is required by society.

As regards human-scale engineering, it is clear that by its very nature engineering is bound up with society and human behaviour, and involves responsibilities that should be borne in mind by every school of engineers. In our initiative the university can move closer to society, while at the same time society improves its opinion of the university.

Selected examples

Over the years we have participated in over 50 ICT4D international cooperation projects in 18 countries: Angola, Algeria, Bolivia, Burkina Faso, Colombia, Cuba, Ecuador, Equatorial Guinea, Gambia, Guatemala, Haiti, Morocco, Mozambique, Nepal, Paraguay, Peru, Senegal and Togo. Some projects have been quite simple, like installing a computer classroom in a school, or our participation was very small. Others were of great complexity, lasting several years and involving the development of several master's theses. Here we focus briefly on selected ICT4D projects, just as a taste of the kind of projects we are dealing with. We present some empirical and anecdotal evidence supporting the lessons learned discussed in the next section.

Project: Water, a scarce resource

In this project the target groups were farming communities in the coastal Pacific areas of Peru, with fertile land, a well-structured social network managing the river waters for irrigation and close proximity to the food markets of the capital, but poor communications and limited access to public services. A community of more than 6,000 farmers from the Chancay-Huaral irrigation district were directly involved in the project.

The goal was to support farmers in improving the quality of life of the community and the local economy. The project involved a number of agents: the local government (Ministry of Agriculture), the local farmers' association, a local NGO (the Centro Peruano de Estudios Sociales), the International Development Research Centre from Canada and a contribution from our university in the later stages.

Tasks involved the introduction of a complete ICT system, including electricity (with water-powered generators) in some areas, a wireless broadband network connecting 14 telecentres, VoIP telephony services and a software application (Yacu) for the management and coordination of irrigation quotas and agricultural production.

The project has been successful in supporting a rural community in adopting an ICT system that helps schools and farmers to be more effective and have a better quality of life. On the other hand, the project has not yet succeeded in exporting this technology to other irrigation districts.

Project: UN Western Sahara refugee camps healthcare system

The UN Western Sahara refugee camps are situated in the western part of the Algerian desert, near the frontier between Algeria and Morocco. Men, women and children of Western Sahara have lived here for nearly 20 years in one of the most inhospitable regions of the world: the summer temperature rises to more than 50° Celsius in the shade, and in winter it is freezing cold. When they came to these regions, the people found nothing beyond sand. It is solely thanks to the solid organization structure and large feeling of solidarity characteristic of these people that they were able to build a coherent society in this desert.

Nearly all the 20-year-old youngsters were born in these camps. At first the mortality rate was very high, especially among children. But thanks to a strong input on hygiene, the Sahrawi people were able to prevent epidemics and control the high infant mortality rate. As a result of a policy adopted for dealing with food products destined for children, there are now practically no cases of malnutrition. The Committee for Health Care focuses its greatest attention on prevention, but treatment is also very important. In the camps women are trained to become assistant nurses to help in the dispensaries, and a number of students are training abroad as nurses or doctors. The Ministry for Health Care has continued to make progress: a new national hospital just opened, with operating rooms and facilities for physical and psychological treatments.

Our work focused on two projects, developed as part of two master theses: an information system for the central pharmacy warehouse, and an information system for the child vaccination programme. The first project's goal was to optimize the storage system of the central pharmacy warehouse. This was one of our earliest projects, and we proposed it to the heads of the pharmacy warehouse, seeing a problem to be solved but without a deep knowledge of the reality of the camps. The project was a failure, because the final users are not using the information system but their old and inefficient pen-and-paper system. So for the second project, we changed our strategy.

The second project's goal was to develop a child vaccination information system adapted to the special characteristics of the refugee camps. We developed the software in close collaboration with paediatricians who have been working as volunteers in the camps for several years. These paediatricians have a deep knowledge of the real problems of the target community, so we act as experts in technology supporting the work of experts in cooperation. In this case, the project was a clear success.

Project: Conservation of the K'che' language and culture

The goal of a range of projects under the label "In your language" is to enable and extend the participation of indigenous communities in the digital society, and contribute to improving the learning of a native language to avoid language extinction. Projects of this type were started by Web Networks (Canada) with the Inuit language, and have been applied successfully in diverse regions of the world. We have participated directly in one in Guatemala (Quiché o K'che') and another in Colombia (Nasa Yuwe language), reusing some of the software tools and the accumulated experience.

The objective in Guatemala was to help the K'che' community to maintain their cultural inheritance. K'che' is part of the Mayan language family. It is spoken by close to a million native people in the central highlands of Guatemala, but is in peril because most children are now speaking Spanish for communication at school and using Spanish-language media. This project was a collaboration with the Ajb'atz' Enlace Quiché NGO, a non-profit organization run by Mayans for the Mayan people.

This NGO had experience in developing K'che' language courses using internet-connected computers, and our work was focused around two complementary master's projects developing an improved set of tools for language learning. The first project developed a simple content management system to empower the NGO in creating and managing its own web content locally using old computers and simple code it could easily understand, manage and extend. The second project was about developing a web application to allow language teachers to create and modify their own multimedia content (animated interactive lessons) for K'che' language lessons instead of just using pre-packaged fixed modules. Both projects resulted in and were based on FOSS (Apache web server, PHP, OpenLazlo, etc.). In both cases the objective was to start up development and initial use of the tools for the target NGO so it could improve its training activities by creating and modifying multimedia training modules and also develop the software tools further.

The project had mixed results: despite some initial success in the creation of the K'che' content and implementation of the tools, a lack of development resources has limited their usefulness so far. However, the lessons learned have been very helpful.

Project: Casa Guatemala orphanage and backpackers' hotel

Casa Guatemala is an NGO which owns an orphanage, the home and school for over 250 children. Casa Guatemala takes care of orphaned, abandoned or abused children, and those from families too poor to provide even the basics of child needs. Its main site is located in the jungle on the banks of the Rio Dulce in Guatemala. The orphanage receives no government support and is totally dependent upon donations from people and groups around the world. Only accessible by river via a little pier, the orphanage houses the people who work there, the teachers employed at the school and the volunteers from all over the world who give their support.

The orphanage covers an area of 40 hectares, including the school and houses for workers and volunteers. There is also some cultivable land and a farm (which are the main food sources), a little shop to sell farm produce and the backpackers' hotel, located right on the water's edge of Rio Dulce with rooms and food to suit all budgets. These last two entities contribute to the general funding of Casa Guatemala.

We started our collaboration with Casa Guatemala in 2006. Our efforts have been focused on six main areas: facilitate access by volunteers/donors/tourists to the orphanage; improve service quality and reduce costs of the backpackers' hotel; improve agricultural production systems; improve water conveyance facilities and water quality; improve energy facilities; and improve the quality of education.

In these years we have done 16 different projects related to the six areas. We have improved physical access to technology through successive donations of computer equipment, provided by the reuse workshop at our university. Since problems with electricity at Casa Guatemala have caused damage to power supplies for desktops, in the last few years we have donated laptops, which resist voltage fluctuations better and allow work even without electrical power. This technology is needed at the orphanage to encourage the digital literacy of children and improve the internal management processes. However, given that teachers in Casa Guatemala did not have adequate skills to operate such equipment and teach their work to children, we have conducted various training courses, aimed primarily at teachers of the school. Our volunteers are also involved in solving technical problems for the duration of their stay.

We have also designed a program for managing the hotel using free software tools, and a FOSS CRM (customer relationship management) is being designed to allow the directors of the orphanage to manage the large volumes of information they need. These applications are designed at the request of the orphanage to meet its needs, thus providing an added-value service. The software meets local regulations and standards in privacy and security, as well as international standards. However, the low technological training of Casa Guatemala workers makes them reluctant to use the programs when our volunteers leave the orphanage – they continue to perform many processes on paper because they do not trust technology. This causes them to see the technology as a burden rather than a solution, and often they do not update data in the software, which eventually makes it inoperative.

Although access to some of the computers we provide is free for all Casa Guatemala's inhabitants, workers limit their to use the functions they need to carry out their jobs. Fortunately this does not happen with the children, who are much more permeable to the acquisition of new habits and integrate technology into their lives, especially the internet.

Finally, the use of technology has had a direct impact on the economy of the orphanage, mainly because it lets the directors maintain constant contact with sponsors through the internet and also contact potential new donors.

Discussion and lessons learned

Some main lessons have been learnt from the projects in which we have participated.
- *Potential for replication.* The use of FOSS in development projects opens the way for replication to similar settings. Solutions initially con-

ceived for a given project can be extrapolated to other partners and environments, producing (at low cost) generic and specific software tools. To do so, the requirements of the project should include from day one the need to generate and publish the documentation for potential reuse.
- *FOSS may be necessary but not sufficient.* FOSS is a key element in many cooperation projects with less developed countries, but it is not enough to ensure success. It is part of a complex process that must be addressed with a holistic view. For example, a solution based in FOSS may not be useful if the infrastructure is not adequate (e.g. stabilized power supply is not guaranteed, no appropriate computers are available or local people are not properly motivated and trained to use FOSS technology).
- *The symbiotic relationship of FOSS with service learning.* FOSS and SL are complementary elements that help to solve problems in developing countries through cooperation projects. Being free of licensing and usage fees and open for customization and extension, among other freedoms, FOSS brings the possibility of easy adaptation to how target communities operate and the needs of each project. SL can complement FOSS at different levels, e.g. contributing refurbished hardware from initiatives such as computer reuse workshops, and involving the collaboration of students who receive, in return for their effort, not just monetary compensation but learning. FOSS and SL are both effort-intensive learning activities, and complement each other in a symbiotic way: SL works effectively using and producing FOSS as an outcome of learning processes, and the learning processes occurring in SL and at the same time on target communities introducing FOSS-based systems feed back to each other along the timeline of projects.
- *Macro and micro contributions of SL.* The macro contributions are large projects (final degree projects, master's theses, etc.) that students do before graduation. These also help in developing professional skills (i.e. several of the ABET criteria) in students – leadership, multidisciplinary teamwork, etc. The micro contributions are small assignments done by students within a particular subject – for example, working on adaptation, updating or development of a small piece of software or developing and installing computers for ICT4D projects. This service learning could not exist without FOSS. Students are trained in topics such as operating systems or network environments (because they have learned to modify some FOSS code, such as a driver). They use this technical training in real problems with real constraints, being aware that their work is part of a larger project focused on helping the community. We consider cooperation projects should be defined in two steps. The first is based on macro contributions where volunteers deal

with problems of a certain size, and perform risk analysis and a project feasibility study. At this stage a commitment must be established with the counterpart, identifying objectives and responsibilities of each project member. The second step can be based on micro contributions. Once the project is running, collaboration can continue by maintaining the joint learning through a less intensive service – for example the maintenance and updating of the software developed, and improving the training of the counterpart.

- *FOSS can be disruptive for counterparts.* FOSS might require extra information, training and assistance to its target users during the development and deployment phases. This process should be agreed and committed to by both parties but should mainly occur in the target communities, with local members taking responsibility for it – assuming it as their own, not as an imposed solution. It is therefore essential to minimize the workload of the counterpart but maximize its participation in decisions. For this reason the change and implementation process should be led (or assumed) by a local person. In the medium term, perhaps during the first year, the use of FOSS should not be seen as a burden but as added value for counterparts.
- *The formative nature of the process.* Service learning benefits both the volunteer and the partner receiving technology training and a FOSS solution at the same time. Gradually, the counterpart's processes change and are optimized to accommodate the use of FOSS that is concurrently being adapted to them. To succeed, counterparts must endorse the technology, replacing manual processes with more automated ones. If the automation process does not successfully replace manual ones, but runs in parallel, it is likely that the project will fail because the partner has not adopted the technology or adapted its processes and, as soon as the volunteers return to their country of origin, automation will be discarded and everything will be back to the previous well-known manual processes.
- *Service learning brings stability to FOSS development.* Sometimes errors in software take a long time to be solved just because the person able to fix a problem is unavailable or overloaded. This usually occurs when no local experts are available or they leave the project. We must take into account that the training makes them more attractive in the labour market. SL can be a solution that allows trained volunteers to participate in projects while local entities have no permanent trained staff.
- *Service learning might imply an additional overhead.* There can be an excess of staff turnover as people get trained, contribute for a short time and then are replaced by new people. The training overhead should not overload the counterpart (even though it has to participate

in this work), because if too much time/money is spent in the formative phase of SL volunteer training, it will not get the desired performance at the production phase. In the extreme case, it is possible that the productive phase of volunteering does not compensate the effort invested in the training phase, and counterparts might prefer to receive directly the resources (money) to be spent on the volunteer and invest them in local people, probably less specialized but giving better long-term performance. If that is not possible, the partner may even prefer not to receive volunteers to save the overhead of their training. However, training by the counterpart has a key formative value for the students. Besides the technical training to implement/design/adapt FOSS to a cooperation project, coexistence with members of the counterpart community will transform the volunteers, who will never again contemplate life as they did before participating in an SL cooperation project. The counterpart should never see volunteers as a burden, but as a help. The presence of volunteers has a beneficial effect, since locals can catch the spirit of voluntary cooperation and leave the competitive attitude that often occurs in some environments. And volunteers can obtain further benefit by sharing their experiences with volunteers from other branches of science, fostering multidisciplinary cooperation.

- *Organizational barriers.* In some cases, the organizational scheme of the counterpart may be in conflict with using FOSS and its assumptions to address a problem. If the organization is too horizontal, competition arises between members of the counterpart that hinder the successful implementation of FOSS, as some people desire and look for the failure of others as a way to claim their own success. This happened, for example, in the Casa Guatemala project. Casa Guatemala has several crop gardens which were managed by different people: each managed their garden in a different way and using different cultivation techniques. Workers did not share any information or material between them, and hid their own successful "tricks" to prevent others from succeeding. This problem was solved by employing a general horticultural manager, who unified criteria and encouraged cooperation rather than competition. An organization that is too vertical, on the other hand, often has problems of lack of responsibility and commitment, especially for members in the lower strata of the pyramid. FOSS helps to detect weaknesses in the organization because it brings out all these problems, and can help members of the counterpart to move from a competitive to a cooperative standpoint, and take more responsibility within the organization. When a solution based on FOSS is installed in a cooperative project, users are often expected to share computers and information. In addition, the lack of knowledge about the tools encourages them to cooperate. While this is true for any

software, not just for FOSS, the use of FOSS helps people to see that there is a worldwide community which creates these products through cooperation among members of that community. This can help them to understand that cooperation between them will achieve major goals and objectives.
- *Refocusing projects to match the crude reality.* When students begin working in the field they must usually reformulate aspects of the project based on the actual situation and the elements at their disposal. There are typical mistakes in the assumptions. Some are very basic: for instance, to assume that is easy to get computer spare parts, internet access or good electrical infrastructure. Other mistakes are more complex: for instance, how to train users to take over maintenance of the proposed solution, how to find a solution in accordance with the local ICT strategy and policies, or how to get institutional support. Very often the counterpart does not have a clear vision of ICT, so we must focus on providing computer equipment and initial training. The lack of a mature ICT environment in these projects makes the development of software applications both uncommon and difficult. For example, in the UN Western Sahara refugee camps the information system for the central pharmacy warehouse failed due to the lack of a mature ICT infrastructure and social ICT culture, whereas projects with the appropriate prerequisites – the information system for the child vaccination programme, and the Yacu system for farmers in Peru – were successful.
- *ICT4D promotes social reflection in target communities.* TxT only contributes human resources and computers to projects, so our scope for action and impact is limited and we cannot expect our ICT projects to improve the situation directly at the macro level. Table 4.1 shows 12 of the most challenging TxT projects, rated according to the "real access" criteria. The assessments were performed by project volunteers, and range from 1 (minimum) to 5 (maximum); the totals are the average values. The table shows that points 6–9 are insufficient (ICT is not perfectly integrated into daily routines, digital divide is high or acceptance of ICT is low). However, points 10 (macro-economic environment), 11 (legal and regulatory framework) and 12 (political will and public support) were the worst rated by our volunteers. These points reflect the level of ICT maturity and vision of governments, institutions and companies. The ability to influence through service learning could focus on the promotion of processes of reflection about the appropriate framework for ICT to flourish. The ideal environment to promote this reflection requires trust and confidence among both parties. ICT4D co-operation from an educational institution based on volunteers looking for new experiences and learning from them is a very favourable aspect. This, combined with our FOSS-based approach, removes barriers

Table 4.1 Assessment of TxT projects according to real access/real impact framework

Real access criteria	1	2	3	4	5	6	7	8	9	10	11	12	
Morocco 2003	3.50	4.50	2.00	2.50	3.00	2.50	3.00	2.50	2.00	1.00	2.00	2.00	2.77
Bolivia (San Ignacio) 2006–2007	3.00	3.50	4.00	3.00	3.50	2.50	5.00	2.50	3.00	3.00	2.50	3.00	3.50
Morocco 2007	4.00	3.00	3.00	3.00	3.00	2.00	4.00	2.00	2.00	1.00	1.00	2.00	2.72
Senegal 2007	4.00	3.00	3.00	3.00	4.00	2.00	3.00	4.00	3.00	1.00	1.00	1.00	2.90
Bolivia (sucre) 2007	4.00	5.00	4.00	5.00	5.00	3.00	3.00	4.00	2.00	1.00	1.00	1.00	3.45
Guatemala (hotel) 2009	5.00	5.00	5.00	4.00	5.00	4.00	4.00	2.00	4.00	1.00	2.00	1.00	3.81
Guatemala (restaurant) 2009	5.00	5.00	5.00	4.00	3.00	3.00	4.00	2.00	3.00	1.00	2.00	1.00	3.45
Bolivia (sucre) 2009	4.00	5.00	4.00	5.00	5.00	5.00	1.00	4.00	3.00	1.00	1.00	1.00	3.54
Cameroon 2009	4.00	4.00	2.00	2.00	1.00	1.00	2.00	1.00	3.00	1.00	2.00	3.00	2.36
Colombia (Nasa Yuwe) 2009	4.00	3.00	4.00	3.00	5.00	4.00	4.00	3.00	4.00	1.00	1.00	1.00	3.36
Nepal 2010	3.00	4.00	4.00	3.00	2.00	5.00	2.00	4.00	3.00	1.00	1.00	1.00	3.00
Bolivia (sucre) 2010	4.00	4.00	4.00	3.00	4.00	4.00	1.00	2.00	3.00	1.00	1.00	1.00	2.90
	3.96	4.08	3.67	3.38	3.63	3.17	3.00	2.75	2.92	1.17	1.46	1.50	

(i.e. interests, restrictions and hidden dependencies) and constitutes a good environment for dialogue to promote this process of reflection.
- *Knowledge and learning processes.* One process involves knowledge transfer that should work both ways (domain information from the target community to the students doing software development, and software engineering and organization techniques from the students to the target community). Another learning process should run in parallel: organizational learning for the target community to re-engineer their social processes, and service learning for the students. Finally, a third long-term process concerns constructing an ICT4D project methodology and the generalization of the software elements being developed to be more applicable to separate but similar (in requirements) target communities.
- *FOSS versus proprietary software.* The development of an information system using FOSS and the deployment of a wireless network partially based on FOSS in the Chancay-Huaral project had some main expected and unexpected effects. Beyond the typical effects, FOSS has the conflicting attributes of being less expensive and easier to replicate, but less known than commercial software solutions. That has a critical effect on the initial adoption, development and maintenance of the system, but our SL process was a good complement, bringing a surplus of training and software development capacities. In countries where there is no specific support to the use of FOSS, additional training is required for all actors, unlike some global proprietary solutions from large multinational companies. This might be solved initially with mixed solutions, with FOSS installations using proprietary operating systems or office applications.
- *Effective dissemination of FOSS.* In the long term, FOSS facilitates the replication of experience to other similar settings, as the adoption of the same software tools comes without additional costs in licensing and facilitating customization or small adaptations. However, extra resources and incentives should be put in place from the start to encourage and support the extra work required to prepare the software tools for use by external people or projects.
- *Staffing risks.* As in most projects, training creates highly skilled local staff with higher chances of getting better employment elsewhere. In using FOSS, the openness of the software development, particularly when there is good documentation, facilitates the transition to new people (either locally or by external supporters) and the incorporation of additional volunteers adding new features. Thus the risk of losing key developers is mitigated by the openness and the standardization effect when a growing community is using a software system in multiple settings.

- *Local policies.* Beyond the well-known effects of software openness and associated knowledge in developing local skills and capabilities, the local policy environment has a significant influence in being neutral, favourable or against FOSS solutions. Balanced or favourable policies to FOSS in developing countries are difficult to find, given the strong interests of global software companies and the usually weak civil social actors.

Conclusions

Using service learning to perform ICT4D projects allows students to acquire very important but difficult-to-learn skills, while helping developing communities. As a key part of the FOSS philosophy is the idea of sharing and disseminating knowledge, we wish to offer some recommendations to other institutions that want to replicate our experience.

It is very important not to disrupt or break the identity of the target community. We must not change the very nature of a community, but integrate new tools, processes and even values in their daily routines. ICT must not be a burden, so local ownership and cooperation with local experts must be ensured. It is essential to analyse the real needs of the community, and adapt experts to the project instead of adapting the project to your knowledge and way of thinking. Projects should be careful with minorities in target communities, so care must be taken to avoid increasing the digital divide of some excluded subgroups on the basis of age, gender, race or religion.

Change minds: projects are designed to help, but also to enable all participants to learn. Sustainable development requires a process of dialogue and ultimately consensus building of all stakeholders as partners who define the problems together, design possible solutions, collaborate to implement them and monitor and evaluate the outcome. There must be concrete goals that are realistic and take small steps. Introducing technology too fast, without a short-term clear benefit and some training, will result in its rejection. Projects should be more evolutionary than revolutionary.

Service learning can help to start up new projects (using master thesis students to develop new schemes, for instance), but can also follow up and improve ongoing projects (as part of the lab of some courses). Monitoring, evaluating and adapting the work to the new needs of users can be the difference between a successful project and a failed one.

In training volunteers, goodwill may not be enough. Volunteers will be very sadly disappointed by the lack of progress if key information is blindly ignored because some things are taken for granted. Volunteers must try to understand the historical forces: previous bad experiences, environmental conditions such as unreliable electricity infrastructure, etc. It is fundamental not to try to impose overnight changes, but spend more time on understanding the existing process. This will result in a contribution to improved processes supported by the resources provided by service learning and the tools provided by FOSS developments.

The FOSS paradigm is a natural choice in solidarity projects when the impact and adaptation of technologies in engineering solutions are a concern, due to a need for freedom to adapt the solution and reduce dependencies. Cooperation from an educational institution based on volunteering, FOSS and service learning seems to be an ideal combination, where mutual learning becomes the central process and a necessary secure and trusting environment can be built to create a shared ICT vision.

Acknowledgements

We wish to thank all the volunteers who participate in the reuse workshop or develop their bachelor/master theses in solidarity projects. Without their time, knowledge and motivation nothing can be done. We also wish to thank the academic staff involved in advising these projects. Thanks to the Technology for Everybody organization, the Cooperation for Development Centre of BarcelonaTech and the Barcelona School of Informatics for their unconditional support and encouragement in implementing our ideas, as well as their logistic and financial support. Finally, we wish to thank the anonymous reviewers for their useful comments.

REFERENCES

Alonso, J., D. López, J. L. Cruz, C. Álvarez, D. Jiménez-González, A. Fernández and F. Sánchez (2008) "Work in Progress – Achieving the ABET Professional Skills Using Solidarity Projects", paper presented at Frontiers in Education Conference 38, Saratoga Springs, 22–25 October.

Bridges (2010) "Real Access/Real Impact Criteria"; available at www.bridges.org/Real_Access (accessed 22 December 2011).

Coyle, E. J., L. H. Jamieson and W. C. Oakes (2005) "EPICS: Engineering Projects in Community Service", *International Journal of Engineering Education* 21(1), pp. 139–150.

Duffy, J., E. Tsang and S. Lord (2000) "Service-Learning in Engineering: What, Why, How?", paper presented at ASEE Annual Conference, St Louis, 19–21 June.

Farreras, M., D. Franquesa and D. López (2009) "TxT as a Vehicle for Service Learning", paper presented at Ninth Workshop in Active Learning for Engineering Education, Barcelona, 9–12 June.

Folke, C., S. Carpenter, T. Elmqvist, L. Gunderson, C. S. Holling, B. Walker, J. Bengtsson, F. Berkes, J. Colding, K. Danell, M. Falkenmark, L. Gordon, R. Kasperson, N. Kautsky, A. Kinzig, S. Levin, K.-G. Mäler, F. Moberg, L. Ohlsson, P. Olsson, E. Ostrom, W. Reid, J. Rockström, H. Savenije and U. Svedin (2002) *Resilience and Sustainable Development: Building Adaptive Capacity in a World of Transformations*, Stockholm: Norstedts Tryckeri.

Franquesa, D., J. L. Cruz, C. Álvarez, F. Sánchez, A. Fernández and D. López (2010) "The Social and Environmental Impact of Engineering Solutions: From the Lab to the Real World", *International Journal of Engineering Education* 26(5), pp. 1144–1155.

Heeks, R. and A. Molla (2009) "Impact Assessment of ICT-for-Development Projects: A Compendium of Approaches"; available at www.sed.manchester.ac.uk/idpm/research/publications/wp/di/di_wp36.htm (accessed 17 February 2011).

Hemmati, M. (2002) *Multi-stakeholder Processes for Governance and Sustainability: Beyond Deadlock and Conflict*, London: Routledge.

Herwijnen, M. V. (2008) "The Sustainability A-Test", in *OECD Sustainable Development Studies Conducting Sustainability Assessments*, Amsterdam: OECD Publishing, pp. 63–74.

Hislop, G. W., H. J. C. Ellis and R. A. Morelli (2009) "Evaluating Student Experiences in Developing Software for Humanity", in *Proceedings of the 14th Annual ACM SIGCSE Conference on Innovation and Technology in Computer Science Education*, New York: ACM, pp. 263–267.

Hoe, N. S. (2006) "Breaking Barriers: The Potential of Free and Open Source Software for Sustainable Human Development – A Compilation of Case Studies from Across the World", UNDP Asia-Pacific Development Information Programme, Bangkok; available at www.apdip.net/publications/ict4d/BreakingBarriers.pdf (accessed 20 January 2011).

Jacoby, B. (1996) *Service-Learning in Higher Education: Concepts and Practice*, San Francisco, CA: Jossey-Bass.

López, D., F. Sánchez, J. Garcia, M. Aller, J. Piguillem and M. Velasco (2011) "Introducing Sustainability and Social Commitment Skills in an Engineering Degree", paper presented at 41st Frontiers in Education Conference, Rapid City, 12–15 October.

Shuman, L. J., M. Besterfield-Sacre and J. McGourty (2005) "The ABET Professional Skills – Can They Be Taught? Can They Be Assessed?", *Journal of Engineering Education* 94(1), pp. 41–55.

Tsang, E. (ed.) (2000) *Projects That Matter: Concepts and Models for Service Learning in Engineering*, Washington, DC: American Association for Higher Education.

Venkatesh, V. and H. Bala (2008) "Technology Acceptance Model 3 and a Research Agenda on Interventions", *Decision Sciences* 39(2), pp. 273–315.

Venkatesh, V. and F. D. Davis (2000) "A Theoretical Extension of the Technology Acceptance Model: Four Longitudinal Field Studies", *Management Science* 46(2), pp. 186–204.

Venkatesh, V., M. G. Morris, G. B. Davis and F. D. Davis (2003) "User Acceptance of Information Technology: Toward a Unified View", *MIS Quarterly* 27(3), pp. 425–478.

5
Open source software migration: Capturing best practices using process reference models

Onkgopotse Molefe and Thomas Fogwill

Introduction

This chapter presents a summary of a study conducted at the Meraka Institute of the Council for Scientific and Industrial Research (CSIR) in South Africa to document a set of best practices for organizational open source software (OSS) migration projects. Such practices can assist with the planning and execution of future OSS migrations, as well as similar projects conducted in other organizations. Recent studies have shown that OSS migrations are increasing in South Africa and internationally, because OSS is secure, customizable and inexpensive. Its rise brought a tremendous change in the information technology sector all over the globe, with numerous government departments, private sector businesses and educational and non-governmental organizations considering a move to OSS (Lawrence, 2010). South African examples include the CSIR, a national science council and the largest research institution in Africa, the State Information Technology Agency, the national government's Department of Science and Technology, the Water Research Council and the Centre for Public Service Innovation (Comino and Manenti, 2005).

OSS is software that is freely available for use and can be modified to meet a user's specific computing needs. This type of software emerged worldwide with customizability, freedom, cost saving, security advantages and avoidance of vendor lock-in as some of the driving factors (Ahmed, 2005). Other reasons cited for OSS adoption include the facts that it is free to use, copy and share, it can be localized, translated and customized

---

Free and open source software and technology for sustainable development, Sowe, Parayil and Sunami (eds), United Nations University Press, 2012, ISBN 978-92-808-1217-6

to suit a particular business function or user need and it supports older hardware platforms, eliminating the need for costly state-of-the-art equipment (Ayala et al., 2011).

A problem is that while many organizations want to adopt OSS, they often struggle to plan and implement successful OSS migrations. Such projects are highly complex. They require strong technical, development and integration skills and top-level management buy-in and support. They also need a robust set of processes to support project execution, change management and ongoing operation and maintenance of the information technology (IT) environment (Bruggink, 2003). Limited resources are available in the literature to document the important steps and hidden problems in migrating from a proprietary to an OSS platform. Many organizations must design their own migration processes from scratch when planning such a project. This often holds back, or even precludes, organizations from embarking on the path of adopting OSS.

Process reference models (PRMs) can be a solution to this problem. They capture the common activities, roles and resources of processes in a particular environment, and represent process model structures that can be reused in different environments (Rosa et al., 2005). PRMs make it easier for people involved in OSS migration to plan and execute projects. To develop a set of PRMs for OSS migration, it is necessary to identify the key generic process models that are repeatable in all such projects. The approach should be to look at a case study and identify the key processes that will result in a set of PRMs for arbitrary OSS migration projects.

The study documented in this chapter suggests a set of PRMs for an organizational OSS migration that were identified using this approach on project Vula – the CSIR's OSS migration project. All processes were captured during the project as process models using the standard process notation IDEF0. A case study approach was used, based on the systematic research approach of van der Merwe and Kotze (2009). Data collection was primarily done through interviews and focus group discussions. Pre- and post-migration interviews were conducted with project team members and migrated users; their responses were recorded and documented. Focus groups were held with Vula project experts to assess the validity of captured process models and obtain advice on identifying generic PRMs. Other data collection methods included participant and non-participant observation and a review of existing literature.

The aim was to ensure that the resulting PRMs are unique, reusable and applicable to other organizations planning OSS migrations. The process models needed to be generic to ensure that other migration projects will get the same results. To be of value, the PRMs needed to reduce the risks associated with OSS migrations and help prevent the occurrence of common, recurring problems. The PRMs developed have been informally verified, and it is firmly believed that they represent a solid baseline upon which organizations can base their own migrations and will help to reduce the risks and challenges associated with such projects.

Background

Open source software

OSS is software that has been licensed in a manner that allows users to study, edit, improve and redistribute it freely (Ahmed, 2005). Some OSS licences, such as the GNU General Public License, are *viral*, in that they require redistributed or derived works to be released under the same terms as the original software. Others, such as the Berkeley Software Distribution style of licence, are less viral and allow distribution of derived works under arbitrary licences. OSS is often available free of charge and typically no licence fee is required for using the software. OSS can be used and shared among users as many times as they want. In contrast to traditional proprietary software development practices, OSS is produced by a self-organized community comprising developers, users and IT vendors that engage online and collaboratively develop and improve the software (Molefe and Fogwill, 2009). It has become very popular worldwide and is currently used and adopted in many private companies, governmental organizations and academic institutions for several reasons: it is free to use, copy and share; the open source operating systems are often more reliable and secure than proprietary operating systems; it can be customized and/or localized to suit specific business functions or users' needs; and it works on older personal computers, which are no longer supported by proprietary software (Dudley, Finlay and Otter, 2006).

There are many OSS operating systems, the most widely used being Linux. Developed in 1991 as a replacement for the commercial Unix offerings available at the time, today Linux is regarded as a possible replacement for commercially produced operating systems. Linux is produced as OSS and freely distributed. It is used and adapted by many companies and organizations for both desktop and server environments. OSS is not restricted to operating systems, but includes network and internet service software, server software, development libraries and tools and end-user application software. Application software such as Mozilla Firefox and OpenOffice.org is available to run on multiple platforms, so many users do not have to migrate their operating system to make use of such OSS.

Process modelling

Processes are the structured, measured activities designed to produce a specified output in a particular context. Process models are tools used to represent processes and the flows between them. They are often represented diagrammatically. For this study, the definition of process modelling provided by Perumpalath (2005) is adopted, which specifies that it is the procedure of constructing the process model using a standard notation. The primary purpose of such modelling is the documentation of process information. Comprehensive documentation of processes could contribute to the success of many projects, especially if models are stored in a repository where they can later be retrieved. Process models are used for process re-engineering, reorganization, monitoring and controlling, continuous improvement, quality management, benchmarking, practice and knowledge management (Barn, 2007).

Building process model structures can be a complex and costly exercise. Common recurring problems encountered in the construction of such models led to the idea of reusing generic process models. These generic models form the baseline and can be adapted to become the specific process models that are required for an organizational environment (Childe, Smart and Weaver, 1997). Generic process models allow modellers to learn from the process designs of similar projects, which means they do not have to build their own process models from scratch. This results in a saving of resources and effort (Tyrrell, 2000).

Documenting process reference models

PRMs are generic process model structures collected in a library to allow reuse. They capture the common activities, roles and resources of processes in a particular environment, and can be reused in different environments (Rosa et al., 2005). One of their advantages is that they enable *design by reuse*, alleviating the need to redesign processes. This assists enterprises that perform similar practices by allowing them to reutilize proven processes, without having to develop their own from scratch (ibid.). Errors often occur during execution of projects, and these may come at high cost without any guarantee that they will not reoccur. Using generic process models allows enterprises to avoid these common pitfalls and benefit from the prior experiences of others. PRMs thus reduce the risks and costs associated with repetitive errors in projects (Jensen and Scacchi, 2003).

Van der Aalst et al. (2006) consider PRMs to be like *plug and play*, in the sense that they can be *dropped into* environments other than those in which they were developed. PRMs, after initial development, often require further improvement to reach a level of satisfactory quality. This point is made by Tyrrell (2000), who indicates that a working process needs to be monitored and improved from time to time to ensure that it meets ongoing and possible future requirements. PRMs have been used by organizations as generic solutions to improve their business performance (van der Aalst et al., 2006). From the experiences of other organizations, it is evident that PRMs are one of the most powerful means to capture the acquired process knowledge of an organization (Childe, Smart and Weaver, 1997). This is why they were selected as the medium to disseminate the process knowledge acquired during project Vula.

At present, PRMs are represented in various modelling languages and standard notations (Fettke, Loos and Zwicker, 2005). For any particular project, a well-defined, widely accepted and easily understood standard notation is required (Rosa et al., 2005). The Integration DEfinition for Function modelling (IDEF0), which is widely used for the creation of process models, was selected for this study. A number of approaches can be used to develop PRMs. When applying any of these, PRM developers must be aware of the fact that modelling can be carried out in many different ways and there is no single optimal path, nor a single correct solution for the constructive activity. As such, the approaches must be seen as supporting the construction of PRMs through a number of guidelines that have been proven to work well in practice, rather than being absolutely and exclusively correct. To date, PRMs have not been used on OSS migration projects. However, based on the positive effect they have had on other technology projects, it appears that they offer the potential to improve greatly the planning and execution of OSS migrations. To investigate whether this is indeed the case requires that initial PRMs are developed for OSS migration projects; that these PRMs are used on an OSS migration to test their validity and effectiveness; that the findings are incorporated into the PRMs to improve them; and finally, that the first two steps are iterated.

This chapter presents the outcomes of the first step, the development of baseline PRMs for OSS migration projects. The repeated application (step four) of verification (step two) and refinement (step three) of the PRMs remains as future work.

OSS migration projects

Background and considerations

Recent literature has shown an increased awareness of OSS over the past decade and a rise worldwide in migrations from proprietary software to

OSS (Mtsweni and Biermann, 2008; Ellis and van Belle, 2009). Typical reasons for migration include lower or free licence costs, easy access to source code, lower total cost of ownership (TCO), security, customizability, stability (Dudley, Finlay and Otter, 2006) and a drive to foster local and home-grown ICT (information and communication technology) talent and innovation. South African examples of OSS migrations are numerous, and include the governmental and non-governmental bodies listed in the introduction to this chapter. With the Vula project, described in the next section, the CSIR prioritized OSS as a key programme, with the aim of leading by example and inspiring other organizations in the public, private and educational sectors to adopt OSS. South Africa is not alone in recognizing the socio-economic benefits and technological advancement OSS brings; other nations supporting OSS include China, Chile, Spain, Thailand, India, Brazil, France, the United Kingdom and large portions of Germany (Kshetri, 2004). These countries have become more active in adopting OSS solutions because they believe it is a way for them to be competitive in the global marketplace: it will reduce the cost of IT purchases, inform society about the uses of OSS and encourage the growth of the OSS and ICT industry (van Reijswoud and Topi, 2004). There are many examples of migration outside South Africa, including Orwell High School in the United Kingdom, Beaumont Hospital in Ireland, the cities of Schoten, Vienna, Munich, Schwäbisch Hall and Treuchtlingen, and others (Cassell, 2008).

Migrating to a new technology can be challenging, and OSS migrations are no exception. OSS migrations are complex and require good knowledge of the OSS environment, and it can take a long time to complete detailed planning and implementation of the migration strategy (Astor and Rosenberg, 2005). Besides the challenges common to all technology adoption projects (such as effective change management, overcoming user resistance to change, ensuring business continuity and maintaining productivity levels), OSS migrations have several unique challenges. For any organization intending to embark on a technology migration, TCO is an important factor. TCO is the total cost of adopting and using a particular technology, and includes acquisition cost, licence fees and cost of customization, integration and implementation, as well as operating, support and maintenance costs over the entire life of the technology (Kok, 2005). Because of the differing nature of these costs (some are one-off, while others are recurring), it is difficult to calculate TCO accurately for any particular technology. This problem is possibly even worse for OSS: it has little or no acquisition cost and licence fees, and is often easier and cheaper to customize, but some have argued that it requires a higher degree of (scarce) skill to maintain and thus carries higher operating and support costs (Kemp, 2009; Morgan and Finneman, 2007). Others claim that OSS

is often of better quality than proprietary software, issues are discovered and rectified more quickly and it is inherently easier to maintain, which could suggest the opposite. As such, it is important that organizations do a proper and impartial analysis of their own requirements, to estimate adequately the cost of migrating to OSS (Bruggink, 2003; Cassell, 2008).

Another important element of OSS migrations is that of technology evaluation, specifically the evaluation of the maturity and quality of a particular piece of OSS. Because OSS is collaboratively developed, it is important to evaluate the software comprehensively before implementation. Such evaluation should go beyond what is typically done for proprietary technology and technology vendors – it should include an evaluation of the maturity of the OSS product, the effectiveness of its quality assurance processes, the strength of its release and bug-fixing policies, the strength of its developer community and the rate at which issues are reported and fixed. These are vitally important considerations, to ensure both suitable levels of current performance and longevity and sustainability of the technology (Kemp, 2009).

For OSS, there is not always a commercial entity formally backing the technology. It is thus not always possible to find local providers offering adequate support for the technology. This makes it imperative to survey the service and support landscape prior to migration to ensure that adequate support can be obtained. In some cases it may be necessary to develop the support capability in-house. A related consideration is finding providers of quality training – often, due to lower market penetration of OSS, this can be challenging (Paré, Michael and Charles, 2009; Mtsweni and Biermann, 2008).

To exacerbate the difficulties in migrating to OSS, there are very few resources available that document the important steps and hidden pitfalls involved in the process. This means there is significant difficulty in planning and implementing migration projects, with processes often designed from scratch for each project, which results in increased cost and risk and often holds back, or even precludes, organizations from embarking on the path towards OSS adoption (Gerber, Molefe and van der Merwe, 2010). In an attempt to address this problem, a study was undertaken to document best practices learnt on project Vula for future migrations (Molefe, 2009).

Project Vula

As a way to show their support for OSS, South African delegates gathered for the Go Open Source Conference in August 2005 in Johannesburg to declare, document and sign a national open source policy and strategy for the implementation of OSS in government (Mokhema, 2005).

This document was presented to then President Thabo Mbeki and members of his cabinet. In 2007 the South African national open source policy and strategy was approved by the cabinet.

The adoption of this policy and strategy paved the way for projects such as Vula, led by the Meraka Institute of the CSIR in South Africa. The CSIR is the national science council of South Africa. It has approximately 2,000 staff, of whom about half are research and development (R&D) staff involved in research, innovation and technology development. The CSIR has a number of operating units, each conducting basic and applied research in different fields of science, with the goal of using science and technology to improve the quality of life of South Africans.

To empower users and promote a vibrant ICT environment for scientific work, the CSIR embarked on project Vula in 2006. The goal was to enable migration from a proprietary desktop computing platform to an open source platform based on Ubuntu Linux. The migration was not primarily motivated by cost, but rather by a desire to refine the CSIR research infrastructure on an ongoing basis; show leadership by being one of the largest South African organizations to adopt OSS; generate and publicly disseminate knowledge about OSS migration; empower other organizations to plan and execute OSS migration projects better; remove the fear and uncertainty associated with adoption and usage of OSS; empower users and scientists within the organization; foster local ICT skills development; and further socio-economic development (ibid.). The migration was deemed possible and timely due, in part, to advances in the usability of Linux as a desktop operating system and the availability of quality productivity suites. Driven by these factors, the project presented an opportunity for everyone in the organization, especially technologically minded individuals (from beginners to experts), to benefit and learn from the experience of migrating to OSS. The CSIR's migration was unique when compared to other organizational OSS migrations, in that the focus was placed on learning and sharing of knowledge. The firm commitment to migrate to OSS was backed by an approach that removed technical barriers to migration, and ensured that skills development opportunities were made available and support systems and structures were put in place for the OSS environment. The approach also enabled voluntary early migration by individuals and groups, before and during the mandated migration. A key step in the project was the adoption of open document standards as an enabler for collaboration and document exchange across multiple platforms.

The project followed an incremental approach, and allowed for a hybrid model where OSS and proprietary systems would coexist side by side in the organization. The main activities involved:

- adapting the enterprise back end to support OSS
- switching to OSS on Windows (using the Firefox web browser and the OpenOffice productivity suite)
- mandating the use of open standards, notably Open Document Format (ODF) as the CSIR document standard
- switching to an OSS desktop operating system, together with OSS replacements for common desktop user applications
- developing and implementing desktop and back-end support processes
- developing and implementing a roll-out plan to migrate CSIR staff
- implementing an appropriate communication strategy
- implementing a portfolio of training mechanisms
- capturing the learning to enable replication of the results in other organizations.

The project was organized into five interdependent tracks: technology, roll-out, training, communications, and research and documentation. In addition, there was an overarching project management and change management function. The project leadership consisted of the project coordinator (appointed by the chief executive), the leaders of each of the tracks and the project manager.

The technology track focused on the analysis, investigation, design, development, customization and integration of all technology required to make the project a success. It involved technology in use across the entire organization by both functional support and research staff. The scope included the complete ICT architecture, desktop application software, system software, server and network infrastructure, migration tools and server/desktop support and management tools. A base enterprise desktop was specified in consultation with representatives from each of the organizational units. Using this specification, the standard Vula desktop system was developed, based on Ubuntu Linux and with support for office productivity, e-mail, secure internet access and web browsing, multimedia support and support for all CSIR enterprise applications (financial, enterprise resource planning, document and configuration management, workflow and procurement). Basic researcher tool support was also developed, including tools for reference management, scientific authoring and research project management. Modifications to the enterprise-wide architecture and server environments were undertaken on a just-in-time basis, as a wholesale redesign was not feasible due to cost, high risk and lock-in via existing long-term vendor licence agreements.

The roll-out track was responsible for planning and implementation of the OSS technology roll-out within the organization, with minimal disruption to productivity. It involved activities such as scheduling roll-out to departments; management of early adopters and users exempt from migration; provision of adequate support to volunteers, mentors and coaches; acquisition, planning and allocation of sufficient support resources to accommodate migration; securing and migrating documents, files and general data; and developing and implementing post-migration support processes.

The training track was responsible for managing and executing the training plan. It did so by developing a skills matrix, identifying required training interventions and sourcing the relevant training. This track also focused on non-skills aspects of training, such as developing user interest, excitement and positive attitude and dispelling fear. An important constraint here was cost; hence there was a strong focus on user empowerment through self- and peer learning to supplement a programme of traditional classroom-based training.

The purpose of the communications track was to develop and execute a communication plan, both internal to the CSIR and external to stakeholders and the general public. Internally, it was critical to ensure buy-in, alignment and excitement about the migration. Within the broader scope of change management, the main objective of the communication component was to ensure that stakeholders were informed and prepared for the new paradigm. To achieve this, the communication strategy was to progress from merely providing information to soliciting involvement and then securing full commitment.

The research and documentation track was responsible for documenting the migration project and analysing it to obtain new knowledge and research outputs. The work presented in this chapter was undertaken on this track. The project faced a number of critical challenges. Some are common to all OSS migration projects: resistance to change, technological risk in adopting new technologies, a legacy of non-interoperable enterprise technologies, the cost of migration, differing levels of technical proficiency among users, *de facto* use of proprietary formats for external collaboration and document exchange, a scarcity of skilled technical resources and limited local support and training service offerings. In addition, due to the nature of the CSIR and the diversity of its research, other challenges were identified, including:

- a broad and highly specialized set of research tools and software in use by researchers – this resulted in some users being unable to migrate fully, due either to their specialized software not running on Linux, there being no OSS alternative, or the high cost of retraining them on the OSS alternatives
- specialized scientific equipment with poor or no support on Linux
- requirements regarding the use of specific proprietary formats for article submissions and documents in some academic communities.

Notwithstanding these challenges, project Vula succeeded in migrating a significant percentage of staff (across most operating units, both functional and R&D) to a Linux desktop. All staff, including those remaining on a proprietary desktop, continue to make use of OSS such as OpenOffice and Mozilla Firefox.

OSS migration process model and PRM extraction

Approach

To extract PRMs from an organizational OSS migration project, it is necessary to:
- identify the project processes and compile all process models
- identify criteria for selecting PRMs
- select PRMs, based on the established criteria
- validate the extracted PRMs against other projects.

The systematic approach used to guide the execution of these tasks was suggested by van der Merwe and Kotze (2009), and consists of five phases (Figure 5.1).

Phase 1: Define scope

The scope of the project is defined, major role players are identified and (if applicable) a feasibility study is conducted. For Vula, this phase formed part of the overall project planning.

Phase 2: Procedure selection

Since few major OSS migrations had been documented, there was little literature from which to draw appropriate procedures for the project. The procedure selected for documenting the migration processes was to use process models and a standard process model notation (IDEF0).

Phase 3: Data gathering

Phase 3 is concerned with the collection of data to facilitate the identification of processes within a project or organization. For Vula, document analysis, interviews and questionnaires were used as data collection tools.

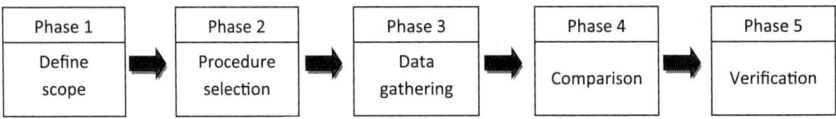

Figure 5.1 Approach to project Vula
Source: Adapted from van der Merwe and Kotze (2009).

Document analysis was done on all project documentation, internal and external communication and other material related to the project. Other data sources included survey data, questionnaire responses and technical documentation. Pre- and post-migration interviews were conducted with the project team and affected users, to obtain information about their OSS experiences. All the questions and responses were recorded and transcribed, and are available as project documentation.

Phase 4: Comparison

Phase 4 involves the extraction of PRMs by comparing the different process structures identified in the previous phase, and noting those that are common or unique. The criteria used for identifying PRMs were compiled from literature. The set of Vula process models were compared against the criteria for PRMs and the generic PRMs were extracted.

Phase 5: Verification

Phase 5 involves the verification of the extracted PRMs at an institution (or in a project) not involved in their identification or extraction. For this study, the models were verified informally using domain experts and project leaders. Future work includes verification outside the CSIR.

With regard to epistemological stance, this research was executed as a qualitative empirical study. The process documentation was primarily captured through observation and there was no interference with the project's execution. The migration was observed in the working environment of the project team and project execution office.

Vula process modelling

It was envisioned that project Vula would not only benefit the CSIR but would also present opportunities for skills development and education to emerging young professionals, particularly in OSS development. To support Vula's knowledge-sharing goals, the project processes had to be thoroughly documented. This documentation was also the first step required for the identification, generation and documentation of the generic migration PRMs.

PRMs are typically developed hierarchically and recursively. First the top-level processes are identified and their detail is captured, including activities performed as part of the process, their order of execution, inputs and outputs to the process, and its roles and goals (Tyrrell, 2000). Once this information is captured for the high-level processes, they are decomposed into subprocesses and the method repeats. The steps in Table 5.1 were followed to identify and capture process models for the Vula project.

Table 5.1 Steps

Step	Description	Tools/documentation used	Deliverable
1	Derive high-level process model	Process listing with goals and resources	High-level process model
2	Refine high-level process model to subprocesses	Subprocess and atomic process (sometimes referred to as sub-subprocesses) listing	Subprocesses and atomic processes

Initially, a high-level process model diagram (parent diagram) was developed (Figure 5.2). This parent diagram was later decomposed into child diagrams representing the detailed subprocesses of the model. The high-level process model diagram represents the key processes of the Vula project, and indicates how an output of one process becomes an input to another. It is possible for a process to have more than one output, and for detailed, refined processes to have no input. It is also possible to have more than one input to a process.

As depicted in Table 5.2, each process has its own goal. For example, the goal of the *kick-start project* process is to provide assurance to CSIR employees and its external stakeholders that the project has begun. The *form project team* process has a purpose to ensure that a reliable and committed team is in place. The *announce project publicly* process goal is to ensure the public are informed about the project and kept up to date throughout with regards to its progress. The *develop migration plan, divide project into tracks* process was refined further into parallel processes, one for each of the five migration tracks. The outputs of each process associated with these five tracks are inputs into the *migrate scheduled users to OSS* process. After users have been migrated, they continue to receive *support and maintenance* and the migration knowledge is documented (*document lessons learnt*).

Each of these high-level processes was decomposed into a set of detailed subprocesses (Molefe, 2009), as summarized below.

Kick-start project involved the subprocesses:
- plan the migration
- create a project brand
- review work done by other organizations
- obtain organizational commitment to support the migration
- do awareness campaigns
- demonstrate the planned OSS desktop to users.

Form project team involved the subprocesses:
- establish project governance
- divide project tasks among team members
- draw a schedule plan for the migration.

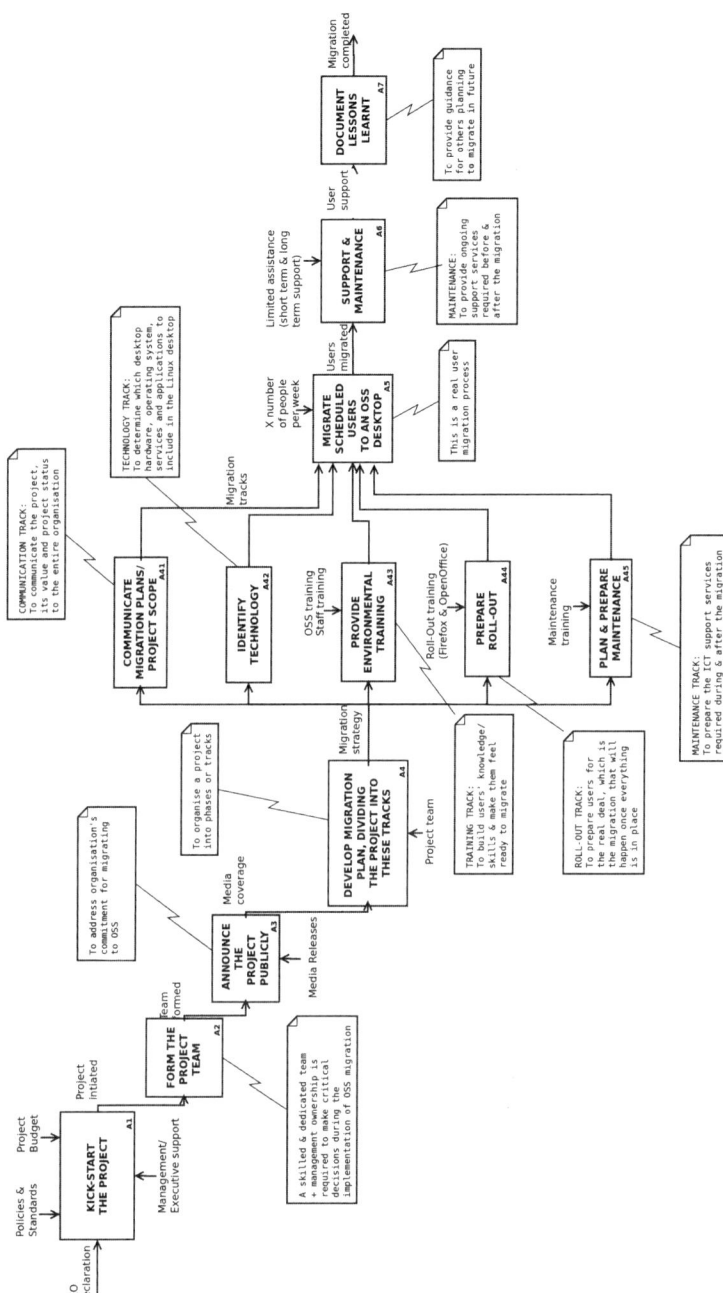

Figure 5.2 High-level process model diagram

Table 5.2 High-level processes: Input and output resources and goals

Process	Input/output resources	Goal description
Kick-start project	Input: CEO declaration Output: Project initiated	To prove the organization's seriousness and commitment to migrating to open source.
Form project team	Input: Project initiated Output: Team formed	To form a team to make critical decisions during implementation of an open source migration.
Announce project publicly	Input: Team formed Output: Media coverage	To ensure the public know about this type of project.
Develop migration plan, divide project into tracks	Input: Media coverage Output: Migration strategy	To help draw a roadmap for the transition from the current to desired environment. To subdivide the project into tracks to allow work to be done thoroughly by responsible parties.
Execute communication track	Input: Migration strategy Output: Migration track	To create user awareness and excitement about changing to OSS.
Execute technology track	Input: Migration strategy Output: Migration track	To find OSS alternatives to proprietary software and check the compatibility of such alternatives.
Execute training track	Input: Migration strategy Output: Migration track	To provide users with relevant training and build their skills to make them productive after migration.
Execute roll-out track	Input: Migration strategy Output: Migration track	To prepare users and put them into action by installing some OSS applications in their desktops.
Execute maintenance track	Input: Media coverage Output: Migration strategy	Plan and prepare for support and maintenance after completion of the migration.
Migrate scheduled users to OSS	Input: Migration strategy Output: Users migrated	To deliver an operational Linux desktop to users.
Support and maintenance	Input: Users migrated Output: User support	To continue to provide all the help needed after completion of the migration.
Document lessons learnt	Input: User support, process model Output: Migration completed	To provide guidance to other organizations planning to migrate to OSS by describing best practices.

Announce project publicly involved the subprocesses:
- announce the project internally and externally
- invite media.

Develop migration plan, divide project into tracks had the five project tracks as subprocesses.

The *communication track* had the following subprocesses:
- develop communications plan
- communicate migration plans and scope
- create user awareness
- communicate reasons for change
- address user concerns
- create positive motivation for change
- build user understanding of OSS
- distribute necessary migration information
- provide regular internal feedback
- communicate progress externally.

The *technology track* had the following subprocesses:
- develop a plan to identify technological and business requirements
- analyse the current architecture
- do an application inventory per user per machine
- categorize users according to their dependence on proprietary applications
- investigate alternative OSS applications and assess compatibility
- identify OSS desktop environments, distributions and applications
- develop pilot base desktop
- test, customize, refine and improve the desktop
- prepare data centre, servers, network infrastructure and support services
- establish a legacy data conversion centre and ICT support team.

The *training track* had the following subprocesses:
- provide training on OSS environment
- train users and technical staff
- encourage self-training or allow users to experiment
- provide practical hands-on training
- call for early adopters
- provide exclusive support to early adopters.

The *roll-out track* had the following subprocesses:
- prepare roll-out
- equip users with latest versions of OSS
- ensure servers, network infrastructure and support services are ready for migration
- conduct pilot courses
- select users deemed ready to migrate

- schedule selected users for migration
- communicate process to users
- assign resources for migration or installation
- migrate scheduled users
- convert templates and standard documents.

The *maintenance track* had a single subprocess, namely to plan and prepare long-term maintenance.

Migrate scheduled users to an OSS desktop had the following subprocesses:

- communicate process to scheduled users
- confirm user training completed
- gain exclusive access to collect desktop machine
- migrate desktop
- record progress
- release desktop to user
- provide additional assistance and support for a short period after migration
- hand over to ICT operations.

Support and maintenance had the following subprocesses:

- provide ongoing support services
- make system enhancements and upgrades
- ensure positive and continuous commitment to change.

Document lessons learnt had the following subprocesses:

- document the migration and lessons learnt
- review and share lessons learnt with other organizations.

Many of these processes and subprocesses would apply equally well to generic technology adoption projects. A few, though, are unique to OSS projects, or manifest differently in OSS projects. For example, the analysis of applications needed to consider several additional factors, including maturity of the OSS, strength and size of the developer community and health of the OSS project. In addition, it is often necessary to combine a set of OSS tools to deliver the same functionality as a single suite of proprietary software, due to the nature of most OSS tools, which are typically small and built for a single purpose, but designed to work together well with other OSS tools. In contrast, many proprietary software suites tend to be more monolithic in design.

Another important factor that distinguishes OSS environments from proprietary technology environments is how releases and version updates are handled. OSS tends to have very frequent incremental releases, whereas developers of proprietary systems tend to release fewer but larger updates. Compare, for example, the release strategies of Ubuntu Linux (six-monthly releases, small functionality increments) and Microsoft Windows (several years between releases, large functionality increments). Due to this difference in release strategy, the task of planning and executing a long-term support and maintenance plan for OSS environments differs significantly from that for proprietary environments.

PRMs for organizational OSS migrations

To extract PRMs from a set of process models, it is necessary to define the criteria to which PRMs must conform. For project Vula this was done through a detailed study involving an analysis of existing documentation and a review of the literature. The following characteristics were identified as being important to PRMs (Rosa et al., 2005; van der Merwe and Kotze, 2009; van der Aalst et al., 2006):
- reusable
- generic
- provide enough information to execute a project or business function
- well-defined scope, outcomes and results.

From these characteristics, the following criteria were developed and used to identify and extract PRMs for project Vula:
- clearly defined context, goals and results
- atomic and complete
- generic to migration projects
- reusable within other contexts to achieve similar results.

The high-level process model diagram was analysed to extract PRMs using these criteria. The extracted high-level PRMs are displayed with heavy black outlines in Figure 5.3, whereas those that do not form part of the reference model are not highlighted. The reasons for selection of specific processes are described in Table 5.3.

Further work required

The Vula project established a partially verified set of PRMs for migration projects, representing a largely sequential process flow during the project. Future work will involve the full verification of these PRMs in other organizations to determine their reusability and applicability to general OSS migrations. In addition, the PRMs will need to evolve to cater for other models of project execution, notably those with an iterative approach.

Lessons learnt

Project Vula found that for OSS migrations to succeed, it is vital to have buy-in and support from decision-makers, notably top management (CEO

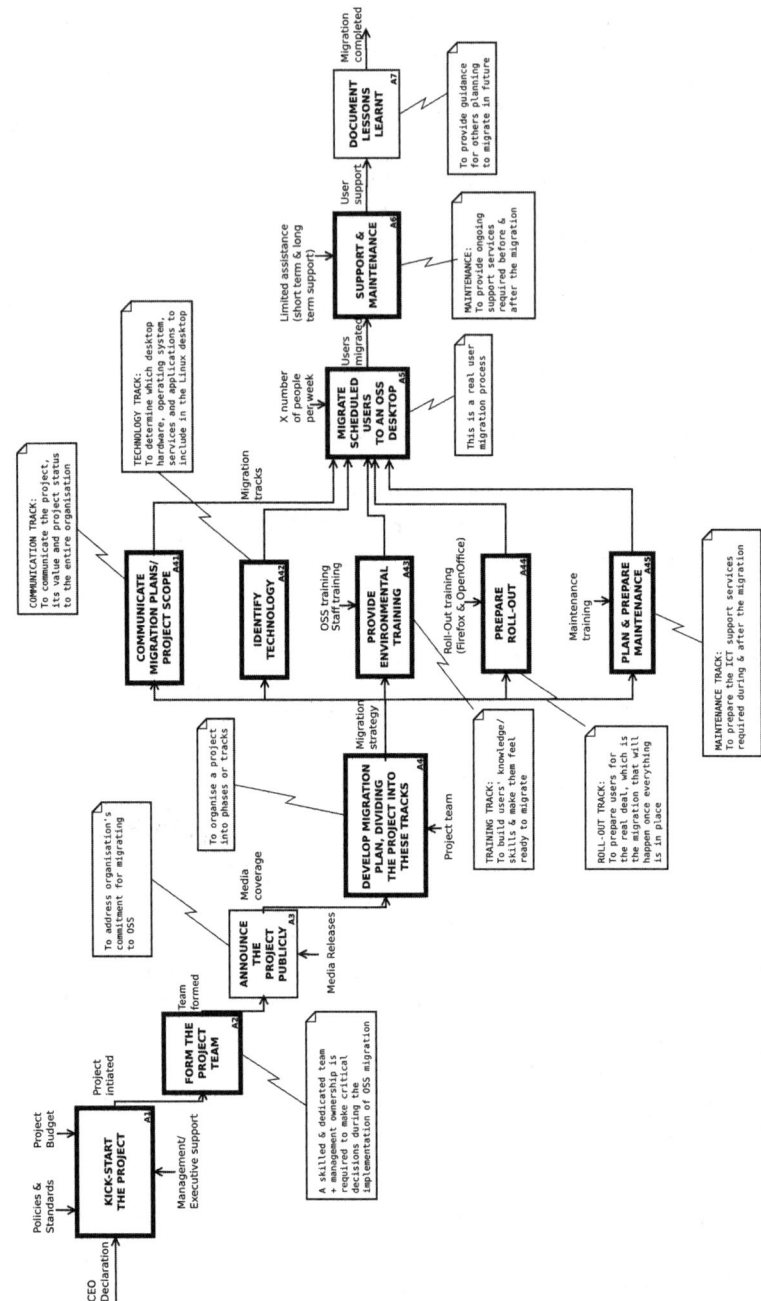

Figure 5.3 Generic process models

and executives). They play an important role in bringing about change in an organization, and in driving the required shift in user mindset. Without the support of top management, the migration project has little chance of success. Organizational and governmental OSS migrations should be encouraged, as they offer a number of benefits. These include possible cost reduction, flexibility, customizability, stability, security and socio-economic development opportunities.

OSS migration projects require careful planning. Analysis, planning and brainstorming are required before measurable objectives are set, lest unrealistic expectations be created. The planning and initiation phases of such projects are critical to understanding these requirements and scoping the project. Because OSS migration projects can take a significant amount of time, hard work and specialized skills to complete successfully, these also need to be carefully planned. OSS deployments may require a larger initial investment in custom technology (or higher-end skills) than proprietary software, but OSS has the potential to reduce longer-term operating costs. However, it is vital to ensure the selected technologies are robust and well maintained (by the OSS community or a service provider), and that appropriate skills are available to operate and support them. If these are not in place, the adoption of the technology will introduce significant risk to the organization.

The quality and composition of the project team are key in determining the success of OSS migrations. The team must be dedicated, capable and empowered. Reporting lines, roles and responsibilities must be clearly defined and communicated, to prevent confusion and a lack of accountability. Where the team comprises people from different organizational units, cultural differences between those units can cause conflict on the team and disagreement on priorities, which can lead to delays. In addition, it is important to ensure that the necessary technical, development and integration skills exist in the team.

Change management is very important in such projects, but is not typically a core expertise of internal ICT support units. As such, the project coordinator and managers must ensure that proper change management processes are adopted. Detailed analysis will ensure efficient and effective development and integration activities. False assumptions can lead to a technology or requirements mismatch and problematic integration, both of which could require additional effort and delay the entire project. The analysis required should consider the computing requirements of users, the functionality and maturity of OSS alternatives, the ICT infrastructure and architecture and the support and maintenance requirements.

Communication and training are vitally important. Communication keeps the entire organization on board and informed, and allows early flagging of potential issues. Training ensures that users can remain

Table 5.3 Extraction of process reference models from the high-level processes

Process	Generic	Reusable	Reason
Kick-start project	Y	Y	Any technology project must be initiated. Subprocesses ensure that any OSS project gets off to a good start, with informed and supportive users.
Form project team	Y	Y	Process is required for any technology adoption project.
Announce project publicly	N	N	The process is particular to Vula and its desire to demonstrate leadership and publish the approach; it is thus neither generic nor reusable, as it is not necessary to ensure migration success. Many organizations may prefer to keep their OSS migration secret.
Develop migration plan, divide project into tracks	Y	Y	Any migration project requires a plan.
Execute communication track	N	Y	Although it is good practice to have good communication during the project, it is not necessary. Most subprocesses can be used on any OSS migration project, but some, such as external communications, are particular to Vula.
Execute technology track	Y	Y	Process is indispensable in any OSS migration project as it identifies the necessary OSS technology solutions. Execution of subprocesses for this track is very particular to OSS migrations and may differ for non-OSS projects.
Execute training track	Y	Y	Training should form part of any technology migration project. Process is differentiated from those in generic technology projects by strong emphasis on user empowerment and self-learning through discovery and customization.

Table 5.3 (cont.)

Process	Generic	Reusable	Reason
Execute roll-out track	Y	Y	Roll-out is indispensable to execute any OSS migration. The approach taken, and recommended for similar OSS projects, involves users directly and thus may differ from the approach typically used on general technology adoption projects.
Execute maintenance track	Y	Y	Any technology change in an organization requires proper planning and implementation for ongoing support and maintenance.
Migrate scheduled users to OSS	Y	Y	Process necessarily forms part of any OSS migration.
Support and maintenance	Y	Y	Process must be executed to ensure OSS migration is sustainable.
Document lessons learnt	N	N	Process is very particular to Vula and is not necessary for general OSS migration projects.

productive with their new technology, helps overcome fear and uncertainty and promotes a positive attitude towards change. In general, the project should strive to change mindsets and get target users positive about the migration. An effective way of accomplishing this is by involving users throughout the project and empowering them to perform their own technology adoption and customization.

From a technology migration point of view, it is preferable to design and migrate the data centre first, to ensure interoperability with the OSS desktop. In addition, the adoption of open standards is a critical enabler for technology migration, promotes interoperability between different systems and platforms and reduces the integration risks associated with the project. Open standards also promote the availability of support and implementations from multiple vendors, reducing the risks associated with vendor lock-in.

To manage the actual roll-out and implementation and prevent significant productivity losses, it is important that a good plan and schedule are developed for rolling out the OSS to users. Analysing computing needs and classifying users into categories can help, as can appointing a champion in each organizational unit to help coordinate activities. In general, it is more efficient to migrate an entire department together, as this allows better contingency planning and maximizes the shared learning that takes place. In environments like the CSIR, where there is a wide range of different uses and technologies, some users need to be convinced of the value of OSS, particularly those who are entrenched in their current technologies. The migration of such users, e.g. R&D staff with varied and heterogeneous computing needs, is challenging and can only succeed if the researchers themselves buy into the project.

OSS migrations based on voluntary adoption have a better chance of success – users are empowered and more positive about the entire process. Involving and enthusing users to become early adopters and coaches, and empowering them to take the initiative and the lead in their departments, create a positive and open mindset and encourage exploration of the opportunities that OSS offers to users. The migration or translation of documents, files and data is extremely important, but can take a lot of time and resources. The approach used in Vula was to convert all standard, shared templates, forms and data before migration, to educate users on how to migrate their own data and to provide a just-in-time conversion support facility to assist where users encountered issues.

Support and maintenance are an important factor to consider in the migration project. There must be adequate and skilled resources available to support the new environment. Typically the amount of support required increases during and for a short period after migration. In addition, support staff will need to be reskilled and will have to adopt a new mindset that accommodates the way OSS is developed and used. It is important to document OSS migration best practices, to improve the quality of future projects by reducing the incidence of common, repeated errors. PRMs offer a suitable means of documenting and evolving good processes for these projects.

Conclusions

This chapter presented a summary of the activities conducted on project Vula to capture and document the lessons learnt and the best practices that emerged. The CSIR embarked on project Vula to migrate its ICT to OSS. In the planning phase it became apparent that no reference process model for organizational OSS migrations existed in the literature. It was decided to capture and publish the knowledge gained on the project, to facilitate similar endeavours by other organizations. The approach used was to analyse the project and extract a set of generic PRMs. PRMs provide a set of baseline processes that can serve as a starting point for any organization wishing to perform a similar migration in future. The process-related information of Vula was captured as process models. From the project-specific process models, a set of PRMs was identified using established criteria.

This study confirms that PRMs for organizational OSS migration can be identified. These models are expected to be useful in reducing uncertainty and risk in organizations planning to migrate from proprietary software to OSS, as they capture organizational learning in a way that could serve as a guide to help in the planning and implementation of arbitrary OSS migration projects. Although these PRMs still need to be fully verified and refined in practice, it is believed they already provide a solid baseline upon which any organization-wide OSS migration project can build its own process models. This chapter presents the research undertaken in the form of a case study of an organizational OSS adoption, and suggests an approach for documenting best practices in order to improve the quality of future migration projects.

REFERENCES

Ahmed, O. (2005) "Migrating from Proprietary to Open Source Learning Content Management Systems", master's thesis, Department of Systems and Computer Engineering, Carleton University, Ottawa.

Astor, A. and D. K. Rosenberg (2005) "The Top-Five Mistakes to Avoid When Migrating to Open Source", *Enterprise Open Source Journal*; available at http://java.sys-con.com/node/175755 (accessed 26 February 2012).

Ayala, C. P., D. S. Cruzes, O. Hauge and R. Conradi (2011) "Five Facts on the Adoption of Open Source Software", *IEE Software* 28(2), pp. 95–99.

Barn, B. (2007) "Business Process Modelling"; available at www.jisc.ac.uk/media/documents/programmes/eframework/process-modelling_balbir_barn.pdf (accessed 26 February 2012).

Bruggink, M. (2003) "Open Source in Africa: Towards Informed Decision-Making", Research Brief No. 7, International Institute for Communication and Development; available at www.ftpiicd.org/files/research/briefs/Brief7.pdf (accessed 18 March 2010).

Cassell, M. (2008) "Why Governments Innovate: Adoption and Implementation of Open Source Software by Four European Cities", *International Public Management Journal* 11(2), pp. 193–213.

Childe, S. J., P. A. Smart and A. M. Weaver (1997) "The Use of Generic Process Models for Process Transformation", in G. Doumeingts and J. Browne (eds) *Modelling Techniques for Business Process Re-Engineering and Benchmarking*, London: Chapman & Hall, pp. 51–60.

Comino, S. and F. M. Manenti (2005) "Government Policies Supporting Open Source Software for the Mass Market", *Review of Industrial Organisation* 26(2), pp. 217–240.

Dudley, G., A. Finlay and A. Otter (2006) "Open Source Software: The Five Step Migration Guide"; available at www.opensourceafrica.org/default.php?view=migrationguide (accessed 25 February 2010).

Ellis, J. and J. P. Van Belle (2009) "Open Source Software Adoption by South African MSEs: Barriers and Enablers", in *Proceedings of the 2009 Annual Conference of the Southern African Computer Lecturers' Association (SACLA '09)*, New York: ACM, pp. 41–49.

Fettke, P., P. Loos and J. Zwicker (2005) *Business Process Reference Models: Proceedings of the Workshop on Business Process Reference Models*, London: Idea Group Publishing.

Gerber, A., O. Molefe and A. van der Merwe (2010) "Documenting Open Source Migration Processes for Re-use"; available at http://researchspace.csir.co.za/dspace/bitstream/10204/4605/1/Gerber1_2010.pdf (accessed 26 February 2012).

Jensen, C. and W. Scacchi (2003) "Applying a Reference Framework to Open Source Software Process Discovery", paper presented at First Workshop on Open Source in an Industrial Context, Anaheim, CA, October.

Kemp, R. (2009) "Current Developments in Open Source Software", *Computer Law & Security Review* 25(6), pp. 569–582.

Kok, F. (2005) "Open Source Software as a Value Alternative to Commercial Software", master's thesis, Faculty of Management, University of Johannesburg.

Kshetri, N. (2004) "Economics of Linux Adoption in Developing Countries", *IEE Software* 21(1), pp. 74–81.

Lawrence, J. (2010) "The Factors that Influence Adoption and Usage Decision in SMEs: Evaluating Interpretive Case Study Research in Information Systems", *Electronic Journal of Business Research Methods* 8(1), pp. 51–62.

Mokhema, T. (2005) "Go Open Source Task Team Conference Results of 22 and 23 August 2005 – The Go Open Source Campaign Partners, Government Departments, the Private and Public Sectors and Academia"; available at www.meraka.org.za/news/goopensourceconference_8sep 2005.html (accessed 16 January 2009).

Molefe, O. (2009) "The Use of Reference Process Models to Capture Open Source Migration Activities", master's thesis, Information Technology, University of South Africa, Pretoria.

Molefe, O. and T. Fogwill (2009) "Open Source Community Organization", in P. Cunningham and M. Cunningham (eds) *IST-Africa 2009 Conference Proceedings*, Dublin: IIMC.

Morgan, L. and P. Finneman (2007) "How Perceptions of Open Source Software Influence Adoption: An Exploratory Study", paper presented at 15th European Conference on Information Systems; available at http://is2.lse.ac.uk/asp/aspecis/20070050.pdf (accessed 26 February 2012).

Mtsweni, J. and E. Biermann (2008) "An Investigation into the Implementation of Open Source Software within the SA Government: An Emerging Expansion Model", in *Proceedings of the 2008 Annual Research Conference of the South African Institute of Computer Scientists and Information Technologists on IT Research in Developing Countries: Riding the Wave of Technology (SAICSIT '08)*, New York: SAICSIT/ACM, pp. 148–158.

Paré, G., W. Michael and D. Charles (2009) "Barriers to Open Source Software Adoption in Quebec's Health Care Organizations", *Journal of Medical Systems* 33(1), pp. 1–7.

Perumpalath, Binoy P. (2005) "Modelling Business Process: An Integrated Approach", MBA dissertation, University of Portsmouth.

Rosa, M. L., F. Gottschalk, M. Dumas and W. M. van der Aalst (2005) "Linking Domain Models and Process Models for Reference Model Configuration"; available at http://wwwis.win.tue.nl/~wvdaalst/publications/p413.pdf (accessed 26 February 2012).

Tyrrell, S. (2000) "The Many Dimensions of the Software Process", *Crossroads* 6(4), pp. 22–26.

van der Aalst, W., A. Dreiling, F. Gottschalk, M. Rosemann and M. Jansen-Vullers (2006) "Configurable Process Models as a Basis for Reference Modeling – Business Process Reference Models Position Paper", in *Business Process Management Workshops*, Berlin: Springer, pp. 512–518.

van der Merwe, A. and P. Kotze (2009) "A Systematic Approach for the Identification of Process Reference Models", paper presented at IASTED International Conference on Software Engineering, Innsbruck, 17–19 February; available at http://researchspace.csir.co.za/dspace/bitstream/10204/3264/1/Van%20Der%20Merwe_2009.pdf (accessed 26 February 2012).

Van Reijswoud, V. and C. Topi (2004) "Alternative Routes in the Digital World: Open Source Software in Africa", *Mtafiti Mwafrika* 12(2), pp. 76–94.

6

Exploring FOSS opportunities in natural hazard risk assessment and disaster management

Coley Zephenia

Introduction

This chapter examines natural hazards and disaster management (DM) as a critical sustainable development intervention. It puts into perspective the state of natural disasters across the globe and highlights challenges dominating the area – especially in developing nations. The primary focus is on the application of free and open source software (FOSS) technologies in developing value-adding information systems that can support effective hazard risk analysis and efficient natural DM. By and large, while developing countries lack information systems for integrated end-to-end management of disasters, there has been a rise in frequency of occurrence of disasters due to a number of human and geophysical factors. Contemporary holistic DM is now premised on abilities to gain in-depth understanding of natural hazard risks, full short- and long-term implications of disasters and proactive planning for disasters. Such an approach demands the analysis of combined data on seismology, meteorology, topography, soil characteristics and vegetation, hydrology, settlements, infrastructure, transportation, population, socio-economics and material resources; this requires robust and dynamic supporting information systems. Thus there is a need to develop innovative systems based on a scalable and flexible architecture in which best practice FOSS technologies can be implemented. The aim is to ensure DM initiatives, particularly in developing nations, become highly sustainable. The chap-

Free and open source software and technology for sustainable development, Sowe, Parayil and Sunami (eds), United Nations University Press, 2012, ISBN 978-92-808-1217-6

ter includes two case studies of the application of FOSS in the natural hazards and DM space.

Background

The chapter examines possible ICT (information and communication technology) interventions in the discipline of natural hazards and DM through exploring FOSS opportunities. It starts by defining a few relevant concepts.

Natural hazards

Natural hazards are described as "those elements of the physical environment, harmful to man and caused by forces extraneous to him" (Burton, Kates and White, 1978). However, the Organization of American States (1991) elaborately defines the term as "all atmospheric, hydrologic, geologic (especially seismic and volcanic), and wildfire phenomena that, because of their location, severity, and frequency, have the potential to affect humans, their structures, or their activities adversely".

A natural hazard that is not understood or effectively managed has great potential to turn into a natural disaster. To avoid disasters, serious research work in hazard risk analysis must inform disaster risk reduction activities at country, regional and continental levels.

Natural disaster

Several definitions of a disaster have been coined by scholars, but the following definition is closer to home than others:

> A serious disruption of the functioning of society, causing widespread human, material or environmental losses which exceed the ability of the affected people to cope using its own resources. Disasters are often classified according to their cause viz. Natural or man-made. (International Water Association, 2009)

In the history of mankind, natural disasters have caused catastrophic loss of life and destruction of property during their short periods of occurrence. Recent studies have shown that the rate and intensity of natural disasters are increasing due to a number of human and geophysical factors. This has made more lives and property across the globe more vulnerable than before (Figure 6.1). It is clear that natural hazards and disasters will remain unpleasant phenomena and human beings will constantly need to deal with them. Proactive strategies based on research knowledge have begun to dominate contemporary efforts to limit natural hazards before they become natural calamities.

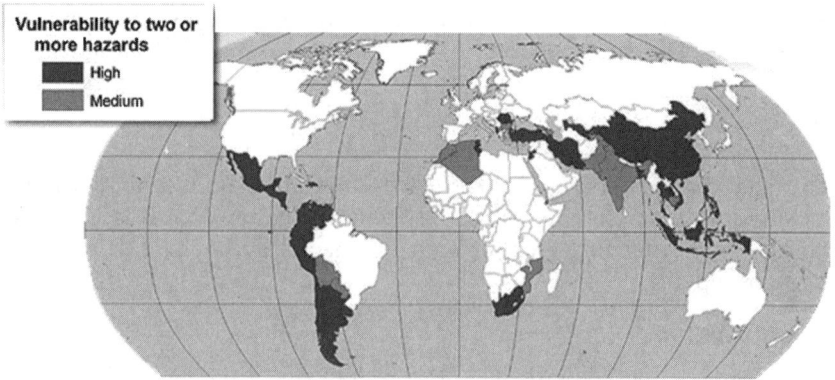

Figure 6.1 Natural disaster hotspots and vulnerable countries
Source: IEG (2011).

While efforts are being made by affected communities, geographers, scientists and international developmental organizations to understand and devise ways to minimize the impact of disasters, many developing countries still suffer heavy casualties, mainly due to lack of knowledge and systems to support DM. As just a few examples of consequential calamities, the 7.0 magnitude quake that rocked Haiti on 12 January 2010 was the biggest urban disaster in modern history: more than 316,000 people were killed and 1.5 million left homeless, and estimated damage and losses ranging between $8 and $14 billion were recorded (AlertNet, 2010). In 2004 the Indian Ocean earthquake, the second largest ever recorded at a magnitude of 9.3, claimed 230,000 lives (Its Nature, 2011). Mozambique suffered floods in 2000 in which at least 700 people died, 650,000 were displaced and 4.5 million were affected, totalling about a quarter of the country's population (Wiles, Selvester and Fidalgo, 2005).

In recent decades innovations in space and supporting ICTs have made gathering, sourcing, processing, retrieving and sharing natural hazard risk and disaster information feasible. Nevertheless, it is still a Herculean task for developing countries to analyse natural hazard risks effectively, take corrective action and minimize impacts of the consequent natural disasters because of the scarcity of IT (information technology) systems and resources. While factors such as economics and political challenges have augmented problems in this area, the real challenge has been how to unlock the power of IT to promote DM. FOSS presents unlimited potential to provide institutions involved in these activities with low-cost IT solutions. It could be used to support DM systems that can harness and streamline data and information from disparate geographical sources. Such information systems have become instrumental in creating multifaceted, integrated DM initiatives. In addition, using FOSS in developing such solutions is in itself an innovation in the practice of DM and ultimately sustainable development.

Global hazards and disasters landscape

A snapshot view of natural disaster statistics across the globe indicates a rise in frequency and magnitude. Between 1980 and 2006 natural disasters killed more than 2 million people worldwide, while between 1991 and 2005 5,210 disasters occurred and caused reported damages totalling US$1.2 trillion. According to Mulugeta et al. (2007), disaster cases have grown from an average of 100 major natural disasters per decade recorded up to 1940 to 2,800 per decade recorded during the 1990s.

In 2008 natural disasters cost the world US$200 billion (Maplecroft, 2009). Some disasters have annihilated years of investment and economic development in a few seconds. Global maps produced by risk specialists Maplecroft (ibid.) show the United States and China bearing about 90 per cent of this burden, while developing countries are most susceptible to economic losses. Developing countries are also more likely to be locked up in a vicious cycle of poverty as a result of the growing prevalence of natural disasters, due to high population growth, decreasing food security, high levels of poverty, destruction of natural resources, global climatic change and collapse of policy and institutional frameworks. However, although the human impact of natural disasters is predominantly concentrated in developing countries, with 90 per cent of deaths occurring in these regions, the rise in both frequency and severity of climate-related disasters is increasingly impacting upon developed and emerging economies, including China. Currently, the World Bank (2010) has a large lending portfolio of natural disaster risk management projects.

Natural disaster management and sustainable development

DM and sustainable development are two intricately related concepts: the former has become an important component of the latter. According to Corina Warfield (2008), the primary objective of DM is "to reduce, or avoid, the potential losses from hazards, assure prompt and appropriate assistance to victims of disaster, and achieve rapid and effective recovery".

Wikipedia (n.d.) advocates that developmental considerations contribute to all aspects of the DM cycle. In principle, integrated DM's main objective, and one of its closest interfaces with development, is the support of sustainable livelihoods, protection and recovery before and during occurrence of disasters. Attaining this goal ensures that "people have a greater capacity to deal with disasters and their recovery is more rapid and long lasting". A proactive and holistic DM approach ideally focuses on managing hazards and preventing and mitigating disasters as well as preparing people and institutions for emergencies. Thus sustainable development considerations are strongly represented in all phases of the DM cycle. Experience, especially in developing countries such as Mozambique, India and the Caribbean states, has shown that inappropriate development processes can lead to increased vulnerability to disasters and loss of preparedness for emergency situations. Effective and efficient hazard management strongly contributes towards disaster-proofing Millennium Development Goals (MDGs). The Asian Disaster Preparedness Center (2010: 5) concurs, noting that the "MDG acceleration framework clearly reveals the importance of considering disaster risk reduction and increasing resilience to all types of natural hazards ... for accelerating the achievement of the MDGs". Thus given that hazard risks and disasters are becoming prevalent across the globe, DM approaches need to be developed to address the causes and effects of disasters. If successfully implemented, these strategies have great potential to transform affected societies into sustainable communities.

FOSS and sustainable development

FOSS use is part of a new paradigm which involves an integrated best-of-breed approach to software implementation being followed across the vendor landscape, and in which software-as-a-service, on-demand and co-sourcing models prevail. New business models and value offerings have surfaced not only to address classic cost challenges, but also to derive value from community networks. FOSS implementation is set to impact positively on the sustainable development of host regions in hazards, DM and other areas. This has been augmented by the emergence of FOSS as a strong competitor in the marketplace *vis-à-vis* proprietary software in many facets of utilization.

FOSS's niche in the market has predominantly been the four fundamental freedoms it gives to an assortment of users. *The freedoms to use, distribute, modify and redistribute the modifications made to software released as FOSS, as well as the availability of FOSS without licensing fees and with source code*, have been responsible for its widespread acceptance and adoption. The growing ubiquity of FOSS has opened up innumerable opportunities for its application in different environments, especially in developing countries. In Africa, for example, the Free Software and Open Source Foundation for Africa (FOSSFA) has in the past five years been a very active catalyst for FOSS adoption in local governments, training, advocacy and application in other areas such as mobile technology. The potential to use FOSS in information systems that enhance DM is being explored in developing economies, albeit in a piecemeal way. Unlike in the developed world, DM in these countries is still hampered by scarcity of data, lack of information infrastructures and skills, and limited financial capacity to invest in IT.

FOSS is premised on a collaborative and community-driven model of software development and maintenance. Its value-adding capabilities have assisted in leveraging developing countries around the world, particularly free licensing, which has resulted in low costs of access to IT. FOSS is resilient and allows localization of software applications, thus accelerating efforts to bridge the digital divide. In recent years it has become more widely adopted and a substantial number of projects use the applications to drive economic development and empower communities in developing countries or regions. Examples of such projects in this chapter provide a reference point to demonstrate to stakeholders that FOSS utilization can offer developing countries a low-cost entry point into the information and internet age.

With a global rise in frequency and intensity of disasters due to human and geophysical factors, developing nations have become more susceptible than ever before. FOSS is a technology and business solution area that needs to be explored with a view to enhancing DM efforts and facilitating sustainable development. A conceptual model for a holistic DM information system could include areas of potential FOSS implementation. It is also encouraging that the International Council for Science (ICSU) Regional Office for Africa published a hazards and disaster science plan which includes a number of research projects in this space, presenting opportunities for FOSS experts and institutions to pursue research of this nature (Mulugeta et al., 2007). To that end, there are unlimited opportunities for organizations such as FOSSFA and ICSU to synergize and establish a *modus operandi* that can ensure IT and FOSS professionals play a critical role in research and development of DM systems.

The information technology challenge in DM

To establish the role that technology play in this realm, it is important to understand best practice DM process. The DM process is divided into two life-cycle phases, namely *mitigation* and *response* (Figure 6.2). The two phases involve a number of complex series of activities. Mitigation focuses on hazard risk assessment, prevention measures and preparedness

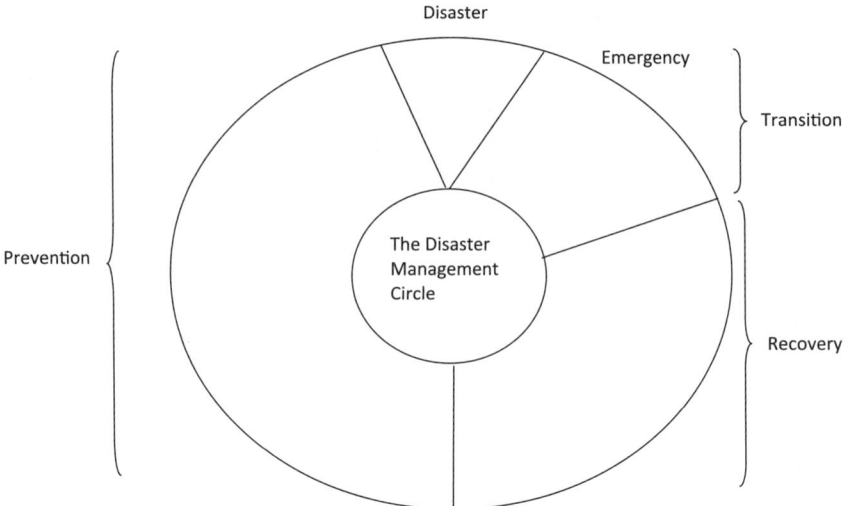

Figure 6.2 Disaster management life cycle

to cope with future disasters, while the response phase concentrates on emergency reaction to a disaster, recovery and rehabilitation.

Histories of some of the worst and most frequently affected communities in developing countries illustrate the following challenges affecting the DM process:
- multiple, successive disasters
- lack of accurate disaster prediction technologies and systems
- slow response to disasters and difficult relief operations
- unnecessarily heavy destruction of infrastructure and property
- huge but avoidable losses of human and animal life.

All these challenges are related to the lack of adequate data, information and effective communication systems before and after disaster. In this twenty-first century, information and technology play critical roles in DM (Figure 6.3). To support this assertion, the International Strategy for Disaster Reduction (2003) states: "Disaster risk reduction begins with information access." Disaster managers and stakeholders require complete and accurate information in all phases of the disaster cycle: pre-disaster activities entailing analysis and research (to improve the existing knowledge base), risk assessment, prevention, mitigation and preparedness; and post-disaster activities involving response, rehabilitation and reconstruction (Rego, 2001). Rego also asserts that the ability of leaders and administrators to make sound DM decisions in analysing risks and deciding upon appropriate countermeasures can be greatly enhanced by the cross-sectoral integration of information. For instance, to understand the

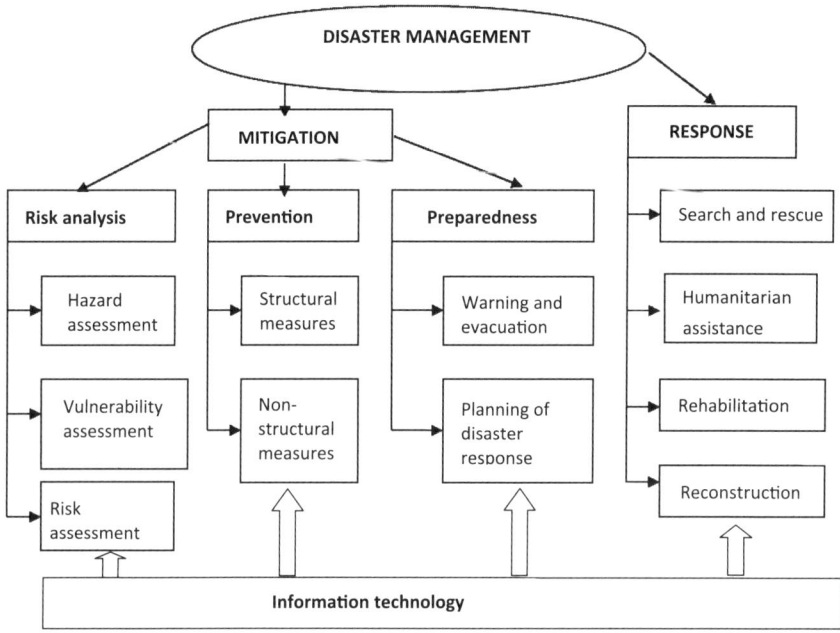

Figure 6.3 Disaster management components
Source: Adeel (2009).

full short- and long-term implications of floods and plan accordingly requires the analysis of combined data on meteorology, topography, soil characteristics, vegetation, hydrology, settlements, infrastructure, transportation, population, socio-economics and material resources. This information can be drawn from different siloed sources. In many developing countries it is a great challenge to consolidate and coordinate these information islands without proper information systems. Yet adequate information is critical to effective DM operations.

Research also indicates that most DM efforts, especially in developing states, have been concentrated more on response than on mitigation. This reactive approach frequently results in unpreparedness and consequent heavy losses when disaster strikes. Nevertheless, there has been a general shift towards proactive DM. Emphasis should now centre on monitoring and establishing knowledge edifices to assess hazard risk, improve hazard prediction and mitigate impact of disasters in advance (Mulugeta et al., 2007). This strategy change has coincided with growing interest by scientists in integrated DM with a focus on sharing data, information, DM technologies and systems. However, there are still very few DM information systems (DMIS) that are designed to assist in end-to-end management of hazards and disasters.

Mulugeta et al. (ibid.) identify a number of knowledge, information and capacity gaps limiting the overall capacity of susceptible communities to tame natural hazards. These include lack of data, knowledge and skills; unavailability of a shared platform to discuss disaster information and prevention strategies; inconsistencies and incompleteness in documentation of historical records; lack of data and information analysis for DM, for example remote-sensing images and hydrological and land-use patterns; and lack of infrastructure, software and skills to download and interpret data. It is thus recognized that increasing natural disaster risk across the globe is exacerbated by piecemeal use of information systems and technologies.

Importance of FOSS-driven DMIS

Management information system concept

Harizanova (2003) defined a management information system (MIS) as a "system to convert data from internal and external sources into information and communicate that information in appropriate forms to managers at all levels in all functions to enable them to make timely and effective decisions for planning, directing and controlling the activities for which they are responsible". An MIS and the information it generates are considered essential components of strategy-driven management operations. MIS technologies have been applied to manage complex phenomena in many corporate organizations – a case in point is the use of IT asset management tools and configuration management databases in IT governance.

However, the MIS concept has not been adequately applied to aid strategic decision-making to enhance DM operations, at least in most of sub-Saharan Africa and other less developed societies. A DMIS, and more so if driven by FOSS technologies, can contribute to cost-effective and holistic DM in a number of ways.
- It offers a platform for structured processing of information from various sources, such as disaster risk assessments, meteorological, geological and geotechnical reports, demographics information, disaster maps, infrastructure and land-use information, specialized disaster research etc.
- It enables systematic collection, rapid processing and timely presentation and dissemination of hazard and disaster information to empower people and institutions to prepare proactively and respond in ways that minimize damage and deaths and ensure speedy recovery.

- A robust DMIS feeds information into the DM life-cycle phases, allowing disaster managers to plan ahead for emergencies taking into account the current risks.
- It provides a framework for a visionary strategy-directed response to managing disasters, for instance enabling measurement of performance of natural DM operations, particularly if integrated with balanced scorecard metrics, such as natural disaster risk reduction and preparedness, disaster monitoring and funding, education and training (Balanced Scorecard Designer, 2009).
- It provides avenues for collaboration and knowledge sharing between scientists and technologists involved in DM, where content management systems and collaboration tools are used.
- It enables susceptible communities to participate actively in DM operations, thus boosting community confidence and enhancing awareness, speedy response and recovery.
- A FOSS-based DMIS can provide information to support integrated multi-hazard management and the full DM life cycle.
- It provides a potential to decrease the digital divide between developed and developing countries in this area and improve the well-being of the latter societies.

Case studies of DM systems

In some developed and emerging economies DM information systems and technologies have been deployed in a bid to make available reliable and up-to-date information to facilitate DM, such as:
- United States FEMA GIS
- Computer System for Meteorological Services (COSMETS)
- Indonesia Disaster Management Information System
- Indian National Natural Disaster Knowledge Network
- Vulnerability Atlas of India
- India's state-level disaster management communication, network and information system in Maharashtra
- China's Integrated Information System for Natural Disaster Mitigation.

However, a majority of these systems do not have homogeneous architectural frameworks that support inclusive disaster risk assessment and disaster response, mitigation and recovery. In addition, some systems, for instance GIS, target specific types of hazards and disasters, while others concentrate on specific areas of DM.

Nah Soo Hoe (2006: 56 and 64) provides two interesting case studies of the application of FOSS in disaster management in developing countries.

Sahana disaster management system: Sri Lanka

Sahana is a disaster management system that grew out of the 2004 Asian tsunami which devastated many of the countries in Asia bordering the Indian Ocean. In Sri Lanka, one of the countries hardest hit by the tsunami, ICT volunteers put together the Sahana disaster management system. Its initial aim was to help track families and coordinate work among relief organizations during and after the tsunami disaster. Subsequently, Sahana has been deployed to manage the earthquake in northern Pakistan (2005), the Guinsaugon landslide in the Philippines (2006) and the earthquake in Yogjakarta, Indonesia (2006). Sahana was developed on a FOSS platform using the LAMP software stack and made available as FOSS itself. A major advantage of having a FOSS disaster management system is that it can be readily distributed, localized and customized according to the requirements of the region or community using it, and poor countries can afford to use it. Sahana consists of a series of integrated web-based disaster management applications aimed at facilitating the management of missing people and victims; managing and administering various organizations; managing camps; and managing requests and assistance in the proper distribution of resources. A new and improved version, Sahana Phase II, is now being rolled out: this is more flexible and powerful and can cater to more general types of disasters. Sahana is developed and maintained by a dedicated team of six full-time developers with assistance from the worldwide FOSS community. A key challenge for the Lanka Software Foundation, the non-profit organization that oversees the project, is to ensure that it receives adequate sponsorship to support the core development team. The success of Sahana and its availability as FOSS open up the possibility of international aid agencies, relief organizations and national governments having a single cohesive disaster management system. This will make disaster management and the associated relief effort much more efficient, and allow regions that frequently experience natural disasters to prepare themselves better to deal with these as and when they arise. The Sahana project has inspired the concept of "humanitarian FOSS", a term coined to denote the application of FOSS to alleviate human suffering. Such a concept can be used to bring together many volunteers around the world to build and contribute to worthy FOSS projects that can benefit mankind.

Tikiwiki GeoCMS: Fiji

This project by the South Pacific Applied Geoscience Commission seeks to address vulnerability reduction in Pacific Island countries through the development of an integrated planning and management system. ICT development and related capacity building are very important to the project. A key component is GeoCMS24, which facilitates the collection and sharing of geographical data among the stakeholders. The creation of this GeoCMS is a main innovative outcome of the project. As there was no suitable software available at the time the project started, a new GeoCMS application was developed from two existing FOSS applications, MapServer and Tikiwiki. The GeoCMS system has made it possible for Pacific Island countries to publish their geographical data for access and sharing over the internet, open to contributions from all over the world. All this helps in the development and vulnerability reduction of these nations, as important information can now be made available more easily and when needed. The mapping and GeoCMS parts of the project have benefited from FOSS, as they were built by enhancing and modifying existing FOSS applications. The use of FOSS makes it affordable and practical to build and deploy the GeoCMS application in every participating country. This in itself leads to local capacity building in ICT and the recipients are able to learn and understand the technology. The development of local content is facilitated as people contribute to the information in the maps, which are made available to all. The GeoCMS software is currently still being enhanced and new features are being added. The main project is at its midpoint stage, with deployment actively taking place in participating countries.

Model DMIS architecture

It is noteworthy that, to date, all kinds of natural hazards and disasters have been identified and at least classified. Much research conducted by geologists, geophysicians and meteorologists has managed to establish general causes and effects of natural disasters. Interestingly, a majority of disasters occur in multiple locations across the globe and result in similar or different degrees of impact. There is thus a need to create a viable, uniform information architecture in which different systems and technologies can exist and interact in a DM ecosystem. The model architecture consists of six generic information-processing layers for DM: source, instrumentation, transformation, disaster information repository, analytics and presentation. A DMIS is supported by information technology, information management, data and governance standards. This architectural framework is governed by the following principles.
- *Modularization:* the framework clearly illustrates a logical view of how various disaster information silos can be stored in a single disaster knowledge base for easy retrieval and dissemination.
- *Service-oriented architecture:* a DMIS model enables integration and interoperability of various DM databases, networks and technologies.
- *Scalability:* it allows implementation at different levels – local, regional, national and global.

- *Information management continuum:* it ideally depicts how hazards and disaster-related data are transformed and aggregated into information and knowledge.
- *Solution orientation:* it must facilitate isolation of gaps and problems in the processing of data and information, thereby allowing improved disaster information management.
- *Resilience to technology dynamics:* any technology change or replacement in one layer must not affect DMIS operations. It must allow various ICTs for disaster prevention and management, such as remote-sensing systems, geographic information and global positioning systems, warning and forecasting systems and internet communication technology, to be deployed in relevant architecture layers.

In the following brief description of the DMIS layers, the volume and depth of processes at each layer depend on the DMIS level of abstraction, which can be local, national or regional in scope.

Data/source layer

This is the base layer of the framework where raw hazard data are generated and collected. There is manual or automatic data entry into individual hazard data storage systems and databases.

Instrumentation

Disaster information harvesting and filtering processes take place in this logical area. Information extraction tools and codes enable the export of information from source databases into the information repository.

Transformation

This layer is concerned with validation, verification and cleansing of information. The outputs of transformation will be usable DM data with unquestionable authenticity, reliability and integrity that form part of the disaster knowledge base.

Disaster knowledge base

This information repository stores classified hazard and disaster information – both real-time and historical. The disaster knowledge base must have the capacity to ensure rapid processing of a wide range of information in various formats from different sources. It will have the following metadata characteristics:
- routinely capture all records from different databases
- classify these records appropriately, for example meteorology, topography, soil characteristics, vegetation, hydrology, settlements, infrastructure, transportation, population and socio-economics
- provide adequate information about the records themselves
- provide ready access to records

- prevent unauthorized access, destruction, alteration or removal of records
- store records in such a way that they cannot be tampered with, deleted inappropriately or altered
- allow records to be shared as information resources across a work space, business unit or organization.

The prime functions of the information repository are to register and classify hazards and disaster records/files. It also provides storage, indexing and tracking, access and security monitoring, searching, retrieval and rendering, management in any form, disposal, integration with other electronic applications and reporting.

Analytics

This layer feeds into the reporting on different aspects of hazards and disasters. It involves performing analytics on relationships between information housed in the knowledge base to support an array of decision-making requirements throughout the DM life cycle. For example, since disasters can be caused by a combination of natural hazards, information extracted from the knowledge base can be analysed and correlated, then consolidated to give relationships between various natural hazards and predict disaster risks. Inputs for analysis are measurements from various DM initiatives. This layer results in the realization of metrics, mostly in different forms, that should match the high-level strategy and specific objectives of the stakeholders.

Presentation

This is the uppermost layer where presentation and dissemination of various outputs of analysed information take place. This layer provides disaster managers, scientists and communities with targeted information to enable preparedness, strategies and collaboration on initiatives at different stages of the DM life cycle. It gives timed reporting and notification at specific intervals, on demand or on an *ad hoc* basis. Analysed and coagulated information is delivered through various communication technologies and special networks – radio, TV, e-mail, mobile phones, websites – through which dashboards, widgets, graphs and other visualizations are accessed in real time (floods, typhoons, tsunamis, earthquakes, tropical cyclones, veldt fires, landslides) or as historical information (drought and famine).

Why FOSS for DM in developing countries?

There has been a growing ubiquity of ICTs in the past decade, with major advances in technology integration and convergence on a global scale.

Some interesting developments include the expansion of the internet and the rise of Web 2.0, and improvements in information systems design, telecommunications, networks and databases. The greatest opportunity has been the rise of FOSS and the evolution of a FOSS community, which is now producing intelligent, cutting-edge technologies that have made computing faster, smarter and cheaper for users. With FOSS, the code can be obtained, viewed, changed and redistributed without royalties or other limitations. Developing countries can now afford to acquire and use these technologies to roll out value-adding solutions – such as DMIS – that enhance sustainable development at low cost. Market-leader applications and technologies within the FOSS landscape that can be applied to different DMIS layers include operating systems databases, content management solutions, networks, application servers, business rules engines, security, business intelligence, portal platforms and integrated development environments.

FOSS is mature

With Google, IBM and Sun Microsystems involved, FOSSFA stepping up its open source capacity initiatives in Africa, the Malaysian government attaining 97 per cent FOSS compliance and the South African government adopting an open source policy, FOSS implementation is the next big thing in IT and business! By 2012 FOSS's share in application software will be $19 billion, with a five-year compound annual growth rate of 44 per cent (Gartner, 2008). FOSS has now matured to become a technology of choice to run servers, networks, content management and operating systems, and business and office applications. The past decade has seen a significant increase in FOSS use by businesses as a result of the general corporate drive towards leaner and more efficient operations when faced with reduced IT budgets but a need to maintain the same functional capabilities. Since the majority of FOSS solutions have demonstrated lower cost of ownership and IT innovation (among many other advantages) compared to proprietary equivalents, many institutions are now switching to FOSS to achieve business goals. Thus in as much as FOSS is being used to create mainstream corporate business solutions, it can also be used with a great degree of confidence to enable DM processes.

FOSS lowers IT costs and improves access to technology

Traditionally FOSS vendors have brought 80 per cent of the functionality at a fraction of the cost. Governments in developing countries are using

Table 6.1 Sample comparison of per capita GDP and Windows XP licence fees

Country	GDP/cap (US$)	PCs (000s)	Piracy (%)	Windows XP cost Effective $	GDP months
Albania	1,300	24	n.a.	15,196	5.17
Algeria	1,773	220	n.a.	11,140	3.79
Angola	701	17	n.a.	28,184	9.59
Antigua and Barbuda	9,961	n.a.	n.a.	1,983	0.67
Argentina	7,166	3,415	62	2,757	0.94
Armenia	686	24	n.a.	28,806	9.80
Australia	19,019	10,000	27	1,039	0.35
Austria	23,186	2,727	33	852	0.29
Azerbaijan	688	n.a.	n.a.	28,708	9.77
Bahrain	12,189	92	77	1,621	0.55
Bangladesh	350	254	n.a.	56,401	19.19
Botswana	3,066	66	n.a.	6,444	2.19
Brazil	2,915	10,835	56	6,777	2.31
Bulgaria	1,713	n.a.	75	11,534	3.92
Burkina Faso	215	17	n.a.	91,801	31.23
Burundi	99	n.a.	n.a.	198,864	67.65
Cambodia	278	18	n.a.	71,184	24.21
Cameroon	559	60	n.a.	35,319	12.01
Canada	22,343	14,294	38	884	0.30
Cape Verde	1,317	31	n.a.	14,998	5.10
Regional aggregates					
European Union	20,863	116,997	n.a.	947	0.32
EU accession countries	4,840	8,286	n.a.	4,082	1.39
EU applicant countries	2,023	3,592	n.a.	9,766	3.32
Caribbean	4,560	308	n.a.	4,332	1.47
Latin America	4,335	18,703	n.a.	4,557	1.55
Africa	652	7,636	n.a.	30,297	10.31
Middle East	2,679	9,708	n.a.	7,375	2.51
Asia	2,128	102,229	n.a.	9,282	3.16
Oceania	13,946	11,886	n.a.	1,417	0.48

Source: Ghosh (2003).

FOSS to lower total cost of ownership (TCO), while private and some public sector organizations are using FOSS for strategic IT investment.

Proprietary software is too expensive for many developing countries

TCO is often used as a measure of software cost. Table 6.1 shows a wide gap between TCO computations for developed and developing countries. Lower GDP per capita in developing countries means that while licences could be comparatively cheaper than in developed countries, proprietary software is still beyond their reach. The price of a typical, basic proprietary toolset required for any ICT infrastructure, Windows XP together with Office XP, is about $560 in the United States. This represents 26.0 months, 67.6 months, 31.0 months, 18.0 months, 9.0 months and 2.5 months of GDP per capita in the Central African Republic, Burundi, Burkina Faso, Zambia, Zimbabwe and South Africa respectively.

FOSS adapts to local needs

Localization is another area which demonstrates the advantages of FOSS in building people/community-oriented applications. In general, facets of localization include capturing content in local languages and stimulating local innovation and growth in IT, especially in cases where FOSS is customized to create home-grown solutions that meet local requirements at point of need. Another view of localization involves the development of software itself, for example GNU/Linux. There have been several variations of these operating systems because of the availability of localization methods inherent in GNU/Linux development. This also allows local value chains to be tapped, instead of forcing customers to rely on expensive foreign software vendors.

FOSS redefines independence

FOSS adoptions in developing countries are by and large driven by a range of socio-economic and political obligations.
- The need to bridge the digital gap and improve access to technology.
- The desire for economic independence.
- A general drive towards security and autonomy.
- Growing local IT industries and stimulating innovations that address local challenges.
- Minimizing reliance on single suppliers (vendor lock-in), who may not be focused on regional and national interests.
- Creating an environment in which suppliers fairly and openly compete on quality and cost for software installation, enabling, support and maintenance.

Conclusions

There is no doubt that the frequency and magnitude of natural disasters are increasing due to natural and human-related factors. The key to effective mitigation of natural hazards and disaster risk and minimizing the impact lies in investing in high-technology information systems based on

FOSS. For institutions embracing FOSS, the ultimate benefits are flexibility, security, reliability, performance, high return on investment, reduced TCO and the proliferation of an innovation culture in this area. Application of FOSS in building these information systems has a huge potential to facilitate systematic collection, storage, retrieval, analysis and dissemination of disaster information to decision-makers and affected populations. This can lead to substantial improvements in DM because the right information will be available in the right format to the right person at the right time. This chapter has provided a sample DMIS architectural and governance framework for consideration by institutions that require a jump-start in DM. However, implementing a DMIS is by no means an easy task, as it requires more than the support of sound architectural and governance frameworks. Factors such as the socio-political environment, the financial commitment of the international community, governments and private and public sectors and availability of ICT expertise (which is scarce in many developing countries) need to be considered.

REFERENCES

Adeel, Kashif (2009) "Role of Information Technology in Natural Disasters and Hazard Reduction: An Eye on Pakistan Earthquake"; available at www.authorstream.com/Presentation/aSGuest10698-138340-kashif-apng-presentation-business-finance-ppt-powerpoint/ (accessed 29 July 2009).

AlertNet (2010) "Haiti Earthquake 2010: Haiti's Biggest Tremor in 200 Years"; available at www.trust.org/alertnet/crisis-centre/crisis/haiti-earthquake-2010 (accessed 20 May 2011).

Asian Disaster Preparedness Center (2010) "Disaster Proofing the Millennium Development Goals (MDGs)"; available at www.adpc.net/v2007/Downloads/2010/Oct/MDGProofing.pdf (accessed 25 February 2011).

Balanced Scorecard Designer (2009) "Natural Disaster Management Balanced Scorecard Metrics Template"; available at www.strategy2act.com/solutions/natural_disaster_management_excel.htm (accessed 3 August 2009).

Burton, I., R. W. Kates and G. F. White (1978) *The Environment as Hazard*, New York: Oxford University Press.

Gartner (2008) "Forecast: Open-Source Impact on Application Software, Worldwide and Regional, 2007–2012"; available at www.gartner.com/id=817618 (accessed 15 April 2012).

Ghosh, Rishab Aiyer (2003) "License Fees and GDP per Capita: The Case for Open Source in Developing Countries", *First Monday* 8(12).

Harizanova, Adriana (2003) "Management Information System in the Tailoring Industry", *Academic Open Internet Journal* 9, pp. 1–10.

IEG (2011) "Natural Disaster Hotspots and Vulnerable Countries", Independent Evaluation Group; available at www.worldbank.org/ieg/naturaldisasters/maps/ (accessed 19 February 2011).

Hoe, Nah Soo (2006) "Breaking Barriers: The Potential of Free and Open Source Software for Sustainable Human Development – A Compilation of Case Studies from Across the World"; available at http://idl-bnc.idrc.ca/dspace/bitstream/10625/37302/1/127878.pdf (accessed 1 May 2012).

International Strategy for Disaster Reduction (2003) "Information Systems and Disaster Risk Reduction"; available at http://nirapad.org/admin/soft_archive/1308136664_Information%20Systems%20and%20Disaster%20Risk%20Reduction.pdf (accessed 30 July 2009).

International Water Association (2009) "WASH Disaster Risk Management Toolbox"; available at www.waterdisaster.org/ibis/wash/eng/gloassary (accessed 26 July 2009).

Its Nature (2011) "The Indian Ocean Earthquake"; available at www.itsnature.org/what-on-earth/10-worst-natural-disasters/ (accessed 30 January 2011).

Maplecroft (2009) "USA and China Top Global Risk Ranking for Economic Loss Due to Natural Disasters Linked to Climate Change"; available at www.reuters.com/article/2009/03/11/idUS185929+11-Mar-2009+BW20090311 (accessed 30 January 2011).

Mulugeta, G., S. Ayonghe, D. Daby, O. P. Dube, F. Gudyanga, F. Lucio and R. Durrheim (2007) "Natural and Human-induced Hazards and Disasters in Sub-Saharan Africa", ICSU ROA Science Plan; available at www.icsu.org/icsu-africa/publications/reports-and-reviews/icsuroa-science-plan-on-hazardsdisasters/Doc%20SP03.1_ICSU%20ROA%20Science%20Plan%20-%20Hazards%20and%20Disasters.pdf (accessed 20 June 2009).

Organization of American States (1991) "Primer on Natural Hazard Management in Integrated Regional Development Planning", Department of Regional Development and Environment; available at www.oas.org/dsd/publications/unit/oea66e/ch01.htm#a.%20what%20are%20natural%20hazards (accessed 29 January 2011).

Rego, Aloysius J. (2001) "National Disaster Management Information Systems and Networks: An Asian Overview", paper presented at GDIN 2001; available at www.adpc.net/infores/adpc-documents/paperatgdin01.pdf (accessed 15 July 2009).

Warfield, Corina (2008) "The Disaster Management Cycle"; available at www.gdrc.org/uem/disasters/1-dm_cycle.html (accessed 30 February 2011).

Wiles, Peter, Kerry Selvester and Lourdes Fidalgo (2005) "Learning Lessons from Disaster Recovery: The Case of Mozambique", Disaster Risk Management Working Paper Series No. 12, World Bank, Washington, DC.

Wikipedia (n.d.) "Sustainable Development"; available at http://en.wikipedia.org/wiki/Sustainable_development (accessed 28 February 2011).

World Bank (2010) "Projects Database"; available at http://web.worldbank.org/external/projects/main?pagePK=218616&piPK=217470&theSitePK=40941&menuPK=51526592&category=simsearch&pagenumber=1&pagesize=100&sortby=BOARDSORTDATE&sortorder=DESC&query=Natural%20Disasters&status=ALL (accessed 30 February 2011).

7

Open source software adoption best practices: Myths, realities, processes and economic growth

Carlo Daffara

Introduction

> The Swiss canton Solothurn is reversing its move to a complete open source desktop, Swiss and German media report. Major reason for the failure appears to be a lock-in to proprietary applications. Protest by users added pressure to the project ... According to the *Solothurner Zeitung*, the canton was unable to connect the open source desktop to a governmental database ... [Users noticed] missing special characters and complained about having to switch back and forth between a Linux and a Windows desktop. (OSOR, 2010a)

This is, unfortunately, the current most common outcome of many migration experiments with open source software. Despite the many perceived advantages of free and open source software (FOSS), adoptions are still marginal and most of the benefits of collaborative development models do not materialize for the majority of companies and public authorities. In particular, government agencies and the public institutions to which they contract out services are large software users with special characteristics derived from their obligations to citizens and their unique legal status. For example, most agencies are expected, or even required by law, to provide services accessible to all residents of their regions, including those who are disabled, lack education or are geographically isolated. Agencies must also be neutral in their relationships with manufacturers, and must often guarantee the integrity, privacy and security of the data they handle over long periods of time. Any institution values the

Free and open source software and technology for sustainable development, Sowe, Parayil and Sunami (eds), United Nations University Press, 2012, ISBN 978-92-808-1217-6

advantages of keeping open options for different vendors, because it tends to lower costs and leave an escape path if a chosen vendor quits the business or fails to provide up-to-date features. But for public agencies, a competitive market is usually more than a preference – it is a legal requirement. The legislation enjoins them to initiate procurement by issuing calls for tenders that do not favour a single vendor. Any interested company that fulfils reasonable criteria can produce a bid to compete on its own merits with everyone else.

However, this critical adherence to disinterested policy is violated in the case of proprietary software. Each product is available only from one supplier (even if it uses a number of intermediaries). If a particular product is specified in a call for tenders, the administration has predetermined the supplier that gets the contract. In the case of computer applications, it is virtually impossible to avoid specifying a particular product because the agency needs compatibility with products that are already deployed, savings in training and maintenance, or other reasons.

Adoption of FOSS by companies has been demonstrated to be both economical and able to increase flexibility and innovation capabilities; in this regard, there is no shortage of data and results to demonstrate that FOSS, when adopted with appropriate best practices, can significantly lower costs and provide quality IT (information technology) solutions, especially for small and medium-sized enterprises (SMEs). For example, in COSPA (2008) the project results demonstrated that by using best practices for FOSS procurement, not only was software acquisition cheaper but the evaluation of tangible and intangible costs over five years showed a cost reduction ranging from 20 per cent to 60 per cent.

An EU study on the impact of FOSS (Ghosh, 2006) indicates that it can reduce software research and development costs by 36 per cent, while INES (2006) shows that companies adopting FOSS increased profits and reduced time to market and development costs in 80 per cent of the trials. More recent research from Venice University (2009) similarly found:

> Finally, comparing the individual data on firms with turnover of less than 500,000 euros with the variable on size classes of customers (by number of employees), one can hypothesize a correlation between the use of FOSS and the ability to attract customers on a relatively larger scale. At the same turnover, in other words, companies which are "Open Source only" seem to have more chances to obtain work orders from companies with more than 50 employees (i.e. medium–large compared to our universe of reference).

Despite this, only 30 per cent of companies are currently using FOSS in a structured way. This chapter analyses the reasons for the majority of adoption failures, and what can be done to increase the probability of successful adoption, using results from EU research projects and participation in the UN International Open Source Network activities in Southeast Asia, as well as some activities specific to African countries.

Developing countries: FOSS perspective

To date, most of the work on FOSS adoption processes has been done in two separate research contexts: its adoption in developed countries (United States, European Union, Japan) by both commercial actors and public administrations, and its use in the ICT4D (information and communication technology for development) context (Sida, 2004). The degree of sharing between these two environments is quite limited, meaning that very few scientific results are available for FOSS adoption processes specifically for developing countries (Camara and Fonseca, 2007). To try to bridge as much as possible the results of these two fields, the chapter focuses first on the differences between developed and developing countries in the ICT context, and how these differences impact on the traditional adoption processes. While recognizing that it may be a rough approximation, the main points have been identified in the literature.

- *Infrastructural differences*: developing countries have a lower share of available resources per user, including large variation in reach and affordability for classes of users. As an example, in Table 7.1 the ratio of fixed-line and mobile subscribers shows huge variation between countries. The limited presence of landlines is an example of the "generational jump" effect: the absence of pre-existing investment in basic infrastructure leaves the door open for new technologies. The International Telecommunication Union ICT regulatory toolkit (ITU, 2010), for example, mentioned that "The absence of a well-established interconnection regime may allow regulators in developing countries to bypass policies that are no longer appropriate, in favour of arrangements that are sustainable, minimize opportunities for arbitrage, and are more in line with emerging technologies." There is a discussion later in the chapter of how this may be used as a basis to facilitate the introduction of new FOSS-based tools in ICT environments.
- *Cultural differences*: developing countries tend to exhibit a higher geographical differential in both linguistic and economic terms. There is a higher income gap between urban and non-urbanized areas in these countries when compared with EU or US areas, as well a higher presence of local languages and dialects accompanied by a reduced literacy rate. This may hamper the adoption of software that is not localized, or

Table 7.1 Fixed and mobile subscribers per head of population

Country	Mobile	Landline
EU	0.95	0.48
USA	0.83	0.53
China	0.41	0.27
India	0.25	0.03
Guatemala	0.76	0.10
Albania	0.63	0.10
Morocco	0.57	0.07
South Africa	0.86	0.09

is designed using cultural assumptions that may not be universally valid. The phenomenon is widely known, and is present in developed countries as well; it mainly affects guidelines that are related to social aspects of ICT introduction, like the ease with which a FOSS package can be localized for a minority language.

Negative and positive factors in FOSS adoption

Despite the substantial interest in FOSS, very few studies exist on the actual factors that facilitate or negatively impact the adoption or migration processes. One of the largest such studies was done through an EU-sponsored research effort, COSPA (Consortium for Open Source Software in the Public Administration), that measured over two years the real costs and difficulties in several adoption experiments performed in European public administrations of widely different size and kind (large and small municipalities, province associations and consortia, healthcare authorities). The analysis of adoption factors identified in the project resulted in two factor tables (Tables 7.2 and 7.3).

By analysing reports from the many migrations performed in the EU projects COSPA, Calibre, FLOSSMETRICS and OpenTTT, a set of best practices designed to facilitate the emergence of positive factors while at the same time reducing the impact and occurrence of negative ones has been prepared. One of the main results of this effort is the recognition that adoption processes are influenced not only by the most commonly mentioned technical guidelines, but by social and management factors as well.

- *Management guidelines.* Understanding the procedures that company or agency heads need to put in place, and how staff must be coordinated.

Table 7.2 Positive variables

Variable	Spearman Rho
Technological benefits of FOSS outweigh its disadvantages (e.g. ability to tailor to precise needs, transparency)	.382*
Availability of FOSS-literate personnel	.363*
Top management support for FOSS adoption	.332*
Personnel support for FOSS ideology	.332*
Network externality benefits from FOSS (e.g. availability of extra deployed functionalities, support from other users of same FOSS project)	.327*
Existence of committed and respected FOSS champion in-house	.324*
Limited financial resources ensure consideration of FOSS	.155

Note: * denotes variables with significant two-tailed correlation at the 0.01 level.

Table 7.3 Negative variables

Variable	Spearman Rho
Perception of work undervalued if using "cheap" FOSS products	.573*
Changing operation model to FOSS might be problematic (e.g. no contracted maintenance support)	.525*
Staff resistance due to fear of being deskilled if using FOSS instead of commercial packages	.498*
No other successful FOSS examples in industry sector	.446*
Staff unwilling to tolerate "teething problems" with FOSS products	.380*
Organization has a favourable agreement with a proprietary vendor (e.g. bulk purchasing agreement, state-wide marketplace discounts)	.374*
Organization is in a risk-averse industry sector	.089

Note: * denotes variables with significant two-tailed correlation at the 0.01 level.

- *Social guidelines.* Presenting change to staff in a positive manner and handling the various forms of resistance they will put up; interacting with the community that developed the software in a productive manner.
- *Technical guidelines.* The actual technical processes and approaches used to perform a migration, including factors like software selection, update and migration processes, may be enhanced and adapted to the specificity of FOSS, increasing acceptance by end users, reducing disruption and discomfort and improving the overall quality of the IT environment.

These guidelines have been adapted for the specific ICT landscape of developing countries, adding a set of suggestions for policy-makers on how to facilitate a large-scale adoption process.

Management guidelines

The main drive for a successful migration to FOSS always starts with a clear assessment of the IT landscape, a clear vision of the needs and benefits of the transitions, and continual support. FOSS development models and support may require a significant change in the way software and services are accounted for and procured, and in general a shift of responsibility from outside contractors to in-house personnel.

Be sure of management commitment to the transition

Management support and commitment have been repeatedly found to be one of the most important variables in the success of complex IT efforts, and FOSS migrations are no exception. This commitment must be guaranteed for a time period sufficient to cover the complete migration; this means that in organizations where IT directors are frequently changed, or where management rotates after fixed periods (for example in public administrations, where changes happen regularly), there must be a process in place to hand over control of the migration. The commitment should extend to funding (as transitions and training will require resources, both monetary and in-house). The best way to ensure continued coordination is to appoint a team with mixed experiences (managerial and technical) to give continuous feedback and day-to-day management.

Troubleshooting point. If the only people working on planning the migration are from IT/management information, there may be insufficient knowledge in upper management and financial planning to continue the migration after the initial step.

Policy considerations. There are relatively few training programmes for ICT managers, and even fewer that are specific to the proper management of open source systems. A consistently small percentage of SME and public administration managers have actual management training; compounded with the limited practical literature on FOSS management, this increases the probability of choosing the wrong approach for introducing a new IT infrastructure. A potential approach is to create an easy-to-follow guide, designed for the main unaddressed user group (SME and small public administration managers), providing a small set of best practices in IT management, explicitly including FOSS guidelines.

Pointers to online courses (especially the many public access courses available) can also be the basis of a personal learning path.

What is expected from the migration or adoption, including measurable benchmarks?

The transition can be started for several reasons, including better control of IT costs, independence from suppliers, flexibility or support of open data standards. To be sure that the migration is effectively producing benefits or is going according to plan, it is fundamental to know beforehand what indicators will be used to evaluate progress. Those requirements must be realistic; in particular, expectations of TCO reductions must be compared with publicly available data.

Troubleshooting point. If the only perceived advantage is that "the software comes from the net for free", there may be wrong assumptions that will probably lead to a final negative judgement on the migration.

Policy considerations. Many countries introduced guidelines for estimating the TCO and real costs of an ICT adoption process, and use these to guarantee a transparent evaluation process in public administrations. These guidelines in several instances tend to ignore hidden costs like lock-in and lack of transparency in acquisition processes when there is a market imbalance (for example, when a single vendor has an absolute majority of the market and thus a large indirect impact on other vendors). Acquisition and cost estimation guidelines must take into consideration these aspects, to guarantee market fairness.

Make sure the timetable is realistic

The introduction of a new IT platform will always require a significant amount of time; as a rule of thumb the time to perform a full transition to FOSS may be considered comparable to that of the introduction of a new company-wide ERP (enterprise resource planning) application; for smaller transitions, time effort should be scaled accordingly. Give more guidelines here.

Troubleshooting point. When migration time is measured in days, and no post-migration effort is planned, the process may be forced to a stop after the planned resources are expended.

Policy considerations. A simple and effective suggestion may be a central, public archive of FOSS adoptions by public administrations, along with costs, migration efforts and time. These data can be used as a reference source for other administrations and SMEs – simply by looking at the most similar project in the list, they can identify a set of similar efforts and the time required for a migration to be performed.

Make sure that budget allocation is reasonable

An unfortunate effect of the widespread belief that "FOSS is free" is an improper association with lower cost in every step of the adoption process. This may or may not be true; it is important to recognize the fact that some costs may be shifted from one cost centre to another, or moved from tangible to intangible (for example from externally outsourced support to internal self-help). The estimation process is complex, and even many proprietary projects fail because of budgeting errors or an unanticipated increase in the workload.

An initial and simple estimate for real, complete TCO of a migration project is to double the costs that are estimated for the explicit migration (COSPA, 2008). While the approach is approximate, and may not be fully valid for all the possible adoption processes or company/agency sizes, it does at least provide a valid ballpark estimate that can guarantee the project managers will not discover (too late) that some efforts cannot be completed because the budget allocated for a task is insufficient.

Troubleshooting point. When a budget is not clearly allocated or estimated, or when the estimate is too small compared with the approximate migration cost, the migration process may be halted by a lack of necessary resources – even a marginal deviation from the plan may result in substantial disruption.

Policy considerations. Similar to that suggested for timescales, a central and public database of real costs can be used as a basis to obtain initial budget estimates and (more importantly) an indication of the variability of such costs, to find lower and higher bounds on the necessary budget.

Review the current software/IT procurement and development procedure

As implementation effort is shifted from commercial to open source software, the procurement and development process needs to be updated accordingly. In particular, the focus may move from acquisition to services, as less software comes "shrink-wrapped" (commercially bought), and this may require changes in how the internal IT budget is allocated.

Internally developed software will require a rolling transition to new software that is either multi-platform or accessible using standard interfaces (for example web applications), and this should be taken into account in the overall IT plan. FOSS should go through the same process used for proprietary software: this will ensure stability of procurement, and reduce a posteriori criticism for the managers and administrators who endorsed the migration process.

Table 7.4 Ecosystem revenues compared with Microsoft revenues by partner type

Microsoft	Product-oriented partner (e.g. ISV, IHV)	Services-oriented partner (e.g. SI, Hoster)	Value-added partner (e.g. VAR)	Logistics-oriented partner (e.g. large account reseller)	Retail logistics partner (e.g. large electronics store)
$1	$4.09	$2.44	$2.30	$2.70	$2.93
1	24.0%	40.9%	43.5%	37.0%	34.0%

Troubleshooting point. When no change of procurement or development is planned, the management may have not understood the scope of change required for the adoption of open source and open data standards.

Policy considerations. A nationwide policy can impact only public administrations, but governments can address public procurement using guidelines like those published by the EU Open Source Observatory (OSOR, 2010b) as a basis for increasing fairness in the market. Facilitation of FOSS acquisition has been found effective in stimulating a local market for open source services as well, with the practical result of increasing the margins of local operators by reducing the fees for (usually US) proprietary software. Previous studies found, for example, that Microsoft partners pass 24.0–43.5 per cent of their revenues to the US company (Table 7.4) – without considering other additional software that may be resold along with the partner offering (IDC, 2011). A nationwide policy that facilitates open source has the side-effect of increasing, when possible, the percentage of revenues that is spent and reinvested locally, thus improving the local economy.

Seek advice or search for information on similar transitions

As the number of companies and administrations that have already performed a migration is now considerable, it is easy to find information on what to expect and how to proceed. Public administrations and companies can contact their local open source competence centre for information and support in the migration process; sometimes industry associations have an internal FOSS working group that can facilitate information sharing and knowledge diffusion.

Troubleshooting point. When no information is sought on similar efforts before starting the adoption process, it is possible to risk repeating errors already made by others, including encountering difficulties that can be avoided easily.

Policy considerations. FOSS competence centres are effective, low-budget tools that have been found effective in increasing adoption rates (for further information see tOSSad, 2006), and their usefulness is greater in developing countries where the role of commercial FOSS providers is limited. In this context, competence centres reduce the cost of finding a reputable information source, accessing documentation and connecting with experts; it is thus important to make centres open to commercial entities as well as public bodies, as the availability of local commercial adopters increases the probability of companies being interested in offering FOSS-based services, and this facilitates the spontaneous development of a market that can be useful for public administrations.

Avoid "big switch" transitions and favour incremental migrations

Most large-scale migrations that are performed in a single, large step (involving the abrupt change from one IT environment to another) are usually marred by extremely high support and technical costs. While the need to support more than one environment does increase support and management cost, "gentle" or incremental migrations usually bring a better overall experience for the users and result in minimal disruption to business processes.

An example of gentle migration can begin with server-side applications that are usually standards- or network-based and thus easier to replace, leaving desktop and user-facing applications until last. Performing an analysis of what impact is due to any change in the IT infrastructure, especially which and how many users are affected, is important – both in a successful migration, but even more so in a partially unsuccessful migration.

Group segmentation is also effective in this scenario: having a small group of "alpha testers", especially taken from the group of "champions" discussed later for social best practice, may be extremely effective in finding outstanding problems in real scenarios, and not only in the limited internal or vendor-based testing.

Troubleshooting point. When the transition is planned in a single "gate point", the risk of disruption if some technical problems arise is substantially increased.

Policy considerations. Public guidelines (for example by local competence centres) should provide guidance on how to plan properly for a migration process, including planning for minimal disruption and risk analysis. A small set of process templates, like ready-to-use templates and process graphs, may help in facilitating this even for managers with limited experience in IT planning.

Interacting with communities or vendors and finding online information sources

A significant advantage of FOSS is the availability of online free resources, in the form of knowledge bases, mailing lists and wikis (collaborative sites) that can give substantial support, in many cases comparable to commercial offerings (or even better). The biggest problem is the identification of such knowledge sources; assigning a person to determine which resources to find and categorize and interact with such sources is a way to reduce the cost of support. A common way to provide a unified source of information is by setting up a small intranet webpage with links to online resources.

Troubleshooting point. When no one knows where to find information on the tools being used, or everyone has to search websites on their own to find usage tips, not only is research being constantly repeated, but critical pieces may be lost or not found in the first place. Also, a lack of visibility on currently adopted packages may reduce the effectiveness of legal auditing, increase the costs and difficulties of implementing a proper security process and in general increase the perception that FOSS is not properly managed.

Policy considerations. An effective help for companies and administrations interested in working with FOSS communities and vendors is the creation of training materials that can guide users towards understanding the differences between the proprietary and FOSS worlds. Some material can be effectively reused from other competence centres, like the UK OSS Watch or the EU Open Source Observatory. There are many parallel efforts worldwide, in both developed and developing countries, that can provide freely available and modifiable materials to jump-start the document preparation process.

Evaluate licences and ancillary conditions

A common business model adopted by some "enterprise" open source companies is called "open core", where the product is available in two different editions – one fully open source but limited in functionality, and the other complete but released under a proprietary licence. In evaluating a FOSS product, management must ensure that the desired functionality is available in the FOSS edition. If not, this becomes a "normal" proprietary adoption process. Also, not all the projects that claim to be FOSS are really under an open licence; a "custom" or non-traditional licence can hide additional restrictions that may make the product not completely open or modifiable by the user.

Troubleshooting point. When no one checks the licences of the software used, there is a substantial risk that some features are not really available. Adopters may reach the point where the migration fails because the software is not really capable of performing the expected tasks. The risk of licence incompatibility is substantially lower in many migrations, since the potential problems are apparent only when assembled software with incompatible licences is distributed outside the adopter environment.

Policy considerations. Competence centres can prepare a catalogue of solutions, similar to that created by the European Commission (FLOSS-METRICS, 2009), including the explicit mention of features that are not included in the open source edition, and any limits in its use. Such a catalogue can be customized for vertical sectors, to increase the relevance for the target users.

Identify functionality, not names

When adopting software one should never go for the shortcuts of looking for "something like [proprietary product name]". It is nearly impossible to find exact clones; prepare (as part of the inventory) a list of features you need, features you would like to have, and use it as a basis for product evaluation. As indicated above, beware of FOSS products that have different licensing (as in the "open core" model), because some features may be restricted to the proprietary version only.

A useful technique is to use a standardized approach to functional evaluation, like QSOS (Qualification and Selection of Open Source). In this approach, products are first evaluated for the essential features (those that are necessary), and those that lack one of these are excluded from further evaluation. Ancillary features – those that would be beneficial but are not essential – are evaluated using a numeric score to give a monotonic ranking that helps in choosing the final software to be adopted.

Troubleshooting point. When evaluation is done without an in-depth analysis or a structured methodology there is a considerable risk of introducing bias, for example towards the software that is more heavily promoted or more used, even if it is not the most appropriate for the target environment.

Policy considerations. There is substantial equivalence among the many assessment tools and methods, including several studied by the European Commission and other entities, which means it is simply a matter of selecting one of them and promoting it as a tool for evaluation. This can be done in the context of competence centres or through industry associations; evaluations can be easily shared and improved upon in a real collaborative fashion to reduce the effort needed. Information can also be included as a part of the previously mentioned catalogue of solutions.

Identify in a proper way your support needs

At least 70 per cent of deployments do not require any additional support – other than the free, community-based one. This percentage, identified in the COSPA project, has been broadly confirmed; for example, in a recent Lighthouse (2011) survey self-support was the form of technical support identified by 56 per cent of Red Hat Linux users. In general, deployments tend to use external support in a temporary way during the initial "exploration" phase, and after the internalization of FOSS-related skills support moves from a generic helpdesk to more specialized and vertical consultancy. It is important to include the ease of finding a support provider as one of the selection criteria: while the majority of deployments do not need external support, it is important to be in a position to access it if necessary.

Troubleshooting point. If there is no estimation of support needs, or a wrong budget allocation, the adoption process may be compromised. Both having a too-small budget (which means that if support is needed, the adopter may have no budget allocated for it) and a too-big budget request (such that the project may not get funded at all) are dangerous for any migration process.

Policy considerations. As mentioned, having a public listing of already executed projects, along with support costs, can help the migration manager to assess costs and needs properly for most projects.

Management guidelines: Overall policy and troubleshooting points

The main points of a proper management approach are knowledge and action. Most of the identified troubleshooting points are centred on a lack of information or wrong assumptions about what must be performed in a proper FOSS migration and how to do it. Management must be able to plan properly for time, effort and budget from the beginning to the end of the migration – exactly like a large-scale proprietary adoption process. Knowledge to complement internal management actions is already available – through both competence centres and expertise shared by those who have performed a migration; it is essential to evaluate and use this knowledge to avoid repeating mistakes already made by others.

Social guidelines

Provide background information on FOSS

A significant obstacle of FOSS adoption is acceptance by the user, who usually has a very limited knowledge of open source and open data standards. In many cases, FOSS is perceived as lower quality as it is "free", downloadable from the internet like many shareware packages or amateur projects. It is important to cancel this perception, and to provide information on how FOSS is developed and the rationale and business model that underlie it. In particular, small guides and online pages can give a simple, understandable background to what open source is and what kind of direct and indirect benefits the migration could bring not only to the company and users, but to the local ecosystem as well; also, small pointers to relevant national and international efforts in support of FOSS may add strength to the idea that open source is not only "free" software, but an important and relevant IT alternative supported by major companies and governments. Additionally, a timeline and description of what phases will be performed in the migration will give users enough time and understanding to face the adoption process without traumatic "last-minute" discoveries.

Troubleshooting point. When internal users believe that the migration is done to pay less for software, they may feel they are not provided with the best tools for their work and fight against the change.

Policy considerations. Competence centres may provide background information and dissemination activities on open source software, including its economic value and collaborative potential. Much work in this area is already being done in many countries, including school projects and special industry-specific efforts. While no conclusive results have yet been obtained, an important consideration is that creating vertical, differentiated messages and materials is helpful in increasing interest – for example an edition for educational environments, one for public administrations and one for commercial adopters, with different examples.

Identify local experts and improve overall skills

The migration may cause some resistance from so-called "local gurus", who could perceive this overall improvement as diminishing their social role as technical leaders. By offering them higher-level training material and enhanced opportunities for learning, these leaders can requalify themselves in the new IT environment, maintaining their original social status and even gaining additional recognition by providing on-time support for their peers. In a similar way, it is possible to identify local FOSS "champions" and offer them opportunities for sharing their knowledge and passion with co-workers. If training for the new infrastructure is required, it can be used as a way to improve overall ICT skills; in many companies and public administrations, for example, little formal training is usually given to users. This not only helps in increasing confidence, but can be used to harmonize skills among groups and improve performance overall. In general, it is useful to create an internal intranet page with links to all the different training packages, to facilitate multiple learning paths for different users (or groups of users).

Troubleshooting point. When no assessment of user experience and competence is performed, there is a high probability of sending the wrong message to those users who invested a substantial amount of time and effort in helping other workers and colleagues. Also, such an assessment is useful for avoiding a mismatch between the level of the training materials and the experience level of the users.

Policy considerations. Most IT courses are centred on proprietary software and training models; for example, it only recently became possible to access the EU Public Licence courses through open source software. As a policy point, courses run by public bodies should be accessible through open source or provide FOSS as a primary means of execution. A public, online e-learning platform with public access materials can increase dissemination and the probability of having more users and increasing their skills.

Social guidelines: Overall policy and troubleshooting points

The social and human aspects of a migration are often overlooked – most migrations are in fact started and managed by IT/management information personnel, who may have a simplistic view of how other parts of an administration operate. Not only can this hinder a migration, but it limits the use of the migration as an opportunity to provide added value to the existing human capital, in the form of training or by recreating and improving existing processes. In particular, complaints and difficulties encountered are important sources of information on how the migration is progressing, and whether specific technical areas may need further work or planning.

Technical guidelines

A significant factor in FOSS adoptions is the different development model used by most open source projects, and the difference in delivery of updates and support. This requires a change in the way adoption and updates are handled, to reduce as much as possible interoperability problems. Also, some migration projects tend to ignore the pre-existing technical infrastructure and its requirements; for example, even in developed countries, only a small percentage of public authorities and companies perform even a minimal survey of installed hardware and software, or the document formats that are used in an ICT infrastructure. This knowledge is critical for the correct evaluation of whether an FOSS solution can be introduced effectively, and what steps can be taken to minimize disruption for end users.

Understand the way FOSS is developed

Most projects are based on a cooperative development model, with a core set of developers providing most of the code (usually working for a commercial firm) and a large number of non-core contributors. This model provides great code quality and a fast development cycle, but requires a significant effort in tracking changes and updates. The adoption of a FOSS package can be suggested in the following cases.
- When the project itself is "alive" – does it have an active development community? Aliveness estimates can be obtained from existing evaluation methods like QSOS (2010) or FLOSSMETRICS; other sources of information are public repositories like Ohloh.[1]
- When there is a clear distinction between "stable" and "unstable" software. In many projects there are two distinct streams of development, one devoted to integrating the latest changes and additions, and another focused on improving stability and bug fixes; periodically, the developers will "freeze" development to turn the unstable version into the stable one, and create a new cutting-edge version. This distinction allows the developers to satisfy both the users willing to experiment with the latest functionality and those using the software for day-to-day operations, but requires an extra effort in collecting information and new versions.

If new functionality or fixes are necessary, it may be easier to ask for a commercially supported version of the software; in many cases, the commercial vendor will also contribute financially to the open source project.

Troubleshooting point. If the IT manager or the developers think FOSS is some kind of commercial software that someone has put for free on the net, and it "just works", they may expect pre-packaged updates, or to have some existing structure that disseminates information or advertises new functionality.

Policy considerations. Along with the list of potential software candidates mentioned before, competence centres can provide a list of potential candidates for support, both as major sponsors (for example the company that created the FOSS package in the first place) and secondary support providers.

Software and hardware that will be affected by the migration process

There can be no successful migration when the initial situation is not known. Most companies and administrations have no process in place for auditing software and hardware platforms, and thus are unable to quantify the tools and software that need to be replaced or integrated in a FOSS migration. A survey must take into account the number of concurrent users, average use across the organization and whether the software uses open or closed communication protocols and data formats. This survey will be the basis for deciding which users will be migrated first and estimating the cost of software redevelopment or migration to a different data format. Automated software inventory tools are readily available, and can reduce the cost of performing the inventory and allow a stricter control on installed software (thus reducing maintenance cost).

Some of the aspects that should be surveyed are:
- used data format, at document exchange, database and network protocol levels
- list of used applications, including those internally developed, macros and active documents
- available functionality
- shortcomings and problems of the current infrastructure.

It is fundamental that the migrated software can fulfil the same functional requirements as the current IT infrastructure, and usually improve on the existing infrastructure in functional terms or inherent quality (like availability, reliability and performance).

Troubleshooting point. When there is no clear picture of what software is really used within an IT infrastructure, there may be functionality that is not included in the initial FOSS migration assessment but is necessary for day-to-day operations (the Solothurn canton cited at the start of the chapter is a perfect example of this kind of problem).

Policy considerations. By surveying and assessing software and formats it should be possible to provide a country-wide indication of the actual spending on proprietary software (something only a few countries usually have), which can give an indication of the potential savings with open source software. Surveying the protocols used can help in identifying the effort necessary for a movement towards open data standards, especially in public administrations, or whether publicly mandated standards are implementable only with a proprietary solution (something that is clearly not equal or correct from a market point of view). A recent example was the introduction of an open source implementation of electronic procurement protocols used in Europe in the Open e-Prior (2010) project.

Use the flexibility of FOSS to create local adaptations

The differentiating aspect or property of FOSS is the flexibility and freedom that it gives to users and developers in creating new or adapted versions of any package. This flexibility can greatly enhance the perceived value of FOSS; for example, it is possible to create customized packages that contain local configurations, special fonts and other supplementary material like pre-set macros and templates commonly used in the company. A custom look and feel may significantly improve user acceptance, both by presenting a nicer-looking desktop and by maintaining common links and menu entries.

These customizations can be integrated in a simple way in the most popular Linux distributions, or by creating a local repository of software. Note that in many cases it is not necessary to produce software or code, as most adaptations are related to selecting the appropriate package, changing the graphical appearance or providing templates and pre-sets.

Another important adaptation, specific to developing countries, is localization in terms of language and culture. Such adaptations are extremely easy to implement for open source software, and in some specific projects are expressly promoted with online tools to integrate multiple languages in a single package. These adaptations are extremely important in areas where there is no dominant language, or where English (the most widely used language in the open source world) is not widely spoken.

Troubleshooting point. When local adopters take the installed software as something that cannot be modified, important opportunities for creating a perfect match with the local ICT infrastructure may be lost. Also, if no localization is available, users may be unable to use the software effectively.

Policy considerations. Competence centres can give a single point of access for such modifications and adaptations, with the overall idea that useful adaptations (for example by country, or by vertical sector) may be shared across interested parties in an easy way. In fact, in many cases such modifications are not made public or only shared in a very limited way; these efforts will probably be done again and again, losing the advantage of sharing. A country-wide effort to localize and adapt the most important products (for example office productivity suites like LibreOffice, or desktop environments) can be performed using crowdsourcing, and increase substantially the appeal of an open source solution.

There is much more software available than what is installed by default

Licensing or design issues limit substantially the amount of software that is usually included in the default install of most Linux distributions. For example, only a few include playback capability for the most common audio and video format, due to licensing and patent issues; for the same reasons, some packages that may be of interest to only a minority of users are not included. It is important to research and include in the default installs additional packages that may help in the transition period, such as additional fonts, multimedia tools and other software that may be useful in a mixed environment.

Troubleshooting point. Especially in desktop adoptions, users may encounter difficulties in accessing and using multimedia contents or in interoperability with proprietary software.

Policy considerations. By promoting open, freely interoperable standards it is possible to reduce this negative effect substantially; for example, using the free WebM video standard instead of the proprietary MPEG4,[2] or using open video communication standards like SIP instead of proprietary tools.

Technical guidelines: Overall policy and troubleshooting points

The technical parts are in some ways simpler to observe and solve – processes, best practices, software and tools are already in place in a substantial number of adoption cases. It must be remembered that the technical part is in a sense only a support to guarantee that management and people can operate and get value out of an IT system; the best suggestion may be to ensure that there is a real, working communication channel between the technical groups and the rest of the organization, and that this communication is not biased towards the simple solution of problems.

From adoption to economic networks

The first part of this chapter noted some of the economic and structural advantages of using FOSS as part of the internal IT infrastructure for companies and public authorities. An important difference between FOSS and proprietary models emerges when a substantial number of actors start to use a FOSS product, and (even a small percentage) begin to enhance and modify it.

In fact, the non-rival properties of open source licensing imply that adopters can cooperate together in providing enhancements and patches to a common technical basis, even if the individual actors are competitors in some other market. In general, the idea is that for non-differentiating IT components it is always economically sensible to cooperate on a shared resource (reducing not only development cost but maintenance cost as well) while eventually competing on a different, differentiating element that is not shared. A substantial number of commercial projects include a large amount of open source software, thus reducing the cost of redevelopment; an example is Apple, which saved $350 million by reusing FOSS components in its OSX operating system, or the Maemo project from Nokia, with 85 per cent of the source code derived from FOSS (Anttila, 2010), later taken up by Intel as a basis for the Meego project. This form of reuse and take-up by external companies creates an opportunity for a phenomenon called "coopetition", where competitors in a market collaborate in software development in vertical areas to share the cost of development and maintenance.

A very good example of such coopetition is the Eclipse project, where a large number of companies, some fierce competitors, cooperate in maintaining and enhancing a large FOSS system of components, originally released by IBM. Most Eclipse adopters enhanced the software with some additional features, and in a positive feedback loop each addition in turn made the project more interesting for other potential adopters. Many companies in the Eclipse ecosystems submit enhancements to Eclipse despite the advantage to potential competitors. This decision is in reality an economic one: it is better to use and participate in a complex ecosystem, thanks to the value obtained from it, even though this participation helps some competitors.

This process can be leveraged by other agents. For example, offering consulting services, integration, quality assurance and more – in fact, creating a new, completely exogenous market – increases the probability of companies and public administrations using the Eclipse component, again providing a new positive feedback loop.

There are a few extremely successful examples of such loops and projects, like the Linux kernel (adopted among others by many mobile phone system developers), the Apache web server, the MySQL database system and the OpenOffice productivity suite. These successes are, however, quite few in comparison to the large number of projects; also, it is clearly much easier for "horizontal" projects (those that impact a large number of users, or can be reused in many independent vertical groups) than for smaller, niche efforts. For example, there is very little cooperation between industry peers in specific vertical efforts in terms of either software development or knowledge sharing.

An approach that has been found effective in facilitating both FOSS adoption and sharing of resources is the OpenTTT methodology, an

EU-funded initiative that aimed to replicate the success of the European Innovation Relay Centres network of technology transfer centres in the open source world. The approach is that of mediation: the identification of technology needs and appropriate matching with the technology offers already identified in an internal database. The process is extremely simple, and can be used to facilitate the growth of a local open source ecosystem in developing countries, taking advantage of the fact that in such an environment many potential adopters are still in the preliminary stages of ICT adoption, and as such are not forced into "lock-in" by proprietary software.

The first activity is the collection of requirements: a simple online form (or, in some competence centres, an e-mail address to send requests to) to collect details of specific software functionalities. The second step is the classification of these forms into horizontal requests, which are needs common to a large number of companies, and vertical requests, which are specific to a single industry sector. As an example, most companies express an interest in software for project management, groupware (both messaging and calendaring or coordination software), infrastructural software (security, backups, network and system management), ERP and CRM (customer relationship management). A third step is identifying (in a catalogue of open source products) potential matches, which are then used to provide a summary of how far a FOSS package can match the requirements of the majority of its potential users.

The most interesting part is the next step, matching: for those needs that can be immediately satisfied, potential users are provided with a list of matching solutions and contacts for those registered in the developers' club that are compatible with the request in competence and geographic area. This way, users are relieved of the task of finding software, evaluating it and finding potential support. What happens to the needs that are not satisfied by existing FOSS solutions? The matching process continues, with the identification of pieces of the solution that fill as much as possible the user request and details of the missing functionalities. This information is passed on to the users and developers, who are then free to propose a commercial transaction to create the missing functionalities. Pooling similar requests allows for a much lower price per company to obtain the desired functionality, and the consultant can complement the development with the provision of additional services like training and support.

Conclusions

This chapter provides a summary of some of the best practices and suggestions gained from the author's experience in both European regions and developing countries. Most of the suggestions can be easily promoted through low-cost efforts, especially mediated by local competence centres. In particular, the creation of local catalogues of relevant open source software, public access documentation and training materials, or efforts like the creation of localized versions of the most relevant software, may facilitate adoption of open source software with a very limited budget. Cooperation efforts, like that designed for the OpenTTT methodology, can also be adopted in a very effective way to facilitate the creation of a local ecosystem of ICT service providers that are naturally adapted to their native environment.

This approach, through transparency and facilitation, may help even competitors to take advantage of their shared effort without compromising their differentiating IT components. Overcoming issues of trust and process requires a strong commitment by a central public administration that may participate as a catalyser of the various interactions without taking part in any commercial transaction, thus guaranteeing that no possible bias is introduced in the market – an aspect that is especially important in developing countries where large-scale software and services markets are still young and fragile.

Notes

1. Ohloh (www.ohloh.net/) is a public wiki site that provides detailed metrics and charts on open source activity and development across a wide range of projects.
2. While MPEG4 is a public specification from ISO, its implementation requires payment to the standard patent holders, so it cannot be freely installed in open source desktop environments. Up to now, WebM patents held by Google (the WebM releaser) are licensed freely for all uses, and no further patent holders have advanced any additional licensing restriction.

REFERENCES

Anttila, E. (2010) "Open Source Software and Impact on Competitiveness: Case Study", master's thesis, Helsinki University of Technology.

Camara, G. and F. Fonseca (2007) "Information Policies and Open Source Software in Developing Countries", *Journal of the American Society for Information Science and Technology* 58(1), pp. 121–132.

COSPA (2008) "COSPA Project Deliverable 6.1: Report Evaluating the Costs/Benefits of a Transition Towards ODS/OS", COSPA consortium, Brussels.

FLOSSMETRICS (2009) "SME Guide to Open Source Software"; available at http://guide.conecta.it (accessed 21 April 2010).

Ghosh, R. (2006) "Economic Impact of FLOSS on Innovation and Competitiveness of the EU ICT Sector"; available at www.ec.europa.eu/enterprise/sectors/ict/files/2006-11-20-flossimpact_en.pdf (accessed 18 May 2008).

IDC (2011) "Partner Opportunity in the Microsoft Ecosystem"; available at www.microsoft.com/presspass/presskits/partnernetwork/docs/IDC_WP_0211.pdf (accessed 4 April 2011).
INES (2006) "IST Project: Final Project Report": available at http://web.archive.org/web/20060510061337/http://www.euroines.com/down/INES_final_report.pdf (accessed 20 April 2012).
ITU (2010) "ICT Regulation Toolkit"; available at www.ictregulationtoolkit.org (accessed 5 April 2011)
Open e-Prior (2010) "Description"; available at http://joinup.ec.europa.eu/software/openeprior/description (accessed 19 April 2012).
OSOR (2010a) "Application Lock-in and Protest from Users Halt Open Desktop"; available at www.osor.eu/news/ch-application-lock-in-and-protest-from-users-halt-open-desktop (accessed 17 September 2010).
—— (2010b) "Procurement and Open Source Software Guideline"; available at www.osor.eu/idabc-studies/OSS-procurement-guideline%20-final.pdf (accessed 21 September 2010).
QSOS (2010) "Method for Qualification and Selection of Open Source Software Version 1.6"; available at www.qsos.org/download/qsos-1.6-en.pdf (accessed 5 January 2011).
Lighthouse Research (2011) "Linux-Related Technical Support Comparative Study Report, August, 2010"; available at www.novell.com/docrep/2011/01/Linux%20Technical%20Support%20Full%20Report%20Aug%202010.pdf (accessed 24 February 2012).
Sida (2004) "Open Source in Developing Countries"; available at www.eldis.org/fulltext/opensource.pdf (accessed 13 April 2011).
tOSSad (2006) "Workshop on Governmental, Educational, Usability, and Legal Issues Towards Open Source Software Adoption in an Enlarged Europe"; available at www.tossad.org/publications (accessed 16 April 2012).
Venice University (2009) "Open Source Study"; available at www.univiu.org/images/stories/viu_paper/Ricerca-Open-Source-DeRossiPicerni.pdf (accessed 18 March 2009).

8

Language data as a foundation for developing countries: The ANLoc 100 African Locales Initiative

Martin Benjamin

Introduction

Free and open source software (FOSS) is only free to users who are able to understand how to use it. When an interface is in a language at which the user is not adept, she bears the cost of either learning technical concepts in the foreign language, making errors when using the software or wasting time installing and attempting to make sense of a product that ultimately proves useless. European developers recognized the problem of language localization (L10n) early, establishing systems and bodies to overlay interfaces for languages from Italian to Finnish. In Africa, however, FOSS has until recently stagnated in the former colonial languages of English, French and Portuguese, with Arabic, Swahili and Afrikaans making much lesser and much later appearances. Not coincidentally, use of FOSS, like use of much information and communications technology (ICT) other than mobile phones, has remained extremely low among most of the continent's inhabitants.

Is FOSS use in Africa low because it is not available in local languages? Or is FOSS unavailable in local languages because the potential user base is satisfied with the existing language options? The premise of this chapter is the former: although the educated elite who currently use FOSS in Africa have the skills and desire to do so in European languages, the vast majority of Africans will only begin to use ICT that is available in their own languages (Kachale, 2008; Prah, 2000).

Free and open source software and technology for sustainable development, Sowe, Parayil and Sunami (eds), United Nations University Press, 2012, ISBN 978-92-808-1217-6

A prerequisite that underlies the development of ICT for a language is the existence of a locale to which software can refer to configure essential parameters, such as character sets and date formats. Having a locale does not guarantee that subsequent FOSS localization will occur in a language, but not having one fairly well guarantees that it will not. With this imperative in mind, the African Network for Localization (ANLoc) embarked on the 100 African Locales Initiative. Managed by the Kamusi Project, an international non-governmental organization dedicated to the production of resources for African languages, and implemented technically by IT46, a Swedish social enterprise focusing on knowledge transfer to promote social change, with the support of the International Development Research Centre (IDRC) of Canada, the project succeeded in completing 90 locales, nearly its target number, and upstreaming most of those to Unicode's Common Locales Data Repository (CLDR).

This chapter tells the story behind the production of so many locales. These locales are a sustainable basis for the further development of FOSS in the completed languages, providing permanent bedrock language data that can be reused in any L10n project. Although the technical challenge was relatively straightforward, finding people for such a large number of languages, and working with them until their languages reached completion, was more complicated than anticipated. The process offers a number of lessons showing approaches towards successful L10n for future FOSS projects, and also the limitations and pitfalls of working with volunteers in dozens of countries speaking a hundred different languages. It is hoped that this case study will be instructive both within and beyond Africa, as FOSS projects take the existence of numerous African locales as a starting point for localizing their interfaces for the languages thereby enabled (Wolff, 2011).

Background

A locale consists of the set of parameters that define how a language appears within an operating system or software environment, as well as variations within a language for the different countries where it is spoken. Items delimited by a locale include formats for numbers, date, time and currency, the set of characters used to render the language, key terms such as yes/no, true/false, days of the week and months of the year, and names for languages, countries and currencies (Figure 8.1). For example, all French locales will contain the ç (cedilla) within the default character set, but the currency symbol for French in France is the € (euro) while the locale for French in Canada uses the $ (dollar).

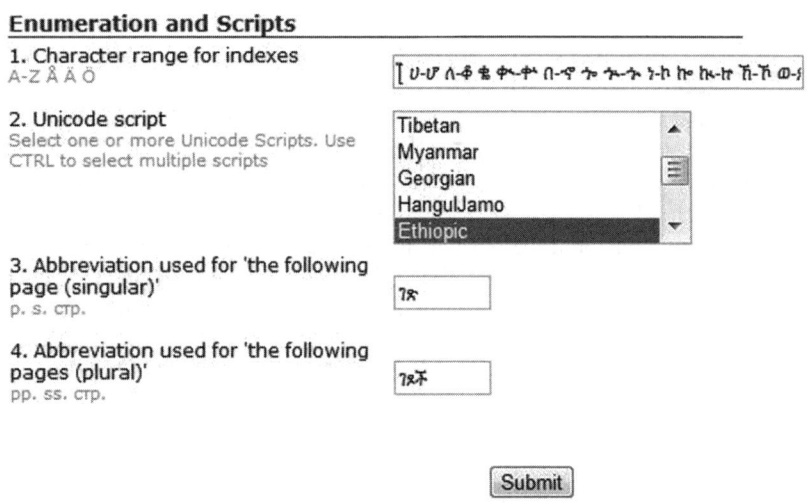

Figure 8.1 Sample of required data in Amharic locale, using Afrigen software

Locales generally remain hidden from the user experience. The first time a user configures her settings within a program, she may be asked to choose her language and her country. From then on, she does not usually have to worry about whether her keyboard actions will correspond to the right keys, whether she will print to A4 or letter-sized paper, or how her spreadsheets will display separators between thousands (1,000 or 1.000 or 1 000 or 1000). Her software takes care of those considerations automatically, through reference to a dataset containing the values for her country/language pair. Texin (2002) demonstrates problems with the assumption that all parameters are stable within a language/country pair, but concludes that the problems are likely only able to be solved by users tweaking their settings, rather than at the level of locale design. Locales have generally been discussed within technical circles, for example a working group position statement from a W3C internationalization workshop (Topping, 2002), not as the subject of academic publications. A search of the literature reveals almost no research on the topic. This demonstrates the point that locales exist almost entirely in the background of the ICT experience, invisible to all but the coders who work directly with them. Comprehensive resources relating to technical aspects of locales are catalogued by Texin (n.d.).

From a developer perspective, the minimum requirement for preparing a program for a language is the availability of reliable data for the variable parameters. For example, someone could use a word processor to type in Amharic as long as the core language settings were available, such as the character set and calendar format, even if the command interface and help menu remained in English. The developer of the word processor would just need access to the Amharic locale data in order to provide this base functionality. However, few developers are in a position to seek out their own datasets for numerous locales; if no Amharic locale data are on hand, the language will simply be left out of the word processor's options.

To address the need for quality language data that could be tapped for any software project, the Unicode consortium developed CLDR. Unicode membership includes major industry players from Adobe to Yahoo, as well as FOSS organizations such as GNOME, Mozilla and OpenOffice. By collecting locale data in a central database, CLDR is able to normalize the locale creation process through reference to open data. GNOME, OpenOffice and Microsoft all have their own locale requirements, but can use data from CLDR to glean most of the information they need. Filling in the data fields once for a language within CLDR is generally enough to make that language a candidate for further development in any number of FOSS or for-profit projects. Osborn (2010) notes that CLDR contained few African languages until the undertakings discussed in this chapter.

The official process of adding a locale to CLDR is via that organization's Survey Tool. Until 2011 the CLDR Survey Tool interface was one that technical specialists could make their way through, but was completely opaque to the average computer user. In 2006 IT46 sought to address a gap in the locale creation process by developing LocaleGen, bypassing the CLDR Survey Tool for the purpose of enabling L10n projects for OpenOffice. LocaleGen is a simple set of web forms that users complete with data for their language, with the output generated in OpenOffice format. In four years LocaleGen has been able to create over 180 basic locales, of which about 25 per cent have been submitted to OpenOffice. The initial set of LocaleGen contributions included new or improved locales for 13 African languages, and this served as the basis for Afrigen, the substantially revised software that IT46 developed for the 100 African Locales Initiative. Importantly, Afrigen output is generated in CLDR format rather than OpenOffice, with the data intended to be universally applicable. The Afrigen interface is intentionally simple to use – unlike the complicated CLDR Survey Tool, anyone with the skills to buy an airline ticket online would be able to navigate through the entire Afrigen process.

The African Network for Localization (www.africanlocalization.net) was formed in 2008 as an outgrowth of an informal organization known as PanAfriL10n, the Pan-African Localization Network (www.panafril10n.org), also supported by the IDRC. Whereas PanAfriL10n was largely a group that facilitated discussions among different L10n projects, the purpose of ANLoc was to work together in a concerted strategy towards L10n on a continental level. Since that time, ANLoc has undertaken activity in areas ranging from fonts and keyboards to terminology, tools, training and policy development.

The 100 African Locales Initiative was a component of the first phase of ANLoc. The group recognized that future L10n activities would be severely hampered for languages that did not have locales. For example, one ANLoc tool developed at the University of Nairobi School of Computing and Informatics was a spell-checker for the Gikuyu language – but how could the tool be distributed without implementation of a locale that properly handles the unique diacritics found in the Gĩkũyũ character set? CLDR is opened for new submissions at most once a year, and the review process can take another six months before the locale is officially released. Without pre-existing locales, tools or software for a language, it could languish for months or even years. ANLoc therefore made it a priority to complete as many African locales as possible, even for languages that held no immediate prospect of further L10n development.

The original concept for the 100 African Locales Initiative was to organize a single day for people around the continent to complete their locales online. When consideration was given to the challenge of finding and preparing so many people at once, the plan was modified to divide the work into eight regional one-day events. Those logistics also proved overly ambitious. In the end, the project was completed bit by bit over three years, with most work conducted in September and October 2009 in order to meet that year's CLDR deadline. In 2010 CLDR announced plans to make its Survey Tool more user-friendly based on the Afrigen experience. When that programming was completed, and CLDR 2.0 opened for submissions in February 2011, Afrigen was switched off and the final 29 locales were upstreamed to CLDR.

This chapter details the experience of the 100 African Locales Initiative, particularly the process of recruiting and working with a large multilingual group of volunteers over three years. Part of the experience revealed weakness in the Afrigen software that will be informative to the design of other collaborative projects. Even the software deficiencies, though, were of a piece with the main lesson from this experience: localization is as much about working with people as it is about working with languages. Success in a multilingual FOSS project depends perhaps more on building and managing relationships and networks than it does on the software itself. The social aspects of implementing an L10n project with hundreds of people are difficult and time-consuming. What follows is the story of how the ANLoc 100 African Locales Initiative successfully accomplished its technical objectives through the evolution of a broad international network of individuals and organizations interested in improving ICT resources for African languages.

Building locales

The main challenge of building a locale for a language is collecting the data. The main challenge in collecting data is to find one or more people who have the linguistic and technical knowledge, software skills, computer and network access, and motivation to see their locale through to completion. The linguistic, educational, financial and technical infrastructure environments in Africa mean that, for many languages, there is no guarantee that all the prerequisites can be fulfilled within the timescale of a software release cycle.

Africa's 1 billion people speak about 2,000 languages, close to one-third of the world's total. This simple declarative statement itself masks many of the problems that were encountered during the 100 African Locales Initiative. To begin with, nobody really knows how many languages exist on the continent, nor the full extent of where they are spoken and by how many people. The best attempt to codify and quantify such information is *Ethnologue* (Lewis, 2009), a publication by SIL International (formerly the Summer Institute of Linguistics) that presents the full extent of demographic and geographic data known to its researchers, on a country-by-country and language-by-language basis. Yet *Ethnologue* is a work in progress, with some radical changes from one edition to the next, and many persistent gaps in knowledge or data. As just one example, *Ethnologue* lists Swahili as a language with a total of 787,630 speakers in all countries (ibid.). However, it notes "30,000,000 rural people [in Tanzania] are L2 [second language] users ... It is also common for people of numerous ethnic groups besides Swahili who grew up in certain towns to speak Swahili as L1." The first number, up from exactly 772,642 in the previous edition, is bizarrely precise – seemingly referring to people who speak Swahili as a first language and identify themselves as members of the Waswahili ethnic group. The second number is enticingly vague, and with Tanzania's population at 42 million, of whom 25 per cent live in urban areas (CIA, 2011), this essentially (and correctly) means that everyone in that country is an L1 or L2 Swahili speaker. *Ethnologue* estimates for Swahili speakers in neighbouring countries are similarly dubious. The fact is that all these numbers are artificial – census questionnaires in Tanzania and Kenya do not ask about mother tongues or languages spoken, and no other comprehensive survey to collect language data has ever been attempted.

Beyond not having real data for each language, we do not always know what a language is. In some cases, essentially the same language may be called different names on different sides of a border or political divide (such as Kinyarwanda and Kirundi), while in other cases the "same" language may be unintelligible from one end of its range to another. For other languages, reliable research has not yet been undertaken. It is widely stated that 120 languages are spoken in Tanzania, for example, but any attempt at a list is plagued by the problems above. Nevertheless, we can state with cautionary vagueness that around 2,000 languages – some as close as Spanish and Catalan, some as distinct as Icelandic and Japanese – are spoken on the continent.

The numbers of speakers of Africa's languages range from single-digit figures for endangered languages to tens or even hundreds of millions. Arabic is spoken as a daily language over the entire northern expanse of the continent, though not in the same form from place to place. The classical form is used in religious contexts by Muslims continent-wide. The reader is free to guess at the numbers who are conversant in one or another dialect, and/or can read it, write in it or use it for prayer, with opening bids starting at 200 million. English, French and Portuguese are official languages in almost every country, but levels of proficiency vary widely. As a broad estimate, maybe 5 per cent of Africans are literate in one or another of the former colonial tongues – assuming a round number for secondary school attendance based on Tanzanian data (Trading Economics, 2011), and using that number as a proxy for L2 literacy continent-wide. The number of people who can converse in Swahili is surely more than 50 million, with perhaps twice that able to use the language to exchange pleasantries or engage in market transactions. At least 15 languages are spoken by more than 10 million people, and *Ethnologue* indicates that 200 are spoken by more than half a million. The 15 largest languages, according to ethnographic reports, are Amharic, Arabic, Chewa, Fula, Hausa, Igbo, Kinyarwanda, Malagasy, Oromo, Shona, Somali, Swahili, Tamazight, Yoruba and Zulu. The remaining 1,800 languages are distributed on a long tail, with many isolated tongues spoken by a few thousand people, and some languages on the cusp of disappearing altogether.

The 100 African Locales Initiative did not attempt to resolve any debates about the boundaries between languages, nor the relative importance of one versus another. Using *Ethnologue* as a handy starting point, blank locale files were created for every language in Africa that was said to have more than 400,000 speakers (Figure 8.2). Special focus was placed on including all the languages that have some form of official status within any country, although efforts to recruit volunteers for such lan-

EDIT LOCALE

■ Select the locale file you want to edit.

○ 1. Acholi Uganda (*ach_UG.xml*)
○ 2. Afar Ethiopia (*aa_ET.xml*)
○ 3. Afrikaans South Africa (*af_ZA.xml*)
○ 4. Afrikaans Namibia (*af_NA.xml*)
○ 5. Aghem Cameroon (*agq_CM.xml*)
○ 6. Akan Ghana (*ak_GH.xml*)
○ 7. Akookse Cameroon (*bss_CM.xml*)
○ 8. Alur DR Congo (*alz_CD.xml*)
● 9. Amharic Ethiopia (*am_ET.xml*)
○ 10. Anaang Nigeria (*anw_NG.xml*)
○ 11. Anyin Côte d'Ivoire (*any_CI.xml*)

○ 99. Isoko Nigeria (*iso_NG.xml*)
○ 100. Izi-Ezaa-Ikwo-Mgbo Nigeria (*izi_NG.xml*)
○ 101. Izon Nigeria (*ijc_NG.xml*)
○ 102. Jju Nigeria (*kaj_NG.xml*)
○ 103. Jola-Fonyi Senegal (*dyo_SN.xml*)
○ 104. Jula Burkina Faso (*dyu_BF.xml*)
○ 105. Kabiyé Togo (*kbp_TG.xml*)
○ 106. Kabyle Algeria (*kab_DZ.xml*)
○ 107. Kagoma Nigeria (*kdm_NG.xml*)
○ 108. Kalabari Nigeria (*ijn_NG.xml*)

○ 197. Oku
○ 198. Oror
○ 199. Pan(
○ 200. Pher
○ 201. Plat((*plt_MG.x*
○ 202. Pök(
○ 203. Port
○ 204. Port
○ 205. Port
○ 206. Rom

Figure 8.2 Some of the 294 locales configured for Afrigen users to complete

guages were not always successful. Smaller languages were included if a volunteer stepped forward; the case of Sami, spoken by about 20,000 people in northern Scandinavia and well furnished with localized software, devices, automatic bank tellers, etc., demonstrates that ICT can ignite even for a small language (European Commission on Multilingualism, 2010). The main criterion for inclusion in the project, quite simply, was whether a volunteer was available to carry out the task. Thus Kwasio, a language of Cameroon and Equatorial Guinea with fewer than 18,000 speakers, had a locale submitted for CLDR 2.0, while Sukuma, with 5.4 million speakers in Tanzania, did not.

Recruiting volunteers and working with them until their locales were completed became the principal ongoing activity of the project. Locating volunteers was difficult for many reasons.

- Many languages are spoken predominantly by poor people who do not have computers or the means to access the internet. Cyber cafés are widespread in Africa, particularly in urban areas, but someone earning a few dollars a day would need to be extraordinarily passionate about her language to pay out of her own pocket for the roughly three hours of internet time needed to complete a locale.
- Possessing the right equipment does not guarantee the electricity supply to use it. Power failures are chronic in Africa, discouraging or preventing some potential volunteers. Similarly, although optical fibres are rapidly increasing the availability of the internet in Africa, many areas still have limited or no access.
- Many Africans are literate in one or more languages, but not in their mother tongues. Hundreds of languages have writing systems but little written – perhaps a bible translation, or transcriptions of local oral literature. Many people needed to be encouraged to combine the writing skills they already knew for L2 with the L1 oral language skills they

grew up with. Admittedly, some results might therefore be appropriate for later revision by a more formal review, but in the meantime the output for each language is fully usable by its speakers.
- Some lay people stated that they did not feel they had the authority to represent their language, despite speaking it fluently and having sufficient skills to write in it. They felt the work should be done by university experts, not ordinary people like them.
- Conversely, university experts could rarely be found, largely because many languages are not subject to formal study. In the Tanzanian example, Swahili scholarship is a venerable pursuit, with several institutes and research departments, but few of the country's other ~120 languages enjoy systematic academic attention. The most fertile source of scholars for many languages was researchers from SIL, several of whom participated. In cases where scholars could be found, securing their participation was often hit or miss, since many had access problems or other demands on their time.
- Not all people agree with the premise that their mother tongues should be languages for ICT. Because advanced education in Africa is conducted in the former colonial languages, many educated people equate command of those languages with prosperity and modernity. They feel that local language development is retrogressive, with the potential to discourage students from learning languages like English, and thereby perpetuating poverty and isolation. This sentiment was especially prevalent in Nigeria, Africa's most populous nation – and, as anyone knows who has ever received an e-mail from the widow of General Sani Abacha, a nation with a well-established cyber culture – which produced a paltry three locales, and only for its largest languages, despite repeated recruitment efforts.
- Some people had all the combination of prerequisites, but were only interested in participating if they could be paid for their efforts. For this project, payments were absolutely impossible. Obstacles included:
  - establishing a fair rate of compensation for people in dozens of different countries
  - apportioning the reward if more than one person worked on a locale
  - controlling the quality if some people were motivated by a cash prize for completing a data form that did not have the possibility of external review, rather than being motivated by producing a respectable end product
  - the logistics of getting at least 100 small payments to people without bank accounts or PayPal, or where wire and exchange fees could easily exceed the labour remuneration.

While an argument against payments could be made based on the principle of FOSS, for this project monetary award was obviated a priori on practical grounds (not to mention that no budget was available). Individuals in societies that do not have a history of volunteering for technical projects can also make a convincing case that they should be paid for their expertise, but in this instance that argument could not prevail.

Networks

Facing these obstacles, the 100 African Locales Initiative determined that the best chance of success lay in using networks to locate people interested in African languages. Existing formal networks, such as online mailing lists, were tapped by sending invitations to participate. Informal professional networks were also called into action, by circulating letters to colleagues asking for participation or contact information for people who spoke unrepresented languages. A third approach to networking was also attempted, with encouraging but not universally positive results: the use of online social networks.

Social networks were employed not for their trendy cachet, but because they were seen as a potentially unmatchable method for locating volunteers for languages along the long tail. Many Africans speak several languages – their mother tongue, perhaps a different father tongue, an indigenous national language and, for the educated, a souvenir language from the colonial era. When Africans go online, though, they generally limit their communication to the latter two. East Africans who wish to communicate with their cohort will use Swahili or English rather than negotiate who speaks which of the many other mother tongues from the region. Nigerians using an African language will select Yoruba, Hausa or Igbo. Cyber communication clusters towards the languages with many millions of speakers, since those are the common denominators on which inter-group conversations most easily flourish, online or off. However, networks of people brought together by speaking the large languages will inevitably include people who also speak underrepresented smaller languages. Furthermore, many speakers of large African languages are at universities in the United States or Europe, where they tend to have friends or colleagues from various parts of Africa whom they meet in classes or African students' associations, who might speak, or be connected to people who speak, languages that are not yet represented. The premises of creating social networks among African language enthusiasts were that:
- a great many speakers of the mega-languages would join, of whom a few would also speak one or another of the diverse languages for which the project was geared

- contacts among the African diaspora would bring in people who originated in areas that were not otherwise well connected to ICT.

A group called African Languages was created on Facebook, and invitations were sent to people within existing networks who were considered likely to be interested. When these people joined, their lists of Facebook friends were viewed. People who had a lot of contacts with African names, or many colleagues within African studies, were sent individual e-mails asking them to recruit those of their friends whom they thought might appreciate an invitation to join. Members were told that the group was seeking to grow, with the specific intent of finding speakers of a wide range of languages. Many responded positively, sending invitations to dozens of people. This strategy resulted in a group with about 1,500 members; these people were sent announcements describing the 100 African Locales Initiative. Many volunteers emerged, often for unwired languages such as Bemba and Shona with a million or more speakers.

Another approach to social networks came through Twitter, which was used in two ways. The first was periodic general tweets from the Kamusi Project asking for volunteers or reporting the status of the project. These messages would often get retweeted, contributing to the goal of reaching the eyeballs of potential volunteers. The other method was to search the Twitter stream for mentions of particular languages that lacked locales. The people who wrote those tweets were sent direct messages with a brief description of the project and a link. This method ran against a barrier that many languages had zero mentions in the archive, even for a tongue like Kirundi with millions of speakers. (The Kirundi locale was eventually completed, after two years of unsuccessful gambits, by means of a colleague-of-a-colleague e-mail connection.) The clearest success was Malagasy, spoken by some 20 million people in Madagascar, where a community of ICT enthusiasts were identified who worked together to complete the locale for their language.

While social networks proved to be a useful recruiting device, the single most effective method was more traditional. The School of Computing and Informatics at the University of Nairobi recruited students on campus. As a national university, students come from almost every ethnic group in the country. Through a recruiting drive that included on-the-ground social networks, volunteers from many unrepresented languages were brought to the project. Students were sat in front of computers and gently walked through the creation of locales for their mother tongues. In this way, 15 of the 16 Kenyan languages that *Ethnologue* says have at least 400,000 speakers now also have locales (Figure 8.3). As of this writing, the locales are serving as the basis for serious proposals to develop online dictionaries for at least five of the enabled Kenyan lan-

Susu	Guinea	52 %	0 %	0 %	
Yalunka	Guinea	52 %	0 %	0 %	
Swahili	Kenya	100 %	100 %	100 %	
Teso	Kenya	100 %	100 %	100 %	
Embu	Kenya	100 %	100 %	100 %	
Kalenjin	Kenya	100 %	100 %	100 %	
Bukusu	Kenya	100 %	100 %	100 %	
Samburu	Kenya	100 %	100 %	100 %	
Kamba	Kenya	100 %	100 %	100 %	
Turkana	Kenya	52 %	0 %	1 %	
Taita	Kenya	100 %	100 %	100 %	
Gikuyu	Kenya	100 %	100 %	100 %	
Gusii	Kenya	100 %	100 %	100 %	
Meru	Kenya	100 %	100 %	100 %	
Luo	Kenya	100 %	100 %	100 %	
Pökot	Kenya	100 %	100 %	100 %	
Giryama	Kenya	86 %	0 %	1 %	
Maa	Kenya	100 %	100 %	100 %	
Luyia	Kenya	100 %	100 %	100 %	
Sotho, Southern	Lesotho	76 %	0 %	92 %	
Kpelle	Liberia	55 %	0 %	0 %	

Figure 8.3 Kenyan languages completed by the University of Nairobi

guages. Similarly, the Goethe Institute in Yaoundé worked with locally recruited volunteers to complete locales for seven languages spoken in Cameroon.

The sword cut both ways when working with established institutions, unfortunately. Across northern Africa is a group of languages that has historically been known as Berber. Now called by the ethnonym Tamazight, or the Amazigh languages when using an adjectival construction, these tongues have long been suppressed, discouraged or ignored. Recent years have seen a resurgence of interest and linguistic pride. When the Afrigen announcement was distributed on a Tamazight mailing list, numerous volunteers stepped forward. A representative from an official institution in a country with a large population of Tamazight speakers identified himself, and the project handed him formal authority for the locales for his country. Subsequently, this individual erased all the work that had been done on the less common Amazigh languages within his country. He announced that his institutional mandate was to standardize Tamazight, so any recognition of minority forms ran counter to that mission. In effect, the majority part of an oppressed minority had made the decision to exclude the even more oppressed minorities within the minority. The individual was blocked from further participation, and IT46 was able to restore most of the vandalized data. The experience pointed to a weakness in collaborative software that awards too much trust to any one individual, and it showed that not all institutions dealing with languages in Africa share the objective of enabling ICT for all in the language an end user prefers.

The Tamazight experience also highlighted the importance of having instructions for participants that are crystal clear across languages. Afrigen was not explicit in stating that the English name and the three-letter ISO code for a language were fixed elements. Tamazight speakers thus took the occasion to change the language name in the English name field to their preferred spelling of their preferred name, and even the script in which the language name was written, and adjust the field for the ISO code and the corresponding file name accordingly. Revert wars ensued, and entire files disappeared from view when their names changed. In this case the simple fix would be to make those fields uneditable by normal users, but the larger lesson is that inadequate instructions such as "language name" can lead to complications that multiply in a multilingual project.

In most cases, participation in the 100 Locales Initiative marked the first exposure of the people involved to any aspect of contributing to FOSS, and marked the first effort at FOSS development for the languages of their countries. The experience and the networks created will not necessarily lead the participants to contribute to more in-depth FOSS development or localization. However, the existence of a locale provides the enabling environment for further technical work, and a number of individuals recruited into the project from African countries are now pursuing more advanced work on technology development for their languages.

Completion

After locating and recruiting people for the many languages, a continuing challenge was to work with them to see their locales through to completion. The goal was for each language to complete all the requested data in several categories, for a total of some 415 data items, about 80 per cent of which were the names of countries, currencies and languages. Time to completion was approximately three hours, often with some additional time needed to research specific items. The task was not difficult, but it was not trivial; some attrition occurred after people started their locales, when they filled in a few items and then ran out of steam. The numbers indicate that the main hurdle was getting started: 189 people enrolled with the project, of whom 55 never logged in after receiving an e-mail with login and usage instructions. Yet 90 locales were completed, meaning that a large proportion of people who began a locale saw it through

to completion. (The numbers are imprecise, because some people worked on multiple locales, other locales had multiple registered participants and multiple participants often collaborated locally using a single login.) Registering with the project was the easiest step, involving no commitment. Logging in after receiving the project instructions was just marginally more complicated, but marked the end of the line for over a quarter of the people who registered – perhaps because the instructions sounded intimidating, perhaps because of the realization that a few hours of serious effort would be involved, perhaps because the person had second thoughts about her interest in the project. About a quarter of those who registered logged in at least once, but did not complete a locale. What is interesting is that about half of users were involved in completed locales. Most of the blank locale files created for the project emerged in one of three states:
- remained blank, i.e. no work was done by anyone
- had a few data items entered
- was completed.

There was very little middle ground. Either people hesitated at the beginning and the moment was lost, or they worked through to the end. This was a highly management-intensive process – many e-mail nudges were needed, many questions had to be answered about particular data items – but in very few cases did a locale languish after it reached a tipping point of being about one-quarter completed. In for a dime, in for a dollar; those participants who invested more than a tiny amount of time did not want to see their initial efforts lost, and therefore had an incentive to continue all the way to submission. Participant feedback noted that the real-time statistics Afrigen provided for a locale's progress were highly motivating, with bars changing from red towards green as various sections were completed, culminating in the satisfying moment of hitting 100 per cent in all categories (Pimenta, 2009).

In terms of data, locale completion ran into two problems: terms that did not exist in a language, and data that were demanded in a way that only made sense in English. The former mostly consisted of country, language and currency names; e.g. few African languages have standard terms for Kyrgyzstan or the Northern Mariana Islands. Participants were guided to use the lexical and morphological patterns of their language to produce stopgap terms where none existed. Future official standardization efforts for a language might lead to subsequent revisions of its locale, but interim data are meanwhile available for current ICT development. The latter problem, English orientation in the data model, had to be addressed creatively on a case-by-case basis. For example, the data model calls for two-letter abbreviations for AM and PM, and BC and AD. Many African languages use a clock system that is based on sunrise and sunset, rather than the meridian (Kamusi Project, 2006), so the notions of AM and PM do not even make sense conceptually within the language, but when referring to "European time" there is no rational basis to expect that two-letter abbreviations should exist for "morning" and "afternoon". Similarly, one-letter abbreviations for days of the week were tricky for languages where most day names begin with the same word for "day", e.g. "Day One", "Day Two", etc. Participants were asked to research whether any precedents for the requested data existed for their language. If no guidance was available from existing sources, the locale creator was asked to propose a plausible solution that, because it will be the first and most widely distributed attempt to address the problem, will generally become the *de facto* standard for the language. The solution that would be more internationally appropriate – revising the CLDR dataset to accommodate a non-English orientation – is an inherent design problem that is not currently the subject of discussion.

Future trends

The success of the 100 African Locales Initiative foretells little about the further development of locales, but it may speak to other future L10n efforts for FOSS in African languages. The ideal trajectory would be to have complete locale data for each language, not just in Africa but for unrepresented people worldwide, which ICT developers could have on hand as a starting point for any project. A comprehensive bibliography of 174 papers and publications relating to African language technology has been assembled by de Pauw (2011), showing a marked increase in research and human language technology projects in recent years that points to expanded use of locales and the potential of involving the people and networks who worked towards their creation.

As ICT becomes more ubiquitous, it is easier to imagine the day that even the most remote languages produce young speakers with the skills and enthusiasm to develop FOSS in their mother tongues, and on-the-shelf locales would give them an embarkation point. However, the ANLoc project has come to an end, and it is hard to envision another effort organized on such a scale to find people and work with them for the languages that do not yet have locales. Without such a push, locale data will dribble into CLDR if and when individuals recognize the need on a language-by-language basis. The improvements to the CLDR Survey Tool in 2011 will hopefully make the process simple enough for non-technical participants. Not all 2,000 of Africa's languages will make it into CLDR, but the system is in place, and the precedent established, for any language to be included when a motivated volunteer is inspired to take on the task.

The Going Kompyuta project by the Goethe Institute of Cameroon, in which local volunteers were organized to complete locales for seven of the nation's mother tongues, is a model that FOSS interest groups in other countries could follow when seeking cooperative activities that their membership can achieve. Linux user groups have emerged in many African countries, replete with young computer enthusiasts looking for interesting voluntary projects. Projects could be organized by libraries, computer science departments or ICT training centres, local technology businesses or international cooperation agencies that would like a low-cost way to make a quick and lasting impact. With an average of 40 languages spoken in each country in Africa, groups could use local networks to increase locale coverage for their languages. First Nations in North America, Aboriginal groups in Australia, indigenous peoples of Papua New Guinea (who speak 850 languages among their 6.7 million citizens!) and even linguistic minorities in Europe could all organize collective efforts to put themselves on the ICT map through the creation of locales, using the improved Survey Tool provided by CLDR and the methodological network template developed during the 100 African Locales Initiative.

In the long run, however, locales are of limited interest – they are a means to an end, not an end in themselves. The Afrigen system was peculiar software, designed to make itself obsolete after a maximum of 2,000 uses. What is truly interesting is what can be accomplished after a locale has been created. Any number of FOSS projects have the potential to be localized into any language, to the extent that, in theory, an entire ICT environment can be created in the language of a user's choice. ANLoc developed a sequence of steps that each language can follow – a locale, a font and a keyboard if necessary, an agreed ICT terminology, training for software localizers – that together lay the foundation for quality L10n activities. What remains to be determined is who will do the hard work of localizing software into Africa's numerous languages. Currently, L10n projects tend to happen when a single young technophile sees that a program like Firefox is available in other African languages, and asks, "Why not do this for my language, too?" Localizing a big FOSS package, though, can be lonely and daunting. The 100 African Locales Initiative demonstrates ways to use social networks to create communities that can participate in such projects. Moreover, an initial network for African languages is now in place; with 1,500 current members of the Facebook group, for example, a renewed membership campaign could expand the group size tenfold in a matter of days. The larger the social network, the more likely it is to find people with the skills and desire to translate FOSS into their mother tongues, and the more rapidly we can envision the community creating a new norm: a world in which anybody can access the benefits of ICT in a language with which they are comfortable.

Conclusions

This chapter has examined the 100 African Locales Initiative, which succeeded in generating locale data for languages throughout the continent. Locale creation was a straightforward technical challenge, but a complicated logistical one: how to locate people with the skills, desire and facilities to work on locales for their languages, and how to work with volunteers in dozens of countries all the way through the process.

Not everything that the initiative attempted was successful. For example, attempts to find participants for Nigeria's many minority languages failed repeatedly, leaving Africa's most populous country as perhaps its most underrepresented within CLDR. Reasons why locales were *not* created for some languages included lack of mother-tongue literacy, hesitation by non-experts to take an authoritative role, paucity of scholars with expertise in many languages, a preference in some quarters to maintain ICT in the provenance of colonial souvenir languages and a desire by some to be paid for their technical contributions rather than volunteering.

Despite these obstacles, the initiative succeeded in reaching its goals, largely through the careful cultivation of networks. Networks included established groups such as the H-Africa academic mailing lists and the membership list of the Free Software and Open Source Foundation for Africa, the individual professional networks of ANLoc members and local networks such as those organized at the University of Nairobi and the Goethe Institute of Cameroon. More innovatively, the project used online social networks, particularly Facebook and Twitter, to locate people who could work on many diverse languages. The combination of all these networks proved a viable means of locating volunteers who could complete locales for nearly 5 per cent of Africa's languages.

Many more locales remain to be completed, both within Africa and for unrepresented languages elsewhere in the world. This work can be undertaken by interested groups within their own countries, modelled on the ANLoc experience and using the improved CLDR Survey Tool. Of even more interest, once a locale is completed for a language, the initiative demonstrates that networks can be employed to the benefit of FOSS localization throughout Africa, building towards the day when ICT in people's preferred languages is a goal successfully achieved.

REFERENCES

CIA (2011) "The World Factbook: Tanzania", Central Intelligence Agency; available at https://www.cia.gov/library/publications/the-world-factbook/geos/tz.html (accessed 28 February 2011).

de Pauw, Guy (2011) "Publications in African Language Technology"; available at http://aflat.org/biblio (accessed 10 June 2011).

European Commission on Multilingualism (2010) "The Euromosaic Study, Sami in Sweden"; available at http://ec.europa.eu/education/languages/euromosaic/doc4665_en.htm (accessed 28 February 2011).

Kachale, Edmond (2008) "Accessibility of ICT to Speakers of Indigenous African Languages", *OpenSpace* 2(3), pp. 88–94.

Kamusi Project (2006) "Swahili Time Wall Clock"; available at www.kamusi.org/en/swahili_clock (accessed 11 June 2011).

Lewis, M. Paul (ed.) (2009) *Ethnologue: Languages of the World*, 16th edn, Dallas, TX: SIL International.

Osborn, Don (2010) *African Languages in a Digital Age: Challenges and Opportunities for Indigenous Language Computing*, Ottawa: International Development Research Centre.

Pimenta, Waldir (2009) "A Language's Journey out of Digital Exclusion"; available at http://ultimategerardm.blogspot.com/2009/09/languages-journey-out-of-digital.html (accessed 3 March 2011).

Prah, Kwesi Kwa (2000) *Mother Tongue for Scientific and Technological Development in Africa*, 3rd edn, Cape Town: South Africa Centre for Advanced Studies of African Society.

Texin, Tex (n.d.) "Information Resources for Locales and Internationalization"; available at www.i18nguy.com/locales/locale-resources.html (accessed 11 June 2011).

—— (2002) "What Is Wrong with Locales?", paper presented at 22nd Unicode Conference, Santa Jose, September.

Topping, Suzanne (2002) "Position Statement", W3C Internationalization Workshop, Washington, DC; available at www.w3.org/2002/02/01-i18n-workshop/Topping.html (accessed 11 September 2011).

Trading Economics (2011) "School Enrollment; Secondary School Gross in Tanzania"; available at www.tradingeconomics.com/tanzania/school-enrollment-secondary-percent-gross-wb-data.html (accessed 28 February 2011).

Wolff, Friedel (2011) *Effecting Change through Localisation: Localisation Guide for Free and Open Source Software*, Pretoria: Translate.org.za.

Part II
FOSS case studies, surveys, policy development and experience reports

9
The open source ecosystem in Tunisia: An empirical study

Imed Hammouda

Introduction

Information and communication technology (ICT) is an effective means for economic and social progress in developing countries, touching sectors like education, administration, business and trade. However, many developing countries lack sustainable local ICT service providers, ICT-driven businesses and ICT experts and managers. This is often attributed to the lack of resources and proper strategies (or their poor implementation) in these countries.

Free and open source software (FOSS) represents a key technology to drive development by strengthening the role (and adoption) of ICT. It is believed that through FOSS solutions and processes, developing and rising economies can foster innovation, create local value and build sustainable and affordable ICT solutions (UNU-MERIT, 2006; UNCTAD, 2003).

Studies on the adoption of open source have mainly focused on developed countries, e.g. Norway (Hauge, Cruzes and Conradi, 2008), Germany (Kessler and Alpar, 2009) and Finland (TKK, 2008, 2009). The situation is less clear in developing countries. Also, it is not known how the successful adoption models in developed countries can conveniently be applied to developing countries. The purpose of this study is to fill this gap, providing a critical scientific review of FOSS adoption in a sustainable development setting. The work was carried out within the Commissioned Development Policy Research programme of the Ministry for Foreign Affairs of Finland. The programme selected Tunisia as the example

Free and open source software and technology for sustainable development, Sowe, Parayil and Sunami (eds), United Nations University Press, 2012, ISBN 978-92-808-1217-6

developing country. As it has been recognized that Finland is a leading country in FOSS adoption (Red Hat, 2008), this study identifies possible areas where the Finnish FOSS experience can be useful for Tunisia.

A decision was made to study FOSS at different levels, since it is widely acknowledged that open source is a mindset seen in many areas, such as education, business, government and non-governmental organizations (NGOs). The focus is on the software business sector, as FOSS is primarily a software development and distribution model. The main research question is: what is the extent of FOSS adoption in Tunisian software industries (both public and private), universities, NGOs and the governmental sector, and how do different facilitating or inhibiting factors affect the adoption process?

The research sought to answer to this question by conducting an exploratory study with both a qualitative and a quantitative approach. Semi-structured face-to-face interviews involved different FOSS stakeholders in Tunisia. A questionnaire was designed to collect quantitative data (OSSTraDe, 2010), and sent to Tunisian software companies. In addition, existing literature related to open source was reviewed.

ICT for sustainable development: Role of open source

As background to the study, this section discusses ICT and open source software from the perspective of sustainable development, and elaborates on the importance of studying open source ecosystems in a development policy context.

ICT for sustainable development

Sustainable development has been recognized as a fundamental principle for the stability and growth of societies and nations. One of the most common definitions of sustainable development is development that meets the needs of the present without compromising the ability of future generations to meet their own needs (WCED, 1987: 43). There are other complementary definitions, all suggesting that development needs can be categorized along four dimensions: social, economic, ecological and political. For instance, at the social level sustainable development should ensure self-sustaining improvements in quality of life of communities and societies (Singh and Titi, 1995: 8). From an economic perspective, it can be seen as the will to follow a rational approach to economic policies (Barboza, 2000). Ecologically speaking, sustainable development means not unreasonably depleting natural resources and not generating waste products that significantly alter natural systems (Lowe, 1990). Finally, from a political point of view, it ensures that people have basic human rights and freedoms to participate in societies (Singh and Titi, 1995: 8).

In today's knowledge society, a central question is what kind of actions and strategies are needed to achieve sustainable development. Recently it has been suggested that ICT could offer numerous opportunities for sustainable contributions to both economic and human development (Tongia, Subrahmanian and Arunachalam, 2005). Recognizing the important role ICT could play, a central question is how to promote it in developing countries. Among other studies, recent UN reports suggest that FOSS represents a key technology to strengthen the role (and adoption) of ICT (UNU-MERIT, 2006; UNCTAD, 2003).

FOSS as a development driver and policy

To make ICT work for sustainable development, it needs both an affordable, market-driven infrastructure and multi-stakeholder efforts at all levels to help developing countries use it according to their priorities and demands. This fits the characteristics of open source software. The principles of open source suggest that everyone should be able to run, study, redistribute and improve the software. It is also assumed that the improvements (and modified versions in general) are released back to the public, so the whole community benefits. This makes open source software available at zero price.

By adopting open source solutions, governments spend less money on buying licences of proprietary software. Almost all proprietary software solutions have open source counterparts that can be used for free. The open source alternatives are usually of high quality and supported by a distributed community of companies and volunteers.

FOSS allows developing countries to adapt software to their own needs and contexts, as source code is freely available. This makes them less dependent on outside software producers and developers. By adapting and contributing to open source software, societies in developing countries enter the information age as producers and not only consumers. Sustainability requires active participation of consumers interacting with producer networks. Furthermore, open source provides a framework for community-driven content and knowledge creation. This is important, as sustainable development requires that society as a whole works collectively towards economic and social development. In this way, local development of ICT skills can be boosted through using, adapting and implementing FOSS.

On the economic side, open source software brings new kinds of business opportunities and models for ICT-based companies, moving from product-based to service-based business. Services may include hosting, support, consulting, training, integration or customization activities. With open source it becomes possible to start a service-based business without the need to develop or purchase software. This is considered an important opportunity for young entrepreneurs and university graduates in developing countries. It is important to note that support services around open source software extend beyond technical and engineering skills to cover things like legal and strategic consulting. In addition, FOSS enables business models such as developing commercial software on top of open source, building hardware embedding free software solutions or simply producing documentation (e.g. books, user manuals, etc.) for open source technologies.

As the software industry is dominated by proprietary businesses, the benefits of FOSS are still unclear and not recognized by many developing countries. The role of open source in sustainable development can be significant through a multi-stakeholder ecosystem of educators, promoters, advocates, adopters and producers. In particular, the ecosystem is driven by government policies, and many argue that FOSS adoption level could be used as an indicator of good governance and sustainable development policies in developing countries. Their main argument is that FOSS is a good instrument for implementing the general priorities and decisions set by government agencies to achieve economic, political, social and environmental goals. This study uses the open source ecosystem in Tunisia as an example developing country.

Research approach

To gather relevant data and material, contact and cooperation were established with a wide range of institutions. The study was carried out mainly during 2010.

Online questionnaire: Design and sampling process

This research adapted a questionnaire used in a recent study in Finland (TKK, 2008), altering it to reflect the language used and the total number of companies sampled due to the economic and demographic differences between the countries. Six questions guided the online questionnaire.
- What is the role of FOSS within the company? And what did it bring as benefits, if any?
- What are the types and names of FOSS products that the organization has chosen to adopt? And why?
- What is the extent of FOSS adoption for these products?
- What are the factors facilitating and inhibiting the adoption of FOSS in software industries?

- Is the company just a user of FOSS, or does it contribute to the community?
- Will the company adopt FOSS in the future, or continue the same initial strategy?

In total, the survey questionnaire was sent to 210 e-mail addresses (which is around the number of software companies in Tunisia). Contact information was obtained from a national repository. Eighty-one answers were received (a response rate of 39 per cent), 28 of which were dropped since it was not possible to confirm their origin, leaving a total of 53 answers. Some answers are partial (34 per cent) and others are complete (66 per cent).

Face-to-face interviews

A total of 26 in-depth interviews were conducted with software industry entities in Tunisia. The interviewees were company chief executives, ICT managers and technical engineers. The interviews were semi-structured and followed a guideline that was adapted over time to take findings of earlier interviews into account. The focus was on the open source use and development process, in particular the question of if and how this process can work in a field that is dominated by commercial firms, not hobbyists. Linked to this, the business opportunities arising from the process were investigated.

The web was the main source in gathering contacts and phone numbers to conduct the face-to-face interviews. The study focused mainly on the northern regions of Tunisia (Tunis, Ariana and Radès), plus some central parts (Sousse and Sfax). The biggest target was companies within technological parks/centres, as it was easier to reach their personnel. The sample interviewed was almost arbitrary: no preference for any company was made. None of the 26 interviews was electronically recorded, but in all cases handwritten notes were made. The average interview length was 50 minutes.

In addition to companies, interviews were organized with private and public universities' faculty staff, hospital personnel, governmental officials and social activists. To increase comparability of the responses and exclude the effect of time trends, interviewees were selected for their knowledge of ICT in their organizations.

Literature review

There is very little literature available about FOSS in Tunisia, but a number of reports and online resources were studied, mainly taken from the Tunisian Open Source Software Portal (2011). The literature discusses adoption models and data in various sectors.

Existing FOSS studies in Tunisia

Studies on FOSS in Tunisia have been planned many times since the late 1990s, with national conferences and talks on the subject. However, no official empirical studies or clear strategies on how Tunisia could benefit from FOSS were made until 2010, when the Tunisian government launched a nationwide study on FOSS in the country. The study covers ICT companies, universities, high schools, training centres and NGOs.

FOSS in Tunisia

In 1999 the Tunisian government started considering the place that should be dedicated to FOSS in the national ICT strategy. A cabinet meeting agreed a national FOSS plan on 12 July 2001 (ibid.). Other cabinet meetings discussed this matter and designated the following objectives:
- to stimulate FOSS use and development progressively in different sectors, particularly education, higher education and research
- to take advantage of FOSS in creating new products and services for ICT companies
- to encourage the use and development of FOSS to boost innovation, job creation and entrepreneurship
- to take advantage of the benefits of open source software to enhance human resource skills and competencies in IT
- to make FOSS a catalyst for developing the software industry and strengthening the competitiveness of companies operating in the ICT sector.

In 2003 the Open Source Software Unit was created within the Ministry of Communication Technologies to implement a national FOSS plan (Tunisia, 2003). The decree creating this unit was later extended (Tunisia, 2007, 2009). The unit set a number of goals for the realization of the national FOSS plan:
- widening and developing the uses of open source software
- setting up an observatory to stimulate technological awakening and follow-up of novelties in this domain
- technical framing of administrative structures, enterprises and public establishments to ensure good exploitation of FOSS
- follow-up of programmes in relation to FOSS, particularly in the sectors of education, training, higher education and scientific research
- preparation and organization of training workshops.

The Tunisian ICT strategy dedicates special interest to FOSS as a technical and technological alternative to be considered in projects for new or redesigned systems. Adding open source software to the title and mission of the secretary of state for information technologies indicates the importance given to FOSS in the national ICT strategy.

Tunisian study cases

Most FOSS-related studies in Tunisia have been conducted by large public organizations. Their goal has been to form a plan to migrate their information systems to FOSS environments. Examples include a proposal prepared by the Tunisian electricity and gas company, STEG (2008). STEG's main objectives are to create a reactive infrastructure, cost reductions and innovative and creative teams, and adapt solutions to technology evolution independent from providers. Many of the adopted solutions are open source. Another proposal was published by the National Centre of Retirement and Social Providence (CNRPS, 2008). Its main objective for going open source was cost reduction, multi-platform usage and compatibility, technical promotion of the development team and saving time in administrative procedures.

However, the most relevant related study was conducted by the Ministry of Communication Technologies of Tunisia in 2010 (Ministry of Communication Technologies, 2011). The goal was to study the usage patterns, development practices and technical skills related to open source software in Tunisia. The survey targeted a comprehensive sample of public and private enterprises, computer services and engineering companies, academia and higher education institutions, and open source communities. The list of interviewees has been kept internal.

As illustrated in Figure 9.1, one of the main findings of this study is that the public sector seems to be the most aware of the concept of open source software (54.4 per cent), followed by the software business sector (33 per cent) and universities (31.8 per cent). Professional training centres are the least aware of FOSS (13.8 per cent). The author is not aware of a similar study covering all sectors in Finland or other developed countries; instead, most studies focus on a particular segment. The collected survey data were used to establish an international benchmark comparing Tunisia to other countries. Moreover, a roadmap for the realization of the national plan on open source software is to be established using the study results.

The present study and that of the Tunisian administration were conducted during the same period. They also applied similar methodology and used similar questions. However, the overall motivation behind the two studies is different. Rather than establishing a benchmark, the

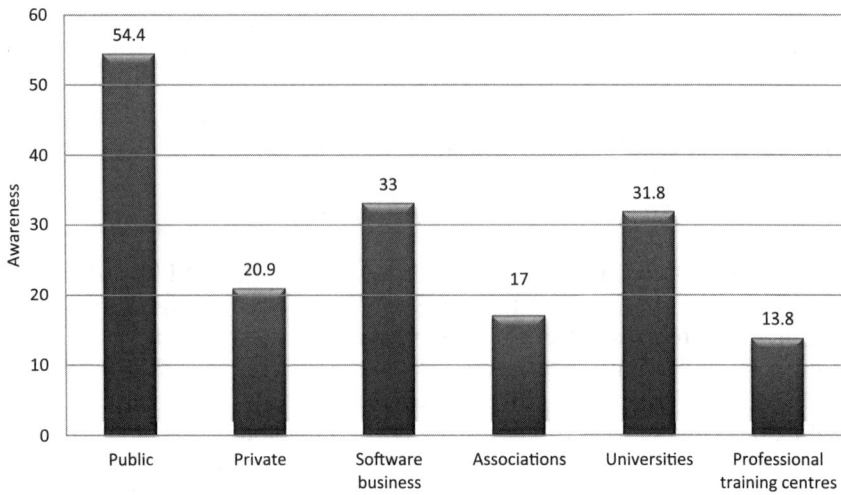

Figure 9.1 Familiarity with the concept of FOSS
Source: Ministry of Communication Technologies (2011).

present study aims at a critical evaluation of the open source ecosystem in Tunisia and identifying ways to improve and sustain it.

Research results: FOSS ecosystem in Tunisia 2010

Based on the face-to-face interviews and online questionnaire, the main stakeholders in the open source ecosystem in Tunisia were identified. As software companies are at the core of open source, an empirical model for FOSS adoption in the Tunisian software industry was derived, highlighting the main facilitators and inhibitors. Qualitative data obtained from interviews are presented, and the empirical model is backed with quantitative data regarding the mindset of Tunisian software companies towards FOSS.

FOSS stakeholders

As illustrated in Figure 9.2, the open source ecosystem in Tunisia consists of various kinds of stakeholders with different roles. The stakeholders can be categorized into four groups. The government represents a key player in the ecosystem. Its role has been mainly as a promoter of FOSS solutions, for example by the adoption of FOSS technologies in governmental organizations, providing training and organizing events. The second key stakeholder is industrial entities, in particular those whose

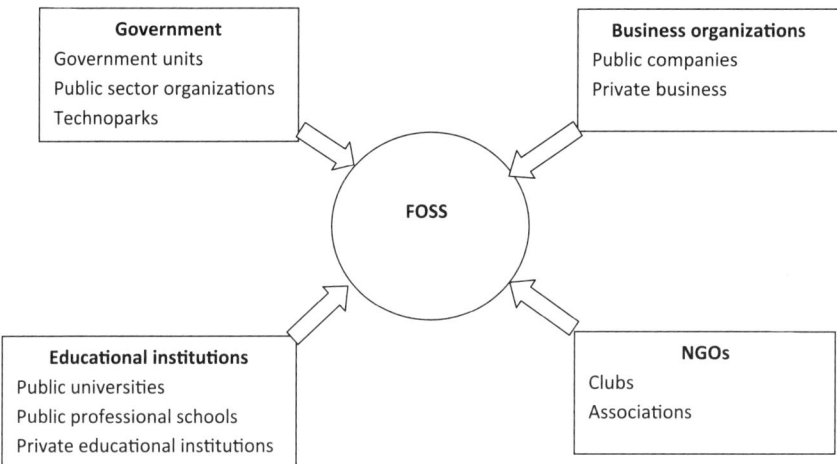

Figure 9.2 Stakeholders in the Tunisian FOSS ecosystem

business portfolio include software production. The Tunisian software industry can be categorized along the traditional lines of being either public or private. Companies have a twofold role, being both adopters of FOSS solutions and producers of open source software.

Higher educational institutions represent the third key element. These can be classed as universities and higher professional schools, both public and private. Their role is mainly focused around education and training of students. To a lesser degree, educational institutions promote FOSS through the adoption of open source solutions in their IT infrastructure. NGOs represent the fourth key stakeholder in the ecosystem, bringing together university students and social activists whose role is to advocate the use of open source software.

Relevance to development policy

From a FOSS perspective, one could argue there is a strong link between sustainable development and sustainability of the open source ecosystem. For FOSS to contribute to sustainable development, it is critical to have a healthy open source ecosystem, and that requires concerted effort and commitment from each stakeholder. Structurally speaking, the FOSS ecosystem in Tunisia seems to be well suited to take on the important roles of enhancing capacity building, promoting the adoption of open source solutions and fostering demand for and supply of FOSS-related products and services. The Tunisian government needs to maintain and enforce the current structure. However, the structural aspect of the ecosystem is not the most significant. What needs to be studied is the extent to which the ecosystem is stable and balanced enough to perform its expected functions. In other words, what exactly and to what degree is each stakeholder contributing to the ecosystem?

Public sector

It is interesting that the Tunisian government has the Open Source Software Unit in the Ministry of Communication Technologies. The unit is responsible for a national open source plan. It is believed that the national strategy has boosted interest in open source and helped spread awareness of its potential across different sectors, such as education, research and ICT businesses. Concrete actions include training human resources, FOSS solution promotion and consulting and technical consulting for both public organizations and private start-ups in technology parks.

Many of the interviewees thought that the governmental involvement in open source could be strengthened by taking further concrete steps to support FOSS-based companies. Ideas include more business opportunity in the public sector and tax exemption. Another major issue in this area is the confusion which arose after the government signed partnership agreements with large international proprietary software vendors. Many interviewees viewed this as a step back and a contradiction in the government strategy. A frequently cited argument supporting this claim is that governmental organizations themselves do not use open source solutions.

According to the literature, and documents received from some Tunisian governmental organizations, the public sector is using and adopting FOSS more than the private. The open source solutions considered are mostly general-purpose desktop applications.

In this regard, a field study was carried out on FOSS adoption in Tunisian hospitals as an example public sector. The findings show that the use of open source is accidental. Most hospitals adopt general-purpose open source solutions such as document and content management systems, but almost no domain-specific open source software is in use. The main reason is that decisions regarding technological solutions deployed in hospitals are centralized and made at the ministry level. Another reason is that the technical level of IT managers in hospitals is quite modest: many did not even know the characteristics of open source software.

However, the situation is more favourable to open source in the Computing Centre of the Ministry of Public Health (le Centre Informatique du Ministère de la Santé Publique), where major decisions regarding IT systems in hospitals are taken. Its strategy is not to migrate from legacy proprietary applications to FOSS solutions, but FOSS is the default choice for a new project or development. This is reported to be a tactical move to avoid upsetting proprietary vendors and their advocates.

Relevance to development policy

The role of the public sector is to stimulate demand and create an enabling environment for open source software to thrive. This is important, as the public sector represents an important ICT market in developing countries - as is the case in Tunisia. From a development policy perspective, the Tunisian government needs to maintain its strategy to promote open source in public organizations through training and awareness creation programmes. Furthermore, the government needs to enhance open source adoption in public administrations. This will encourage local businesses to foster and promote localized products and services.

Software business organizations

During the field study it was found that many small IT companies (10–20 employees) specialize in FOSS only. All their offered solutions and services were fully open. Some companies, however, tried to hide this fact because they were afraid of clients' complaints about the costs and product development fees.

One of the biggest problems faced by these companies is the "ignorance" or misunderstanding of the meaning of FOSS by the clients. Once they know a product is based on open source, they fear security issues concerning their own source code, or object to the price of the final product on the grounds that it was developed and built on a free basis. They do not even ask for further support or maintenance contracts because of the FOSS notion.

Most small companies find a huge challenge in the Tunisian software and development market. As almost all the big Tunisian companies use proprietary and closed source solutions, clients choose these instead of open source. It was reported that most clients trust "big" known entities that have been on the market a long time with stable solutions, and avoid "newly emerged" companies with new solutions and developing strategies. Clients trust a known entity in preference to an open source community, which is considered as an unknown group of amateurs, or even students. Another common prejudice against FOSS is that it is inferior because it is free.

Empirical model

An empirical model of FOSS adoption and participation in the Tunisian ICT sector was developed, based on Strauss and Corbin's (1998) paradigm. This paradigm has already been used to study FOSS adoption in hospitals (Munoz-Cornejo, Seaman and Koru, 2011). The purpose of the

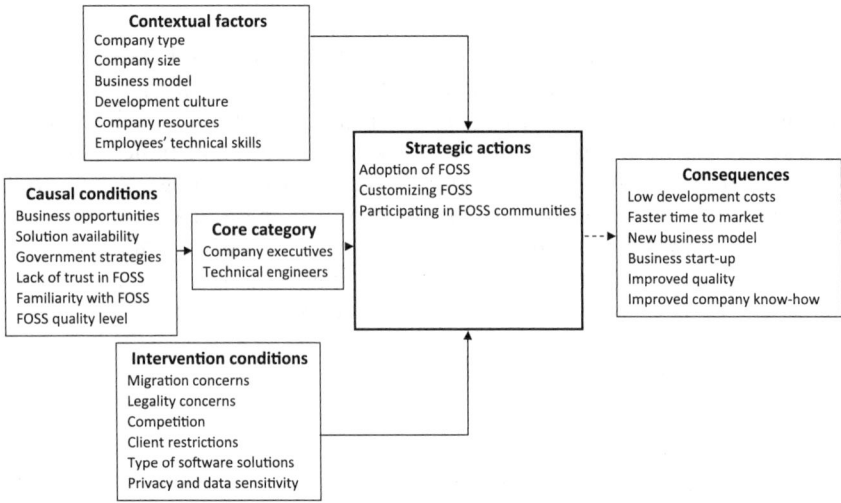

Figure 9.3 An empirical FOSS adoption model in the Tunisian software industry

model, which is depicted in Figure 9.3, is to identify corresponding influential factors based on the present study.

The core category block identifies the decision-makers – either company executives or technical engineers. Three kinds of strategic actions are considered by the decision-makers: adopting open source solutions as such, customizing open source for company needs and contributing back to the community. Almost all the companies were simple adopters and many had needed to do fine-tuning, but very few contributed back to the community. The stated main reason for low contribution is that most companies do not own the copyright of the software they produce, as most of the work is done for international IT clients. The other major reason is that most companies have an opportunistic mindset, in the sense that they benefit from zero-price software but are reluctant to spend resources on communicating back to the community. Among the interviewees, only one company is planning to build an open source community around core software that is implemented as closed source in the first place.

The main benefits of engaging in FOSS (in order of importance) were lowered development costs, faster time to market, implementing new business models, creating new business start-ups (e.g. spin-offs), achieving better product quality and improving the overall company know-how in terms of technical and business skills.

The influential factors are organized into three categories. Causal conditions are fundamental factors influencing the decision of a company regarding FOSS adoption and participation. These factors, in order of importance, were the emergence of a new business opportunity, availability of an open source alternative to proprietary solutions, the influence of government strategies (for example requiring open source in a call for tenders), trust level towards FOSS in general and a specific open source solution in particular, familiarity of technical engineers with open source solutions and overall quality of the FOSS products.

Contextual factors are facilitators or inhibitors specific to each company. The most visible factor is the company type. Certain kinds of companies (named SS2L) specialize in FOSS-related solutions and are the most active in the field. The second contextual factor is the size of the company. With few exceptions, the smaller the company, the more it depends on FOSS solutions. The business model adopted in the company also has influence. For instance, "software-as-a-service" companies are most likely to adopt FOSS, whereas most subcontracting companies are governed by the technical requirements (i.e. the use of open source) set by their clients. Other factors include the development culture and past traditions of the company, the resources it has for trying open source solutions and contributing back, and finally the technical skills of the engineers. Most interviewees agreed that high technical skills are needed to evaluate FOSS solutions.

The third set of influential factors are called intervening conditions: external factors that have an impact on the causal conditions. The most apparent intervening condition is the tough competition by proprietary providers. Almost all interviewees referred to a number of IT giants, calling the competition unfair. The main reason is that these giants have long-term market penetration.

The next factor is legality concerns about open source; this has a great impact on trust in FOSS. The type and domain of the software often determine the familiarity and quality levels. Most technical engineers are familiar with and have high quality perceptions of server-side FOSS (e.g. Linux, Apache, MySQL, etc.) and tools such as content management systems and integrated development environments. Another intervening condition that affects the quality of the FOSS solution is privacy and data sensitivity concerns raised by clients if FOSS is used. The cost associated with migrating from a solution (whether proprietary or not) to open source was also reported as a key consideration once a FOSS-based solution becomes available.

Quantitative data

Based on the answers given in the survey of 53 Tunisian companies, charts were generated to interpret the data and make the analysis easier.

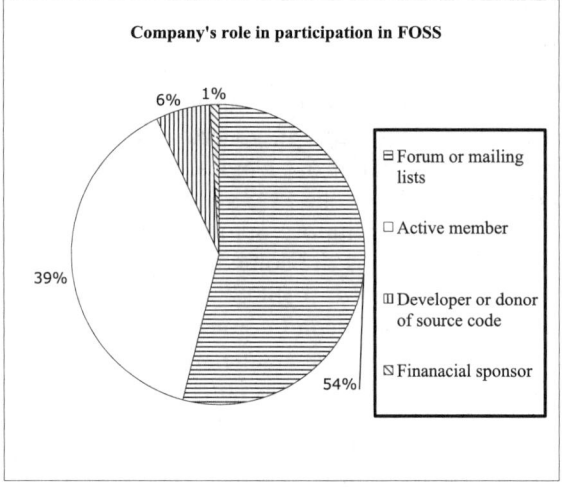

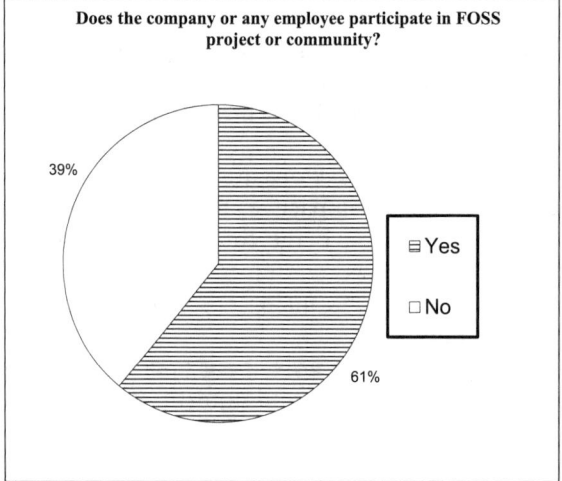

Figure 9.4 Role of company participation in FOSS

All the charts can be found at the project website: http://tutopen.cs.tut.fi/osstrade. As a general observation, the survey results confirm the empirical model presented earlier.

Company participation in FOSS is depicted in Figure 9.4. It can be seen that 61 per cent of the companies report a form of participation in FOSS communities, with more than half participating in discussion forums or mailing lists and about 40 per cent being active members in those places. Only 6 per cent and 1 per cent are source code developers/donors or financial sponsors, respectively.

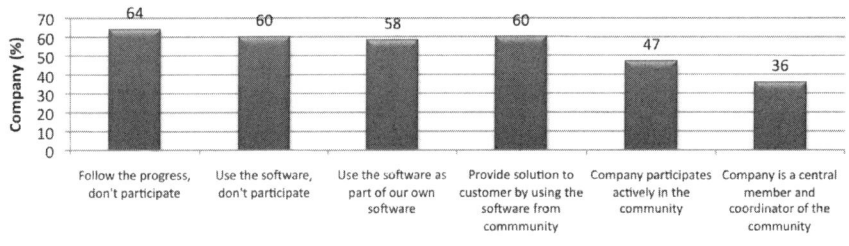

Figure 9.5 Type of company participation in FOSS

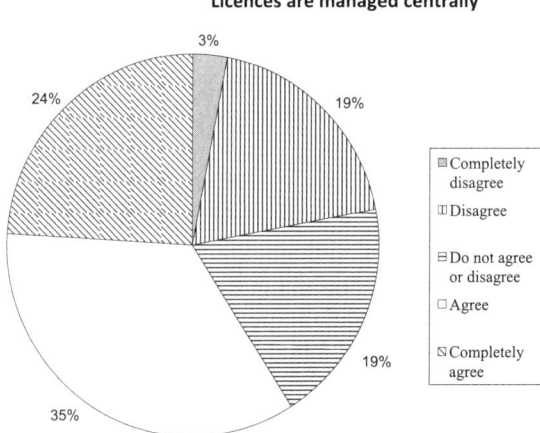

Figure 9.6 Central management for software purchase and licences

Figure 9.5 shows that more companies (64 per cent) follow the progress of the software than participate in any kind of activity in the community (47 per cent). This confirms the empirical model that very few companies participate in development.

The survey findings show that around 60 per cent of the companies agree that software purchase decisions are made centrally; the same is true for licence management (Figure 9.6). This suggests that core decision-makers for FOSS adoption in business organizations are the top managers.

Concerning the use of FOSS inside companies (Figure 9.7), 80 per cent of the respondents agreed that it contributed to lower software purchase and deployment costs. So cost cutting is one of the most important consequences, as seen in the empirical model. Furthermore, 86 per cent of the companies agreed that the scalability and performance of FOSS are good, which improved software quality as a whole.

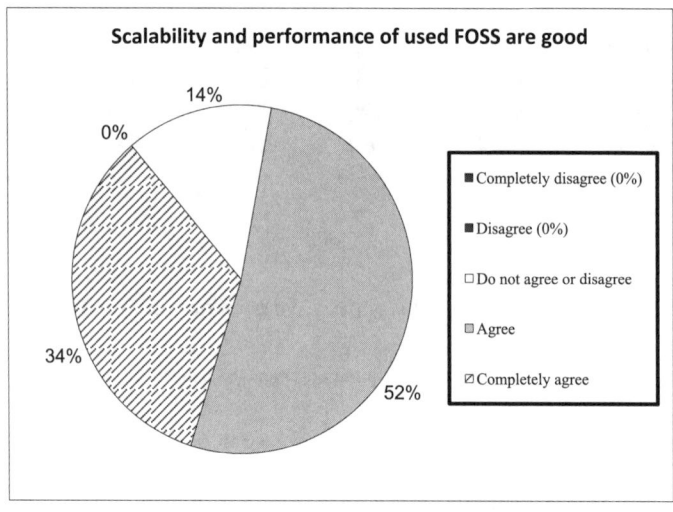

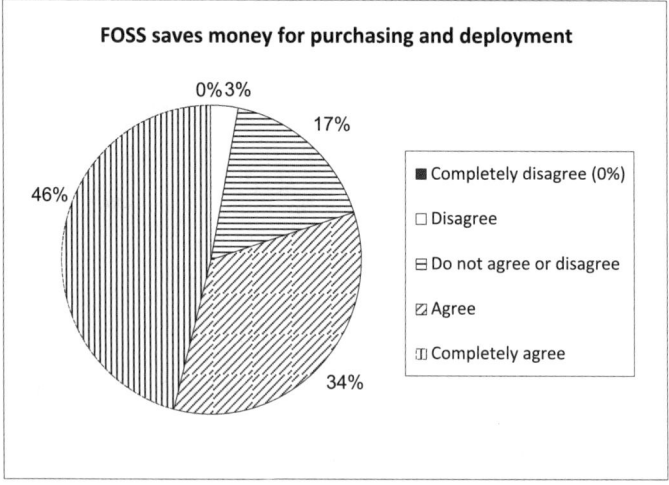

Figure 9.7 Consequences of using FOSS in an organization

As pointed out earlier, the business model is one of the contextual factors. In Figure 9.8 two different business model scenarios are shown. From the survey answers it can be seen that Tunisian companies deliver very little software under FOSS licence or dual licensing. Only 27 per cent reported that they offer software under dual licence, and 29 per cent deliver their own products under FOSS licence. Apparently, there is a lack of FOSS-based business models in Tunisian companies.

As shown in Figure 9.9, 25 per cent of the companies said that deploying FOSS internally is a huge task. Several interviewees also mentioned

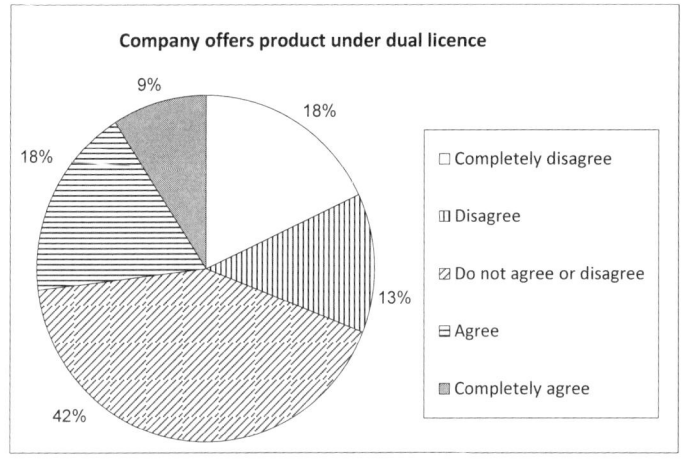

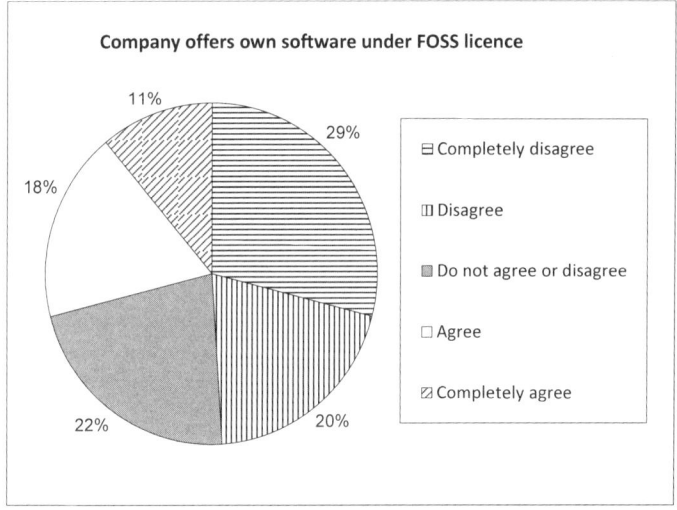

Figure 9.8 FOSS business models in Tunisian companies

migration issues – and hence place migration concerns at the top of the intervening conditions in the empirical model. Furthermore, 17 per cent of companies think challenges related to intellectual property rights are a problem in using open source software, and 14 per cent said they faced problems related to copyright issues. The competition between proprietary and open source software is another inhibiting factor: 11 per cent of respondents are not using much FOSS because they have already invested in commercial software. Since some commercial software has long-term market penetration, companies cannot shift to FOSS even if they want to.

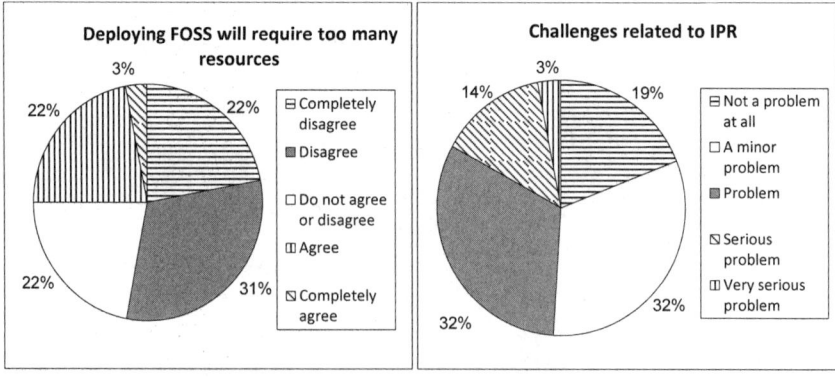
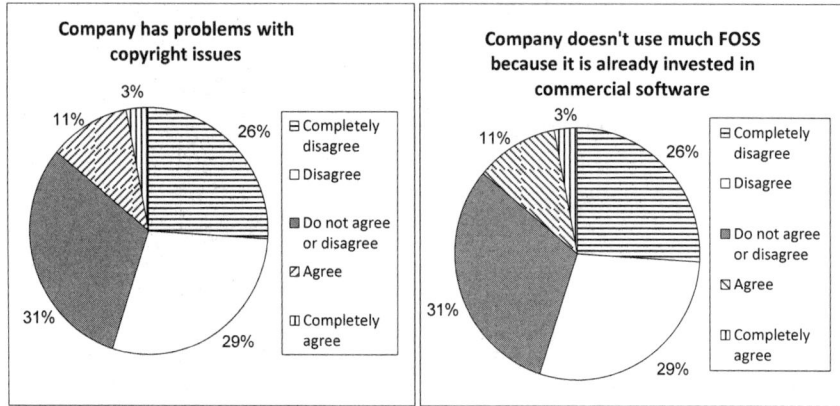

Figure 9.9 Inhibiting factors for FOSS adoption

Relevance to development policy

As an important stakeholder in the FOSS ecosystem, the role of software businesses is to create technical expertise and solutions to address market needs. They could also participate in creating demand for other businesses. From a development policy perspective, Tunisian software companies still have lots of room to grow and improve in addressing the needs of the local market. This will create solutions suited to the requirements of the local setting, leading to modernization in many sectors. The Tunisian government should support local businesses in developing localized solutions based on FOSS technologies that allow free use and modification of source code.

Educational institutions

Educational institutions, whether private or public, are still lagging behind in open source education despite a number of promising attempts, mostly around the technical aspects of open source technology. The latest effort was the launch of the Professional Master in Open Source Software in a collaboration between two universities and the Ministry of Communication Technologies in March 2010. Apart from this young initiative, most open-source-related education is given within the scope of other technical subjects such as networks and security. Important aspects of open source such as licensing, development methods and business models are rarely taught to students. This is a major obstacle for the emergence of business start-ups around open source solutions, and a major inhibitor for migrating to open source business models.

However, all university presidents and head of departments interviewed recognize the importance of open source software and are in favour of improving the curricula of their institutions with regard to FOSS education. As concrete actions, open source solutions were favoured when building IT infrastructure, and a number of open source educational products such as Moodle have been adopted to support teaching methods. Clubs promoting open source are hosted and their activities are encouraged.

Relevance to development policy

The role of educational institutions in the open source ecosystem is to produce graduates with FOSS technical and business capacity. Unfortunately, this role is not yet being taken seriously enough in Tunisia. From a sustainable development perspective, university students could learn to be producers by contributing to open source projects and tailoring the solutions to the local setting. This is important, as graduates represent future entrepreneurs. The Tunisian government should encourage educational institutions to be technology neutral so that students are introduced to open source. Also open source educational solutions, which can be used for free, should be promoted to improve the educational system and learning practices in the country.

NGOs

There are a large number of associations and clubs advocating the use of open source and participation in open source communities in Tunisia. These NGOs play a vital role in FOSS promotion and training. Example clubs include Ubuntu-tn, Fedora-tn, LibertySoft, SecuriNets, FreeWays, OpenSource-tn and Esprit Libre. Most of these are regularly active and have a large member base – Ubuntu-tn, for instance, has hundreds of members. Associations include the DFSA (Digital & Free Software Association), the Youth Science Association Tunisia and the Internet and Multimedia Tunisian Society. As representative NGOs, community members from Ubuntu-tn and the DFSA were interviewed.

These groups started as individual efforts but gradually evolved into relatively large communities. Their main activities include organizing thematic seminars and install parties. However, lack of resources remains a big obstacle to their vitality and continuity. Whereas associations get funding from governmental programmes, clubs rely on self-financing and modest donations from a few sources. As their role is vital, it is very important to ensure the continued existence of NGOs.

Relevance to development policy

From a FOSS ecosystem perspective, the role of NGOs is to advocate the use of open source software. Communities and organizations represent the healthiest stakeholder in the Tunisian open source ecosystem. It is very important that the Tunisian government encourage and support these volunteers both morally and financially. These groups can also play an important role at the social and political levels, as they advocate free speech and openness in general.

Discussion

Limitations of the study

This study was subject to a number of limitations. First, it was not possible to cover all stakeholders of the Tunisian open source ecosystem: elements were selected which were thought to be reasonable representatives.

A major factor was the Open Source Software Unit of the Tunisian government conducting a similar study on the Tunisian open source ecosystem, in parallel with the study discussed here. This might have caused delay, as the people contacted for this study could think they were approached twice about the same topic and receiving the same request many times. Research e-mails might be ignored, or even confused with those from the Tunisian survey.

Another obstacle is that it is much easier to contact people when in Tunisia than by phone or e-mail from Finland. Some of the contact information available on company websites is either not up to date or presented as an embedded form to be sent to the company's administrator – and many such e-mail requests for interview and/or questionnaire participation do not get any kind of feedback or cooperation. The only way is to know the exact name of the person to contact.

Generalizability of the Tunisian case

Recently FOSS has attracted the attention of policy-makers and governments in both developed and developing worlds. Similar to Tunisia, many countries chose to define a national strategy for open source software –

for example Switzerland (FITSU, 2005) and South Africa (Department of Public Service & Administration, 2006). However, a strong FOSS presence in the software business sector (and other sectors as well) does not seem to depend on whether or not a national strategy is established and implemented. Countries like Finland and the United States still enjoy high levels of open source adoption in the absence of such a strategy. (In the case of Finland this may be attributed to historical factors, as Finland is the birthplace of two popular open source technologies, Linux and MySQL; in the US case, strong open source presence in the industry might be due to the fact that venture capitalists are investing in new business models.) Indeed, a recent study (Red Hat, 2008) shows that Finland, though with no national strategy, ranks higher than Switzerland with respect to open source activities in different sectors. However, a national FOSS strategy is believed to help in the context of developing counties. The same study shows that both South Africa and Tunisia are leading countries in the African context. This is partially attributed to the presence of such a strategy.

Other countries, like Algeria, maintain a portal for open source software, helping communities, industry and academics to stay updated with the latest in the field of open source. In the absence of such portals, countries like Tanzania rely on local associations and international educational programmes such as ict@innovation. In many African countries similar FOSS initiatives and bodies are mushrooming spontaneously. However, for most of these countries two main weaknesses are being reported: first, governments are not investing in adopting open source solutions; and second, the industry lacks open source technical capacity. To some degree these are the same challenges as those faced by the open source ecosystem in Tunisia.

The recommendations presented here could be applied to other developing countries, as Tunisia seems to share the same symptoms. The Finnish open source ecosystem could be helpful from a software industry point of view, as Finland is ranked first in this aspect (ibid.). As far as government activities are concerned, the Finnish model is not the best to follow, as countries like France have a stronger engagement. However, the biggest problem in implementing developed-world models in developing countries is the insufficient level of computer literacy, ICT skills and internet penetration.

From the ecosystem point of view, it seems that open source activities in developing countries are mostly driven by local communities, clubs and associations. Governments are still lagging behind such volunteer initiatives, although some are working on filling this gap by defining national FOSS strategies. Open source education seems to be the other handicap in these countries. The open source software industry is facing three main challenges: not enough market share in the public sector, tough competition from proprietary international players and limited technical capacity.

Naturally, one cannot generalize the open source mindset presented here to other countries. Contextual factors seem to be significant in shaping views towards open source. However, it is anticipated that most findings are repeated in many developing countries, particularly in Africa.

Policy recommendations

Based on findings concluded from the survey results, face-to-face interviews and a literature review, an action plan has been formulated to promote the open source ecosystem in Tunisia, categorized among the four stakeholders (Table 9.1). A set of policy recommendations has also been formulated, illustrated by the Finnish experience. Some of the recommendations are related to the action points.

Creating umbrella organizations

Finland has an umbrella open source organization, COSS, which works for the advancement of FOSS in Finland and represents an emerging business community (COSS, 2011). It gives support to all its member organizations with networking and competence development, information services and business promotion, as well as professional services for open source research, development and internationalization. In short, COSS helps its members to improve business related to FOSS. This is exactly what the Tunisian open source ecosystem is lacking. An umbrella organization like COSS can be created in Tunisia, taking into consideration the specificities of the local context. Its main role would be awareness creation and activity coordination.

This survey revealed that Tunisian companies are not familiar with open source business models like dual licensing, and open-source-friendly business models like software as a service are not that popular. Another attractive example of Finnish umbrella organizations is Validos (2011), a collaboration of companies and other entities that coordinates efforts related to open source compliance in business use. Borrowing the concept of open source umbrella organizations could be included in the agenda of future discussions between the two countries.

Promoting FOSS educational programmes

Promoting educational programmes on FOSS can be a great help for its adoption in Tunisia. From the survey and face-to-face interviews, it can be seen that most companies use FOSS mainly for server infrastructure; its use in other fields is minimal. This is a serious limitation, as the range of open source applications covers a much wider field. The main cause is

Table 9.1 Open source action plan for Tunisia

Stakeholder	Action point
Government/public sector	Maintain and execute a clear open source strategy
	Enhance open source adoption in public organizations
	Organize more training sessions, certification programmes and seminars
	Favour open source in calls for tenders
	Create trust channels with the private sector focusing on open source
	Avoid categorizing companies based on FOSS/non-FOSS and encourage company adoption of open source through tax exemption
	Maintain a national open source forge/free software bank
	Implement national open innovation models
	Encourage different open initiatives (open standards, open resources, open access, etc.) and enhance the role of the national open source centre
	Enhance the infrastructure needed for ICT and internet penetration
Business organizations	Favour open source technology in developed solutions
	Build cooperation channels between open-source-intensive companies
	Train company personnel in open source technology and practices
	Participate in global open source communities
	Localize open source solutions to local market needs
	Use open source as a business channel to external markets
Educational institutions	Adopt open source solutions in teaching tools and technical infrastructure
	Implement open educational frameworks and resources
	Teach various aspects of open source principles and technologies
	Encourage open source certification programmes
	Train faculty staff and other technical personnel in open source
	Participate in open innovation frameworks with the industry
NGOs	Raise awareness of open source in educational institutions and technoparks
	Coordinate efforts with similar organizations
	Establish cooperation with global communities

the limited technical know-how of university students and lack of relevant training for company personnel. Participation in FOSS projects is also very low in Tunisia. Most companies adopt open source software as is, and do not contribute to the community. The concept of community-driven development should be introduced early to university students.

The Finnish experience regarding the diversity of FOSS applications used in industry and academia and the sense of community can be a useful instrument to enhance the open source ecosystem in Tunisia.

Based on the findings, NGOs are the primary open source educators in Tunisia. There are several NGOs promoting FOSS education among university students, and these can be supported properly to widen the range of their activities. Among other needs, NGOs lack financial support to execute their operations and interaction with international counterparts. Organizing visits between relevant organizations in Finland and Tunisia could strengthen their role and be an opportunity to exchange ideas regarding activities and sustainability models.

The second promoting instrument for open source in Tunisia is seminars and conferences, organized by the government, academia, industry and civil society. International presence in such meetings is an important dissemination tool. Exploiting these forums, Finnish literature and studies could be shared with relevant counterparts in Tunisia. For instance, experience related to open source migration models in Finnish governmental organizations and industry could be useful, since migration is a big concern to most Tunisian companies and governmental agencies.

Decentralizing decision-making processes in organizations

As seen in the survey and confirmed during face-to-face interviews, the decision-making process in Tunisian organizations is very centralized. This is believed to be an inhibitor for open source adoption, as in most cases decision-makers show little interest in open source and are reluctant to consider associated risks. The situation would probably be different if local governments had more freedom in ICT-related decisions. Public organizations such as hospitals could have a more visible role in building their ICT solutions. It is argued that open source adoption would be improved if the decision-making process was decentralized. Umbrella organizations can help achieving this.

Local governments in Finland have a high degree of autonomy and responsibility in defining and building their IT infrastructure, as can be seen in public services such as healthcare. Taking good examples of decentralized and local IT strategies from the Finnish context may be useful for Tunisia, and in turn foster open source adoption.

Initiating business-to-business projects

Tunisian software companies have a high interest in open source software, but the amount of business generated from FOSS is still relatively small, not only because of lack of experience of open source business models but also because of the small size of the Tunisian market. Many companies try to overcome the latter problem by considering business operations in other African countries. This represents good ground for business-to-business initiatives between Tunisian and Finnish FOSS companies. Tunisian companies could act to some extent as a business gateway to Africa and assist Finnish companies in penetrating African markets.

A concrete action is to organize matchmaking events between businesses from both countries. It is acknowledged that open source represents a good medium for business discussions and partnerships. Finnish governmental agencies like Finpro and the Embassy of Finland in Tunisia should play a significant role in realizing these initiatives. This would be an effective way of knowledge transfer among Finnish and Tunisian organizations.

Establishing open innovation models

Open source is not only about free software applications; it is also a development method that brings together a distributed community of developers. Open source practices have been considered in many contexts, such as education and innovation programmes. These practices, however, remain rare and are not well implemented in Tunisia. The situation looks better in Finland. For instance, an open innovation model known as Demola (2011) was launched in Tampere in 2008. The programme brings together academic and industrial organizations to work on common innovation projects in a win-win situation. Such a model could be tried in the Tunisian context.

Conclusions

Open-source-related activities have mostly taken place in developed countries. Tunisia is one of the developing countries trying to get involved in the area. The findings of this study revealed that the role of FOSS in Tunisia is quite important. Naturally, the extent of FOSS adoption is subject to specific facilitating and inhibiting factors.

In particular, open source software plays a vital role in the Tunisian software industry: many companies reported that they would not exist without such software. However, FOSS adoption in Tunisia is mostly focused around server infrastructure and other general-purpose software, such as office applications and content management systems. The Tunisian government is taking initiatives to promote open source in the country.

At present, Tunisian companies have specific reasons for adopting open source software. One important factor is the financial benefit due to reduced development cost. Since lack of resources is the biggest concern for small Tunisian organizations, open source solutions represent an important opportunity. Most Tunisian companies do not want to spend money buying software, so when it comes to adopting new software inside the company they consider an open source solution first. This mindset obviously increases the degree of open source adoption in Tunisia.

As proprietary software business companies have long-term penetration in the Tunisian market, many companies prefer such solutions. Migrating to FOSS has been reported as a big challenge in terms of resources and affordability. However, recently more and more companies are breaking this vendor lock-in situation. This brings more independence to the adopter companies.

The most straightforward way to foster FOSS adoption in Tunisia is to improve FOSS-related education in universities and other educational institutions. Also, FOSS-driven business models have to be introduced to companies. In this regard, Finnish companies can serve as a model. Another important contribution from the Finnish open source ecosystem could be adopting similar umbrella organizations in Tunisia.

REFERENCES

Barboza, N. (2000) "Educating for a Sustainable Future: Africa in Action", *Prospects* 30(1), pp. 71–85.

CNRPS (2008) "Démarche de la CNRPS en matière des logiciels libres"; available at www.cnrps.nat.tn (accessed 26 February 2012).

COSS (2011) "Finnish Centre for Open Source Solutions"; available at www.coss.fi/en/ (accessed 26 February 2012).

Demola (2011) "New Factory Innovation Platform"; available at www.demola.fi (accessed 26 February 2012).

Department of Public Service & Administration (2006) "Policy on Free and Open Source Software Use for South African Government"; available at www.info.gov.za/view/DownloadFileAction?id=94490 (accessed 26 February 2012).

FITSU (2005) "OSS Strategy of the Swiss Confederation", Federal IT Steering Unit, 15 March; available at www.isb.admin.ch/themen/architektur/00164/index.html?lang=en (accessed 26 February 2012).

Hauge, Ø., D. Cruzes and R. Conradi (2008) "Adoption of Open Source in the Software Industry", in *Proceedings of Fourth International Conference on Open Source Systems*, Berlin: Springer, pp. 211–221.

Kessler, S. and P. Alpar (2009) "Customization of Open Source Software in Companies", in *Proceedings of Fifth International Conference on Open Source Systems*, Berlin: Springer, pp. 129–142.

Lowe, I. (1990) "Sustainable Development: How Do We Get There?", *Australian Society*, 5 June.

Ministry of Communication Technologies (2011) "Strategic Study on Open Source Software in Tunisia"; available at www.opensource.tn/index.php?id=41&L=0&tx_ttnews[tt_news]=196&cHash=f8f2956d40 (accessed 26 February 2012).

Munoz-Cornejo, G., C. B. Seaman and A. G. Koru (2011) "An Empirical Investigation into the Adoption of Open Source Software in Hospitals"; available at http://userpages.umbc.edu/~cseaman/papers/IJHISI08.pdf (accessed 26 February 2012).

Open Source Software in Tunisia (2011) "Tunisian Open Source Software Portal"; available at www.opensource.tn/index.php?id=21&L=2 (accessed 26 February 2012).

OSSTraDe (2010) "OSSTraDe Project Questionnaire"; available at http://tutopen.cs.tut.fi/osstrade/questionnaire (accessed 26 February 2012).

Red Hat (2008) "Open Source Index Ranks"; available at www.redhat.com/f/pdf/ossi-index-ranks.pdf (accessed 26 February 2012).

Singh, N. and V. Titi (1995) *Empowerment: Towards Sustainable Development*, London: Zed Books.

STEG (2008) "Open Source: Démarche d'adoption à la STEG"; available at www.steg.com.tn (accessed 26 February 2012).

Strauss, A. L. and J. M. Corbin (1998) *Basics of Qualitative Research: Techniques and Procedures for Developing Grounded Theory*, New Delhi: Sage Publications.

TKK (2008) "National Software Industry Survey 2008"; available at www.softwareindustrysurvey.org/sites/default/files/Report_2008.pdf (accessed 26 February 2012).

—— (2009) "National Software Industry Survey 2009"; available at www.softwareindustrysurvey.org/sites/default/files/SoftwareIndustrySurvey2009.pdf (accessed 26 February 2012).

Tongia, R., E. Subrahmanian and V. S. Arunachalam (2005) *Information and Communications Technology for Sustainable Development: Defining a Global Research Agenda*, Bangalore: Allied Publishers.

Tunisia (2003) "Decree No. 2003-1249 of 2 June 2003", *Journal Officiel Tunisien* 18.

—— (2007) "Decree No. 2007-1908 of 23 January 2007, Modifying Decree No. 2003-1249 of 2 June 2003", *Journal Officiel Tunisien* 47.

—— (2009) "Decree No. 2009-540 of 24 February 2009, Modifying Decree No. 2003-1249 of 2 June 2003", *Journal Officiel Tunisien* 61.

UNCTAD (2003) "E-commerce and Development Report 2003", UN Conference on Trade and Development; available at www.unctad.org/Templates/webflyer.asp?docid=4255&intItemID=2261&lang=1 (accessed 26 February 2012).

UNU-MERIT (2006) "Study on the Economic Impact of Open Source Software on Innovation and the Competitiveness of the Information and Communication Technologies (ICT) Sector in the EU"; available at http://ec.europa.eu/enterprise/sectors/ict/files/2006-11-20-flossimpact.en.pdf (accessed 26 February 2012).

Validos (2011) "VALIDOS – Open Source Compliance for Businesses"; available at www.validos.org/ (accessed 26 February 2012).

WCED (1987) *Our Common Future*, Oxford: Oxford University Press.

10

Adoption and diffusion patterns of FOSS in Jamaican SMEs: A study of perceptions, attitudes and barriers

Maurice McNaughton, Sheryl Thompson and Evan W. Duggan

Introduction

As far as developing countries are concerned, over the last decade two trends have been highlighted as conduits for economic growth and development: the expanding use of information and communication technology (ICT), and the survival and competitiveness of small and medium-sized enterprises (SMEs). With the onset of the knowledge economy, where economic growth is increasingly dependent on a country's capacity to create, process, accumulate and disseminate knowledge, together with the accelerated pace of globalization, companies that are slow to adopt ICT as an integral part of their business operations and capabilities, or adapt to the increased competitive dynamics and complexity of the way modern business is conducted, will find it difficult to survive. Newer technologies, especially the internet with its ubiquitous character, have resulted in easier access to and lower costs of ICT. As such, information and communications technologies for development (ICT4D) have been widely touted as a means to accelerate development in countries and competitiveness in organizations, in particular SMEs.

Micro, small and medium-sized enterprises (mSMEs) are considered to be one of the main forces in economic growth and job creation, not only in developed countries but also in emerging economies and economies in transition (OECD, 2004). In the UK SMEs account for 99.9 per cent of all enterprises, 59.1 per cent of private sector employment and 48.6 per cent of private sector turnover (BIS, 2010). Globally, close to 140 million

Free and open source software and technology for sustainable development, Sowe, Parayil and Sunami (eds), United Nations University Press, 2012, ISBN 978-92-808-1217-6

SMEs in 130 countries account for 65 per cent of the total labour force (Kotelnikov, 2007). In the case of Jamaica, a small island state of 2.6 million inhabitants, it is estimated that micro-enterprises operating in the formal and informal sectors account for approximately 40 per cent of the country's GDP (gross domestic product) and collectively provide over 80 per cent of employment opportunities. Furthermore, the impact of SMEs in the domestic economy goes well beyond employment and GDP, and contributes substantially to the production and distribution of goods and services and the enhancement of innovation, productivity and competitiveness (Witter and Kirton, 1990).

Given the importance of SMEs to the country's domestic economy, there is considerable interest in facilitating the progressive adoption and use of ICT by Jamaican SMEs, ranging from basic telecommunications facilities to the use of advanced information technologies such as enterprise resource planning (ERP), customer relationship management (CRM) and e-commerce business applications. ICT can play a significant role in helping SMEs to improve their operating performance and business competitiveness. But despite the obvious benefits and competitive imperative of adopting ICT, research has shown that SMEs in many developing countries have been slow to use it (Kotelnikov, 2007). In the most recent landscape survey of the mSME sector in Jamaica, the adoption rates of basic ICT such as computers, fax machines and mobile cellular were moderate to low, while the use of the web and e-commerce for online selling was miniscule (Commosioung, Satchell and Waller, 2008).

Perhaps more telling were some of the explanations offered by several SME respondents for their limited use of e-commerce and other modern ICT. These included the lack of importance of online sales, the belief that they cannot afford to sell their goods and services online and the presumption that online selling is not for small businesses. Other perceived barriers to ICT adoption by SMEs include excessive access costs and inappropriate ICT solutions that do not fit the business needs of the organization. These issues relating to cost of access and lack of fit are not only relevant to individual organizations but also to developing economies at the aggregate level.

Free and open source software (FOSS) is increasingly being recognized as the means by which developing countries can expand their use of ICT without the need for huge capital expenditure. There is growing evidence that countries in the Latin American and Caribbean regions such as Cuba, Venezuela and Brazil have used FOSS as a catalyst for the wider diffusion of ICT (Sojo, 2004; McNaughton, 2010). The rapid growth and development of open source communities over the past decade have resulted in a number of innovations that have become increasingly relevant to business enterprise. Further, as these open source communities stabilize and streamline their software production methods and business models, this leads to more mature technology products that can be readily adopted and incorporated into business processes and operations. FOSS is particularly relevant to smaller companies that are lagging behind in ICT adoption. Despite growing evidence of significant adoption trends at the enterprise level (Forrester Consulting, 2007) and national adoption initiatives at the macro level, there is still a significant barrier in the use of FOSS by SMEs. Unfortunately there is a paucity of research examining FOSS and its implementation at the individual firm level, and certainly none of which the authors are aware regarding the adoption patterns of FOSS among Jamaican SMEs.

This chapter describes an empirical study of adoption and use patterns of ICT in general, and FOSS in particular, among a group of SMEs in Jamaica. The study used a survey and a series of facilitated workshops with a sample of 65 SMEs to gather evidence of current ICT adoption and usage patterns within these organizations and provide an informed basis for the role of an intermediary to improve the adoption rate and effectiveness of these technologies. In addition to demographic characteristics of the organizations examined, the survey captured general information about the ICT environment, business owners' attitudes towards the use of ICT and general awareness of FOSS and hosted service models.

The next section reviews salient literature relating to ICT adoption in developing countries that influenced the design of the survey. The following sections describe the research methodology and provide a detailed analysis and interpretation of the survey findings, augmented by qualitative feedback from the facilitated workshops. Together, the outcomes form the basis for a more informed framing and articulation of the challenges faced by the Jamaican SME sector in realizing ICT-enabled business innovation, particularly through the use of FOSS. Informed by these findings, a solution framework for the implementation of FOSS applications in SMEs is prescribed, incorporating a series of ICT artefacts and implementation approaches. The concluding sections offer insights and implications for practice derived from select implementation case studies used to evaluate the prescribed FOSS solutions framework.

Prior empirical evidence suggests that for Jamaican SMEs, external change agents play a vital role in the ICT adoption process by disseminating knowledge and mitigating some of the associated risk (Thompson and Brown, 2008). Against this background, and the recognition that ICT is an important driver of the development and growth of SMEs, the outcomes from this research become relevant to both practitioners and policy-makers interested in facilitating practical implementation of FOSS in public and private sectors in developing countries.

Background

The drive for increased adoption and use of ICT in developing countries is embedded in the thesis that ICT could help these countries leapfrog stages of development experienced by developed nations (Steinmuller, 2001). More specifically, it has been theorized that ICT provides the opportunity to enhance economic growth by making other sectors of the economy more efficient and aid capital accumulation, and an ICT industry may be used as a vehicle to boost investment (Jalava and Pohjola, 2001). This discourse concerning the role of ICT in development has been long debated (Avgerou, 2000; Mansell, 1998; Brynjolfsson and Hitt, 2003); however, as far as Walsham and Sahay (2006) are concerned the issue is to identify *how* ICT can be beneficial in a particular context, rather than the more hypothetical question of *whether* it can be beneficial. Various empirical studies have highlighted the impact of ICT on economic variables. Jorgenson, Ho and Stiroh (2005) examined the ICT sector and measured its productivity gains with GDP and found a strong causal relationship, and also that the greater the size of the sector producing ICT goods and services, the larger the positive impact of ICT on growth. Similarly, UNCTAD's (2006) study of the impact of ICT at the macro level in developing countries confirmed that ICT adoption can make an important and positive contribution to GDP even in poorer countries. Moreover, it was found that ICT helped organizations to reinvent their products, increase market share and integrate activities throughout the value chain (OECD, 2003).

Free and open source software adoption

One category of information systems and technology that has been touted as being particularly relevant to ICT4D and developing economies is FOSS (UNCTAD, 2004; Camara and Fonseca, 2007). In 2005 Brazil joined forces with the UN Conference on Trade and Development (UNCTAD) to promote the use of FOSS in developing nations after having mandated its use by government institutions as a part of its strategy within the ambit of its national ICT policy. The argument for developing countries to promote the use of FOSS at both macro and micro levels is compelling. FOSS is considered to be an important conduit for open access to knowledge and innovation necessary for effective participation in the knowledge society. Its uniqueness in being both a technology and a product means that at the macro level governments can focus on building capability and capacity to foster the wider diffusion and adoption of ICT while creating new business opportunities at the micro level.

The opportunity to use, adopt and customize FOSS can be beneficial to organizations, especially SMEs, once the developmental, practical and operational perspectives are understood. According to Camara and Fonseca (ibid.), "open source software should be used to gain knowledge about the technology itself and as a way of creating technology products that fit the specific needs of developing countries". The notion is also applicable at the organizational level, since utilizing FOSS can enable a company to implement software that fits its business needs, culture and practices. This eliminates the often-prohibitive costs for customization faced by organizations when adopting proprietary software – an issue that is particularly important in the case of SMEs, since cost is usually cited as one of the barriers to their adoption of ICT.

Determinants of ICT adoption in SMEs

Research focusing on ICT adoption by SMEs has consistently identified certain factors that act as barriers, on the premise that the characteristics of small firms differ from those of their larger counterparts. The factors affecting the adoption and use of ICT in large organizations would not necessarily be the same as those that affect SMEs. Consequently, theories that explain adoption in large organizations may not be applicable to small businesses. Small firms in comparison to larger firms require different managerial approaches, since there are fundamental differences between the two. Kotelnikov (2007) identified supply-side issues such as poor communications infrastructure, excessive access costs and inappropriate ICT solutions designed for larger firms and not SMEs as deterrents to the adoption of ICT by SMEs. Additionally, demand-side challenges including limited ICT literacy and awareness of SME owners and employees, cost of acquisition of technology, lack of suitable financing options and lack of the business analytic skills and absorptive capacity to deploy ICT-enabled solutions effectively were also identified. In general, it is not a trivial decision for any organization to adopt ICT; there are numerous factors to consider when ICT is being contemplated. This is especially so in the case of SMEs, since there is often a lack of financial and human resources which contributes to weakness in terms of financing, planning, control, training and information systems (Blili and Raymond, 1993; Thong and Yap, 1995).

Several factors, including characteristics of the firm, the orientation of the chief executive officer (CEO) and type of industry, have been deemed to be influential in the ICT adoption decision of small businesses. Among SMEs there is a higher probability that larger organizations will have a greater propensity to adopt ICT than smaller ones (Thong, 1999). Constraints on financial resources and the lack of in-house IT expertise increase the level of risk that an investment in ICT represents to smaller companies (Blili and Raymond, 1993; Dandridge, 1979; Fink, 1998; Thong, 1999). Similarly, individual characteristics of CEOs as well as their attitude to ICT, innovation and level of ICT knowledge are strong determinants of adoption because they are the main decision-makers in the organization (Cragg and King, 1993; Thong, 1999; Thong and Yap, 1995). SMEs led by CEOs with positive dispositions towards ICT arc more likely to adopt, particularly because of their perception that ICT which is compatible with their operations and comparatively easy to use will be beneficial. SMEs within certain industries have also been quicker to adopt and integrate the internet in business operations. Firms in the IT industry and those from other industries with CEOs who are "IT aware" tend to be more embracing of new and more complex technologies compared to their IT-naïve peers (Cragg and King, 1993; DeLone, 1988).

MSME landscape in Jamaica

More specific to the Jamaican business context, a national study of the mSME landscape (Commosioung, Satchell and Waller, 2008) provided estimates of the sector, broken down by categories (Figure 10.1). The sector is clearly dominated by micro-enterprises and wholesale/retail trading activities. When asked to identify the critical resource constraints on business growth and competitiveness, the majority (72 per cent) pointed to financial capital as the primary requirement. Only 18 per cent identified ICT as a potential enabler of business expansion or innovation, and many still see ICT expenditure as diverting limited resources away from critical development needs. Not surprisingly, the incidence of ICT use in business determined in the study increases with the larger, more formal enterprises.

Role of intermediaries

The studies discussed so far all focused on the user or organization perspective of technology adoption. Brown and Lockett (2004) are among the few researchers to have conducted empirical investigations into ICT adoption by SMEs from the perspective of provider involvement. One important finding was that intermediaries play a crucial role in the adoption of complex applications by SMEs, and the provision of aggregation-specific e-applications to SMEs as a group rather than individually will encourage their engagement in e-business, for example. The concepts of aggregation and trusted third parties within the framework of networks were essential to engagement in e-business by SMEs examined by Brown and Lockett (ibid.). The findings suggest that strategically placed community intermediaries are important to clusters of SMEs with regard to

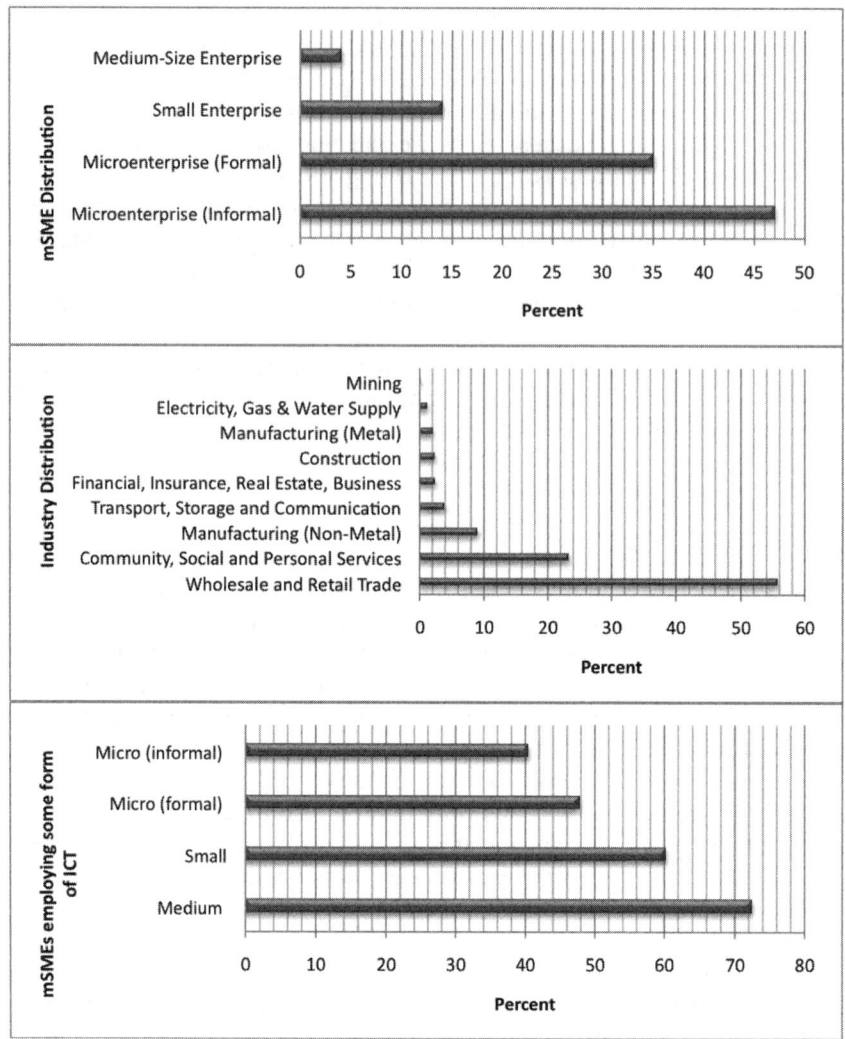

Figure 10.1 MSME landscape in Jamaica
Source: Adapted from Commosioung, Satchell and Waller (2008).

the adoption of complex e-business. The facilitative role of these intermediaries as trusted third parties assures potential adopters that there is likely to be sufficient support to maintain the application, thereby eliminating issues regarding lack of in-house competence or additional financial costs. Further, the intermediaries can act as change agents to assist in garnering a critical mass of users within clusters, and this can positively affect the rate of adoption among SMEs. According to Thompson and

Brown (2008), change agents perform integral roles in the ICT adoption process, specifically internet technologies, by SMEs in developing countries, including knowledge dissemination, financial partnership, technical advice and solution provision.

The scope of these studies highlights both the value opportunities and many of the constraining factors that impact SMEs and their adoption of ICTs. But the reality is that SMEs are still cautious when it comes to implementing ICT. Some evidence of this in the Jamaican context comes from Commosioung, Satchell and Waller's (2008) study, which cited the lack of importance Jamaican SMEs placed on online selling. This indifference, which negatively affected the propensity of SMEs to adopt internet technologies, is rooted in the perception that they cannot afford to sell goods and services online, and online selling is not for small businesses. The reticence towards internet technology is particularly troubling, since the advent of the internet was seen as a way to reduce the gap between large and small companies in ICT adoption. "The Internet and e-commerce have enabled small companies to become an increasingly powerful driving force in the emerging global marketplace, creating new jobs and spurring innovation and economic development all over the world" (da Costa, 2001: 3). The internet, especially internet-enabled cloud computing services and delivery mechanisms, provides new opportunities for SMEs to adopt ICT and presents a more accessible means for companies to collaborate with both suppliers and customers than older technologies like legacy electronic data interchange information systems. Apart from the opportunities to form new alliances and expand into new products and services, effective adoption and use of the internet enable a small business to extend its reach globally, rather than being confined to a specific geography with restricted market size and limited competitive scope.

Methodology and data collection

Design science research

Design science research was adopted as the methodological framework for this study because it offers a rigorous but pragmatic investigative approach in the real-world domain of ICT adoption and utilization. According to the prescriptive guidelines offered by Hevner et al. (2004), design science research is motivated by problem solving and geared towards the building, evaluation and application of innovative, purposeful ICT artefacts that can address practical business needs. Table 10.1 summarizes how their seven guidelines are addressed in this research; the activities are described throughout the remainder of this chapter.

Table 10.1 Design science research guidelines – Activity mapping

Guideline	Description	Relevant research activities
1 Design as an artefact	Design science research must produce a viable artefact in the form of a construct, a model, a method or an instance	Artefacts derived from this study include a portfolio of maturity-certified FOSS business applications and prescriptive implementation methods
2 Problem relevance	The objective of design science research is to develop technology-based solutions to important and relevant business problems	Importance and relevance of effective ICT adoption and use among SMEs have been well established
3 Design evaluation	Utility, quality and efficacy of a design artefact must be rigorously demonstrated via well-executed evaluation methods	Evaluation of the proposed solutions and implementation methods is done through select case studies
4 Research contribution	Effective design science must provide clear and verifiable contributions in the design artefact, design foundations and/or design methodologies	Implications and contributions of this research are articulated in this chapter
5 Research rigour	Design science research relies upon application of rigorous methods in both construction and evaluation of the design artefact	For FOSS components examined, the rigour derives from the maturity assessment and certification process
6 Design as a search process	The search for an effective artefact requires using available means to reach desired ends while satisfying laws in the problem environment	Both the scanning of open source repositories and the iterative prototyping implementation approaches prescribed represent useful proxies for "design as a search process"
7 Communication of research	Design science research must be presented effectively to both technology-oriented and management-oriented audiences	This chapter is the first of several mechanisms to communicate the research findings to practitioner and academic communities

Source: Adapted from Hevner et al. (2004).

This research project used a combination of quantitative and qualitative methods over three distinct phases.

In Phase 1 a survey was undertaken to gather data to provide an empirical basis for a clear definition and articulation of the challenges faced by the Jamaican SME constituency in realizing ICT-enabled business innovation. This facilitated the specification, development and evaluation of a series of ICT artefacts that offer prescriptive solution approaches based on FOSS. A series of workshops were also conducted with selected survey respondents during this phase, to provide a more qualitative interaction with the business owners, validate issues arising and findings from the survey and explore in greater depth factors that constrain the adoption of ICT or facilitate greater awareness of and exposure to potential FOSS solutions for their businesses.

Phase 2 involved establishing a general-purpose, component-based application portfolio to provide a variety of horizontal and vertical[1] FOSS solutions for SMEs. This consisted of a suite of FOSS applications that were subjected to a structured maturity assessment process, and validated through a series of facilitated workshops where participating SMEs were exposed to the FOSS solutions and their utility in addressing common business problems. In Phase 3 several case studies were undertaken to provide contextual and in-depth information about the implementation of these ICT-enabled business innovations for a number of candidate organizations in order to evaluate and develop prescriptive implementation methodologies which would enable repeatable dissemination of the solutions to the wider business community. Candidates for the case studies were drawn from survey respondents and workshop participants.

The three phases of the study can be loosely mapped on to the design science research methodology recommended by Hevner et al. (ibid.), as shown in Figure 10.2.

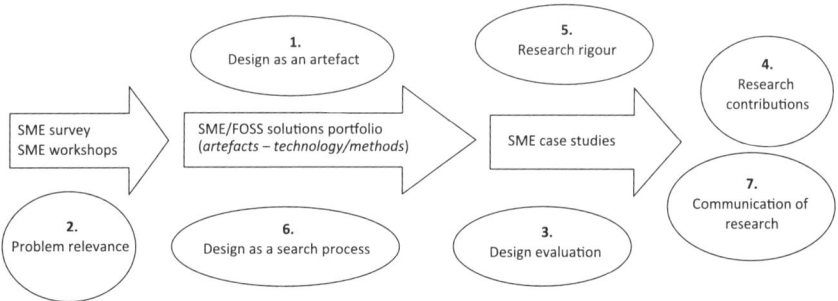

Figure 10.2 Research phases using design science research methodology

Survey design

In general, the survey set out to capture information on a cross-section of companies in the SME sector in order to identify and understand ICT use, level of awareness, attitudes and adoption patterns among Jamaican SMEs towards FOSS, as well as existing enablers or barriers to adoption. The survey was designed to capture the following blocks of information:
- general information about ICT environment – adoption, sources and patterns of use
- attitude towards ICT use in business
- awareness of FOSS and hosted service models
- organization demographics.

There is typically a low response rate by SMEs to surveys of this nature, as seen in the survey of the Jamaican SME sector conducted by Commosioung, Satchell and Waller (2008) through a joint initiative of the government of Jamaica and the European Union. The researchers noted that "in many instances, data collectors were unable to meet their quota as enterprise managers and owners refused to participate in the survey", for two primary reasons. The first was a *lack of trust* regarding the intention of the survey. Many business owners and managers were inherently distrustful of initiatives associated with "government" and fearful that the real agenda behind the survey was either a tax audit or a way to inform and/or expand future tax-related initiatives. The second reason was *apathy*. Some business owners and managers complained they had participated in similar surveys in the past and "nothing has come from them", so they considered it "time consuming" and a "waste of time" to participate in any further government-led survey of entrepreneurship or enterprise/business development in Jamaica.

In an effort to mitigate this propensity to non-responsiveness, researchers wrote to the target organizations, introducing the overall research programme being carried out by the Mona School of Business with the goal of facilitating SME business innovation through ICT, and the purpose of the survey towards those ends. A team of undergraduate marketing students was used to call the target respondents to brief them further on the purpose of the survey and articulate the value proposition to their organizations. The survey was pre-tested and validated with a small number of organizations and knowledgeable business people before being issued to these SMEs and administered through one of three modes to give flexibility in responding. Respondents could choose an online web-based questionnaire if they had easy access to the internet; a self-administered paper questionnaire completed and returned via mail or fax; or an interviewer-administered questionnaire completed via telephone.

To get meaningful results, it was desirable to find a sample of between 60 and 100 small businesses that were willing to respond to the survey and participate in the subsequent workshops. The grant-funded research budgeted for up to four workshops of 20–25 participants each. The sampling frame for the survey was drawn from the membership database of the Small Business Association of Jamaica (SBAJ). While there are several representative bodies covering the mSME sector in Jamaica, the SBAJ, formed in 1974 and with a registered membership of 568 organizations, is one of the more well-established and long-standing institutions. Its membership database at the time of the study, when validated and verified, yielded 230 contactable companies.

Overall there were 65 responses to the survey, which was satisfactory for the research purpose – especially given the characteristics of the respondents (Figure 10.3). Survey respondents were predominantly businesses at the upper end of the SME category as defined by the SBAJ and the Statistical Institute of Jamaica: 46 per cent of the sample were in the 11–50 employee category, with 43 per cent having more than 50 employees. Forty-two per cent of respondents were in the manufacturing sector, 20 per cent in wholesale/retail trading and 12 per cent in financial services. The maturity profile of the companies was relatively high, with 16 per cent in business for less than 10 years, 29 per cent between 10 and 20 years and the rest having operated for more than 20 years. It should be noted that these characteristics are not generally representative of the overall SME sector in Jamaica, which is heavily skewed towards the formal/informal micro sector (<5 employees) and dominated by wholesale/retail trading activities (ibid.).

The geographic coverage of the sample in terms of the parishes[2] in which the businesses operate showed the traditional commercial loci of Kingston, St James (Montego Bay), St Ann (Ocho Rios) and St Catherine dominating, with some representation in all other parishes. Companies were categorized as multi-location if they had business operations in three or more parishes – 23 per cent of respondents fell in this category. The orientation of the survey sample towards more mature, formal and medium-sized enterprises is a combined manifestation of the SBAJ's registered membership, which provided the sampling frame, and a degree of self-selection bias by respondents who chose to participate. In any event it suits the purpose of this research, because these companies appear to have the business scope, scale and intent for which appropriate ICT intervention is likely to provide a significant value proposition.

Another interesting characteristic of the sample was that CEOs or other senior executives accounted for 64 per cent of the individual respondents. This was taken as a signal of seriousness of intent, as surveys of this nature are typically delegated to IT or other administrative

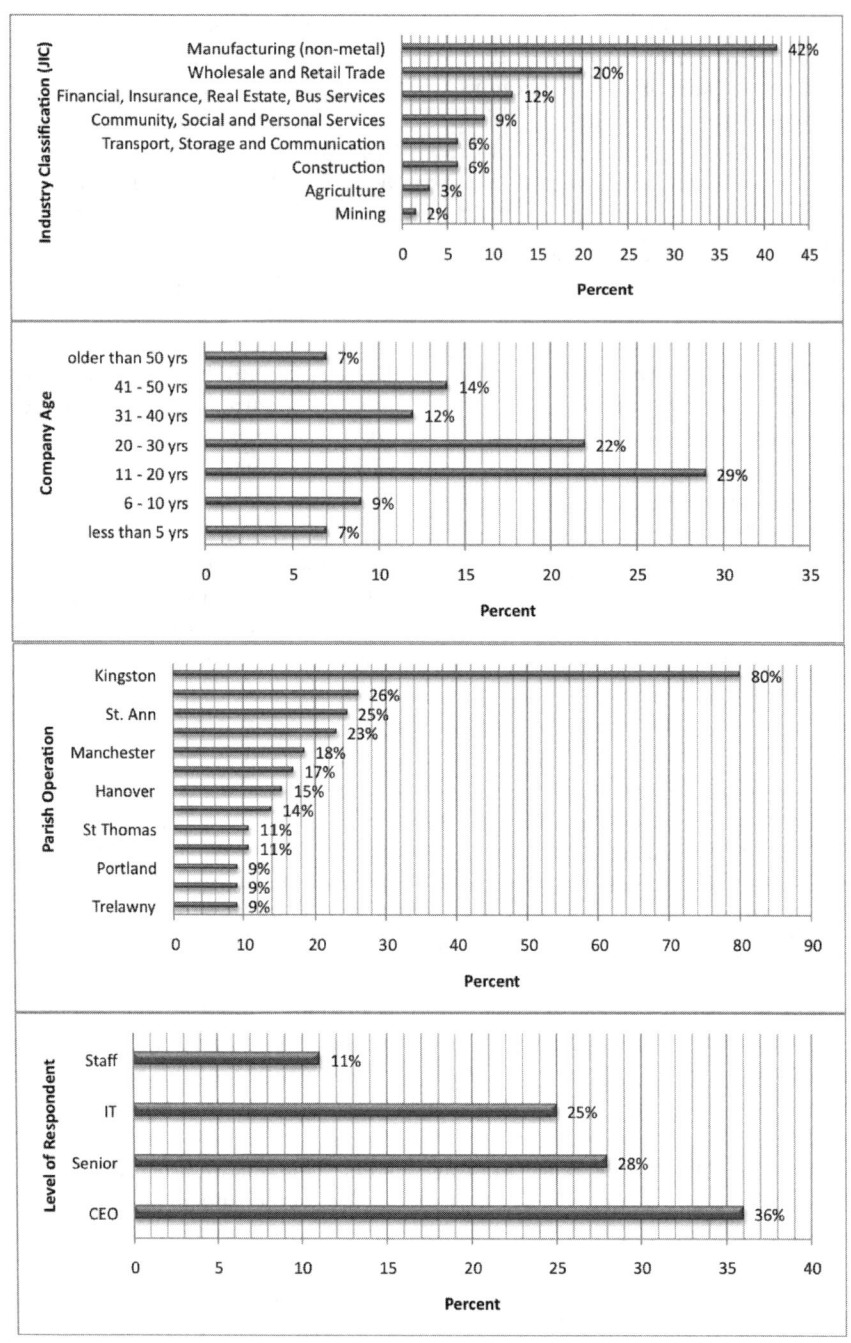

Figure 10.3 Sample characteristics

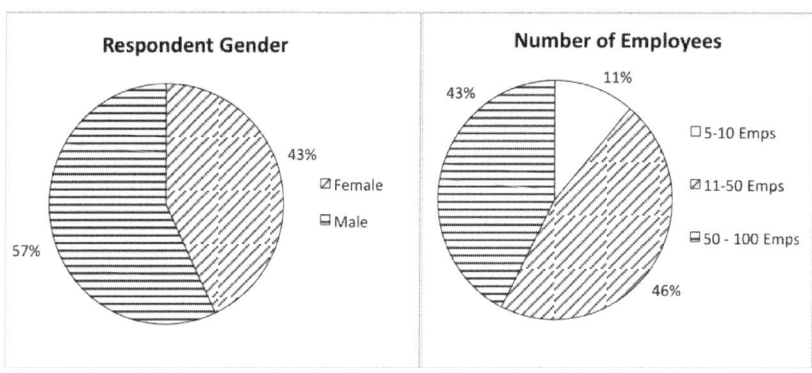

Figure 10.3 (cont.)

personnel. Colleagues researching the characteristics of women-owned businesses in Jamaica would be interested in the inferences to be drawn from the fact that not only were 43 per cent of the respondents female, but 72 per cent of these were the CEO or a senior executive, compared to 58 per cent for male respondents. As noted by Cragg and King (1993), the attitudes of CEOs to ICT and innovation are important determinants of adoption.

Findings and discussion

The results and findings reported here are based on exploratory analysis of the data derived from the survey responses.

General information about ICT environment

The majority of respondents (>90 per cent) had broadband internet access, which is consistent with the robustness and high penetration of telecommunications infrastructure in Jamaica. There was rather less evidence of internal company-wide ICT infrastructure, such as wide area networks (23 per cent) and intranets (26 per cent). Almost all respondents use the internet for communication (e-mail) and 55 per cent had some form of web presence. The use of e-commerce for online sale of goods and services was relatively low at 15 per cent, although 42 per cent of companies would use the internet for the procurement of goods and services from other parties (Figure 10.4).

The study sought to determine what types of information system applications were being used for common business functions such as

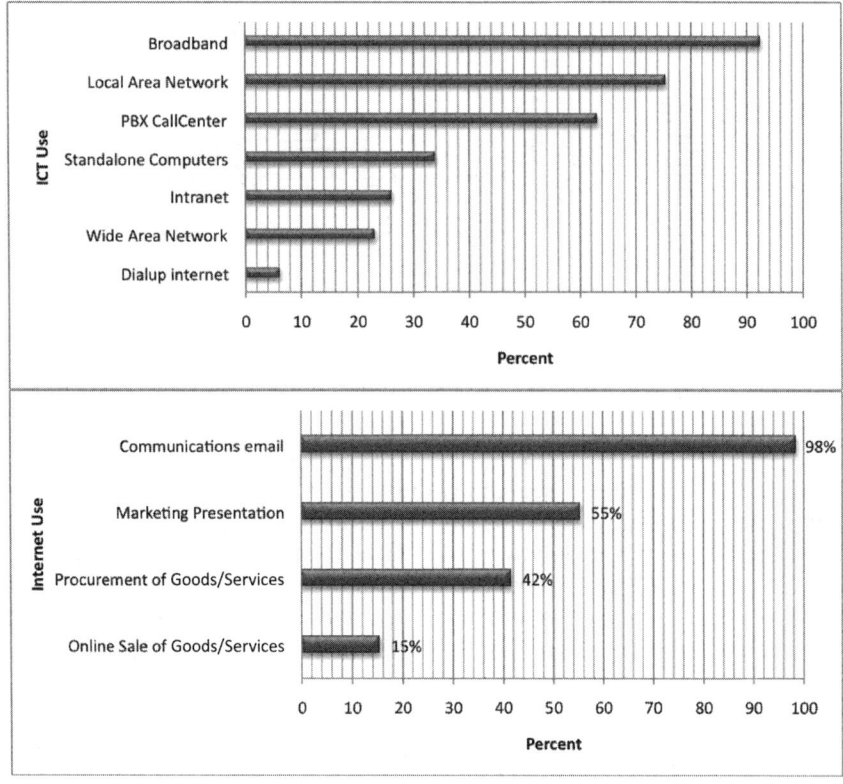

Figure 10.4 Use of ICT and the internet

accounting, payroll and office productivity (Figure 10.5). The business applications currently in use appear to follow what might be considered the typical implementation trajectory of *accounting → payroll → inventory management*, with very limited deployment of more advanced enterprise-level software such as ERP and CRM systems. FOSS was relatively limited to use for office productivity applications such as word processing. In rating factors that influenced their acquisition of ICT, businesses ranked the top three as enabling business innovation, price and after-sales support. Brand name was the least significant factor.

Attitudes towards ICT use in business

Respondents were asked to rank their primary expectations of ICT use in their businesses and the main constraints affecting adoption (Figure 10.6). The top three drivers were improved efficiency of work

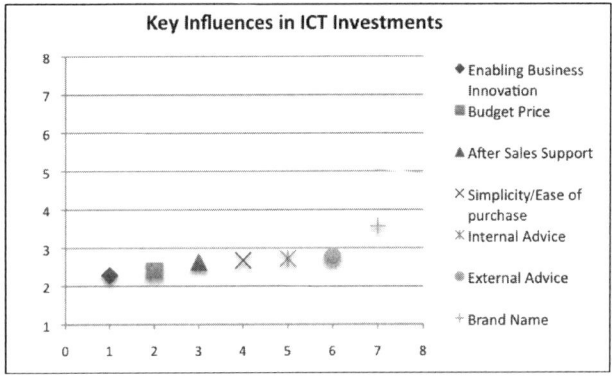

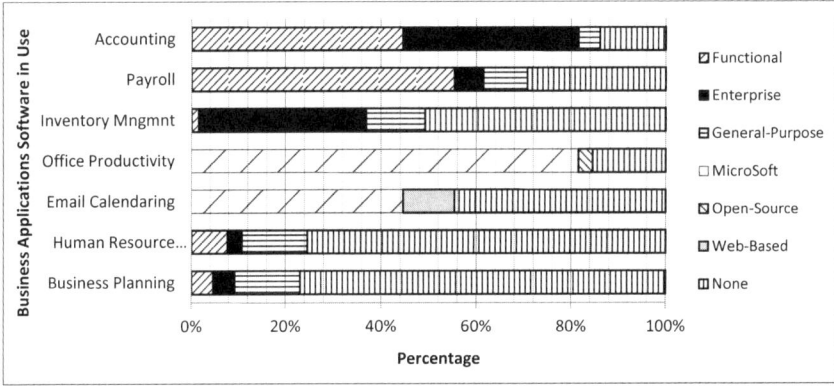

Figure 10.5 Business applications and key influences

processes, improved management information/decision support and improved responsiveness to customers. These might be considered first-order benefits of ICT versus the more transformational second-order impacts, such as improved product quality or the introduction of new goods and services. In terms of the primary constraints to ICT adoption, the costs of acquisition of software and hardware were the dominant factors, consistent with the conventional challenges typically associated with SMEs. However, respondents also ranked "availability of training" and "expertise to maintain systems" as being significant barriers.

Awareness of FOSS and hosted service models

The study also assessed the extent of awareness, perception and/or use of FOSS in these businesses (Figure 10.7). Only 43 per cent of respondents

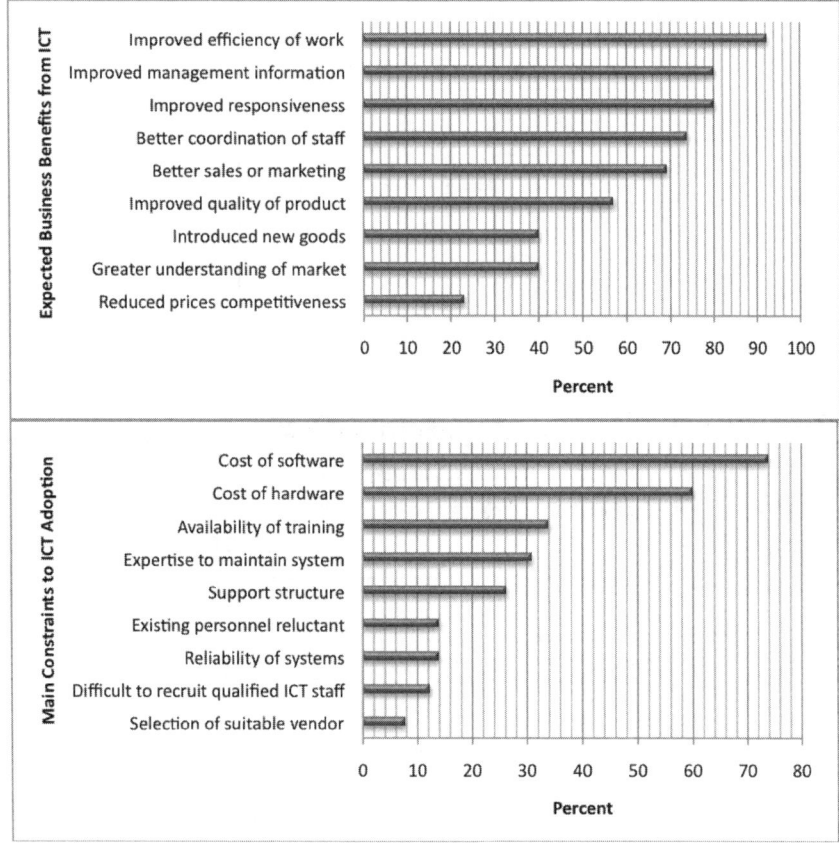

Figure 10.6 Main determinants of ICT adoption

were familiar with the term "free and open source software". Interestingly, 69 per cent were familiar with Firefox and 49 per cent with Linux, which suggested that, for some respondents, the use and/or awareness of these applications was based more on utility rather than on their association with FOSS.

In attempting to elicit the respondents' perception of FOSS, the most common associations were *low cost, unsupported, unfamiliar* and *risky*. This reflected some common perceptions about FOSS and shows there is considerable scope for greater education and awareness about the potential benefits and opportunities available through use of FOSS business applications in SMEs.

Finally, the familiarity of respondents with hosted information system service delivery models such as cloud computing, software as a service

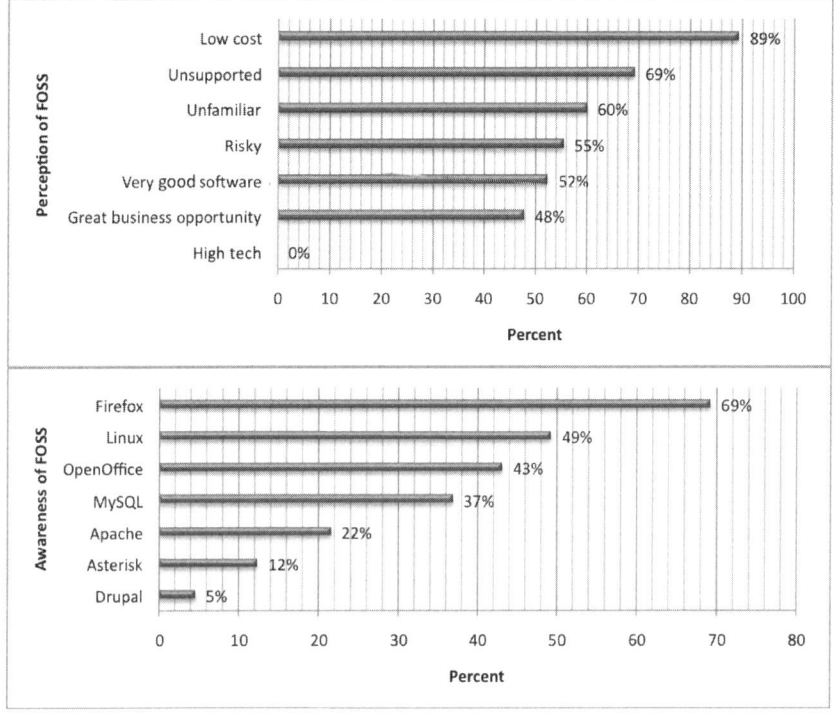

Figure 10.7 Awareness and perceptions of FOSS

and applications service provider was assessed (Figure 10.8). The analysis indicated the respondents' limited awareness or knowledge of these service delivery options. Of greater significance, when presented with the notion of outsourcing their business applications to a trusted service provider, less than 30 per cent of respondents were receptive. Given the importance of the hosted model as a viable means for SMEs to access and use modern business information systems, these responses and apparent perceptions were examined in greater depth during the qualitative workshops.

Qualitative workshops

The quantitative survey was supplemented with a series of facilitated one-day workshops attended by 35 survey respondents. These gave an opportunity to gather more qualitative and in-depth information on the issues uncovered through the survey, expose and orient business users to a selected range of FOSS solutions with potential applicability for their

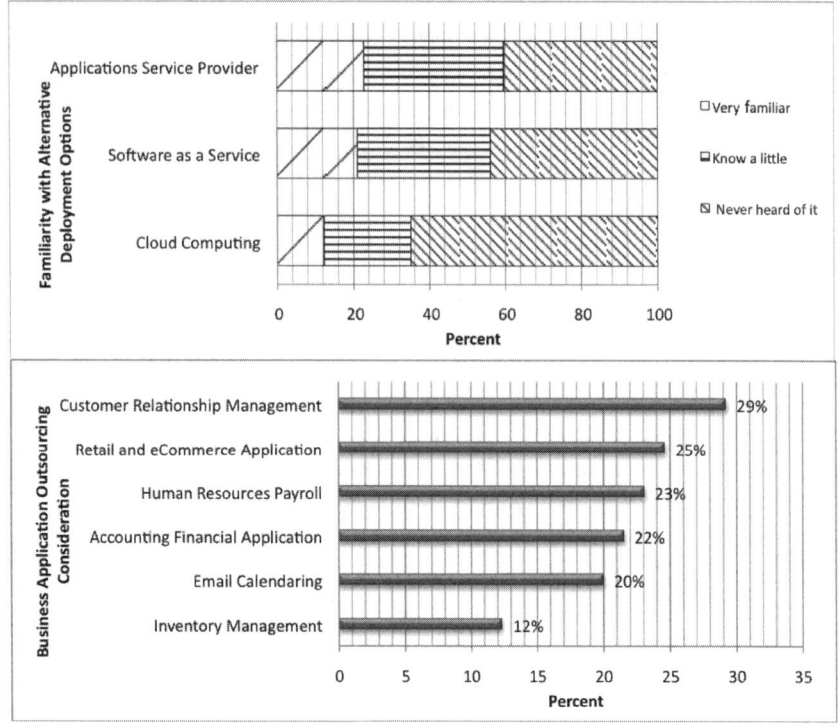

Figure 10.8 Hosted information system service option

businesses and identify prospective candidates for participation in the case studies in the next phase.

Together with the findings from the survey, these workshops yielded several key considerations to support the role of an intermediary to facilitate the effective adoption of ICT in general and FOSS specifically by SMEs in Jamaica. In the first instance they reinforced the notion that the opportunities for implementing and leveraging business value from FOSS-based ICT are quite significant. Due to the robustness of the telecommunications infrastructure in Jamaica, SMEs are generally well positioned to use the internet as a vehicle for access to and delivery of a range of business software and services. Most businesses surveyed appeared somewhat reluctant to consider this delivery model for core applications such as financial and accounting information systems, even in cases where no formal ICT solutions existed. However, business owners were generally much more receptive to the more advanced applications such as human resource management, CRM, sales order management, collaborative tools and e-commerce. This was consistent with the primary business expectations from ICT: improved efficiency and productivity (collaborative tools); improved management information and decision support (CRM/collaborative tools); improved responsiveness to customers (CRM); better coordination of staff and business activities (human resource management/collaborative tools); and sales/marketing (sales order/CRM). Sourcing mature FOSS business applications in these domains appeared to be the most viable strategy for encouraging ICT adoption and use by SMEs.

A facilitated ICT service delivery business model anchored in FOSS is also well positioned to address the primary constraints to adoption expressed by business owners. The much lower acquisition cost of FOSS relative to comparable proprietary software, as well as the opportunities for internet-enabled hosted service delivery models, can significantly mitigate the cost-related barriers to software and hardware acquisition. However, to be effective these approaches must be accompanied by a deliberately structured programme of training, relevant FOSS expertise and pre- and post-implementation support capabilities.

Arising from the workshop discussions, business owners generally expressed scepticism about the availability of effective training, technical expertise to implement and maintain systems and a structured support mechanism. Although many of these concerns arose from prior experience with the implementation of either packaged or bespoke developed solutions, they nevertheless led to a strong perception that adopting FOSS-based solutions had inherent risks that made them susceptible to similar support deficiencies. This sentiment was echoed when discussing hosted solutions such as software as a service or cloud computing. Several workshop participants expressed a strong view that they were only amenable to hosted solutions for business applications if these were delivered by trusted, known intermediaries rather than anonymous third-party providers, even if these were well-established services entities such as Amazon.com's EC2 or Rackspace.

Given these considerations, it was determined that an effective intermediary role to facilitate FOSS adoption among Jamaican SMEs would require several key elements.

- Ensuring awareness and education of business owners and decision-makers about the value proposition and opportunities presented by FOSS business applications.
- Establishing a structured programme for the ongoing maturity assessment and certification of FOSS business applications that are suitable for production deployment.
- Implementing a flexible technical environment that facilitates the staging, demonstration and large-grained prototyping of FOSS business applications for small business owners and decision-makers.

- Providing customized, on-demand training options for targeted end users of FOSS business applications.

SME FOSS business solution portfolio

This section describes a series of ICT artefacts that were developed specifically to respond to the challenges and requirements that emerged from the survey and workshops, in order to enable the creation of an intermediary role that could facilitate the effective adoption and utilization of FOSS business applications by Jamaican SMEs. This is in keeping with the design science framing of this research, which Hevner et al. (2004) characterize as a problem-solving paradigm that seeks to create innovations for defining *ideas, practices, technical capabilities* and *products* through which the analysis, design, implementation and use of the information system can be effectively achieved.

Open source laboratory

An important requirement established early on was the creation of a technology environment that would facilitate the ongoing maturity assessment and certification of FOSS business applications suitable for production deployment. This environment would also enable the staging, demonstration and large-grained prototyping of these applications for small business owners and decision-makers. Unlike commercial off-the-shelf applications, FOSS puts considerable responsibility on adopting organizations to search for an effective artefact, determine its suitability and mitigate business adoption risk. This is an important role for the facilitating intermediary.

To meet this requirement, a flexible technology environment was developed with the capability to define and configure multiple virtual guest operating systems that could deploy standard open source stacks on demand (e.g. LAMP[3]). This gave the ability to create and test development instances rapidly for various FOSS business applications that could be evaluated and demonstrated to clients. The technical characteristics of this environment included the use of a VMWare virtualization platform and thin-client workstations. An important feature was the ability to package a specific test configuration instance for deployment to a hosted production instance in the cloud.

Use of this laboratory environment enabled the evaluation and specification of a portfolio of FOSS business applications that provided viable solutions to the SME business requirements identified. This portfolio

FOSS IN JAMAICAN SMES 233

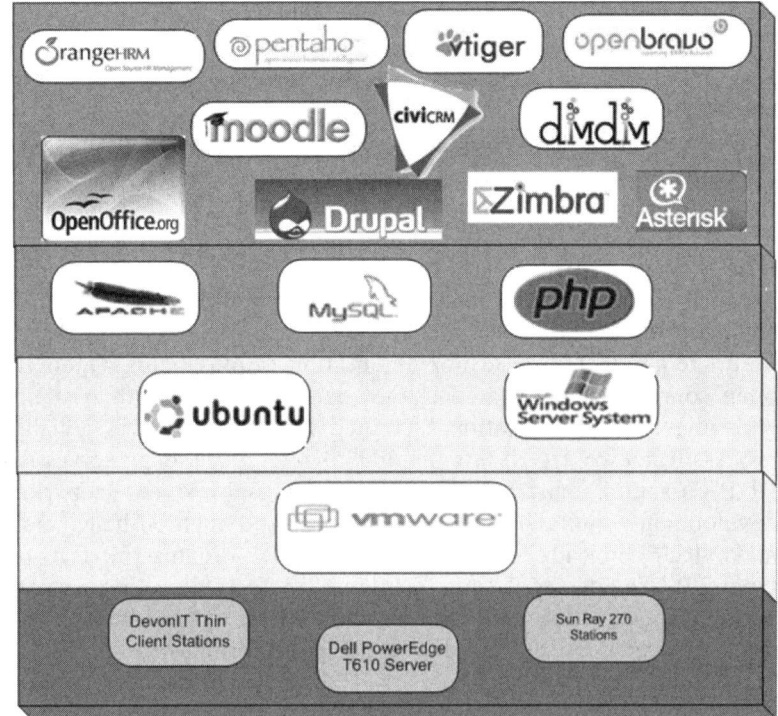

Figure 10.9 SME FOSS business solutions

(Figure 10.9) can be characterized as the outcome of an iterative "design as a search process" that involved the scanning of open source repositories such as SourceForge.Net and use of an open source maturity model for assessment and certification, as prescribed by Golden (2005). The model was designed to enable organizations to evaluate various dimensions of open source products, including software attributes, capabilities of the support community and availability of support services and resources. This helps to determine whether a specific product can fulfil an organization's requirements.

A hybrid adaptation of agile and component-based methodologies

Several implementation case studies of open source business applications were undertaken for SME participants selected from the survey and workshops. These studies were used as a basis for developing and validating effective implementation approaches that could become prescriptive and repeatable solution delivery methods. Ongoing interactions with the small business owners and decision-makers suggested that an effective, facilitated approach needed to have the following characteristics:

- active involvement of the key business owners/decision-makers within the organization
- a lean and method-light delivery process, with liberal use of application demonstration and solution prototyping
- an incremental approach to delivering the application functionality which allowed for frequent business interactions and feedback.

Open Unified Process (OpenUP) provided a suitable match and very useful template for these implementation requirements. OpenUP is an open source product that packages agile principles with best practices and guidelines from Rational Unified Process (RUP) in a lightweight process framework (Gustafsson, 2008; Kroll, 2007). It preserves many of RUP's essential characteristics of iterative, use-case and scenario-driven development, but avoids the complexity and method-heaviness which make RUP typically inaccessible for smaller organizations. In essence, OpenUP provides tools and resources to facilitate a pragmatic, agile, minimalist approach emphasizing stakeholder engagement and understanding over unproductive deliverables and formalisms.

Another important attribute of RUP that is especially applicable to implementation of open source in SMEs is the principle of component-based software engineering (CBSE), whereby the business solution is assembled from independently deployable and reusable components. Open source applications that typically provide industry-standard interfaces for integration with other business applications can be managed as large-grained components and hence are amenable to the best practice guidelines of CBSE. An important differentiator for open source is the ability to adapt these discrete large-grained components to individual requirements, which provides a greater degree of flexibility than is typically associated with traditional commercial off-the-shelf software. This latter characteristic turns out to be an extremely important and powerful attribute of open source software. In the case studies, a specific FOSS business application (vTigerCRM) was adapted to suit three very different SME contexts with widely varying information domain and business process requirements.

Table 10.2 summarizes the various ICT artefacts that were derived and used to support the business case implementation process, based on adapted methodologies and software delivery practices considered suitable for SMEs. Table 10.3 shows the use of these artefacts in a sample of case study organizations.

Table 10.2 Summary of ICT artefacts to support SME FOSS business implementation

ICT artefact	Type	Purpose	Design process
Open source laboratory	Technical capabilities, environment	A technology environment that facilitates ongoing maturity assessment, certification and staging of FOSS business applications	Technical design
Portfolio of open source business applications	Software products	Certified FOSS business applications that provide viable solutions to a common subset of SME business requirements	"Design as a search", open source maturity model assessment
Adapted OpenUP methodology	Methodology, practice, eclipse process framework	Facilitate a pragmatic, agile, minimalist approach that emphasizes stakeholder engagement	Adaptation, integration
Web-based forms and spreadsheet utilities	Software products	Enable cost-effective self-service mechanisms for business requirements gathering and data collection as part of iterative software implementation process	Iterative software design

Insights and implications for practice and policy in developing countries

The effective adoption and use of ICT to facilitate the survival and ultimately the competitiveness of SMEs is a critical imperative for developing countries like Jamaica. The use of FOSS and internet-based software delivery mechanisms such as cloud computing offers new opportunities for SMEs to access advanced ICT capabilities and reduce the effects of the internal and external digital divide. It also presents policy-makers with a compelling rationale for explicitly incorporating FOSS as a component of a national ICT strategy. However, many SMEs continue to be challenged by lack of awareness, lack of ICT expertise and lack of confidence in the potential benefits and opportunities presented by FOSS business applications. This is further compounded by some ill-conceived

Table 10.3 Sample of SME business case studies

Business challenge	Expected business benefits	Target FOSS solution
Engineering, motors and controls, power transmission equipment and accessories (16 employees)		
No single human resources (HR) system in place – various applications used to achieve HR objectives System needed to centralize HR information and improve ease of collection, dissemination and management of information and time and attendance	Complete HR system that stores employee data and converts these into reports to help in making more informed decisions System should allow staff members to view their benefits and entitlements, change status as necessary, assist in time management and recruitment	Human resource management system (OrangeHRM)
Entertainment services provider to individual consumers, presence in three parishes (~100 employees)		
Implementing a call centre to centralize and streamline customer contact management, ticket reservations and service issues management Previously these support services were managed separately at each location	Improved customer service response Increased operating efficiency in problem tracking and resolution	Customer support desk and ticket reservations system (vTigerCRM)
Janitorial and sanitation services operating in Kingston and St Catherine (~85 employees)		
Job planning and CRM processes are operated manually	More organized method of managing clients, especially non-business customers Most important aspect is inventory management: program should allow properly disbursement of inventory (which is not for sale) into jobs Ideal if inventory program can be used to determine cost of carrying out a job	CRM integrated with material requisitioning and job costing functionality (vTigerCRM)

Table 10.3 (cont.)

Business challenge	Expected business benefits	Target FOSS solution
Fourteen-bedroom banquet and conference lodge in Kingston (22 employees)		
Most business processes are manual, which is time-consuming and prone to error	Small size gives a unique competitive advantage: customers are treated to personalized service which seeks to meet and exceed their expectations, translating into referrals and repeat business	Vendor-CRM system integrated with events management (vTigerCRM)
Because departmental operations are decentralized, information is scattered and managed separately	A CRM that can maintain a single centralized electronic repository for all client information and customer-related interactions can enhance this capability	
Need for more effective and responsive communication channels and better collaboration of information between departments		

public sector FOSS adoption initiatives that are plagued by poor conceptualization, planning and execution, thus helping to perpetuate traditional myths of FOSS being risky and unsupported. In the absence of national FOSS initiatives, such as those that have emerged in Brazil, Cuba and Venezuela, there is considerable scope for intermediary organizations that can facilitate greater adoption and more effective utilization of these technology solutions, as well as helping to inform ICT public policy.

The interactions with the Jamaican SMEs that participated in this research suggested some important considerations for this intermediary role. Firstly, the search for, selection and certification of FOSS applications that are mature, robust and appropriate for small businesses are a key support that should not be underestimated. Individuals and organizations can develop negative perceptions and experiences with FOSS if the process of adoption is not supported by a degree of rigour in sourcing business solutions. A consistent programme of awareness and education of business owners and decision-makers about the potential value of appropriate ICT adoption to their businesses is also important in helping to disavow some of the prevailing myths and negative perceptions and stimulate positive demand. Such programmes are most effective when accompanied by actual scenario-based solution demonstrations of the potential applications. Public sector agencies that work closely with the small business sector to facilitate the growth and development of new and existing mSMEs can provide excellent channels for this programme of awareness and education.

The increased availability of mature "industrial-strength" FOSS, vertical business applications and an expanding range of robust, cost-effective cloud-based IT service delivery options presents tremendous opportunities for SMEs to access advanced ICT such as ERP, CRM and business intelligence applications without the traditional constraints of infrastructure, costs and resident in-house expertise. However, a strong aversion to hosted business solutions was detected among the surveyed Jamaican SMEs, unless these were delivered through familiar local providers. Thus the role of trusted intermediaries in facilitating the adoption and use of these business applications in a hosted environment would be critical to persuading SMEs to pursue such opportunities. Policy initiatives that encourage and cultivate the emergence of these business models and intermediaries can be an important catalyst for the development of local ICT sector capacity and capabilities.

It is important to underscore that FOSS is not being presented as a panacea for all SME contexts, and alternative ICT solutions will no doubt be more suitable for some SMEs to suit their particular requirements. Nevertheless, this research seeks to contribute to the growing awareness of the potential business value of FOSS to SMEs. In particular, flexibility and adaptability are powerful FOSS attributes that address one of the major barriers to ICT adoption in SMEs, namely the incidence of inappropriate ICT solutions designed for larger organizations that are relatively costly, unnecessarily complex and do not fit business needs or operating processes of smaller organizations.

One visible limitation of this research is that the sample studied is not necessarily representative of the entire SME sector and is skewed to businesses in the upper end of the category, whereas the Jamaican sector is clearly dominated by micro-enterprises and wholesale and retail trading activities. For the design-science-oriented study, broad generalization was a lesser goal relative to the primary objective of solution design for typical SME contexts. This goal was realized through the subsequent case studies, which covered a range of SME organizations operating in varying business contexts.

Conclusions

The research yielded some important insights into approaches to deploying FOSS to SMEs in Jamaica and, by inference, other developing economies. In the first instance it is important to address any initial uncertainty by business owners about FOSS by demonstrating the functionality and potential utility of FOSS business applications that were subjected to prior maturity assessment and certified for production use. Secondly, the "staging" of these FOSS applications, using the virtual open source laboratory environment established for this purpose, provided a highly effective level of "large-grained" prototyping that readily facilitated the orientation and adoption decision by business decision-makers, as was evidenced by the Jamaican situation. Further, accompanying these initiation activities with other formal "best practice" software engineering methods such as use-case-centred modelling and incremental delivery is an important aspect that may help to maximize the engagement and active involvement of key small business stakeholders throughout the implementation process.

OpenUP provided a useful template for developing a lean implementation process tailored specifically to working with small business clients in Jamaica, and may be applicable in other developing countries, especially small-island states. This research emphasized the use of web-based tools to manage the client interaction through business requirements gathering, prototyping, user training and solution validation, which allowed for a more efficient and cost-effective solution delivery process that was repeatable for participants. This proved to be beneficial, since many SMEs do not possess the organizational capability to generate a coherent ICT strategy or implement ICT-enabled business solutions. A low-cost, non-disruptive approach would enable SME owners to concentrate their limited resources and management attention on participating meaningfully in the targeted business innovation made possible by these emerging ICT solutions.

By combining an increasingly mature portfolio of FOSS business applications with lean, low-cost implementation methods that utilize internet-based software delivery mechanisms such as cloud computing, new opportunities have been demonstrated for SMEs to access advanced ICT capabilities at considerably reduced costs and diminish the effects of the technology gaps between larger enterprises and themselves. This will allow SMEs to compete more effectively in an increasingly global and knowledge-based economy. Intermediary support organizations that can leverage a portfolio of proven FOSS business solutions with prescriptive implementation methods can become quite instrumental in facilitating greater adoption and utilization of ICT among SMEs. This is proposed as an important business opportunity for local technology service providers that can replicate these solutions across various SME business contexts.

Notes

1. Horizontal refers to the more traditional general-purpose applications of FOSS at the lower layers of the application stack (i.e. operating system, database, web servers, etc.), whereas vertical refers to the newer emerging FOSS solutions for more specific line-of-business applications such as CRM, ERP, etc.
2. Jamaica is divided into 14 geographic regions called parishes.
3. LAMP is the acronym for the common open source software stack utilizing the Linux operating system, Apache web server, MySQL database and PHP/Perl/Python programming language.

REFERENCES

Avgerou, C. (2000) "IT and Organisational Change: An Institutionalist Perspective", *Information Technology & People* 13(4), pp. 234–262.

BIS (2010) *Small and Medium-sized Enterprise Statistics for the UK and Regions*, Sheffield: Department for Business Innovation and Skills.

Blili, S. and L. Raymond (1993) "Information Technology: Threats and Opportunities for Small and Medium-sized Enterprises", *International Journal of Information Management* 13(6), pp. 439–448.

Brown, D. and N. Lockett (2004) "Potential of Critical E-Applications for Engaging SMEs in E-Business: A Provider Perspective", *Journal of Information Systems* 13(1), pp. 21–34.

Brynjolfsson, E. and L. M. Hitt (2003) "Computing Productivity: Firm Level Evidence", *Review of Economics and Statistics* 85(4), pp. 793–808.

Camara, G. and F. Fonseca (2007) "Information Policies and Open Source Software in Developing Countries", *Journal of the American Society for Information Science and Technology* 58(1), pp. 121–132.

Commosioung, M., N. Satchell and L. Waller (2008) *A Landscape Assessment of Jamaican Micro, Small and Medium-Size Enterprises (mSMEs)*, Kingston: Private Sector Development Programme – Target Growth Competitive Committee.

Cragg, P. and M. King (1993) "Small-firm Computing: Motivators and Inhibitors", *MIS Quarterly* 17(1), pp. 47–60.

Da Costa, E. (2001) *Global E-Commerce Strategies for Small Businesses*, Cambridge, MA: MIT Press.

Dandridge, T. C. (1979) "Are not 'Little Grown-UPs': Small Business Needs Its Own Organizational Theory", *Journal of Small Business Management* 17(2), pp. 53–57.

DeLone, W. (1988) "Determinants of Success for Computer Usage in Small Business", *MIS Quarterly* 12(1), pp. 51–61.

Fink, D. (1998) "Guidelines for the Successful Adoption of Information Technology in Small and Medium Enterprises", *International Journal of Information Management* 18(4), pp. 243–253.

Forrester Consulting (2007) "Open Source Software's Expanding Role in the Enterprise", study commissioned by Unisys Corporation, Forrester Research; available at www.anpop.org.eg/Data/Sites/1/media/forrester_research-open_source_buying_behaviors.pdf (accessed 23 April 2012).

Golden, B. (2005) *Succeeding with Open Source*, Boston, MA: Addison-Wesley.

Gustafsson, B. (2008) "OpenUP – The Best of Two Worlds", *Methods & Tools* 16(1), pp. 21–32.

Hevner, A. R., S. T. March, J. Park and S. Ram (2004) "Design Science in Information Systems Research", *MIS Quarterly* 28(1), pp. 75–105.

Jalava, J. and M. Pohjola (2001) *Economic Growth in the New Economy: Evidence from Advanced Economies*, Helsinki: UNU World Institute for Development Economics Research.

Jorgenson, D. W., M. S. Ho and K. J. Stiroh (2005) *Information Technology and the American Growth Resurgence*, Cambridge, MA: MIT Press.

Kotelnikov, V. (2007) *Small and Medium Enterprises and ICT*, Bangkok: Asia-Pacific Development Information Programme.

Kroll, P. (2007) "OpenUP in a Nutshell"; available at www.ibm.com/developerworks/rational/library/sep07/kroll/index.html (accessed 1 March 2011).

Mansell, R. (1998) *Knowledge Societies: Information Technology for Sustainable Development*, Oxford: Oxford University Press.

McNaughton, M. (2010) "Broadening the Revolution: An Assessment of Open Source Initiatives in the Caribbean and Latin America", paper presented at International Conference on Information Resources Management, Montego Bay, 16–18 May.

OECD (2003) *ICT and Economic Growth: Evidence from OECD Countries, Industries and Firms*, Paris: OECD.

—— (2004) "Promoting Entrepreneurship and Innovative SMEs in a Global Economy: Towards a More Responsible and Inclusive Globalisation", paper presented at Second OECD Conference of Ministers Responsible for Small and Medium-sized Enterprises, Istanbul, 3–5 June.

Sojo, C. A. (2004) "Venezuela Embraces Linux and Open Source Software, but Faces Challenges"; available at http://venezuelanalysis.com/news/827 (accessed 15 November 2011).

Steinmuller, W. E. (2001) "ICTs and the Possibilities of Leapfrogging by Developing Countries", *International Labour Review* 40(2), pp. 193–210.

Thompson, S. and D. Brown (2008) "Change Agents Intervention in E-Business Adoption by SMEs: Evidence from a Developing Country", paper presented at AMCIS 2008; available at http://aisel.aisnet.org/amcis2008/242 (accessed 23 April 2012).

Thong, J. (1999) "An Integrated Model of Information Systems Adoption in Small Businesses", *Journal of Management Information Systems* 15(4), pp. 187–214.

Thong, J. and C. S. Yap (1995) "CEO Characteristics, Organizational Characteristics and Information Technology Adoption in Small Businesses", *Omega* 23(4), pp. 429–442.

UNCTAD (2004) *E-Commerce and Development Report 2003*, Geneva: United Nations.
—— (2006) *Information Economy Report 2006*, Geneva: United Nations.
Walsham, G. and S. Sahay (2006) "Research on Information Systems in Developing Countries: Current Landscape and Future Prospects", *Information Technology for Development* 12(1), pp. 17–24.
Witter, M. and C. Kirton (1990) *The Informal Economy in Jamaica: Some Empirical Exercises*, Mona: Institute of Social and Economic Research, University of the West Indies.

11
Development NGOs as potential groups for expansion of FOSS: The case of Iran

Saeid Nouri Neshat, Parvin Pakzadmanesh, Mehdi Almasi and Mohammad Amin Ameri

Introduction

Non-governmental organizations (NGOs) are striving hard in many developing countries, particularly Iran, to prove they can be regarded as one of the stakeholders in sustainable development. Thousands of NGOs have been established and officially registered in various fields. In certain areas such as poverty reduction, NGOs play a facilitating role. In other areas such as health, education and environmental protection they are involved in awareness raising, information campaigns, advocacy and training. Some NGOs carry out research activities while trying to run advocacy for sustainable development. NGOs need technology to attain their goals, so free and open source software (FOSS) can be very useful for them because of cost-effectiveness, legality, improved stability, licensing conditions, avoidance of technology lock-in, increased organizational flexibility, enhanced cooperative culture, extension of the lifespan of existing hardware and reduction of waste (especially from the environmental point of view) and ability to attract high-level skills at low costs. A major question is how much NGOs in Iran know about and use FOSS, and how much it is helping them in achieving their goals. There is sparse literature on the issue beyond sporadic interviews and articles.

FOSS is a major challenge in Iran, a country which may be a special case for several reasons. Firstly, the US sanctions make the whole process of buying and using Western software very difficult. There are many examples of Iranian developers having to rely on open source software. A

Free and open source software and technology for sustainable development, Sowe, Parayil and Sunami (eds), United Nations University Press, 2012, ISBN 978-92-808-1217-6

movement to promote FOSS in Iran has already started: the Iran Free/ Open Source Software Users Community (IFOSUC), a non-governmental, non-profit organization established in 2006 and formally registered in 2008, is active in this area. This organization, like some other NGOs, tries to prevent foreign private companies from dominating the Iranian software industry and works to develop and promote education, training and research in the FOSS field. The IFOSUC portal (www.foss.ir) is run by the Advanced ICT Research Centre affiliated to Sharif University of Technology in Tehran, one of the most advanced ICT (information and communication technologies) centres in the Middle East with six research groups in software engineering, organizational software, multimedia systems, advanced computer networks, cell-phone content and electronic health. The centre deploys experts in various fields of advanced technology research and production, and cooperates with governmental sectors and international companies.

The second issue is copyright. The government has already started a process of adopting international codes on intellectual property as part of its bid to join the World Trade Organization (WTO). In May 2005 the WTO General Council established an accession working party for Iran; in March 2006 the government issued a directive to the Ministry of Foreign Affairs to prepare for WTO negotiations; and in November 2009 Iran submitted a memorandum on its foreign trade regime to the WTO which is expected to launch the formal process of accession. These developments show how important the use of FOSS could be in present-day Iran, since Iranian users have to become ready for a shift to WTO rules. However, there are laws in Iran that protect domestic software producers and not foreign software. American embargos prohibit companies such as Microsoft from doing business in the country, a fact that contributes to widespread software piracy. As a result, unfortunately, there is a general tendency in Iran to use pirate software, since users pay little money for what is otherwise a very expensive product.

The third issue is language. Iranians would generally like to use software in their own language (Persian/Farsi), so the Persian language gaps in open source software have to be filled. This is a significant aspect to be considered, since not only does the language create a motivation for changing software, but it can also be an impetus to use open source.

Iran is a developing country with a defined vision for the year 2025 to be the first developed country in Western Asia and the Middle East. To achieve this, many gaps have to be filled and certain challenges have to be faced. One important point is that progress towards achieving development goals has been accomplished almost entirely without international assistance (UNDP, 2003). For example, in 1995 and 2000 Iran received only 0.2 and 0.1 per cent, respectively, of its gross national product in development assistance (World Bank, 2002). In addition, it has endured nearly a quarter of a century of economic sanctions. There are many development challenges for Iran at present, and among them ICT challenges are of great importance. NGOs have potential to tackle these challenges and contribute effectively to the sustainable development of Iran through increased use of FOSS; therefore it is valuable to find out more about the role of development NGOs in the expansion of FOSS in Iran.

Conceptual framework

The FOSS spirit of a voluntary movement, ethics of collaboration and a philosophy of openness and freedom seeking (GNU, 2010a, 2010b) are values shared with the non-profit environment (Peizer, 2003), as they are also among the underpinning foundations of the NGO movement. An NGO is defined as an independent voluntary association of people acting together on a continuous basis for some common purpose other than achieving power, making money or carrying out illegal activities (Willetts, 2006); and volunteerism is a major feature of non-governmental activities. These shared values of the two movements are a major reason why FOSS can be promoted both by and among NGOs, while NGOs can profit a great deal from it in their own development activities. Development NGOs, as an essential ingredient of civil society, have a vital role in realizing sustainable development objectives such as justice, social equity and conservation of the environment to meet the needs of the present generation and those of future generations (Smith and Rees, 1998). These NGOs should fulfil four criteria (Atack, 1999).

- *Representativeness*, referring to the NGO's method of operation. Representativeness can be achieved through considering the three main concepts of good governance: transparency, accountability and participation.
- *Distinctive values*: solidarity (Thomas, cited in ibid.) and voluntarism (Bratton, cited in ibid.) have been suggested as distinctive values that development NGOs should rely on for their organizational movement and existence.
- *Effectiveness*, implying being effective in attaining development goals. This criterion considers NGOs as development agents and can be measured by negotiating with stakeholders in programmes being implemented by NGOs.
- *Empowerment* is the process of local people making changes in communities through community-based practices (Nouri Neshat and Pakzadmanesh, 2009). Most development NGOs are involved in community empowerment in some way.

In recent years development organizations have been active at local, national and international levels to reduce poverty, protect the environment, provide social services, etc. – challenging issues that are also tackled by governments. Development NGOs play a valuable role in empowering people at local level through community-based projects; they are also involved in offering services to guarantee social welfare, promote justice in a society or protect people's rights. NGOs have been very helpful in policy-making processes at national and international levels through creating participatory approaches and mobilizing various social groups and people to run campaigns that have been key drivers of intergovernmental negotiations over various issues, ranging from regulation of hazardous wastes to a global ban on landmines and the elimination of slavery (Lewis, 2001).

Another characteristic of development NGOs is their potential to act as a wide network to share information, knowledge and experiences with other NGOs, communities and people. As Nouri Neshat (2009) says, "networks between NGOs are the most powerful instruments for exchanging information, sharing knowledge and making consensus toward new approaches in development issues. Networks have a main potential role to promote development process in Iran as groups of NGOs are more empowered to effect on communities than a single NGO." The open structure of NGOs networks will help as a facilitating factor to expand FOSS use among their members and finally among people in communities. There is a very tangible fit and relationship between the potential of networking among development NGOs and the need of FOSS to be expanded among public users.

Literature review

Various researchers have studied the reasons why FOSS is of great benefit for NGOs, especially in developing countries. FOSS is a suitable solution for the needs of small organizations due to its free availability, ability to be shared and modified, and its commitment to openness and knowledge sharing. Laszlo (2007), in reviewing the benefits of FOSS, refers to general features such as its free and low-cost use. FOSS offers better security and is promoted on a series of participatory principles shared by many NGOs (Abdool, 2005). Van Reijswoud and de Jager (2008) list the advantages of FOSS over proprietary software according to South Africa's National Advisory Council on Innovations: cost reduction, more independence from imported technology and skills, greater affordability for everyone from individuals to enterprises and governments, easy accessibility, ability to customize to local languages and cultures, absence of difficulties with licensing, and participation in global networks of software development. Also, there are fewer barriers for entry into the software business.

The UK Office of Government Commerce (OGC, 2002) refers to other advantages of FOSS, including supplier independence and quicker availability of patches and updates which limit breakdowns and security risks. Considering these advantages, the low budget and lack of experience of developing countries, and the high cost, security issues and need for training, update and support in proprietary software, it is believed that FOSS would be the best choice for these countries (Van Reijswoud and de Jager, 2008). Different US industries such as banking, construction, healthcare, insurance, retail and others invested over $360 billion in IT in 2008 (IDC, 2009). Using FOSS can significantly reduce software costs, freeing up money for the development of other sectors in a country. Also, as everyone has access to the source codes, it is much easier to fix existing bugs in the software and make it more reliable.

However, FOSS is not without its limitations and problems. According to Van Reijswoud and de Jager (2008) and the UK Office of Government Commerce (OGC, 2002), these include a lack of available support compared with proprietary software, a shortage of FOSS advertising, which makes it very difficult to choose the appropriate application for an NGO's needs, lack of documentation, since most FOSS developers are more interested in technical aspects than usability, hardware-software fit and limited best practice. In addition, as FOSS is a young movement, there are misperceptions and misunderstandings about it among software users and business people: FOSS is considered as user-unfriendly, and typified by a black-and-white screen with command prompts and weird output that only developers would understand. Thus another important issue is to correct these wrong views of FOSS.

By considering the needs of NGOs and the advantages of FOSS in terms of cost reduction and broad potential for customization, the question still remains as to why the FOSS movement has not become as widespread as expected in developing or least developed countries. There are three reasons for this.

Firstly, Van Reijswoud and de Jager (2008) argue that information about the advantages and disadvantages of FOSS and proprietary software is limited, due to access to pirated proprietary software at schools and universities and lack of interest in alternatives, no powerful copyright on this software and insufficient provision of information about FOSS by ICT donors. Secondly, it is essential to have access to medium- or high-speed broadband to get the latest information about FOSS, find a proper application, share problems and look for answers, etc. Unfortunately, in most developing countries the internet is slow, unstable and/or expensive.

The third major reason is the lack of role models, as governments have typically shown no interest in FOSS and nobody has made a fortune from it. However, there are some positive examples. FOSS has been used by NGOs working in various fields and issues and in very different conditions. For example, SchoolNet Namibia used FOSS and the internet in developing a new model for the empowerment of students, aimed at providing sustainable low-cost ICT solutions to all Namibian schools (ibid.). The project enabled schools and other educational centres to use FOSS software and applications running on the Linux operating system as well as the open source OpenLab application. Sahana is a FOSS application that aims to be a comprehensive disaster management information system for use by NGOs involved in relief operations (Wattegama, 2007). This software can facilitate disaster management in a very effective and practical way with a spirit of freedom (Hoe, 2006), and has the possibility of being customized easily even by people in local communities. However, there is a language challenge: if Iranian NGOs, the government or people want to use such software it is not known how this language barrier will be removed. The software has to be localized; but as it is open source, translation is a possibility (ibid.). These and many similar cases are encouraging for NGOs in Iran, but it seems they are not yet familiar with them. Although there are many papers on FOSS and related benefits for NGOs, there is no literature on the role of NGOs in Iran in promoting FOSS, even in Persian.

Methodology

In this study a mixed research methodology was used to collect data. In the first phase, using a qualitative method, a great deal of useful data were collected through in-depth unstructured and semi-structured interviews with experts in IT and managers of Iranian NGOs. As it was intended to study the role of development NGOs in promoting FOSS in Iran, and how much FOSS could facilitate NGO participation in development, the research was limited to Iran and groups that are active inside Iran. Data were saturated after 10 interviews (eight interviewees). Drawing mind maps helped the researchers to categorize the data and find major factors. Through this method, which was borrowed from facilitation techniques, an obvious and logical connection was created among the collected data. Data validation and reliability checking were then applied. In qualitative research, "trustworthiness has been further divided into credibility, which corresponds roughly with internal validity; dependability, which relates more to reliability; transferability, which is a form of external validity; and confirmability, that is largely an issue of presentation" (Lincoln and Guba, Graneheim and Lundman, cited by Rolfe,

2006). In this research various techniques were used to consider the four data validity criteria of credibility, confirmability, transferability and dependability.
- Engagement with the collected data for a long time: researchers have a long-term engagement with the data collected from the interviews. The data were categorized and analysed immediately after each interview – getting data and analysing them were simultaneous. This process helped to introduce new questions and improve later interviews. Using mind maps helped to categorize data better and find the relationship between data collected from the latest interview and previous ones. Having four members on the team led to considering data from different points of view to get more reliable findings.
- Member check: data and findings were confirmed by participants immediately after every interview. Data were shown to the participants to check the understanding of the interviewer.
- Triangulation: after data sorting and analysis led to producing one hypothesis based on findings, FOSS experts and NGO managers were asked about the information to ensure the research process was accurate (Streubert and Carpenter, 2006; Tobin, 2004).

Finally the main hypothesis was introduced in the interviews and continued discussions about findings:
- H1: Iranian NGOs do not use FOSS very much, although they have a good potential to use this software to expand their activities for sustainable development and also to promote FOSS in Iran.

Using quantitative research methodology to test the hypothesis, an electronic five-point Likert-scale questionnaire was designed to collect information from NGOs. To test its internal consistency (reliability), a draft questionnaire was sent to experts and NGO managers to complete. The Cronbach alpha was calculated and the result (0.8049) showed high reliability. Moreover, IT experts and NGO managers were asked to review the questionnaire to give feedback; after a few corrections, the questionnaire was finalized. The NGO population was targeted to complete the survey. Around 1,000 NGO members of a Yahoo group (http://groups.yahoo.com/group/ngonews) were sent the questionnaire through the e-mail group; 30 NGOs filled it in. To analyse the data thus obtained, SPSS software was used for a descriptive statistics analysis. By using tables, charts and figures, data were sorted and explained in an understandable way.

Data analysis

In the qualitative research, data were obtained through in-depth interviews. After five interviews, major questions were identified for use in semi-structured interviews. The interview findings were then categorized and used in designing the questionnaire.

One major finding during the three initial interviews was that some NGOs use FOSS without being aware of it. For instance, when asked whether they knew anything about FOSS, the response was negative; asked about the kind of software used for browsing the internet, they said Firefox. When it was explained that Firefox is FOSS, they were surprised: "Seriously! We didn't know."

Those with more information on FOSS were more interested in using it, and especially were very keen to cooperate actively in the research. They believed that concerns of other NGOs regarding using FOSS were due to the lack of information. One interviewee said: "As they have little information or they have wrong information, they cannot stop using the present [operating] system ..."

From their point of view, FOSS reduces costs, and there is no need to be concerned about technical support for previous software if they change to using a FOSS system. Meanwhile, as NGOs grow they need an expanded network, and may require FOSS for a better technical operating system. An interviewee mentioned: "When an association grows up, a more powerful operating system such as Linux is required to support the new needs."

Those with more specialized knowledge on FOSS referred to security as one of its characteristics: "FOSS applications have gone through trial and error and they are improving and thus they are more secure." Another important point was the possibility of translating software into Persian to facilitate its use by Iranians. Also, the interviewees emphasized the ethical aspects of using FOSS: "As an NGO, we have to observe ethical principles, it is a value for us; we are working for these principles; we have to observe them in everything."

When asked about the reasons why FOSS is not generally used by NGOs, they said NGOs are not well aware of FOSS. "We have got used to our existing operating system; it is very difficult to change it; we are concerned about our applications. We fear that in case of using a new operating system, our previous applications cannot work with Linux." Others claimed: "We need to spend more time to change our system; we need expertise to customize our software." Some people also said "We are sceptical about the security of FOSS."

During the interviews it was found that most NGOs are unfamiliar with FOSS and concerned about the costs of changing, technical support, back-up and customization: "The education system in Iran is using Linux, since they have a very extensive network that needs a powerful operating system, but NGOs do not have the necessary funds for such support and customization."

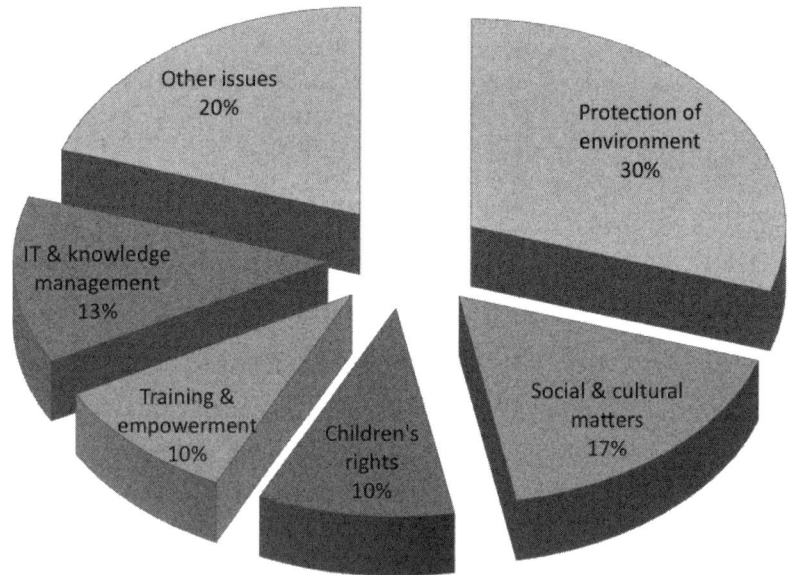

Figure 11.1 Fields of respondent NGOs' activities

All these responses helped the researchers to design the questionnaire.

In total, 30 NGOs responded to the questionnaire. These NGOs have had over seven years of activity on average, and work in various fields: 30 per cent in protection of the environment and biodiversity; 16.7 per cent in social (strengthening of civil society) and cultural matters; 10 per cent in children's rights; 10 per cent in training and empowerment; and 13.4 per cent in IT and knowledge management. The others were active in student affairs, urban sustainable development, women's rights, cultural heritage, journalists' rights and rehabilitation (Figure 11.1).

All participants chose "to some extent" as their response to the question on how much using computers and related software had helped to develop their work. This certainly means that NGOs use IT and rely on it for expansion of their activities. In the third question the participants' knowledge of FOSS was evaluated: considering the previous answers, which indicated an average of seven years of activity and "some extent" of use of computers and applications, it was expected that participants would know about FOSS. Nevertheless, as Figure 11.2 depicts, about 37 per cent had "very little", 33 per cent had "some" and only 27 per cent had a "great" extent of knowledge on FOSS. Among all participants, only one respondent claimed to have a "very great extent" of knowledge.

Asked whether they would rather use FOSS applications such as Firefox than a closed source and proprietary software like Internet Explorer

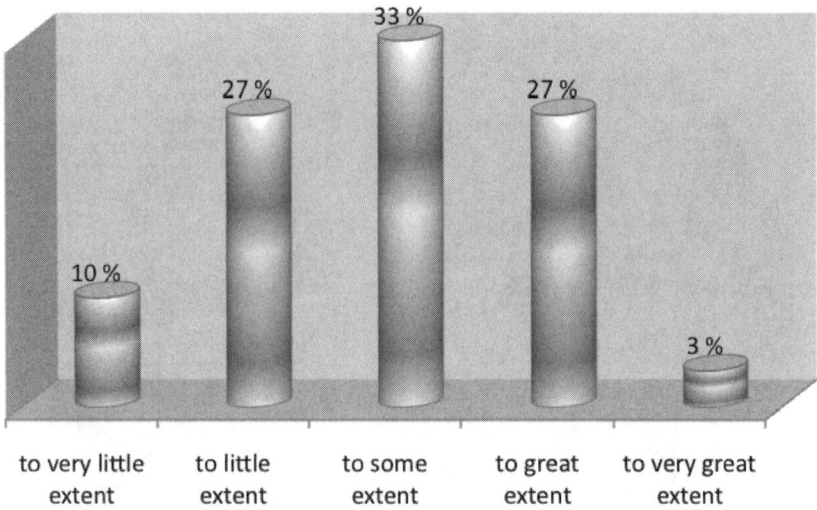

Figure 11.2 Knowledge of respondents about FOSS

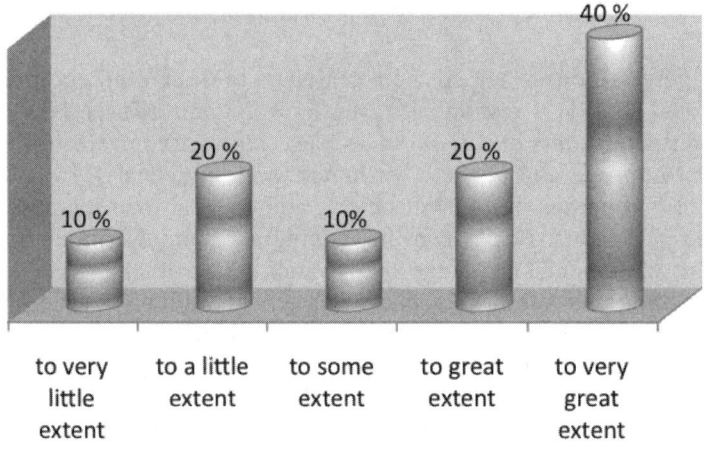

Figure 11.3 Preference for Firefox over Internet Explorer

(Figure 11.3), over 70 per cent of NGOs prefer to use Firefox and about 30 per cent had less desire to use it.

The fifth question covered the Linux operating system and the reasons why it is not very widespread among NGOs. In the initial interviews, six factors were identified as possible reasons and participants were asked to assess these (Table 11.1). As can be seen, the third factor (anxiety over Linux compatibility with other applications) is the most important reason

Table 11.1 Six reasons for not using Linux operating system among NGOs in Iran

Reason	To a very great extent (%)	To a great extent (%)	To some extent (%)	To a little extent (%)	To very little extent (%)	Unanswered (%)
Lack of information about existence of Linux operating system	6.7	20.0	20.0	23.3	6.7	23.3
Little information about power and functions of Linux operating system	10.0	33.3	16.7	13.3	3.3	23.3
Anxiety over Linux limitations as it might not be compatible with other applications	16.7	33.3	10.0	3.3	10.0	26.7
Need for experts to set up and support Linux operating system	13.3	26.7	20.0	10.0	3.3	33.3
Anxiety over losing application outputs which are compatible with previous operating system	26.7	13.3	16.7	3.3	6.7	33.3
Lack of documentation on the Linux operating system to increase users' knowledge and ease of use	16.7	16.7	16.7	10.0	10.0	31.8

for limited use of Linux. Most NGOs, with many projects under way and a lot of work to do involving computers and software, are worried that by using Linux they might face limitations in using other applications. As a result, they resist switching from their current operating system to Linux.

Also, as the table shows, the "unanswered" percentage is high (varying from 23.3 to 33.3 per cent). Participants were required to skip this question if they knew nothing about Linux – thus almost 30 per cent of respondents did not know Linux at all. The fourth factor is also very important in the eyes of NGOs: a concern that by using Linux they will incur increased costs for hiring experts. Potential problems in compatibility

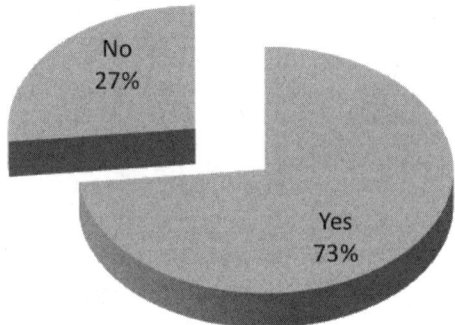

Figure 11.4 Percentage use of FOSS

of Linux with other programs they are currently running and the lack of documentation in Linux are other factors that discourage NGOs from using this powerful and free operating system. Figure 11.4 shows 73 per cent of the participants have actually used FOSS and 27 per cent of them have never used it.

The seventh question related to the applications of FOSS in NGO activities. In the initial interviews it was found that FOSS applications are used in seven different aspects.
- 1App – Communication and text writing.
- 2App – Development and promotion of communication and information sharing (websites, forum groups, etc.).
- 3App – Report writing.
- 4App – Report preparation and presentation.
- 5App – Development and promotion of databases.
- 6App – Fundraising.
- 7App – Accounting.

Analysing the results (Figure 11.5), most NGOs use FOSS in development and promotion of communication and information sharing via the internet.

The eighth question concerned 10 advantages of FOSS which had been revealed through the interviews with IT experts.
- 1Ad – Cost reduction (using free software instead of paying for proprietary software).
- 2Ad – Translatable to Persian.
- 3Ad – High potential to customize to the NGOs' needs.
- 4Ad – FOSS is user friendly.
- 5Ad – The spirit of FOSS production (the world FOSS movement) is the same as that in NGOs' voluntary activities and we would like to be part of it.
- 6Ad – FOSS has fewer bugs and errors in its codes and update patches are available regularly.

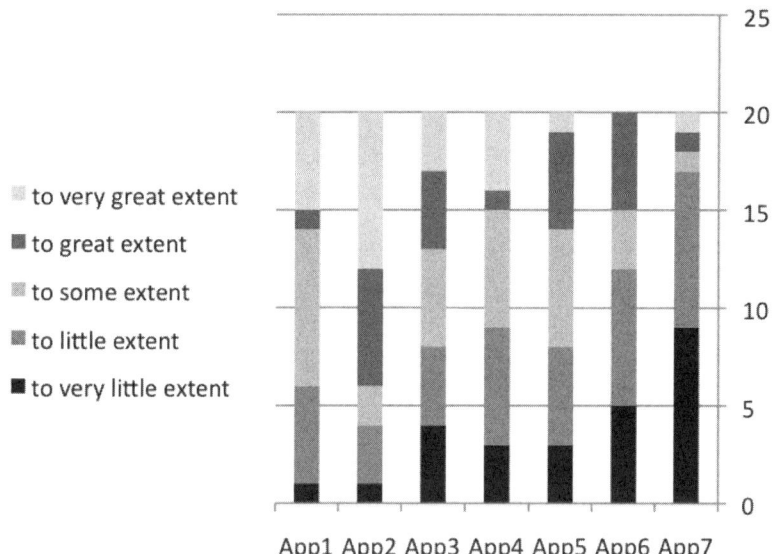

Figure 11.5 FOSS applications for NGOs

- 7Ad – Using FOSS is more ethical than using pirate versions of proprietary software.
- 8Ad – FOSS is more secure in comparison with pirate and closed source software.
- 9Ad – Fewer problems in updating the software.
- 10Ad – Less risk in connecting to the internet compared to pirate proprietary software.

In addition, it should be mentioned that participants were given an empty space in the questionnaire to list any other advantages of FOSS, but this field was left blank. Between all these advantages, 7Ad (FOSS is ethical in comparison with pirate versions of proprietary software) has been the most important for the respondents. "Cost reduction" (1Ad) came second, with "reduced risk in connecting to the internet" (10Ad) and "the same spirit of voluntary work" (5Ad) in third and fourth places (Figure 11.6).

From the initial interviews, six reasons (listed below) were identified why NGOs were not interested in using FOSS. In the questionnaire participants were asked to evaluate each reason and given an extra space where they could add any other reasons – again, this field was left blank.

- We were not aware of its existence.
- We knew that FOSS existed but we did not have enough information on how to use it.

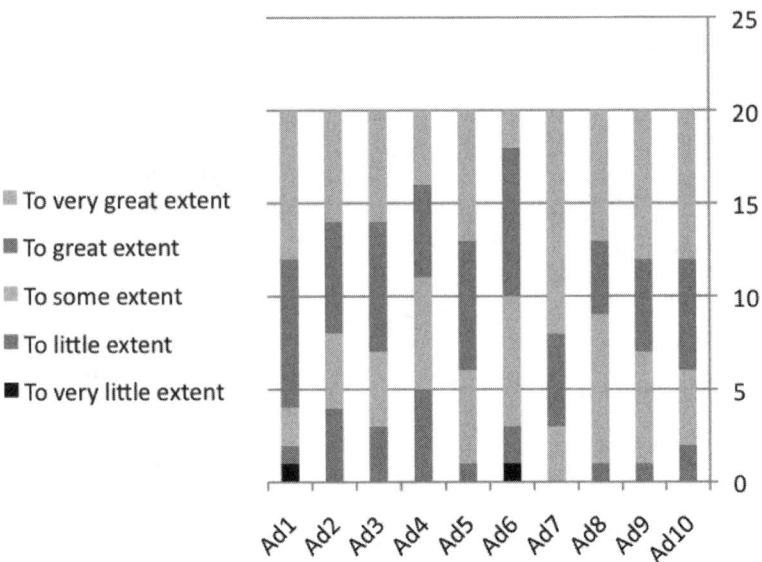

Figure 11.6 Advantages of FOSS for NGOs

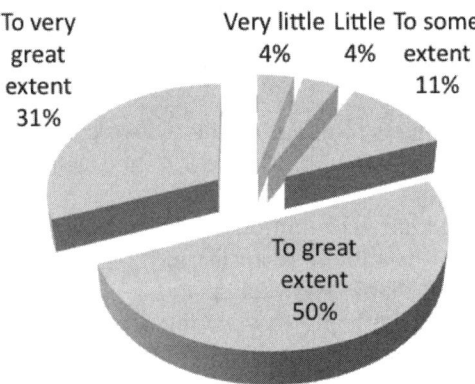

Figure 11.7 NGOs' willingness to attend a FOSS training workshop

- Lack of support for FOSS. No back-up in case of technical issues.
- Need of experts and money for customizing the FOSS application.
- Doubt about FOSS security.
- We are accustomed to the software that we have been using for a long time and are not interested in switching to new products.

Only six NGOs answered this question, and in their opinion the lack of support was the most important reason for not using FOSS. Security and customization cost were second and third in importance.

To know whether participants would like to get more information on FOSS, the last question evaluated their interest in attending a FOSS training workshop. As shown in Figure 11.7, over 80 per cent were highly interested, while about 11 per cent would consider attending and just 8 per cent showed no interest. Probably this uninterested group were participants who already had very good knowledge about FOSS, so had no need to attend a related workshop.

Results and discussion

A major result obtained from the survey is that NGOs emphasized using FOSS for developing and promoting their communication and information sharing. Information and communication software is a vital asset in any NGO, since it enables the organizations to publicize their activities (Figures 11.3–11.5c). Also, by publishing their needs and queries they can get benefit from their activity and expand their network and membership constituency.

The results of the questionnaire showed that NGOs feel very close to FOSS when they know it is based on ethical principles (Figure 11.6). This fact has to be emphasized in any activity to promote FOSS among NGOs in Iran. The word "software" brings a series of technical aspects to mind; it is in fact a useful program or procedure pertaining to the operation of a computer system. An NGO needs software for its daily activities. If an NGO is informed about software that is developed based on ethical values and a freedom-seeking spirit, it will not only think of technical aspects but will consider this shared value system and be encouraged to enter such a movement. Indeed, to deepen the appeal of FOSS it is logical to reach out to those with shared values. As Abdool (2005) mentions, FOSS depends on the same values and standards, which is a reason why it can be an option for the non-profit sector. NGOs are values-based organizations, and mostly populated by those with strong beliefs and commitments (Edwards, 1997). If they can understand the values behind FOSS, they may become very interested in it, and it may therefore spread among NGOs.

However, Iran is a unique case since the country is under sanctions. FOSS is a good solution to bypass these sanctions. The first law of free software is "for anyone for any purpose", which means even sanctions cannot stop people from using the software. Also, using FOSS obviates the need to use a pirate version of proprietary software, which is unethical (Figure 11.6). Indeed, when and if Iran joins the WTO, it will be obliged to enforce these international intellectual property rights on users. But if there has been no experience with any alternatives (i.e. using

OpenOffice instead of Microsoft Office, or Firefox instead of Internet Explorer), it will be a huge problem to shift from pirate proprietary software to FOSS in terms of cost and adaptation. If users (individuals, companies, NGOs or even government entities) want to stay with the same software, then the licence fee should be paid – which could be hundreds of times more than the amount they used to pay for pirate versions, thus significantly increasing the costs. And if users cannot face the cost increase, they have to switch to free software, and in that case would face adaptation issues (Figure 11.6).

Being aware of these two potential problems, it is very important to consider how NGOs can play an important role in migrating to FOSS. This migration can be done either suddenly or gradually. "Sudden" means that all applications, servers and operating systems are switched to FOSS at once. This certainly would reduce the cost, but it definitely affects the users, who are faced with a totally new system (Van Reijswoud and de Jager, 2008). Gradual migration would be the better approach, as it can be done in the back end of each NGO IT system (in web servers, e-mail servers, database servers, etc.). Users would not notice anything, because they were never aware of what was going on behind their screens – and the fact is that they do not care. What is happening behind the screen is all technical. They feel the real changes when it comes to the front end and they can see it. In a gradual migration process, while the back end is being switched to FOSS, training, courses, workshops and education can be staged to prepare everyone for the change.

Iran is unique case for another reason: the language (Figure 11.6). NGOs wish to change the language to Persian, as confirmed by the respondents to the questionnaire. The first law of free software is that it is "for anyone for any purpose" – which also means "anyone with any language can use it".

As mentioned, for various reasons NGOs can benefit from FOSS and have a good potential for expanding its use in Iran. Two great challenges were discovered during the research: the lack of enough information about FOSS, and the needed technical support, back-up and customization (Figure 11.2 and Table 11.1).

Conclusion

It seems that a good solution to expand FOSS among Iranian NGOs would be increased dissemination of information. They have to know more about FOSS so they can gradually shift towards it. But mere knowledge of FOSS is insufficient: NGOs in Iran have to know more about best practices where FOSS has been used as a tool for sustainable development, and the technical advantages that FOSS can add to their work. Such best practices need to be translated into Persian, so NGOs have better access to this powerful facility. Holding workshops to train NGO managers and IT experts on FOSS applications is necessary, especially on the related best practices. NGOs will certainly welcome such workshops.

Implications for policy

The use of FOSS by NGOs is not an issue of policy that can be directly applied by the government. FOSS is based on free spirit and NGOs have to select it freely, without it being part of a government policy, even if it is useful for NGOs and development. However, those agencies within the government that are focused on development issues through NGOs or with the agenda to empower NGOs can encourage these entities to use FOSS.

FOSS could be an issue of policy for NGOs, and in particular those involved in sustainable development in Iran. It can be integrated within their agendas, if those active in the NGO community can understand the importance of FOSS. NGOs have to recognize it as a vital tool.

However, this cannot be done without an institution. A group should take the responsibility and move forward to disseminate information among NGOs. It seems that one of the active NGOs in the field of ICT should start such a move: it would assist a great deal if IFOSUC – as an active organization promoting FOSS in Iran – could move beyond its present mission and focus on NGOs as a target group. A new NGO with a focus on FOSS could even be established, or another NGO active on ICT could take the lead in promoting FOSS among development NGOs in Iran. Such an organization can respond to NGOs' software needs and try to fill the existing gaps.

If NGOs find out how FOSS can help them in their activities, they may expand its use among other NGOs. In time they will discover how FOSS is cost-effective, and they will certainly be ready to pay for technical support, back-up and customization.

Acknowledgements

The authors would like to thank to Robin M. Mills for editing the chapter and Dr James Howison for his good comments. They are so grateful to all interviewees for their time and active participation in providing information, and to all respondents from the NGO community in Iran who patiently completed the electronic questionnaire.

REFERENCES

Abdool, S. A. (2005) *The Theory of Foss and Its Acceptance in Developing Nations*, Goteborg: Department of Informatics University of Goteborg.

Atack, I. (1999) "Four Criteria of Development NGO Legitimacy", *Journal of World Development* 27(5), pp. 855–864.

Edwards, M. (1997) "Organisational Learning in Non-Governmental Organisations: What Have We Learned?", *Public Administration and Development* 17(2), pp. 235–250.

GNU (2010a) "The Free Software Definition"; available at www.gnu.org/philosophy/free-sw.html (accessed 2 February 2011).

—— (2010b) "Why 'Free Software' Is Better than Open Source"; available at www.gnu.org/philosophy/free-software-for-freedom.html (accessed 2 February 2011).

Hoe, N. S. (2006) "Breaking Barriers: The Potential of Free and Open Source Software for Sustainable Human Development – A Compilation of Case Studies from Across the World", UNDP Asia-Pacific Development Information Programme, Bangkok; available at www.apdip.net/publications/ict4d/BreakingBarriers.pdf (accessed 20 January 2011).

IDC (2009) *US Black Book Q2*, Palm Springs, CA: Desert Publications

Laszlo, G. (2007) "Issues and Aspects of Open Source Software Usage and Adoption in the Public Sector", in Kirk St. Amant and Brian Still (eds) *Handbook of Research on Open Source Software: Technological, Economic, and Social Perspectives*, Lubbock, TX: Texas Tech University, pp. 445–459.

Lewis, D. (2001) *The Management of Non-Governmental Development Organisations: An Introduction*, London: Routledge.

Nouri Neshat, S. (2009) "Networking of Non-Governmental Organisations"; available at www.modiryar.com/index-management/tourism/ngo/2554-1388-06-30-03-28-00.html (accessed 26 January 2012).

Nouri Neshat, S. and P. Pakzadmanesh (2009) *Facilitation in Community-Based Rehabilitation – A Manual for Local and Middle Facilitators, and Experts*, Tehran: Barg-e Zeitoon.

OGC (2002) "Guidance on Implementing Open Source Software", Office of Government Commerce, September; available at www.ogc.gov.uk/embedded_object.asp?docid=2498 (accessed 6 March 2011).

Peizer, J. (2003) *Realizing the Promise of Open Source in the Non-Profit Sector*, New York: Open Society Institute.

Rolfe, G. (2006) "Validity, Trustworthiness and Rigour: Quality and the Idea of Qualitative Research", *Journal of Advanced Nursing* 53(3), pp. 304–310.

Smith, C. and G. Rees (1998) *Economic Development*, Basingstoke: Macmillan.

Streubert, H. and D. Carpenter (2006) *Qualitative Research in Nursing*, 4th edn, Philadelphia, PA: Lippincott Williams and Wilkins.

Tobin, G. A. (2004) "Methodological Rigour within a Qualitative Framework", *Journal of Advanced Nursing* 48(4), pp. 388–396.

UNDP (2003) "United Nations Common Country Assessment for the Islamic Republic of Iran"; available at www.undp.org.ir/DocCenter/reports/npd/CCA.pdf (accessed 20 October 2010).

Van Reijswoud, V. and A. de Jager (2008) *Free and Open Source Software for Development: Exploring Expectations, Achievements and Future*, Milan: Polimetrica.

Van Reijswoud, V. and E. Mulo (2007) "Evaluating the Potential of Free and Open Source Software in the Developing World", in Kirk St. Amant and Brian Still (eds) *Handbook of Research on Open Source Software: Technological, Economic, and Social Perspectives*, Lubbock, TX: Texas Tech University, pp. 79–92.

Wattegama, C. (2007) "ICT for Disaster Management", UNDP Asia-Pacific Development Information Programme; available at www.apdip.net/publications/iespprimers/eprimer-dm.pdf (accessed 6 March 2011).

Willetts, P. (2006) "What Is a Non-Governmental Organization?", UNESCO Encyclopaedia of Life Support Systems, Article 1.44.3.7; available at www.staff.city.ac.uk/p.willetts/CS-NTWKS/NGO-ART.HTM (accessed 26 January 2012).

World Bank (2002) *World Development Indicators*, Washington, DC: World Bank.

12
Improving public healthcare systems in developing countries using FOSS: The EHAS Foundation case

Carlos Rey-Moreno, Inés Bebea-González, Ignacio Prieto-Egido, Seth Cochran, Ignacio Foche-Pérez, Jose García-Múñoz, Andrés Martínez-Fernández and Javier Simó-Reigadas

Introduction

Providing healthcare in rural areas of developing countries is a very challenging task, since they are inhabited by the most vulnerable and most impoverished sectors of the population – those who suffer the most acute diseases. In addition, in these countries a high proportion of the medical expertise is located in urban areas, barring the most needy, those living in rural and isolated areas, from access to quality healthcare. Many initiatives have tried to improve public primary healthcare systems in rural and isolated areas by using information and communication technologies (ICT) to connect rural health centres with urban hospitals to address this issue and foster the development of rural communities (Wootton et al., 2009). The isolation and lack of infrastructure (roads, energy) of these regions make them less economically attractive for telecommunication operators to invest in deploying information and communication networks in these areas. This leaves only two solutions for connecting healthcare facilities: either they make use of satellite connections, or they build the networks themselves.

The first option is the most common (Bagayoko, Müler and Geissbuhler, 2006; Kopec and Salazar, 2002; Sachpazidis et al., 2006), but the high operating cost of the connections has meant most of these initiatives fail to become sustainable (Rey, 2008; Bebea-González, Martínez-Fernández and Rey-Moreno, 2011). Other stakeholders have chosen to build their own communication infrastructure, incurring high capital costs but reduc-

Free and open source software and technology for sustainable development, Sowe, Parayil and Sunami (eds), United Nations University Press, 2012, ISBN 978-92-808-1217-6

ing to a minimum the operational expenditure (CAICBO, 2007; Macha Works, 2011; Pun et al., 2006; Surana et al., 2008; Simó et al., 2006). To do so, most use free and open source software (FOSS) to adapt their communication solutions to the environment where they operate. Once healthcare centres are connected, through these means or by traditional networks, many other institutions work to improve healthcare provision through the design of software and hardware solutions to address the communication needs faced by health workers (Seebregts et al., 2009; Braa et al., 2007; Martínez et al., 2005b).

This chapter presents a case study of more than 10 years of EHAS Foundation (Enlace Hispano Americano de Salud – Hispano American Health Link) activities. EHAS not only uses FOSS to provide connectivity, but also to design software and hardware to improve public primary healthcare systems in rural and isolated areas. This allows analysis of lessons learnt from both activities. The chapter introduces the model EHAS follows regarding FOSS, and the role the latter has played in the sustainability of its actions.

Background

Structure of the primary healthcare system in rural areas of developing countries

Public healthcare systems in Latin American countries use a multi-tiered system that includes national and regional reference hospitals and primary care institutions. The latter can be grouped into two categories: health centres (HCs) and health posts (HPs) (Martínez et al., 2004). An HP (Figure 12.1) is an access point to the healthcare system for a rural population. It does not have a physician, but is staffed by at least one medical technician. HPs are typically located in towns with less than 1,000 inhabitants that have no telephone lines and very limited transport infrastructure. An HC (Figure 12.2) is usually located in a provincial or district capital and has telephone lines installed. HCs are always under the direction of a physician and are equipped to make some more advanced diagnostic tests than HPs.

Several HPs depend on a single HC, and together comprise a health "micro-network" of basic primary care. The micro-networks are under the direction of the physician responsible for the HC, who coordinates the activities of the HPs. Most medical technicians at HPs need better ways to communicate with the physician for consultation, conveying epidemiological surveillance reports, ordering medical supplies and relaying information concerning acute epidemic outbreaks, medical emergencies

Figure 12.1 Health post in a rural area of Peru

Figure 12.2 Health centre in a rural area of Peru

and natural disasters. Without technology to assist in this communication and the exchange of information, healthcare workers have to travel from one facility to another, which can take hours or even days.

Communication and access to information needs in primary healthcare

Results from many studies (Martínez et al., 2005a; Dorsch, 2000; Wootton, 2008) show that primary healthcare systems in rural areas of developing countries are very inefficient for various reasons, including difficulties in information sharing. A more detailed analysis shows the following.

- Epidemiological surveillance systems, for gathering and analysing data about diseases to assess whether an epidemic outbreak is to come, are not very efficient for three main reasons: information arrives late, information contains frequent errors and information is not useful for taking timely corrective action. Traditional surveillance systems are expensive because they are labour-intensive and highly dependent on significant travel costs. Information arrives late because HPs are far away from the hospital (not necessarily in distance, but in hours of travel), communication infrastructure is scarce and information is processed manually at all HPs and most of the HCs. Data errors are frequent for at least two reasons: the same data are introduced several times by hand in different locations; and once an error is detected, it is not possible to correct it by asking the person who introduced the original data. In the most isolated rural areas it is difficult to take timely corrective action because diagnostic or referral information from the higher-resourced hospital simply arrives too late.
- There are always difficulties correctly diagnosing and treating cases at the primary healthcare sites for three main reasons: rural personnel have inadequate training; there are difficulties consulting other, perhaps more experienced, professionals; and stocks of medicines are low due to the inefficiency of the drug delivery system. Inadequately trained staff result from inadequate access to medical information and the inefficiency of continuous training programmes. Furthermore, qualified personnel (physicians, obstetricians and nurses) usually move to large cities, preferring the numerous personal and professional opportunities to isolation and insufficient ongoing professional training. The consultation process is quite complicated because of the large distances between centres that lack even basic telecommunication capabilities. The inefficient drug delivery system demands significant time for sending orders and receiving drugs, causing the perpetual absence of important medicines or medical consumables.

- Management of emergency cases in rural areas is complicated for two reasons. The first is the difficulty of coordinating patient transfers. It is not easy to predict when a transferred patient is going to arrive to the referral centre and to know patient clinical history in advance. This creates a delay in the care a patient receives on arrival at an HC. The second reason is unavailability of transport to transfer patients. This is worsened by lack of communication, which makes sharing ambulances between neighbouring establishments impossible. Another challenge is that ensuring every healthcare site has unique access to transport is costly. The transport challenges mean that many patients are delayed or never reach the referral facility.

Using ICTs to address these problems is commonly known as telemedicine. According to the American Telemedicine Association, telemedicine is "the use of medical information exchanged from one site to another via electronic communications to improve patients' health status" (TeleMed, 2011). Closely associated with telemedicine is the term "telehealth", which is often used to encompass a broader definition of remote healthcare that does not always involve clinical services. Videoconferencing, transmission of still images, e-health including patient portals, remote monitoring of vital signs, continuing medical education and nursing call centres are all considered part of telemedicine and telehealth.

Background to EHAS

The EHAS Foundation is a non-profit institution which aims at improving public healthcare systems in remote areas through the application of appropriate ICT. EHAS started its activities in 1999 as a result of a collaboration between the Polytechnic University of Madrid and Engineers without Borders, and since then has interconnected more than 200 healthcare facilities (both HPs and HCs) with their reference hospitals in Peru, Colombia, Ecuador and Cuba. Over this time the group of collaborators has broadened, and nowadays the EHAS board of directors includes representatives from Rey Juan Carlos University, Catholic University of Peru and Cauca University in Colombia.

EHAS works specifically with the primary care facilities of public health systems in developing countries. In rural areas EHAS operates in the relatively well-equipped and well-staffed HCs, as well as remote and less-resourced HPs. These HPs are located in areas with no roads or fixed or mobile phone systems and have very limited medical capabilities. EHAS strives to create more effective communications systems between HCs and HPs, specifically focusing on connecting medical staff in the most isolated HPs with their better-resourced counterparts in HCs to achieve four main results:

- improved epidemiological surveillance, given that the previous system relied on late or erroneous reports
- increased diagnostic and treatment capacity in the most isolated HPs, allowing a quick and costless consultation with a proper doctor and better coordination of essential medicinal stocks
- reduced need for trips by patients and medical personnel, and thereby reduced costs (river travel is expensive) that offset the costs of deploying the infrastructure
- reduced average time for emergency transfer of patients when transfer is necessary.

To achieve these results, EHAS supports the design, execution and maintenance of telecommunications infrastructure appropriate for each deployment context – even in unfriendly areas like forests or mountain ranges. These telecommunications networks are based on radio technologies like high frequency (HF), very high frequency (VHF) or WiFi over long distances (WiLD) that are adapted through FOSS to the requirements of each health micro-network. Thanks to this solution EHAS has extended voice and data connectivity to the most isolated environments. Access to the internet and public switched telephone network is achieved by distributing satellite or landline connections available in cities located in a range up to 500 km. In the whole process EHAS works closely with local partners in each focus country, like the Rural Telecommunication Group of Catholic University of Peru or the Telematic Department of Cauca University in Colombia. Besides providing telecommunications infrastructure and voice and data communications services between healthcare centres, EHAS has recently worked on designing and developing telemedicine services for remote consultations.

Once the network is properly functioning, EHAS transfers network control to the local and regional healthcare authorities, which implies training users of the systems and preparing all constituents for the transfer. EHAS Foundation experience shows that using FOSS and open knowledge throughout the process of designing, constructing and maintaining telemedicine networks allows regional health authorities to leverage their limited budgets and make the networks sustainable. FOSS also allows network administrators to reduce problems with viruses and licences, and focus on the many other kinds of hardware network problems, like protecting communication devices in areas where lightning storms are frequent and the humidity level is very high.

The EHAS model for improving healthcare systems

The challenges affecting primary healthcare provision in the developing world involve a wide variety of constituents. This section describes how the EHAS model is pivotal for these various stakeholders to achieve a common goal: a sustainable improvement of healthcare provision in rural areas of developing countries.

Stakeholders involved and their respective roles are presented as the model core in Figure 12.3 and grouped as follows.

- Universities – research institutions in the global South and North that partner with EHAS. They are responsible for furthering shared research and development of FOSS-based ICT solutions for application in isolated rural areas with low-income populations.
- Local government and health authorities – beneficiaries of EHAS projects that receive and own technology and retain the commitment to administer and maintain ICT deployments.
- Health staff – another category of beneficiaries of EHAS projects, as they use the technology in the workplace, thus helping reduce their professional isolation, improve management of health reports and build capacity through increased telemedical diagnosis and information sharing.
- Patients – the primary target population of EHAS projects, who benefit from better healthcare services in their rural villages.

Figure 12.3 shows the process for a targeted improvement of a rural healthcare provision system, and which stakeholder is involved in each step of the process.

- Step 1. The starting point of any project is a case analysis of healthcare, informational and communications needs of the rural primary care providers of the public healthcare system.
- Step 2. This understanding of needs provides inputs to researchers who seek solutions through research and development (R&D).
- Step 3. These solutions are then proved in controlled test-bed scenarios.
- Step 4. Once these solutions are stable in controlled scenarios, they are ready for real project implementation in rural and isolated areas of developing countries.
- Step 5. Feedback from active users of real networks provides new insights and poses new problems to be addressed for the R&D group.
- Step 6. Operation and maintenance of the networks also raises new issues to be improved.
- Step 7. Once context-related challenges have been addressed, the network is ready for real technology adoption and appropriate everyday usage.
- Step 8. This real usage should lead to improved health processes such as increased telemedical consultations, punctual and accurate epidemiological surveillance and improved emergency transport coordination.
- Step 9. The main challenge is to improve the initial situation raised in Step 1 and achieve positive impact on health by improving effectiveness of healthcare processes.

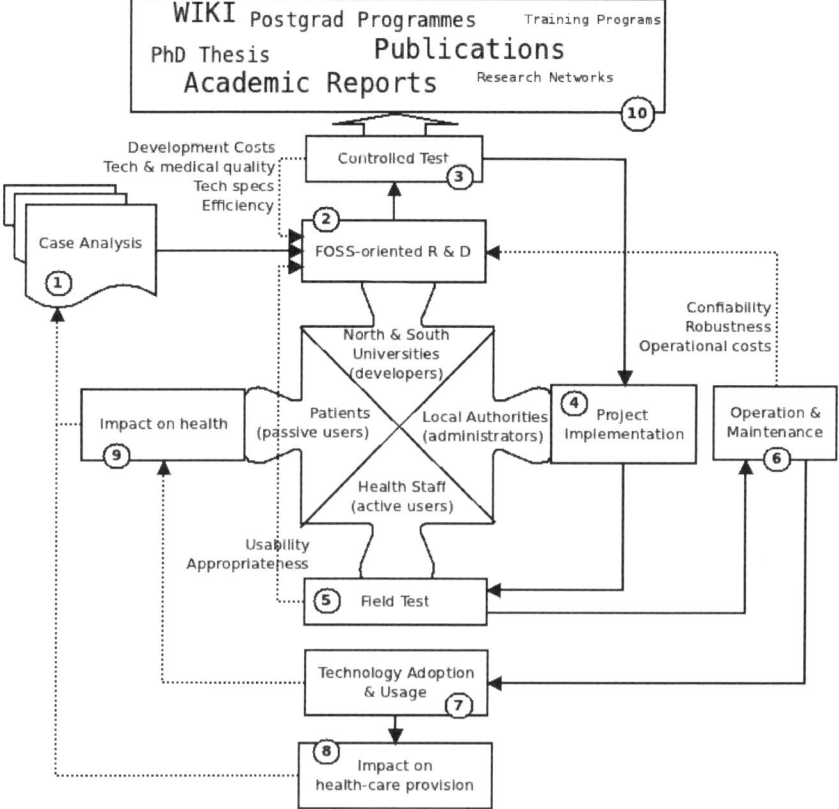

Figure 12.3 EHAS model for sustainable improvement of public healthcare services

- Step 10. Results and lessons learnt through each of these steps are shared openly and widely through academic research and FOSS, so solutions can be further used and adapted anywhere by any individual or institution because they are FOSS based.

FOSS is crucial for this model. Sustainability of ICT applied to development is only feasible if academic and governmental institutions have the tools and know-how to adapt the ICT to achieve the change (Bebea-González et al., 2011). The key is that all processes and roles described above are part of the machinery of open knowledge and open technology, built above the pillar of FOSS. Here, knowledge and technology are not only shared among EHAS partners but also replicable by other institutions. As an example, the Sistema de Interconexión Rural (Rural Interconnection System) in Bolivia has been deployed for the rural health facilities in Riberalta using EHAS technology adapted to the specific context, and the Engineers without Borders Spain multisectoral approach to improve rural healthcare services in Mozambique combines the EHAS model with micro-financing local entrepreneurs for maintaining the network (ISF, n.d.).

The model used and described here is based on three principles: adaptation of technologies to local context (Steps 2–7), impact evaluation of the proposed solutions (Steps 8–9) and replication of these life-saving technologies through the open sharing of knowledge (Step 10). Each of these principles will be presented in the chapter, justifying the steps taken, showing the results obtained and highlighting the lessons learned during more than 10 years of experience of the EHAS Foundation.

Adaptation of technologies

As noted, FOSS is used in almost every aspect of every project carried out by the EHAS Foundation, from network design to final deployment and performance analysis. It is used in the user terminals, the routers that relay information to the closest internet gateway and the servers that provide intranet services to healthcare facilities.

Telecommunication network for voice and data connectivity

The main aim of an EHAS network is to connect isolated HPs to each other and to the referral HC. This connectivity facilitates communication and relevant information sharing throughout the healthcare system. Appropriate technical solutions are different for each place, depending on their geography, climate, isolation, population, needs and resources. However, several characteristics intrinsic to an appropriate communication technology for an isolated rural area have been identified: robustness, low cost, low power consumption and ease of maintenance. To network the scattered populations at a reasonable cost, only wireless technologies seem viable (Brewer et al., 2005).

The most important communication service is local telephony, as it permits staff at rural health facilities to interact in a well-known way with administrative and clinical staff at hospitals. However, data communications have also demonstrated their importance. Access to information systems, exchange of epidemiological information, access to e-learning platforms for capacity building and even access to the internet for general purposes are important communication needs. Hence any communication technology deployed should guarantee local telephony, but should also provide the site with data communication services.

Combining these two features proved difficult with existing technologies back in 1999 when the EHAS Foundation started. The technology needed to be adapted to the local context in which it was deployed and to the communication needs it was trying to solve. Both technology and the FOSS community have evolved wildly in the last 10 years, and the solutions existing in the market today address many of the same challenges existing back in 1999. In this scenario, some of the past developments may seem outdated. However, as seen below, every step was taken to improve public healthcare systems through the use of ICT at the lowest possible cost, making use of the most appropriate technologies available at each instance.

Adaptation of narrowband technologies for the provision of data services
When the EHAS Foundation started, the most appropriate wireless technologies available in the market were HF and VHF radios and satellite transceivers. HF and VHF radios were designed to provide primarily voice, and in some cases also offered low-speed data communications that used high-cost proprietary solutions. Satellite transceivers allowed voice and data communications, but high operating costs hindered the sustainability of such initiatives.

In this context, the first approach used FOSS to develop a solution of transmitting low-rate data over HF and VHF voice-only radios (Figure 12.4), which are much less expensive than voice and data radios. This was done using a computer and an appropriate interface. A radio modem was needed to connect a radio to a computer: to reduce costs and increase flexibility, software modems were used. Software modems can run in any modern workstation, including users' stations, but a cheap,

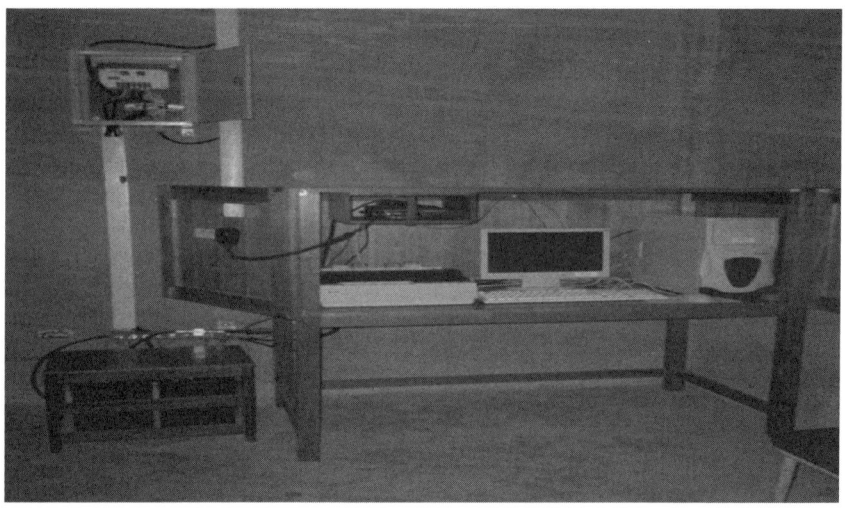

Figure 12.4 EHAS VHF station

low-consumption embedded computer was used instead as a separate platform for interfacing the computer and the radio, which let the user choose freely the operating system for his/her workstation.

To build the software modem, the solution relies on the availability of a sound modem package for GNU/Linux (Sailer, 2000) which implements different modems, each optimized for use in a specific band. Although the package was developed for data transmissions, some modifications were necessary to optimize modems for an environment where propagation conditions were difficult, including the creation of a completely new AX.25 control packet mechanism in the Linux Kernel and the adaptation of UUCP (Unix-to-Unix Copy Protocol) to provide TCP-like services, like e-mail, on top of the data link layer (Martínez et al., 2007).

With the technical solution achieved, several telemedicine networks were deployed in Colombia and Peru using the HF/VHF bands the governments had granted to the health authorities, allowing healthcare centres to use voice and low-speed data services (Rendón et al., 2005; Martínez et al., 2004). However, this solution proved far too complex and it was very difficult to train local technicians to maintain the data services. As a result, medical technicians did not adapt to services they had never used before, and networks functioned exclusively as voice-only.

Adaptation of WiFi for long-distance links
Over time other technologies appeared in the market that could offer improved solutions. One such technology was WiFi, which operated in the non-licensed ISM (industrial, scientific and medical) radio to allow voice and data communications in a wireless local area network with very low-cost devices. The low cost and open frequency band encouraged an effort to use WiFi beyond the local area networks. It was found there were no physical constraints for wide area networks, but performance was not optimal for long distances due to protocol issues. Two parameters – slottime and acktimeout – needed to be adapted to achieve an optimal and predictable performance for long-distance links (Simó-Reigadas et al., 2010). Both parameters can be easily set up on some wireless cards, especially those based on Atheros chipsets, which include the FOSS MadWifi driver. Finally, for WiFi-based networks, a solar-powered wireless router was developed (Figure 12.5). It used an embedded computer similar to the one used as communication processor for VHF/HF networks. With this device, along with a Debian-based GNU/Linux operating system, it was possible to set up not only WiFi fine tuning and routing but other functions like quality of service support, voice over IP (VoIP) using an Asterisk package and a network management system (NMS) (Simó-Reigadas et al., 2008). With this solution many WiFi routers were deployed, and many other healthcare facilities were provided with IP broadband ser-

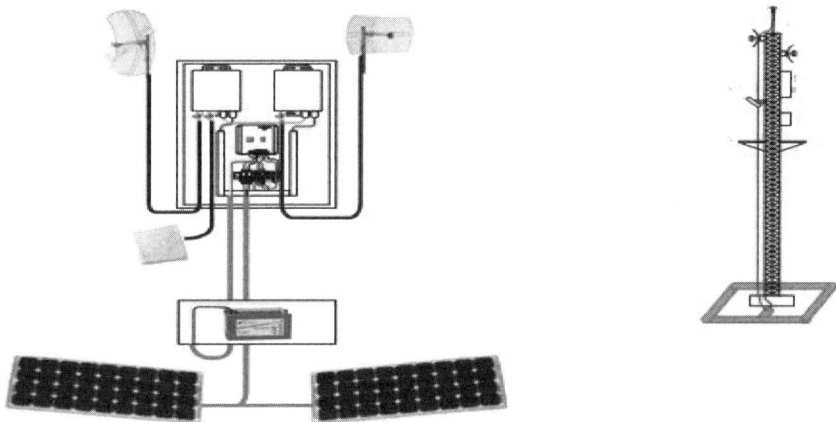

Figure 12.5 EHAS WiFi router

vices (Rendón et al., 2005; Simó et al., 2006) including videoconferencing and VoIP with quality of service.

Today, long-range broadband wireless technologies have come of age and several manufacturers, such as MikroTik and Ubiquiti, offer proprietary WiFi-like solutions that outperform by several times the standard solution developed. The EHAS Foundation has always advocated the use of standard communication technologies that facilitate interoperability among different manufacturers and the use of FOSS for adapting them to the context in which they are to be deployed. But for a small organization like EHAS, maintaining a stable solution over the years by installing all the security updates of the packages and their dependencies was too tough and time-consuming a task.

To solve this dilemma, a Spanish company was approached to maintain the solution in exchange for complete access to all its R&D. Unfortunately, this arrangement proved infeasible. So each time a network is going to be deployed, new tests need to be done with the solar-powered router to check the compatibility of the latest packages available. Now that cost-effective solutions have emerged, it is time for EHAS to reconsider if the resources devoted to developing and maintaining FOSS communication solutions are compensated by the performance obtained. This potential change of strategy will go against the principles EHAS has applied over the last 10 years, but will allow better focus on other solutions for improving healthcare provision.

The use of FOSS for network design, simulation and management

FOSS has been considered in the stages of design, simulation and monitoring of the network, with different results. The design of networks is strongly based on free but not-open software called RadioMobile – the FOSS alternatives are by far lower performing, and EHAS lacks the resources to develop such tools. Other supplementary tools of great value for network design and simulation are network simulators like NS-2 and NS-3. EHAS has developed a solution that integrates RadioMobile and NS-3 for cross-layer network design. However, while NS-2 was almost abandoned because of its many limitations as a complex FOSS that is at the end of its life cycle, NS-3 is at the beginning of its life cycle and cannot be entirely trusted for the moment. It has to be recognized that, in this case, the use of FOSS is very much conditioned by the extremely high price of proprietary network simulators like QualNet or OPNET. There are also technical reasons related to the need to modify internal parameters that are not accessible in the proprietary solutions that made EHAS use FOSS alternatives.

A similar choice drove EHAS to use FOSS solutions for network operation and maintenance. Guaranteeing availability of connectivity and other services is not an easy task in rural areas of developing countries. However, licensed professional solutions for NMS are extremely expensive and not flexible, so solutions based on FOSS products such as Zabbix and Nagios Core (Maya Ortiz, Sánchez and Lara, 2009) have been developed. The flexibility of FOSS permitted EHAS to develop and extend management agents and management GNU/Linux scripts. In this effort, EHAS developed an extension of the IEEE 802.11 Management Information Base (based in RFC 1213) to include specific parameters for WiLD links. As Figure 12.6 shows, this system allows clear visibility of network activities, which leads to easier management of problems when they occur (Bebea-González et al., 2011).

FOSS has also been used to adapt the NMS to obtain a solution ideally suited to the project's needs (Figure 12.7). A gateway from Nagios to a FOSS request tracker for incident response was developed to record NMS alarms and incidents reported by users, as well as time to response and recovery time in EHAS networks (ibid.).

Regarding the operating system used in user desktops, context-related situations have also obliged the use of proprietary technologies on some occasions. Although FOSS is always the first option, EHAS must accept that its preferences as project proponents cannot be imposed when the reality of the network users contains restrictions that make the adoption of FOSS impractical.

Teleservices offered by the EHAS Foundation

No matter what technology is chosen to interconnect healthcare facilities, broadband is granted in the intranet. Thus other telemedicine services can be implemented for medical technicians at the HPs not only to talk

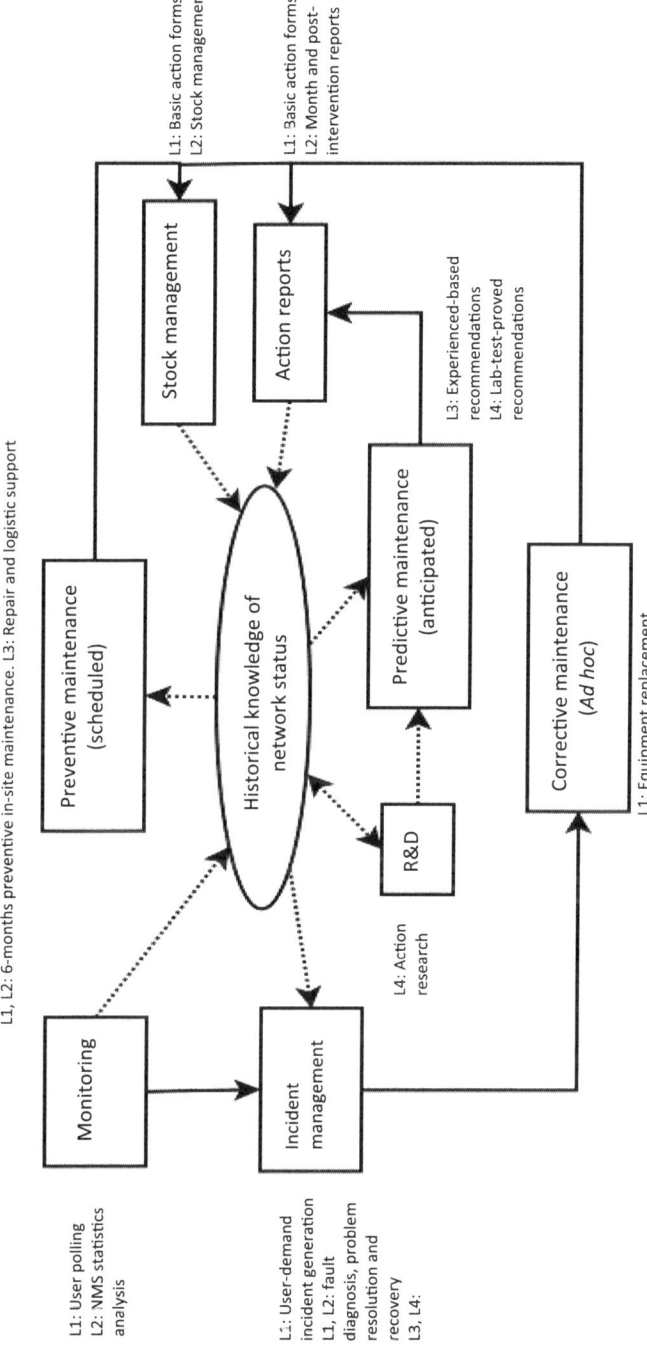

Figure 12.6 Management framework for operation and maintenance of rural e-healthcare

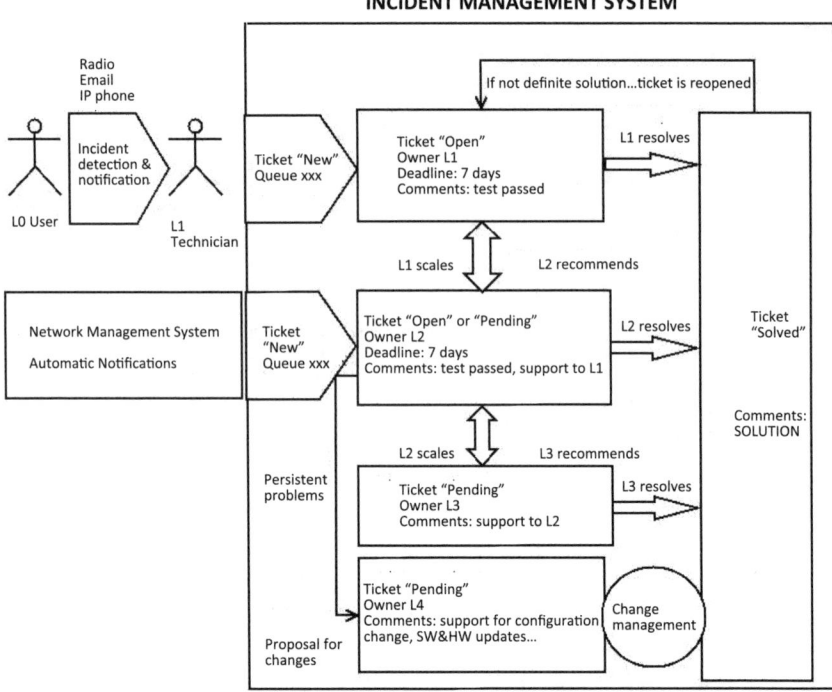

Figure 12.7 Workflow for incident escalation in management framework

with doctors at the HC and the hospital but also send images, videos or sounds for a doctor to have better information of the disease the technician is facing. Most of the telemedicine software and hardware to acquire and send these data are proprietary and prohibitively expensive in the scenarios where these networks are installed. In this context, the EHAS Foundation has used FOSS to developing alternative tools.

Diagnostic support tools
In recent years EHAS has worked on the development of appropriate diagnostic tools to address these problems in remote locations. This is a collaborative effort with two Spanish hospitals (Cáceres and Fuenlabrada) and an Argentinian foundation (Fundatel): it focuses on ways to improve diagnosis and treatment of common infant diseases (such as respiratory conditions and diarrhoea) and improve maternal health.

One example of this FOSS effort is a real-time wireless stethoscope for use in HPs where there is no physician (Figure 12.8). This instrument allows a doctor (usually the reference physician located in the HC) to listen remotely to the respiratory and cardiac sounds of a patient (located

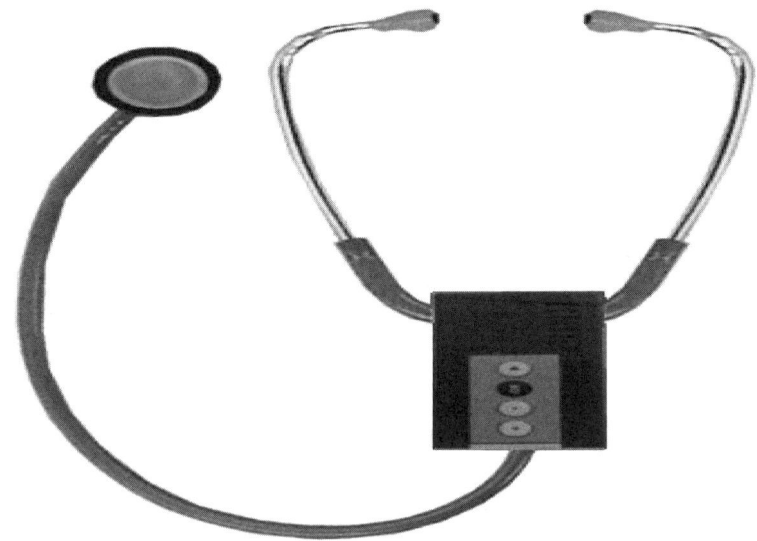

Figure 12.8 EHAS tele-stethoscope

in the HP) while viewing him using a common webcam, and guiding the medical technician (in the HP) in the correct positioning of the stethoscope. The PulseAudio networked sound server (GPLv2) and the softphone Ekiga (GPLv2), to support video-conferencing, have been used. The software and the hardware, specifically developed for the stethoscope, are open source (GPLv3) and open hardware respectively. This device is now in a validation process in collaboration with San Pedro Alcantara Hospital in Cáceres, and is being tried in the research health network EHAS installed in the Napo River HP and HC in Peru as a real-use scenario. The outcomes of both processes will bring the device to its next prototype version.

Another system has been developed for transferring microscopy (to help with diarrhoeal disease diagnosis) and ultrasound (for foetal control) images. In these cases, Java-based open architecture ImageJ has been used for the acquisition, analysis and image processing, and the iPath server, written in PHP, to provide a free and open web platform to support diagnosing cases online. A third example is a specially designed electrocardiograph adapted for use in these difficult rural circumstances. Again its software, necessary for system control, has been developed under the Django web platform (BSD licence), and Arduino has been used for the hardware design.

Validation tests are currently being carried out in Spanish hospitals and field tests are planned in a pilot project in the Napo River in Peru.

After these steps, further lessons in the design of open hardware/software solutions will be learnt. In addition, once validated all these teleservice systems will be kept free, thus providing a cheaper and more flexible alternative to proprietary solutions to those interested in improving primary healthcare in rural areas of developing countries.

Health information systems

As discussed, improving efficiency in health information exchange related to epidemiological reports, telemedicine diagnosis and patient referral is one of the biggest opportunities for EHAS to improve health outcomes. A health information system (HIS) is both software architecture and a discipline at the intersection of information science and healthcare. It deals with the resources, devices and methods required to optimize the acquisition, storage, retrieval, statistical calculation and use of information in health and medicine.

In this area, the EHAS Foundation and its local partners are involved in the design of a software prototype to manage health information related to most common epidemic and clinical outbreaks in the target countries. OpenMRS, a Java-based, web-based electronic medical record, is being used to adapt the technology to the needs of the different health facilities and their clinical staff. Its basic functionality is to be a generic medical record system to support the clinical history of patients, gathering observations, encounters, notes, and finally rendering those in summaries, reports and data views that improve the effectiveness of health workers using the system.

Evaluation of the EHAS interventions

Significant positive results have been achieved and verified in the EHAS interventions using the methodology defined by Martínez (2001): from 93 per cent of healthcare workers who previously said it was impossible to obtain a consultation to 95 per cent who now say it is easy and fast to get this help in cases where there was doubt (this is reflected in a 700 per cent increase in the number of consultations); a 75 per cent reduction in the number of trips required for the delivery of reports; a 60 per cent reduction in the average time for transferring emergency patients; and significant reduction in the maternal and newborn child morbidity and mortality rates in the project areas (Martínez et al., 2004).

These positive quantitative impacts have continued, and nowadays EHAS has a signed commitment of the healthcare and regional authorities in the Loreto region of Peru to keep the network alive through budgeting for the maintenance of EHAS networks, guaranteeing its sustainability. Furthermore, EHAS has had lasting qualitative impacts: for instance, in Peru and Colombia its local partners have grown to develop several projects of their own and are now financially independent and self-sustaining.

FOSS has played an important role in achieving all these positive impacts. As has been shown, it has helped achieve sustainable development for the initiatives not only through the entire process of building local capacity, but also in research, development, testing and adaptation of communication technologies and services specifically tailored to the needs of project beneficiaries (Bebea-González, Liñán and Rey-Moreno, 2010).

EHAS also acknowledges some mistakes during these years; mistakes which have served to educate the institution and help adapt solutions to the ever-changing world of technology. The EHAS Foundation considers it important to share freely all knowledge generated, so others benefit from the steps that obtain positive impact and avoid those leading to negative impact. External actors benefiting from it will expand both the base of knowledge and the positive impact of ICT interventions. The steps taken and lessons learnt are described in the next section.

Open knowledge

As said, one of the main objectives of the EHAS Foundation is to disseminate broadly and promptly all knowledge gained during the research, development or adaptation of software and hardware solutions. This implies the use of General Public License for every software solution proposed, but also making available the documentation and academic work related to developments. Everything that has been learnt during these years is on the EHAS website (www.ehas.org) for everybody to use: graduate and postgraduate theses, articles, conference presentations, posters, wiki discussions, training materials, etc. Furthermore, in a step to put together in a single and neat document all the knowledge and experience achieved, a book in Spanish was edited (Camacho and Rey-Moreno, 2008), and later updated and reviewed by the local partners in Peru (Carbajal, 2009). Creative Commons licensing was used to allow broader access to the contents of the book, which was also made available online.

As a way to disseminate knowledge further, the EHAS Foundation participates in a master's programme offered at Universidad Rey Juan Carlos de Madrid in Spain (TSC-URJC, n.d.). It started in 2008 and has since had an average of 25 engineers per year from all Latin American countries who learn from the experience obtained in these years of

FOSS-oriented networks. The idea is to create a critical mass of professionals and researchers in Latin American universities who are able to advocate FOSS as a technology of choice and improve further sustainable development of ICT initiatives.

Quantifying the impact of these initiatives on open knowledge is a very difficult task. Although some feedback on the use of EHAS solutions has been received, it is believed that more could be done to disseminate further the knowledge gained. EHAS has no budget to market its website, so visibility of its repository is limited to those who have internet access and know it is there. Furthermore, it is claimed that all the solutions are open source, but some are not hosted in a public repository for the broader open source community to engage with the project, so they cannot be considered completely free and open. As highlighted in previous sections, the institution is constrained by a limited number of human resources and a small budget. With such a limited staff, it is difficult to produce, maintain and disseminate all the knowledge gained. This is a problem yet to be solved.

Future trends

In the field of ICT for development (ICT4D), software developers face problems that are specific to underserved areas. The community of developers involved in projects in this field is usually very small because the problems faced are too specific. Financial resources for software development are usually scarce and of short duration. These extra handicaps must be taken into account before adopting a FOSS approach. While FOSS is always desirable, its cost must be effectively measured for not only development but also maintenance and long-term support of the solutions developed.

Many people who develop and promote the use of FOSS tend to give a high priority to the fact that software and information must be open for ideological reasons, as has often been the case for the EHAS Foundation. The obvious advantages of open software and open information are magnified, while the development costs, the difficulties in achieving stable products and other obstacles to sustainability are neglected. This is especially frequent in the domain of ICT4D. However, as actors gain experience, more accurate analysis permits recognition of the power and the limits of FOSS in a more realistic manner.

The questions that arise for future ICT4D projects concern when FOSS must be adopted and when it presents too many disadvantages and must not be imposed. From the experiences presented in the previous sections, the following strategies derive.

- Whenever a new product or service must be developed for the first time, FOSS is the best choice. If there are software modules that can be used as a starting point, it fosters development. But even if development starts from scratch, the possibility of collaborating with others and obtaining their support may be a key to success. Sometimes this is the starting point, but the industry proposes later packaged products that are cheaper, more robust and with higher performance than the previous FOSS solutions. That was the case for EHAS with WiLD communication systems. Developers must recognize that situation and identify the moment when their efforts are better invested in other projects.
- When a product exists in the market in the form of a commercial non-FOSS solution, and FOSS alternatives do not exist or do not meet the specifications, two options must be considered: develop a complete FOSS product, or use and evaluate a commercial alternative first. In the first case, it must be understood that user needs will be met only after the whole development cycle and, if successful, a continuous effort will be required to guarantee long-term sustainability. In the second case, a FOSS project may still be initiated once the utility has been proved and the specifications are derived from real user needs. This way, the FOSS development does not impact the beneficiaries in a negative way in the short term, and a successful product may become an interesting alternative in the future.
- And, of course, when a good FOSS product already exists, that is the solution to adopt.

In particular, broadband communications systems tend to be non-FOSS solutions because good low-cost products are available in the market under different standards that make infrastructure much more stable than any solution based on embedded computers with FOSS. Telemedicine devices follow the same trends: FOSS has been useful for prototyping, but user needs seem only to be met through the appearance of low-cost commercial products in the market. Manufacturers have a high resistance to developing a commercial strategy based on free software, and efforts must be made to promote FOSS-based industrial products in which manufacturers may obtain the help of a wider community in lowering the development costs.

Regarding services that are specific to the health sector, it is especially important to promote the adoption of FOSS in HIS. While immediate solutions may or may not be FOSS based, it would be extremely interesting in the long term to count on solid and well-supported FOSS solutions. Examples from other sectors, such as tele-education, show that a FOSS solution may become the best, and the advantages would be enormous in the case of the health domain for adaptation and integration purposes.

General services like IP telephony, mail, web, etc. may be based on FOSS already, as there are very solid options whose adoption is straightforward.

Concluding remarks

The EHAS Foundation has always worked on the basis of a profound conviction that knowledge and software must be free and open for fostering human development. FOSS maximizes both outreach and impact. As explained throughout this chapter, this commitment to sharing information has marked most of its technological choices and all its R&D, documentation and academic activity. However, also based on this experience, FOSS cannot always be adopted when real impact is a must. EHAS aims to improve the lives of poor people in disadvantaged regions, thus impact on their livelihoods is a higher priority than any technological choice. These are the main reasons that have in reality limited a complete adoption of a FOSS and open knowledge paradigm.

- FOSS does not mean that one can modify the software for free. The cost of modifying, stabilizing and testing complex software packages may be very high in terms of the time and human resources required, as has been the case for EHAS in its e-learning platform, network simulators and software modems.
- FOSS is only meaningful when it happens in collaboration with a wide community that shares the effort and responsibility along the development process, but creating such a community is also a costly task.
- Interaction with beneficiaries that have already adopted non-FOSS solutions sometimes further limits the adoption of FOSS proposals. That was the case for the adoption of GNU/Linux as the operating system of end users in some health networks where several applications required the use of MS Windows. One can always think that software emulators may solve the problem, but that is not always the case.

Even with these restrictions, most of the development activities and final products developed by the EHAS Foundation have been FOSS based, and immense benefits have been experienced from this approach. FOSS inspires collaboration, openness and distribution of resources and business models based on the effort and not on withholding information for specific organizational gain. FOSS is, in general terms and in the humble opinion of EHAS, the best possible philosophy to make R&D, innovation and human development compatible. However, one must always remember that information and software are means and not goals in most real projects, and openness must be seen as a very desirable tendency in which exceptions are sometimes necessary to provide people with real solutions to their problems.

REFERENCES

Bagayoko, C., H. Müler and A. Geissbuhler (2006) "Assessment of Internet-based Tele-medicine in Africa (the RAFT Project)", *Computerized Medical Imaging and Graphics* 30(6/7), pp. 407–416.
Bebea-González, I., L. Liñán and C. Rey-Moreno (2010) "Design of a Sustainability Action Plan for EHAS-Napo Project: A Rural E-Health Initiative", in *Proceedings of the IPID PG at IEEE/ACM International Conference on ICTD2010*, Karlstad: Karlstad University Studies, pp. 14–18.
Bebea-González, I., A. Martínez-Fernández and C. Rey-Moreno (2011) *Manual TIC y Salud*, Madrid: Ministry of International Relations and Development.
Bebea-González, I., J. A. Paco, L. Liñán-Benítez, F. J. Símo-Reigadas and A. Martínez-Fernández (2011) "Management Framework for Sustainable E-Healthcare Provision", in *Proceedings of the IADIS International Conference e-Society*, Ávila: IADIS, pp. 157–164.
Braa, J., O. Hanseth, W. Mohammed, A. Heywood and V. Shaw (2007) "Developing Health Information Systems in Developing Countries: The Flexible Standards Strategy", *MIS Quarterly* 31(2), pp. 381–402.
Brewer, E., M. Demmer, B. Du, M. Ho, M. Kam, S. Nedevski, J. Pal, R. Patra, S. Surana and K. Fall (2005) "The Case for Technology in Developing Regions", *IEEE Computer* 38(6), pp. 25–38.
CAIBCO (2007) "S.O.S. Telemedicina para Venezuela", Centro de Análisis de Imágenes Biomédicas Computarizadas, Universidad Central de Venezuela; available at http://caibco.ucv.ve/SOSTelemedicina.pdf (accessed 16 May 2011).
Camacho, L. and C. Rey-Moreno (eds) (2008) "Redes Inalámbricas para Zonas Rurales", Grupo de Telecomunicaciones Rurales, Universidad Católica del Perú; available at http://gtr.telecom.pucp.edu.pe/system/files/1041.pdf (accessed 1 May 2010).
Carbajal, D. (ed.) (2009) "WiLD: WiFi Based Long Distance", Grupo de Telecomunicaciones Rurales, Universidad Católica del Perú; available at http://gtr.telecom.pucp.edu.pe/system/files/Wild.pdf (accessed 1 May 2011).
Dorsch, J. L. (2000) "Information Needs of Rural Health Professionals: A Review of the Literature", *Bulletin of the Medical Library Association* 88(4), pp. 346–354.
ISF (n.d.) "ISF ApD en Cabo Delgado, Mozambique", Ingeniería sin Fronteras; available at http://sites.google.com/site/isfapdmozambique/ (accessed 9 December 2010).
Kopec, A. and A. Salazar (2002) *Aplicaciones de telecomunicaciones en salud en la subregión andina: Telemedicina*, Washington, DC: WHO Regional Office.
Macha Works (2011) "Macha Works"; available at www.machaworks.org/en/healthcare.asp (accessed 16 March 2011).
Martínez, A. (2001) *Bases metodológicas para evaluar la viabilidad y el impacto de proyectos de Telemedicina*, Washington, DC: WHO Regional Office.
Martínez, A., V. Villarroel, J. Seoane and F. Del Pozo (2004) "A Study of a Rural Telemedicine System in the Amazon Region of Peru", *Journal of Telemedicine and Telecare* 10(4), pp. 219–226.

—— (2005a) "Analysis of Information and Communication Needs in Rural Primary Healthcare in Developing Countries", *IEEE Transactions on Information Technology in Biomedicine* 9(1), pp. 66–72.

Martínez, A., D. M. López, A. Sanz, J. Seoane, A. Rendón, R. G. Shoemaker and I. Fernández (2005b) "Improving Epidemiologic Surveillance and Health Promoter Training in Rural Latin America through Information and Communication Technologies", *Telemedicine and e-Health* 11(4), pp. 468–476.

Martínez, A., J. Símo, J. Seoane, A. Sánchez, S. Salmerón, S. Lafuente, V. Villarroel and F. Osuna (2007) "Low-Cost Telecommunication Systems and Information Services for Rural Primary Healthcare in Developing Countries", paper presented at World Information Technology Forum, Addis Ababa, 22–24 August; available at http://hdl.handle.net/10115/2351 (accessed 26 April 2012).

Maya Ortiz, E., A. Sánchez and E. Lara (2009) "Architecture in Network Administration for Heterogeneous Environments and Its Application in EHAS Networks", *Latin American Journal of Telehealth* 1(1), pp. 129–135; available at http://cetes.medicina.ufmg.br/revista/index.php/rlat/article/view/10 (accessed 3 March 2011).

Pun, M., R. Shields, R. Poudel and R. Mucci (2006) "Nepal Wireless Networking Project: Case Study and Evaluation Report", Knowledge Networking for Rural Development in Asia/Pacific Region (ENRAP); available at www.eldis.org/go/display&type+Document&id+33292 (accessed 26 April 2012).

Rendón, A., A. Martínez, M. F. Dulcey, J. Seoane, R. G. Shoemaker, V. Villarroel, D. M. López and J. Símo (2005) "Rural Telemedicine Infrastructure and Services in the Department of Cauca, Colombia", *Telemedicine and e-Health* 11(4), pp. 451–459.

Rey, C. (2008) "A Systematic Review of Telemedicine Projects in Colombia", master's dissertation, Aalborg University, Denmark; available at http://projekter.aau.dk/projekter/files/14952659/Systematic_Review_of_Telemedicine_Projects_in_Colombia.pdf (accessed 16 May 2011).

Sachpazidis, I., S. Kiefer, P. Selby, R. Ohl and G. Sakas (2006) "A Medical Network for Teleconsultations in Brazil and Colombia", in *Second IASTED International Conference on Telehealth*, Anaheim: IASTED/ACTA Press, pp. 16–21.

Sailer, T. (2000) "Soundmodem on Modern Operating Systems", paper presented at ARRL and TAPR Digital Communications Conference, Orlando, 22–24 September; available at www.baycom.org/~tom/ham/dcc2000/soundmodem.pdf (accessed 4 February 2011).

Seebregts, C. J., B. W. Mamlin, P. G. Biondich, H. S. Fraser, B. A. Wolfe, D. Jazayeri, C Allen, J. Miranda, E. Baker, N. Musinguzi, D. Kayiwa, C. Fourie, N. Lesh, A. Kanter, C. T. Yiannoutsos and C. Bailey (2009) "The OpenMRS Implementers Network", *International Journal of Medical Informatics* 78(11), pp. 711–720.

Simó, J., P. Osuna, R. Quispe and D. Segundo (2006) "Application of IEEE 802.11 Technology for Health Isolated Rural Environments", paper presented at IFIP WCCWCIT 2006, Santiago de Chile, August; available at www.ehas.org/wp-content/uploads/2012/01/Application-of-IEEE-802_11-technology-for-health-isolated-rural-environments.pdf (accessed 4 February 2011).

Simó-Reigadas, J., A. Martinez-Fernandez, J. Ramos-Lopez and J. Seoane (2010) "Modeling and Optimizing IEEE 802.11 DCF for Long-Distance Links", *IEE Transactions on Mobile Computing* 9(6), pp. 881–896.

Simó-Reigadas, J., A. Martínez-Fernández, P. Osuna-García, S. Lafuente and J. Seoane-Pascual (2008) "The Design of a Wireless Solar-Powered Router for Rural Environments Isolated from Health Facilities", *Wireless Communication Magazine* 15(3), pp. 24–30.

Surana, S., R. Patra, S. Nedevschi and E. Brewer (2008) "Deploying a Rural Wireless Telemedicine System: Experiences in Sustainability", *IEEE Computer* 41(6), pp. 48–56.

TeleMed (2011) "Telemedicine Defined", American Telemedicine Association; available at www.americantelemed.org/i4a/pages/index.cfm?pageid=3333 (accessed 23 May 2011).

TSC-URJC (n.d.) "COMPAD: Máster Universitario en Redes de Telecomunicación para Países en Desarrollo"; available at www.tsc.urjc.es/Master/COMPAD/ (accessed 2 April 2011).

Wootton, R. (2008) "Telemedicine Support for the Developing World", *Journal of Telemedicine and Telecare* 14(3), pp. 109–114.

Wootton, R., N. G. Patil, R. E. Scott and K. Ho (2009) *Telehealth in the Developing World*, Ottawa, ON: International Development Research Centre.

13
FOSS in school communities: An experience report from Peace Corps volunteers in Ghana

Caroline Hardin

Introduction

The problem this chapter addresses is how the presence of free and open source software (FOSS) in school communities can be increased, how to leverage the role of local attitudes and perceptions about FOSS, and best practices for foreign volunteers in encouraging sustainable adoption of FOSS in schools in developing countries. The country in the context of this Peace Corps volunteer's experience is Ghana.

Educational settings seem a natural environment for FOSS to succeed. Schools in the developing world need a large amount of cheap, reliable, low-maintenance and high-quality educational software with low hardware requirements – all things that FOSS excels at when compared to current proprietary options. The introduction of FOSS into a school can mean the difference between the children getting a quality ICT (information and communication technologies) education and computers sitting idle because they have been rendered useless by viruses and other problems. The importance of the software being free and requiring little in the way of hardware and professional maintenance is enormous in schools which frequently have to choose between buying food for the students and maintaining the computer lab. For teachers who are overwhelmed with many hundreds of students, anything to reduce maintenance overheads is vital. In addition, FOSS brings the possibility of new information and multimedia content to schools where the alternative is a 50-year-old encyclopaedia which is missing volumes. Schools are also an attractive

---

Free and open source software and technology for sustainable development, Sowe, Parayil and Sunami (eds), United Nations University Press, 2012, ISBN 978-92-808-1217-6

target for promoting FOSS because of the opportunity to reach a large number of children who are enthusiastic and unbiased learners, and who can continue to promote FOSS for decades as they move into their careers.

Peace Corps volunteers (PCVs) are an apt subject for a case study because of their unique and highly valuable experience: after three months of intensive cultural training, each volunteer is immersed for two years in a deprived community and, using only locally sourced materials, funds and talent, helps to develop that community with a constant emphasis on sustainability. This allows them to gain a rich understanding of local people and their motivations, limitations, needs and desires, while also grounding them deeply in the practical realities of people's lives. Local attitudes towards FOSS include both awareness of and reaction to FOSS-type software. These attitudes are a key element in its voluntary adoption: whether it is seen as easy and "cool" or difficult and strange (Pykalainen, 2008). This chapter draws on this perspective and wisdom using both the author's three years of experience teaching FOSS in Ghanaian high school and college contexts, and documents, surveys and interviews with other Ghanaians and PCVs who worked with FOSS in their communities.

An anecdote that helps illustrate the importance of doing local needs assessment, collaborating with the local ICT leaders and stakeholders, and providing comprehensive follow-up support occurred in 2007 during the author's second year in Nalerigu Senior High School (NASS):

At that time, the school science resource center was in terrible condition – the sinks had all broken or fallen through the rotting lab tables, the building lacked running water or reliable electricity, no classroom had sufficient chairs and, as you might expect, the computers were broken relics. I had tried to repair the half-dozen computers; unfortunately, all but one was beyond repair. They weren't even good for parts as a previous repair person had stolen the working RAM and hard drives. The science department desperately wanted a computer for typing of lesson notes, exams, and project work, but the one I had repaired could only run Windows 98 and thus had no flash drive support, and was not of much use to them.

The head of the science department told me that the government periodically made grand promises to restock all the science resource centers with the glassware, chemicals, and computers they needed so badly; and the schools, chronically short on cash, did not want to invest in the science labs if an outside force might someday bring them everything free. Especially if they developed the lab on their own, they might render themselves ineligible for a need-based restocking. The lab had been deteriorating for most of a decade when I was called suddenly to the headmaster's office, where I was introduced to a British man. He said he worked for a foreign company which the government had contracted to do the science lab resupply, and indeed, he had come with a SUV packed with dozens of boxes. As we unloaded them into the lab, we couldn't believe the wealth that had suddenly been brought – including three powerful computers, a projector, an electronic microscope, and a printer. The man said that because his company had not understood how long it would take to get through customs, he was months behind on his deliveries. I exchanged a glance with the head of the science department – they probably had failed to take into account the culture in which bribes were a standard part of the red tape at customs and everything moves slowly. The original plan was for him to give the teachers a half-day's training in the new equipment, but now he would barely have an hour.

The man neglected the traditional formalities; he rushed us through the set-up, assured us that good anti-virus was installed already, sped us through a wealth of powerful new science instruction software and equipment, and finally detected a problem with the projector and took it with him, saying it'd be replaced.

The school never did see a replacement projector – we can only assume it was a lost detail, or stolen. My fellow teachers and I weren't too surprised – we'd grown to expect such things.

My emotions of the visit taught me a valuable lesson. First I was shocked at how fast he moved, how fast he talked, how he seemed to want to rush through everything. I realized that must be how I was sometimes seen. I was ecstatic over the windfall, but also, rather offended. Who was this man, to come casually swooping in, bringing prizes far beyond the meager gains we'd sweated and fought for? Didn't he recognize how hard we'd worked for what he thoughtlessly declared inadequate? Indeed, why had I spent all those hours struggling to repair the old, terrible computers if this man was just going to bring us expensive new ones? And the equipment, though wonderful, was not well chosen. He gave us SATA hard drives, which don't reinstall Windows XP properly. He gave us anti-virus which we couldn't update without an internet connection. He didn't disable the auto-run feature because he wasn't aware that the pen-drive auto-run was a major virus vector in Ghana.

The software was possibly the most beautiful and the most offensive. It was so wonderful – one let you build custom chemical reaction animations. Another did incredible interactive biology demonstrations. But what did this say to the hardworking, humble biology teacher, who struggled for years to teach mitosis on a crumbling blackboard with sub-par chalk, and had gotten admirably good at it? It made his expertise and efforts seem shoddy, pathetic, and worthless. He was given no training in this software. He never used it. The computers were deemed too valuable to be used in the main classroom where students might damage them, and were put in the lab offices. A few weeks later they had become so corrupted by viruses that they tried to reinstall them, and were stuck because of Windows XP's problems installing to SATA drives. The teachers asked me for help, and after talking to them at length about what they needed, I showed them how to reformat the computers with Ubuntu, gave them individualized training, and provided detailed notes. I continued to support them in the next couple of months by answering questions and giving additional training. The teachers were satisfied to be able to type exams, prepare hand-out packets, and complete papers for their continuing education. The new computers may not be transforming the science lab as intended, but they have increased the capacity of the teachers to do quality work.

This experience illustrates that new resources must be introduced only after those affected have been consulted, their individual needs considered, proper training given to the stakeholders and comprehensive support options offered. To do otherwise is to squander resources and potentially offend the very people you are trying to assist.

Theoretical framework

While many projects and pieces of educational software hold great promise for schools in the developing world, this chapter focuses on those that were in use by PCVs in Ghana in their school communities during the period 2007–2010. This list includes Ubuntu, OpenOffice, Wikipedia for Schools, FET timetables, GIMP, Tux Paint, KTouch and the Gutenberg Project. The hardware, policy and cultural contexts are examined for their roles in encouraging sustainable adoption of FOSS.

This experience report also makes use of both an online survey conducted by the author and structured and unstructured interviews with schools teachers, students and curriculum and FOSS technology experts. For the survey data, an online open source software for Ghana survey (https://www.surveymonkey.com/s/madamCaroline) was created and promoted via media such as Facebook and blogs. The survey was active in January–February 2011, and collected both quantitative and qualitative data. The respondents came from a variety of backgrounds, from rural school students to IT professionals in the capital city, as well as Ghana PCVs both current and returned. From 76 responses, duplicates and empty surveys were removed: 18 PCVs and 40 Ghanaians completed at least some portion of the survey. In calculating preference for software, each percentage is based only on the portion that had experience using that software. The number of respondents represented by a percentage might vary, as blank responses caused by internet connectivity challenges in Ghana were removed from the total for each question. A demo of the survey is maintained online (www.surveymonkey.com/s/DEMO-FOSS-SURVEY).

To gain more qualitative data and anecdotes, additional questions were asked by e-mail, Google chat and Facebook (in lieu of the phone interviews mentioned in the survey text). Updates were solicited in January 2012, and included where relevant. These interviews were combined with the author's experiences from three years administering high school and college computer labs, and working as the ICT Think-Tank coordinator for approximately 140 Peace Corps Ghana volunteers.

Technology background and implementation strategies

This section looks at the hardware challenges and best practices for distribution of software, promoting local knowledge and initiative in FOSS, the impact of viruses and the influence of the government-issued syllabi. All these elements are important background context that affects the successful adoption of FOSS solutions.

Challenges and best practices: Software distribution

One of the biggest challenges to introducing FOSS is the state of CD-ROM drives across Ghana. While they were very common, their condition was often very poor. For example, in early 2007 at NASS seven out of 25 computers had working drives. The large amounts of climatic dust and the lack of maintenance equipment meant they got dirty quickly and were rarely cleaned. The only lens-cleaning disks available at stores were cheaply made and entirely ineffectual – a proper one sent from the United States would regularly remove incredible amounts of dust from the lens. "Cans-of-air" were not to be had in most of Ghana, and the electric blowers for sale worked much better for motherboards than for the insides of CD-ROM drives. The potential of DVDs was additionally limited by their increased cost and relative rarity, making projects such as OpenDisk, SuperOS, Wikipedia for Schools and Gutenberg less promising. It was not uncommon for a computer lab to lack a single DVD drive, and in some cases entire towns lacked them. As DVD drives gradually become more common, DVDs will become a more viable distribution media.

Flash drives, despite being very popular and common, are frequently victim to theft, heat and virus problems. They also lack the saturation rate of CDs due to their higher prices (in 2011, $8 per gigabyte). Finally, software placed on them was often deleted, either deliberately or accidentally, or by the ubiquitous viruses. Flash drives thus play a limited role in cheap and widespread distribution of FOSS. Floppy disks could hardly be found in any major city and were quickly ruined by the heat, though they were used occasionally as boot disks for computers without working CD-ROM drives.

Internet connections frequently had such unreliable and slow bandwidth that simply sending an e-mail could take 30 minutes or more, and it was not uncommon to experience days of no connection at all. While internet access has rapidly become more prevalent, affordable and faster, still in 2012 the situation in many rural areas was too exiguous for downloading software:

> Given the internet connection – it's unbearable. As I have set up my computer lab and others, it's best to spend several days (sometimes a week or more) getting one computer fully ready – everything installed and updated – and then imaging it on to others ... [but] in order to use Clonezilla [imaging software], the computers must have similar hardware ... (Travis Donnelly, Peace Corps volunteer)

It was entirely possible to travel for several hours without passing through a town with even an internet café; cell-phone-based internet is helping to expand this reach, but is far from having the affordability or bandwidth for downloading software. Distribution of software via downloads was thus difficult.

When the CD-ROM drives work, therefore, they are the most promising media for FOSS distribution. CDs are cheap, sold in almost every town and, when distributed with sleeves, are taken fairly good care of. CD burners were available in the larger cities at not too dear a price, allowing most labs or internet cafés to act as hubs for further CD distribution (Bridges.org and CIPESA, 2005: 45). This challenge is echoed by Marek Tuszynski at Tactical Technology Collective: "One problem is that because of the lack of bandwidth, it's difficult to even download the software and burn it onto CDs in order to use and distribute it" (Weiss, 2005: 39). The ubiquitous nature of CDs and the high demand for quality software led to several volunteers creating the Peace Corps ICT Resource CD, which contained a selection of dozens of useful FOSS and freeware programs, plus a collection of ICT lesson plans, texts for other educational topics, lab maintenance notes, teaching resources and even HIV/AIDS and health resources, including the Hesperian Foundation's *Where There Is No Doctor* books. Everyone was encouraged to make copies and distribute them; in a computer lab setting they were usually sold for a nominal fee to raise money for equipment and maintenance. A couple of volunteers then created custom remixes of personal favourite FOSS software. The CD was updated three times a year, and distributed to all incoming volunteers in several training groups. Feedback from volunteers and Ghanaians alike was overwhelmingly positive – one volunteer said:

The Resource CDs helped to fill a gap for people who had computers, but no internet access. It also allowed me to give the software I was using in my lab – Firefox, TuxType, Klavaro, OpenOffice – to my students without feeling like I was contributing to the problem of software piracy. Plus, it was handy to have searchable PDFs of *Where There Is No Doctor*.

The ICT Resource CD has some features in common with the Open CD project, which was discontinued in 2007, but it was specifically designed for the Ghanaian educational setting. Furthermore, the disk contained notes and explanations throughout to help users understand both what the contents were and how to install and use them. These notes were written in the local English dialect to make them more accessible. The lab maintenance section contained almost 40 documents on maintenance, administration and the use of FOSS in a computer lab setting. In addition, eight detailed step-by-step tutorials with screenshots on Ubuntu were created and included. Users reported that these were an important resource for learning and feeling confident about using Ubuntu. It was found to be advantageous to include some typing games and anti-virus programs for promotional purposes, as these were the most requested software. The disks became a highly effective method of cheaply and easily spreading FOSS and other beneficial information in the Ghanaian educational setting, and a similar project was undertaken by FOSSFA (Free Software and Open Source Foundation for Africa) in 2010.

It is anticipated that as internet connectivity improves (by 2012 access to 3G and fibre optic was already available in a few locations), this will dramatically improve the outlook of FOSS in Ghana, as "Internet connectivity is one of the key enablers of the FOSS movement ... Participation in global FOSS development projects and access to FOSS applications are severely hindered by lack of affordable Internet access" (Bridges.org and CIPESA, 2005: 18). CDs will continue to serve as an important bridge between locations that have access to internet and those without, however, extending the reach of FOSS into remote and impoverished areas.

Challenges and best practices: Hardware and OS installations

One of the many challenges facing ICT as a tool of development is the low level of hardware currently predominant in developing countries. In particular, RAM has emerged as a bottleneck for wider adoption of FOSS operating systems, especially Ubuntu. While Windows XP will run with 64MB of RAM, Ubuntu requires 256MB (and recommends 512MB), an amount not commonly found in schools. In the rural NASS lab only two out 32 computers had 256MB. The urban Mampong Technical College of Education (MTCE) lab, by contrast, had all computers with 256MB or 512MB, which made Ubuntu installations possible. The computers in the MTCE typing pool and the teaching and learning resource centre did not have sufficient RAM, however, nor did the vast majority of private computers encountered. This experience of insufficient RAM was common across all PCVs surveyed.

One way to address this RAM problem is, of course, Xubuntu. While Xubuntu runs with less RAM, no volunteers were using it, and when asked they reported that it was difficult to get the software and its updates (installations and software for Ubuntu are much easier to get as its popularity creates more organized and *ad hoc* distribution channels), and that Ghanaians disliked the look and feel of Xubuntu. A particular complaint was the necessary substitution of AbiWord for OpenOffice in Xubuntu. AbiWord was generally considered too basic, which not only made it less attractive to learn but meant it had more trouble substituting for MS Word when teaching the government syllabus. Peace Corps volunteer Grant Dobbe, however, used AbiWord in his lab due to the hardware constraints, and says:

> AbiWord worked well for teaching the basics of word processing. It ran decently on machines that weren't very powerful, it looked similar to Microsoft Word, and it did 80 per cent of the stuff Microsoft Word did. I still used OpenOffice for most of my day-to-day work, but AbiWord definitely helped me in the days before thin clients.

A particularly promising solution to the RAM issue was thin-client labs created using LTSP (Linux Terminal Service Project). Dobbe reported that he created a lab of 10 computers which was a great success during his time at the school – both because it only required very basic and affordable equipment for the clients, and because it was so effortless to maintain:

> Thin clients were a turning point in my Peace Corps service. It meant that I didn't have to worry about deploying software to 10 computers, setting up internet access on 10 computers, copying files to 10 computers, and everything else you'd expect to do in a large lab. Combining the thin-client idea with Ubuntu meant I got all of the advantages of running Linux in a classroom: a high level of configurability, the ability to lock down user profiles, and no need to worry about anti-virus and other annoyances that come with maintaining Windows. There were Windows-based terminal server setups out there, but none of them fit my price range or teaching needs.
>
> Once I got the LTSP server up and running, all I had to do was install software once, and I was guaranteed to have it available throughout the lab. It also made

it possible for me to provide internet access with one cell phone, which was a wonderful thing to be able to do for the school. If I had to give advice on how to effectively spend money for a computer lab in the developing world, I wouldn't hesitate to suggest this.

The author set up an eight-seat LTSP configuration at MTCE as a demonstration, and the ICT teachers met it with acclaim. But despite the interest and potential, both Ghanaians and volunteers found it very difficult to implement without thorough training. Luckily this training is fairly straightforward and does not require much time or technical expertise, and this marks it as one of the most promising FOSS solutions to hardware issues in the developing world.

Installing Ubuntu as an operating system (OS) was made more difficult and frustrating because of the degraded state of the CD-ROM drives; Windows XP CDs, in contrast, tended to be more resilient to dust and scratches. To install Ubuntu as a FOSS OS would sometimes require moving the single working CD-ROM drive from computer to computer throughout a lab. OS installation via bootable flash drives (despite the popularity of flash drives) was generally not possible as the original BIOS software found on the older computers often does not allow "boot from external media". Even for computers which were capable of it, enabling bootable flash drives was not advisable due to the very serious virus risk. Overall, installing FOSS software, and in particular operating systems, was frequently limited by the hardware available. Careful attention to this issue should be paid by anyone planning to develop or distribute FOSS in the developing world.

Promoting local knowledge in FOSS

Partially because of the hardware challenges faced, it is the author's belief that one of the most essential elements to new technology adoption is the availability of free, local technical support. In the United States this frequently takes the form of a relative or friend who is called upon to provide free repairs and installations, and something very similar has been observed in Ghana. In Nalerigu several individuals were singled out as being "computer wizards" and called upon by the school's staff members, and even villagers, for services. Formal repairs were not available within several hours' radius up until 2008, and when the local internet café finally started offering repairs the price was very expensive. During this time, the author started a popular student Elective ICT Club which taught installations and technical repairs, and it was very suggestive that as more free student computer repair labour was available, more teachers felt comfortable in investing in a computer. In addition, a number of computers that had been sitting broken in teachers' houses were seen being repaired by the students thus trained. Of those surveyed, 26 per cent reported that students installed software on the computers they used, 26 per cent reported that community members did installations and 55 per cent said computer teachers. Only 14 per cent said professional computer technicians did their installations, which supports the idea of lay-people doing most of the technical support.

This model must be considered when trying to introduce FOSS into a community. Without someone local and free (or low cost) to answer questions and fix problems, the response to new software is usually initial enthusiasm followed by hesitation and disuse. The Peace Corps volunteers often find themselves filling this supporting role while they are living in their communities, and through both the survey data and anecdotes it can be seen that the vast majority of volunteers are asked to provide technical advice on the computers in their schools, regardless of their actual technical background. While this means that foreign volunteers of any particular mission could be recruited as promoters of FOSS, without developing local experts the software is likely to have low long-term adoption rates (ibid.: 44).

Increasing local expertise as a method of attaining sustainable Ubuntu installations was successful with all interviewed volunteers who attempted it – especially when paired with distributing detailed notes and providing an introduction into the Ubuntu internet forums. The high staff turnover at the schools means "left notes" (in the form of technical guides for support and maintenance of the lab that are handed over to each new lab administrator) served as both a reminder to the staff trained and a guide to future teachers. The online Ubuntu forums are also a powerful source of information, but users need careful and repeated training in how to use them, and are dependent on internet availability. The following are several best cases and lessons learned.

Volunteer Grant Dobbe reported that for his Ubuntu LTSP lab he gave extensive one-on-one tutoring to his replacement teacher, Mohammed Zakaria. When asked what he did when he encountered a problem in Ubuntu, Zakaria said:

> I usually connect to the internet to get the update or ask the "Help" for assistance. Ubuntu doesn't usual get problems. But if the unfortunate happens then you have to visit the internet to get the update or for help since the software is not common in Africa.

Lacking other teachers trained in Ubuntu, he used the internet as his reference. This is in contrast to how he sees Windows computers being fixed:

Depending on the problem it has, some minor problems are solved by ordinary users who acquire knowledge through the frequent use of the computer while the major problems are taken to a computer technician which could be an ICT teacher or commercial technician.

In addition, Dobbe left 20 pages of detailed notes, including justifications and instructions for rebuilding a Ubuntu thin-client network. One copy of the notes was printed and placed in the lab, one copy burned to CD and left with the school administration and one copy was given to Zakaria via flash drive. This duplication was intended to ensure that future teachers would be able to find and use the notes, and proved important after Zakaria subsequently transferred to another school.

At MTCE peer experts were created through a Ubuntu club model. Staff and community members were invited to join the Ubuntu Club for a one-time modest fee. This money was used to provide them with installation disks, handouts and text messages reminding them about meetings. Compared with a previous free-cost club model, attendance dramatically improved with the fee (from none or one per meeting to two or three per meeting), as it appeared that members took it more seriously and valued it more. Forty-eight people expressed serious interest in the Ubuntu Club, and 27 attended at least one meeting. The first (and frequently repeated) topic was an introduction to Ubuntu, which covered the main differences between common tasks on Ubuntu and Windows, and included a full installation practice. Participants were given installation disks and handouts with screenshots and detailed directions written in the local dialect of English. Overall 12 different one- or two-hour topics were offered in cycle. The time of day was carefully chosen to accommodate prayers, meals and cooking (a particularly important consideration for female teachers), and a text message was sent to remind members half an hour before the meeting started. The success of the club was measured by the proliferation of Ubuntu on staff members' personal computers.

Besides the students trained in Nalerigu, extensive training was given to three consecutive local ICT teachers. These lessons were always accompanied by detailed notes, which were placed in a binder kept in the lab and on the ICT Resource CD. When asked who does the installations, Nalerigu ICT teacher Joseph Louknaan said, "But now I am doing the installation myself after the Peace Corps [volunteer] has gone."

Most volunteers reported that their first couple of attempts to run staff clubs were not very successful, and they had many meetings where, despite staff members all promising to be there, nobody came. It was learned that allowing members to earn a printed certificate stating their accomplishments and signed by the head of the educational institution was a powerful motivator. These certificates could be used when applying for jobs and higher education, and were thus sought after. Another lesson learned was to have a plan for when the electricity would fail – either something to do on paper, or an automatic reschedule plan. Meeting times needed to be posted in a prominent place and kept up to date. And despite the reminder text messages, members were frequently tardy, and the more gracefully accommodated, the better the meetings went. Having even very modest refreshments was always enthusiastically received. Finally, it was found that every meeting should have detailed, printed notes for participants to refer to later. These notes could even be bundled together into a booklet and sold as a successful revenue-generating activity.

Viruses, pirated software and the FOSS solution

The author visited over a dozen school computer labs in Ghana between 2007 and 2010, ranging from school labs with a single computer to major university labs with over 100 computers, and had an opportunity to provide technical support to most of them. The single greatest challenge was viruses (for conciseness, the term "virus" is considered to include worms, trojans, logic bombs and other forms of self-replicating malware). It was rare, in fact, to encounter any computer without a virus, and every lab visited had them. The viruses varied from mild annoyances to completely disabling the computers. When Ghanaian ICT students and professionals were asked "How much do viruses disturb computers in Ghana?", the general sentiment was well expressed by ICT professional Michael Tsigbey:

> Viruses disturb computers a lot in Ghana. Most anti-viruses being used are either pirated or expired. Most computer users either don't have the money to buy or means to buy even if they have the money.

Afi Jane, a Ghanaian teacher, responded: "Almost every computer in Ghana has virus, including our phones."

The reasons for the surprisingly rampant infections are twofold. While Ghanaians generally had a solid understanding of the basics of anti-virus, they were undone first by the pirated software and second by the lack of reliable internet access preventing their computers from getting both Windows updates and anti-virus updates. Further supporting the premise that viruses were rampant are the tests run by Symantec (2006: 10), which showed an unpatched Windows XP system would, on average, be infected in less than an hour of connection to the internet. Those without internet connection were highly vulnerable to flash-drive-based infections, which according to Microsoft (2010: 168) are eight of the top 10 most common virus types found on scanned computers in Ghana. Returned PCV Brian

Bourne said, "Everyone was used to pirated proprietary software, which was often virus-ridden, limited (promotional copy), or overwhelmingly complex."

Genuine Windows licences were inaccessible because vendors did not carry them and their price was far out of the reach of most Ghanaians. Between 2007 and 2010 the ICT Think-Tank organized volunteers to catalogue the available products and prices in computer stores across Ghana; despite specifically seeking MS Windows, only one vendor of genuine Microsoft Windows was located. As Evan Leibovitch (2003) states, "In many developing countries, software piracy is more a matter of survival than an intent to break the law." The government of Ghana surveyed over 60 organizations in 2003 for their input into the national ICT policy and plan, and listed all 1,378 responses in its report (Republic of Ghana, 2003). While one of the most common themes is concern over cost for individuals and the nation, only six responses specifically mention the cost of software.

> Invest in the provision of basic tools for the ICT drive – make computer hard and software affordable to the average student, lecturer and researcher. Make all the software packages available to everybody. (Ibid.: 44)

This distinction between number of comments on the costs of hardware and comments on the costs of software is striking, considering that the cost of software (individual licences for Windows 7 Professional are $119, Office 2010 Home and Student $149.99) is greater than the cost of the hardware (a common, used computer could be bought for $100–$200). This further indicates that few Ghanaians have experience purchasing legal licences.

The PCVs heard from Ghana Education Service (GES) representatives that Microsoft made educational licences available for $2.00, but no volunteer from 2007 to 2010 was able actually to acquire such a licence, and their enquiries to official lines went unanswered. Only one computer lab known to volunteers had a legitimate volume licence key, and even this was frequently given out to other people. The most common situation was the local ICT teachers and experts had a key and, as PCVs said of their labs:

> All the XP installs are off of one pirated license. But I know that it is a popular key. I saw another student in my first-year class who had the exact same key we used on the machines.

> I dare you to find any school in Ghana that has a computer centre (which all Teacher Training Colleges do, more and more JHSs, and some of the Schools for the Deaf) with completely legal copies of anything on the computers.

In 2010 the Ghanaian government distributed new computers to some of the teacher training colleges. Even these government-issued computers failed the Windows XP Genuine Advantage check, however, because the vendor had imaged them all with the same key.

The version of Windows that was most prevalent was, by far, Windows XP. It was popular because of the ease in finding a pirated copy and its relatively low hardware requirements (PCVs frequently installed it on Pentium 2 systems with 64MB of RAM). The only Windows 7 or Windows Vista seen in Ghana in 2010 were on personal laptops where it had come pre-installed, although by 2012 PCVs were reporting the availability of pirated Windows 7. Some variations of the pirated Windows XP were colourful and creative, such as Crystal XP, Dark XP and Windows 7 Vienna – all, invariably, infested with viruses. Although statistics are lacking for infection rates of pirated installations of Windows XP, a report from the anti-piracy solutions company Media Surveillance estimated that 32 per cent of pirated Windows 7 installations contained malicious code (Williams, 2010). This rampant and problematic virus issue thus becomes the single most effective promoter of FOSS, and especially of Ubuntu. Attempting to promote Ubuntu by pointing out that it is free means little to people who are used to free CDs of pirated Windows. When trying to explain the idea of open source software in Ubuntu Club meetings and class lectures, few grasped its moral and practical advantages over pirated software. When asked, "What is open source software?", 31 per cent did not know and 18 per cent gave a partial answer (compared to 11 per cent and 39 per cent of Peace Corps volunteers). If informed that Ubuntu was a virus-free "Windows", however, Ghanaian students and colleagues grew excited and wanted to know more. Of the Ghanaian ICT professionals interviewed about viruses, all those who had worked closely with Peace Corps volunteers involved with FOSS believed, in Zakaria's words, "Computer with buntu [sic] don't usual get problems like virus and what-have-you."

Thus one of the most promising promotional methods for FOSS is an emphasis on its inherent security advantage over viruses. This is even a compelling argument for computers with internet connection, for although they have access to updates of anti-virus, they are still vulnerable to infection because they will fail the Windows Genuine Advantage check and are thus ineligible for Windows updates. Peace Corps volunteer Blake Fleisher was able to use this idea very successfully to set an entire internet café to use ZenCafe 2.0 (Fleisher, 2009). At MTCE the lab was converted from 45 pirated, infected XP computers to 45 dual-boot XP/Ubuntu computers (with only the Ubuntu having internet access), and the response was overwhelmingly positive.

Educational syllabi and government policy implications

One of the biggest stumbling blocks encountered by PCVs in promoting FOSS was the perception that since proprietary software dominated in businesses it should also dominate in the educational system. Although the GES syllabus is officially "platform neutral", it specifically references Microsoft products and the GES exams featured Windows images and language. When Ghanaian ICT students and professionals were asked if they agreed with this policy, they said:

> I agree, because I think the students need to get the basic ICT knowledge before introducing other softwares and it seems Microsoft product are common and everywhere in Ghana. (Abdulai Salifu, Ghanaian teacher)

> Yes, because we do not have experts to teach Ubuntu in our schools. (Afi Jane, Ghanaian teacher)

An ICT teacher who had worked closely with a Peace Corps volunteer, however, said:

> I disagree [with the Microsoft preference in the syllabus] because as the world of IT grows day in and day out there is the need for the ICT department of GES to update the syllabus to make every Ghanaian student current, because they stand the chance of finding themselves in a country where this softwares are common. (Mohammed Zakaria)

The consequences of the official government syllabus and exams requiring knowledge of Microsoft products cannot be overstated. The need to prepare students properly for the exams was a deciding factor against FOSS in numerous volunteer and teacher interviews, and will remain a major stumbling block to its use across all parts of West Africa that take the common West African Senior School Certificate Examination.

It is important to engage the government education system in truly being platform neutral: "The best way to ensure that users can effectively operate computers is to equip them with basic generic skills that are not dependent on one specific software application or environment" (Bridges. org and CIPESA, 2005: 43). A platform-neutral policy also frees schools from being locked into expensive proprietary software, a situation that often results in the illegal use of pirated software (and all the problems that ensue) due to the extreme penury of the schools.

A further benefit of government policy that does not unfairly favour one foreign software company is the opening up of the market to local software engineers. These entrepreneurs would then have viable opportunities to adapt open source projects to their local needs, bolstering the country's IT economy and creating culturally customized business and educational software. While we take encouragement from the vice president of Ghana hosting and chairing FOSSFA's Idlelo conference in 2010, the policies in the government curriculum still have a long way to go.

Discussion of survey results

In this section the responses to the survey questions regarding software preferences are correlated to the qualitative responses obtained through interviews and the author's own experience. The software discussed includes Ubuntu, OpenOffice, GIMP, Tux Paint, TuxType and KTouch. This selection is not exhaustive, but represents the most popularly or successfully used FOSS. Both the experiences of PCVs and the preferences of Ghanaian students, teachers and ICT professionals are examined to help us understand which FOSS has the greatest potential for adoption and the most to offer.

Ubuntu

Of the Ghanaians surveyed, half had not yet tried Ubuntu, while 94 per cent reported having used Microsoft Windows. When looking at those who had tried Ubuntu, however, the satisfaction rates were almost identical to the satisfaction among the Windows users (Figure 13.1), suggesting that Ubuntu is a viable alternative to Windows.

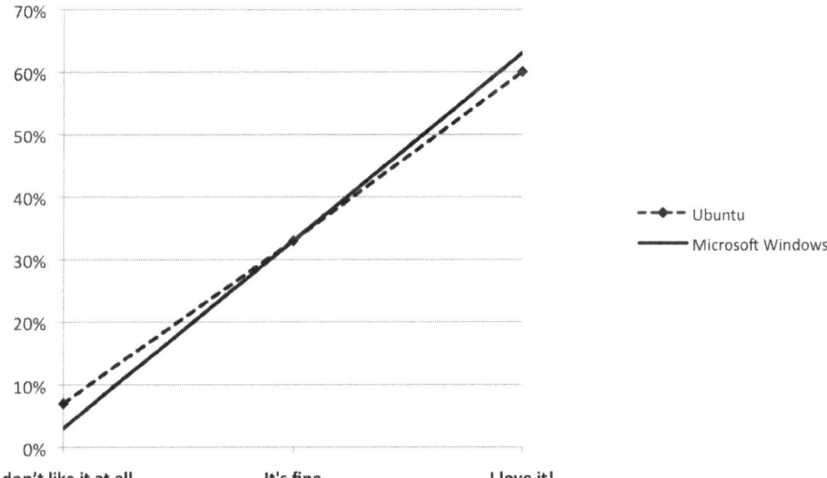

Figure 13.1 How much do you like Ubuntu, Microsoft Windows?

Peace Corps volunteer David Boyer reported that his computer lab at a teacher training college has been converted to a dual-boot XP/Ubuntu 10.10 with only Ubuntu PCs being able to access the network:

> Only a minority did not like to use Ubuntu when they first were approached by it. I would say two or three students did not like it. Our computer-literate population of students is over 100. By the end of the first week of "Ubuntu-Only", there were no complaints. I have not had any complaints from staff that have used Ubuntu. I just tell them where the applications are located and how to turn off the machine and they are happy.

Regarding the Ghanaians' response to Ubuntu, the PCVs identified three major practical objections: MP3 support, game and software installations, and office file formats. Peace Corps volunteer Grant Dobbe said:

> If there's anything that gave me more grief when trying to sell people on using Ubuntu, it was the fact that it didn't support proprietary media codecs out of the box. You can get people all excited about the fact that Ubuntu doesn't have the virus problems of Windows, and that it runs better on older computers, but once they discover it doesn't play MP3s or AVI files until they can connect to the internet, they're not interested.

Music is a huge part of Ghanaian culture, and playing music is quite possibly the single most common use of computers. The fact that Ubuntu installations do not play MP3 files (or the common music video format AVI) therefore becomes a major complaint. While you can download the restricted extras from the internet, installing these files to an offline computer is a challenging task. One solution used by the author was to create an APTonCD with Ubuntu restricted extras and then teach users how to install the files immediately after installation. The APTonCD disks were found to be very difficult to create, however, and became outdated with each new Ubuntu release. Several other solutions were attempted, such as the Ubuntu Customization Kit (with which technical difficulties were reported) and SuperOS (which was excellent but restricted by the lack of DVD players, and the large download size), and the Ninite.com project (very promising except you need a paid account to do offline installs). Anybody who wishes to install Ubuntu in the developing world would be wise to prepare a solution to this problem that is hardware and internet-access sensitive, and test it vigorously. Ideally, it should be easy enough to do such that local ICT professionals would feel confident in recreating and applying the solution for future updates.

The second objection to Ubuntu as a replacement to Windows is the inability to install games easily on to an offline computer. This problem dramatically reduced the social sharing aspect of software – while it was common to show off games and programs to friends and colleagues on a Windows computer and then share the installation files, this was not trivial for most Ubuntu software (with the notable exception of Google's Picasa). Again, several projects exist to help create independent installation packages, but the volunteers were unable to find one that worked well enough to recommend. In particular, WINE as a solution to installing popular Windows games and other software was hindered by the difficulty of getting WINE installed on an offline computer. Although Ghanaians expressed great interest in the idea of WINE, they struggled with its non-intuitive interface.

Finally, office file format was a frequent issue. Printers were expensive and usually only available in the school office or at the internet café, which meant users would bring their documents via flash drive for printing, and the ubiquitous MS Office 2003 cannot open .ODT files. The solution to this problem is an easy configuration of OpenOffice to save always as Office 97/2000/XP format. These instructions can be included on installation handouts to improve things significantly. It can be noted here that since Office 2007/2010 saves files as .docx, .xlsx, etc. it presents the same problems with printing on a computer with only Office 2003 and creates a great opportunity to promote OpenOffice, though it is a limited one as pirated Office 2007 gradually becomes more common. Occasionally the school typing pool would be faced with a .docx file from someone's personal laptop or e-mailed from a government official, and without having OpenOffice they would not have been able to open the file.

A few complaints against Ubuntu of a more minor nature include the moving of the window controls to the left, the differences in "safely removing" flash drives and where to find the "recycling bin", but all these are easy to teach or change to suit preferences. Some PCVs reported success in skinning Ubuntu to make it look like Windows. "Welcome to Ubuntu" and "After Ubuntu installation" notes were distributed with every Ubuntu CD along with detailed installation notes. These were also reproduced on the ICT Resource CD. When asked about encouraging Ubuntu or other FOSS operating systems, returned PCV Brian Bourne said:

> I spent a fair deal of time encouraging Linux. However, I could never advocate more than live disks and dual-boots. I found Linux installs (Ubuntu, Zenwalk, and Mint, for example) to be attractive, but they were frequently frustrating and confounding for me (particularly installing and updating applications), and it would only prove more so for someone with limited computer skills. I strongly encouraged and modeled the dual-boot system because they would be exposed to Linux, but they could fall back on Windows if it became frustrating – otherwise, as on a single OS Linux system, they might wash their hands of it all together.

OpenOffice

When asked about the staff/student reaction to using OpenOffice, PCV David Boyer responded:

> To be honest, I don't know if there is a great comprehension to the difference. During classes, I will instruct using OOo software. I will explain to them that this is free software that does the same thing of Office. If I actually come to a difference between the two pieces of software, I will highlight what is different, and then explain why both operations are quite the same. Some students will use the OpenOffice suite due to 2007 Office being on some of the machines. I encourage that since 2007 is so different that my demonstrations don't make much sense on the [projection on the] wall when they look at their screen. Most will use the MS Office suite on their own when I am not looking though. They know it and they are familiar with launching it. They don't complain about OpenOffice, they have just been taught MS Office for their entire learning careers.

In the author's experience, it was possible to teach Microsoft Office 2003 side by side with OpenOffice without difficulty. The message that seemed to work was to emphasize that what they are using now is not what they will be using in five years, so they need to learn the concepts rather than the user interface anyway. The most resistance came from the secretaries in the typing pools, as they had invested a lot of time in learning Microsoft Office and been proficient and productive in it for many years, and saw learning OpenOffice as being an unnecessary hassle.

The Ghanaians surveyed were asked if they disliked, liked or loved a variety of software. Seventy-seven per cent said they loved MS Office, compared to 48 per cent for OpenOffice, but 19 per cent liked MS Office versus 52 per cent who liked OpenOffice (Figure 13.2). The conclusion one can draw from this is that while Ghanaians prefer MS Office over OpenOffice, they are by no means opposed to OpenOffice.

GIMP and Tux Paint

Although few volunteers reporting using GIMP in the classroom, PCV David Boyer found a popular use for it: "We have a scanner in the lab and boy do students love to put up photographs on Facebook!"

Tux Paint, on the other hand, was a popular piece of software in both its Windows and Ubuntu versions. It was particularly successful among children just beginning to use the computer and mouse. Ghanaian adults surveyed, however, preferred MS Paint by 10 per cent, possibly because of their greater familiarity with it and the ease of doing basic photo and screenshot manipulations in it.

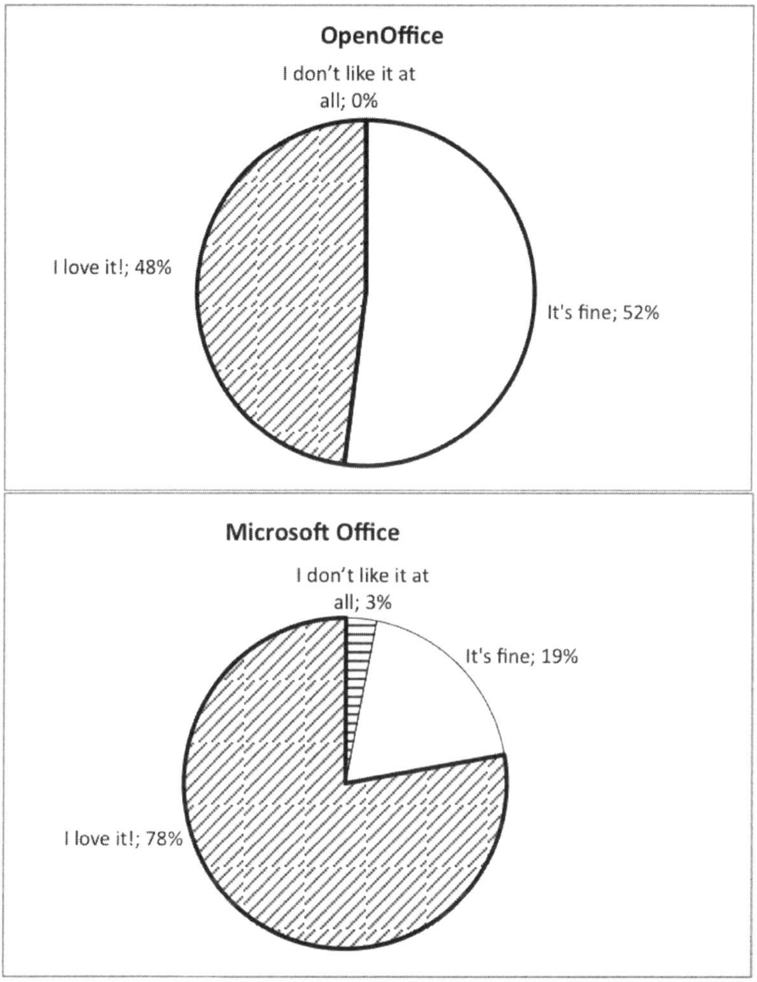

Figure 13.2 How much do you like OpenOffice, Microsoft Office?

TuxType and KTouch

Volunteer David Boyer pretty well sums up the opinions of KTouch versus Mavis Beacon: "KTouch is the FOSS equivalent of Mavis, but ... boy, Mavis has neat games with ants. The kids love that!"

Computer lab administrators, however, found that Mavis Beacon, besides being pirated, required a rather lengthy and complicated sign-in and strictly controlled progression, which did not recommend itself to a lab where many students used each computer and did not always sit at

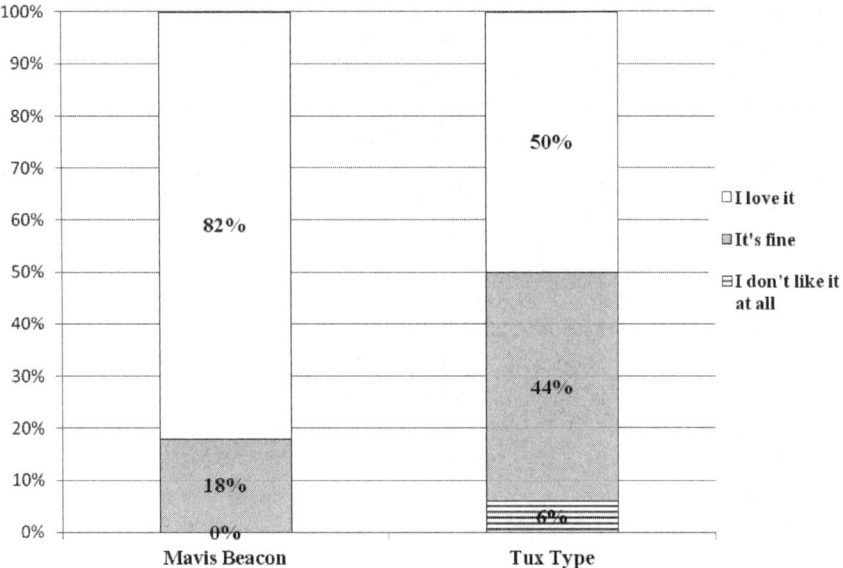

Figure 13.3 How much do you like Mavis, Tux?

the same one. This caused few students to progress beyond the home-row letters. TuxType was simple to start and stop, and gave practice on all keys at once, which better suited learning touch typing with only intermittent practice. On the other hand, TuxType did not give such a clear sense of progression, and during games the students quickly learned they could win simply by mashing all the keys down at once. Ghanaian preference is, however, strongly in favour of the ubiquitous and pirated Mavis Beacon: 82 per cent loved it compared to only 50 per cent for users of TuxType (Figure 13.3).

Lessons to be learned: Other FOSS projects

Five FOSS projects (Wikipedia for Schools, timetable software, Gutenberg Project, Question Time Bank and Library Linux) discussed in the interviews are examined for lessons to be learned.

Wikipedia for Schools

SOS Children and the Wikimedia Foundation combined forces to produce the Wikipedia for Schools selection of 5,500 school-focused articles. This is distributed as a DVD image which is available for download and free distribution. Having this disk filled a few different gaps and gave PCVs a viable alternative to pirated Microsoft Encarta. Because it was made up of plain HTML files, it also allowed teachers who did not have internet access to use it as a way to teach about web browsers. Volunteer Grant Dobbe said:

> When it came time for me to teach students about the web and how hyperlinks worked, I decided to use the Wikipedia for Schools DVD. It had the benefits of letting me control the content my students had access to, and also didn't have the latency problems I was faced with over our GPRS data connection. I also used it as a backup for days when the cell phone tower was out of service.

Timetable software

One of the most useful pieces of software that schools can have is for timetabling. Many schools in Ghana often take weeks (frequently far past the school opening date) to get their timetables figured out due to their sheer complexity – they have dozens of teachers and hundreds of students – all organized on paper. This ends up affecting class sizes, teacher workloads and the amount of material that can be covered in a given term. With a computerized solution, the time drops from weeks to hours. PCVs used both ASC freeware and open source FET. The advantage of FET was that it was free, open source, cross-platform and produced timetables in a wide variety of formats that were fully customizable with cascading style sheets. Its biggest disadvantages were a steep learning curve, complicated printing customization and non-intuitive interface. Between the two, the free version of ASC was preferred by Ghanaian counterparts due to the more developed graphical user interface and ease of use.

FET is an example of how:

> OSS can be developer-centric, with an emphasis on bare-metal interfaces and text-heavy script configurations that privilege the technically savvy at the expense of those who are inexperienced or who prefer to showcase their mettle through other means than hand-editing lengthy scripts. Software that is more time-consuming or complex for general users than its proprietary counterparts can feel like software of last resort, even when the software has superior characteristics that may endear it to power-users or make it the better choice ... (Schneider, 2009: 4)

FET and other timetable FOSS have enormous potential to impact the schools of the developing world, although the software must be introduced with due respect given to the head of the timetable committee, and that individual should be the primary focus of training, lest he or she feel replaced and thus antagonistic towards its adoption.

Gutenberg Project

When faced with libraries in the developing world which have such a shortage of current, relevant and reading-level-appropriate books, the Gutenberg Project's promise to bring 38,000 books on a single DVD seems very exciting. PCVs, however, were not able to leverage this promise into actual educational results. First, it was hard to transmit the project on to computers. The files were too large for the commonly found flash drives (though this will improve over time as flash drive sizes increase), and DVD drives were, as always, in short supply. Even after installation the volunteers did not find it easy to use. The interface was confusing, the search was very slow, it required an additional unzipping program to open the actual files, the books were not sorted by language and the files had large, repetitive headers. In addition, the majority of the texts were not immediately relevant or useful. While the project could be positioned as a research aid, or perhaps aligned with a literature class, in its current form it is not well designed for recreational reading or information browsing. The Gutenberg Project also requires users to be trained not only in the clunky interface but in how to navigate and use 38,000 books – not easy for users who are used to libraries of only a few hundred books.

Test Question Bank

Another project that had lots of lessons was the PCV Test Question Bank. The idea was to create a computer program that allowed students to practise for their high school standardized tests by drawing on a database of past questions, with explanations added in by volunteer teachers. This was a powerful idea and occupied several volunteers for extensive periods of time. The primary reason for the failure of this project was that key members of the team completed their service and left before the program was fully finished and deployed. Peace Corps volunteers reported that "almost completed" projects tended never to be completed once the driving person had left. Any project which is intended to be continued and completed generally requires an extensive and lengthy hand-over process. In addition, the volunteers ran into copyright problems over the rights to reproduce past questions.

Library Linux

A final FOSS project for examination is Library Linux. Intended to solve the problem of libraries having computers without a clear sense of how they should contribute to education, and nobody to maintain them, the author forked the Qimo for Kids project. The goal was to load it up with lots of educational software, remove everything non-educational (music player, games, word processors, etc.) and lock them down so they would not need maintenance (by removing access to the CD drive, disabling flash drives and the internet, and removing all user privileges). It was necessary to be very strict about what qualified as "educational", as many library computers got used, sometimes exclusively, by staff members for typing graduate school work, or even (as several PCVs reported) watching pornography.

The motivation for this project was the enormous potential of digital books to help overcome the sometimes impossibly high costs in purchase, shipping and storage faced by libraries, and thus provide desperately needed, up-to-date information to impoverished communities. As Witten et al. (2002: 7) say:

> In the developing world, digital libraries provide perhaps the first really compelling raison d'etre for computing technology. Priorities in these countries include health, agriculture, nutrition, hygiene, sanitation and safe drinking water. Although computers are not a priority, simple, reliable access to targeted information meeting these basic needs certainly is.

This project was installed in a library computer lab, but its success is undetermined because the library still lacks electricity. In addition, the project was very technically complicated to install and configure and currently lacks an easy way to distribute or reinstall it. While in Ghana the project suffered due to difficult access to the internet for research and downloads, in the United States the logistical challenges of continuing to test and deploy it are very high. A lesson to learn from this is that FOSS work done on location is significantly more likely to succeed than work done remotely, despite the challenges of working with the limited on-site resources.

Conclusion

In conclusion, the potential for FOSS in the developing world has never been greater, and its promise is particularly poignant in the educational setting. This detailed report of the situations found by Peace Corps volunteers, the projects they attempted and their stories of success and failure during the years from 2007 to 2010 comes from direct experience, surveys and interviews. The chapter should serve as a guide for anyone wishing create, promote or encourage the use of FOSS in the developing world. Which FOSS is used, and how it is used, is determined by a combination of available hardware, local expertise and culturally influenced user preference. Often these factors are overlooked when FOSS projects are designed for the developing world, but, as has been seen, they are fundamental in determining success or failure. Some of the most promising projects examined in detail include Ubuntu, OpenOffice, Wikipedia for Schools, FET timetables, GIMP, Tux Paint, KTouch, ICT Resource CD, Library Linux and the Gutenberg Project. Each of these has much to offer to the developing world's schools, but their impact would be greater with improved sensitivity to the hardware issues, better support and training for local technical support.

As internet and flash drive availability becomes more affordable and widespread, the potential of FOSS becomes even greater, but with a little foresight even the most challenging infrastructure situations can be overcome, and it is in these rural and impoverished areas that FOSS is needed the most.

REFERENCES

Bridges.org and CIPESA (2005) "Free/Open Source Software (FOSS) Policy in Africa: A Toolkit for Policy-makers and Practitioners", Bridges.org and Collaboration on International ICT Policy for East and Southern Africa; available at www.bridges.org/files/active/0/FOSSPolicyToolkit_10Aug05r.pdf (accessed 15 May 2011).

Fleisher, B. (2009) "Linux in an Internet Café"; available at http://ictwiki.org/Linux_in_an_internet_Cafe (accessed 10 February 2011).

Leibovitch, E. (2003) "Commentary: Open Source Software Bridging the Technology Gap", *Computer Technology Review* 23(5), p. 12.

Microsoft (2010) "Microsoft Security Intelligence Report"; available at http://download.microsoft.com/download/6/0/5/605BE103-9429-4493-898B-E3D50AB68236/Microsoft_Security_Intelligence_Report_volume_10_July-Dec2010_English.pdf (accessed 5 May 2011).

Pykalainen, T. (2008) "Adaption of Linux SSL Servers across Cultures", *First Monday* 13(12), 1 December.

Republic of Ghana (2003) "Compilation of On-the-Spot Questionnaire"; available at www.ict.gov.gh/pdf/on-the-spot-%20questionnaire.pdf (accessed 25 May 2011).

Schneider, K. G. (2009) "The Think of the Fray: Open Source Software in Libraries in the First Decade of this Century", *American Society for Information Science and Technology* 35(2), pp. 15–19.

Symantec (2006) "Internet Security Threat Report, Volume 9"; available at http://eval.symantec.com/mktginfo/enterprise/white_papers/ent-whitepaper_symantec_internet_security_threat_report_ix.pdf (accessed 30 May 2011).

Weiss, T. R. (2005) "Linux Makes Its Way into the Classroom", *Computerworld* 39(29), pp. 38–39.

Williams, J. (2010) "Genuine Windows Blog"; available at http://windowsteamblog.com/windows/archive/b/genuinewindows/archive/2010/02/11/windows-activation-technologies-update-for-windows-7.aspx (accessed 29 May 2011).

Witten, I. H., M. Loots, M. F. Trujillo and D. Bainbridge (2002) "The Promise of Digital Libraries in Developing Countries", *Electronic Library* 20(1), pp. 7–13.

Part III
Conclusion

14
Conclusion

Sulayman K. Sowe

In contemporary discourse on sustainable development, much attention has been given to climate change and its mitigation, the conservation of ecological and marine ecosystems, protecting biodiversity, saving the planet from idiosyncratic human activities and reducing hunger and poverty. Yet it is obvious that most of our activities depend on and are supported by a host of technologies. In essence, technology plays an important role in addressing complex systems and problems confronting humankind, all the more so in this interconnected world of ours. Harmonizing complementary spheres of human activity to achieve sustainable development can only be possible if we are able to harness and effectively utilize the technologies around us. We must search for and provide technologies that can solve complex and practical problems. However, if technologies are to support sustainable development and bring about the desired effect, they must be responsive to the needs of the majority of the world's population, who live in developing countries. They must also be accessible and less restrictive, and encourage broader public participation in decision-making.

It is often difficult to convince technology implementers that challenging and complex problems do not always require equally complex technologies. Technology becomes simple when the user is an active participant from its conception and design to its deployment and maintenance. The use of complex and alien technologies has constantly failed to solve sustainability problems in developing countries. Many people and governments seek to promote a smooth transition to sustainability by

Free and open source software and technology for sustainable development, Sowe, Parayil and Sunami (eds), United Nations University Press, 2012, ISBN 978-92-808-1217-6

tapping into complex technologies acquired through technology transfer schemes or by purchasing technologies from the developed world. Little attention is given to supporting local initiatives to develop, customize and maintain technologies needed to solve local problems.

The chapters in this book value technological simplicity and address the interplay between technologies and local communities that are searching for opportunities to bring about technological sustainability and innovation in their environs. The book has a diverse authorship specialized in education, computer science, agriculture, environmental and climate science, business, information systems, anthropology, law, humanitarian efforts and information and communication technology for development (ICT4D). With these multidisciplinary contributions, the book serves as a useful knowledge resource, a call to action and a bridge between technology theory and practice.

FOSS (free and open source software) technologies have the potential to bring new actors into the sustainable development field. They are beneficial not only for developing countries but also for developed countries – creating a win-win situation for both technology developers and users. The openness and the meritocratic process that characterize FOSS communities allow people in the developing world to join their counterparts in developed countries in the process of developing and using technology. This bazaar-like ecosystem encourages a degree of autonomy, and actors become producers of their own systems or technologies. However, as echoed in many chapters in this book, ICTs like FOSS, Web 2.0 tools, social media and mobile phones are just tools, and may not be the ultimate solution to all the technology problems associated with sustainable development. The actions of human beings are what are truly important if we are to achieve technology sustainability. If more people from all sectors of society are determined to support and work on FOSS solutions, then the goal of bringing sustainable technologies to the neediest will be achieved. After all, whether or not FOSS technologies can bring about sustainable development in developing countries depends on ordinary people, who can work together to achieve extraordinary things. Readers are also constantly reminded that there are many factors which, in reality, limit the full-scale adoption and use of FOSS technologies to foster human development, improve lives in disadvantaged regions and maximize both outreach and impact.

Working together to drive forward the technology sustainability agenda requires certain propensities which have eluded development experts for decades: the ability to learn with and from ICT4D initiatives or projects. In Chapters 1 and 4, Miscione and Franquesa et al. buttressed this collective community action by introducing service learning in ICT4D projects. The authors show that ICTs do not have to be a burden; rather they should be recognized as the key to analysing the real needs of the community. Furthermore, sustainable development requires a process of dialogue and ultimately consensus building among all stakeholders. Partnerships are even more important: partners who together define the problems, design possible solutions, collaborate to implement them and monitor and evaluate the outcome. There must be realistic goals which are introduced incrementally in small steps, so that communities can learn as the technology evolves. This lowers the technology learning curve, and at the same time gives communities and people in developing countries time to work together and design strategies to cope with technology risks and pitfalls. Introducing technology too fast, without clear goals that are negotiated by all parties involved, will eventually result in its rejection. FOSS technologies for sustainable development should be more evolutionary than revolutionary.

This book documents important milestones in the changing landscape and the shift towards FOSS technologies in developing countries. For instance, Hammouda in Chapter 9 discusses how FOSS technologies are playing a vital role in the Tunisian software industry. Companies surveyed in the study are leveraging FOSS technologies to support their business innovation and sustainability. However, the use of FOSS in Tunisia, as in many developing countries, is mostly focused around server infrastructure (predominantly Apache or the GNU/Linux stack) and other general-purpose software such as office applications, e-learning and content management systems. As far as the adoption of FOSS technologies by businesses is concerned, many chapters in the book repeatedly call for governments' involvement in the promotion of FOSS, the institutionalization or improvement (where it exists) of FOSS-related education in universities, the implementation of appropriate policies to support FOSS technologies, investment in R&D, maintenance and upgrade of internet infrastructure and continuous training.

Education and learning, government involvement and effective policies are all important factors to consider when promoting technology sustainability. Many ICT4D projects are still fragmented and often fail because they fall short of approaching grassroots efforts or linking up with other technology initiatives with the same context or relevance. Miscione cited poor governance as one reason why many ICT projects fail. Fragmentation of ICT projects can be tackled by supporting coordination through the establishment of "federations", in which technology has to be considered as a relevant actor. The author recommends the revision of sustainable development strategies so as to conceive ICT projects as potential parts of larger networks, possibly included in or converging towards a broader infrastructure. In the design and implementation of sustainable ICT projects, technology and ICT4D experts should think of each project or system as a dot to be connected with other dots to achieve a sustainable system. Understanding which infrastructural elements can be translated into the heterogeneous public and private sector contexts in developing countries is a matter of governance or development strategy. Therefore, to deliver benefits over their lifetime, sustainable ICT infrastructures need to enable processes of experimentation, discovery and invention through trial and error. Similar to the concept of federated structures, Molefe and Fogwill (Chapter 5) introduced process reference models (PRMs) to capture rare elements and lessons to be learnt in organizational migration to FOSS technologies. PRMs, which can help reduce uncertainty and risks in organizational planning, provide a set of baseline processes that can serve as a starting point for any organization that wishes to perform such a migration. It is important to note that the adoption of a FOSS national policy and strategy by the South African government paved the way for projects such as the Vula case study presented in Chapter 5.

Adequate provision of basic infrastructure and financial resources, quality education on FOSS technologies and encouraging wide participation from the grassroots level are some of the issues raised by Adenle and Aginam (Chapter 2). The authors assert that FOSS technologies will have an important role to play in sustainable agriculture in developing countries for many years to come. However, for this to be realized, some of the issues facing the adoption of FOSS technologies, such as intellectual property rights (IPR), must be properly addressed. The authors go on to argue, using "terminator technology" as an example, that IPR restricts research tools and leads to innovations that can benefit developing countries being rendered invisible. Since FOSS technologies are not restricted by strict IPR, they may offer a promising solution to the problems plaguing scientists and farmers in developing countries.

Apart from the agricultural sector, FOSS technologies are seen to play an important role in mitigating natural environmental disasters, which occur more frequently in developing countries. According to Zephenia (Chapter 6), the ultimate benefits of FOSS technologies for environmental scientists are flexibility, security, reliability, performance, high return on investment, reduced total cost of ownership and the proliferation of an innovation culture. The author provides the architecture and governance framework of a disaster management information system, which can be considered by institutions that require a jump-start in natural disaster management.

The book also incorporates various methodologies, theories and best practices which can aid the successful implementation of ICT4D. The OpenTTT methodology discussed by Daffara (Chapter 7), with its best practices (e.g. service learning) and suggestions (e.g. how to ensure the successful deployment of FOSS technologies), can be adopted in a very effective way to facilitate the creation of a local ecosystem of ICT service providers which are naturally adapted to their native environment. For the business sector in developing countries (especially small-island states), the Open Unified Process (OpenUP) introduced by McNaughton, Thompson and Duggan in Chapter 10 provides a useful template for developing a lean implementation process tailored specifically to working with small business clients in these countries. The process demonstrates new opportunities for small and medium-sized enterprises (SMEs) to access advanced ICT capabilities at considerably reduced costs. This can diminish the effects of the technology gaps between larger enterprises and SMEs, thus allowing them to compete more effectively in an increasingly global and knowledge-based economy.

Beyond the technical, educational and economic gains, technology sustainability is about recognizing and addressing socio-cultural issues. FOSS technologies are of great importance to developing countries since marginalized and small linguistic groups, considered too tiny to form a viable market for proprietary software vendors or suppliers, can work individually or collectively to tailor the technologies to match their own needs. Important issues arise in localizing software technologies in native languages, as discussed by Benjamin (Chapter 8), and targeting minorities to avoid increasing the digital divide (Franquesa et al. in Chapter 4). The primary motivation for localizing software is to increase technology access and promote literacy among the rural poor, the majority of whom are not schooled in the official language(s) spoken by the urban community. As FOSS grants free access to the source code, local software developers can customize and adapt these technologies to meet the language and cultural needs of a particular group of people or specific regions of the developing world.

In conclusion, a common thread running through all the book chapters is that the potential of FOSS in developing countries has never been greater, and its promise is particularly poignant in the educational setting. In Chapter 13, Hardin's personal experience demonstrates that technology experts often overlook hardware availability, local expertise, support and training, and culturally influenced user preferences when designing or implementing FOSS technology projects for developing countries. These factors, more often than not, determine the success or failure of ICT4D projects in such countries.

This book has compiled scholarly contributions on FOSS technology research, theory and practice (Part I) and FOSS technology case studies, surveys, policy development and experience reports (Part II), which not only bring to light a new era of technology sustainability but also help researchers and practitioners in the field of FOSS and technology for sustainable development to understand better the paradigm shift in technology sweeping developing countries. The book marks the beginning for exploring the sustainability and practical aspects of ICT4D for the future. FOSS technologies for sustainable development represent a scientifically and intellectually stimulating area of study, and each chapter in this book is more like "development in motion" – highlighting the sustainable development flux in developing countries and at the same time proposing the way forward.

Glossary

Adaptation of technologies: The consideration of the characteristics of local context (geography, climate, isolation, population, needs and resources) when designing technological systems.

Biotechnology: A range of different molecular technologies such as gene manipulation and gene transfer, DNA typing and cloning of plants and animals.

BOP business: Businesses targeting people in BOP, which stands for "bottom/base of the pyramid".

Convention on Biological Diversity: A global agreement addressing all aspects of biological diversity, including genetic resources, species and ecosystems.

CGIAR: The Consultative Group on International Agricultural Research, a strategic alliance that unites organizations involved in agricultural research for sustainable development with the donors that fund such work.

Cloud computing: A means of accessing an expanded range of modern ICT business solutions, delivered via the internet.

CRM practice: Management practices which can help organizations develop business intelligence about their customers and their preferences and practices, enabling businesses to understand and retain current customers and acquire new ones.

Customer relationship management: A class of information systems supporting all aspects of interaction that a business has with its customers, whether it is sales or service-related, and typically enabling the business to streamline and enhance the operations of its sales, marketing and customer service teams.

Disaster management information system: An information system developed and used for disaster management purposes.

Design science research: The design of novel or innovative artefacts and the analysis of the use and/or performance of such artefacts to improve and understand the behaviour of aspects of information systems. It is generally motivated by "awareness of a problem".

Enterprise resource planning: Business management application or software that allows an organization to use a system of integrated applications to manage the business.

Ethnologue: A compendium of information about the world's languages, available online and in print form.

FOSS adoption: The recent and growing practice of individuals, companies, organizations and governments transitioning to or adopting free and open source software.

Free and open source software: Software that is both free and open source. It is liberally licensed to grant users the right to use, copy, study, change and improve its design through the availability of its source code.

Free Software and Open Source Foundation for Africa: A non-profit foundation with a vision to promote the use of FOSS and the FOSS model in African development.

Genome: Complete set of genetic material of an organism.

Geographic information system: A system that integrates hardware, software and data for capturing, managing, analysing and displaying all forms of geographically referenced information.

Germplasm: A collection of genetic resources for an organism (e.g. germplasm for plants may be stored as a seed collection).

GNOME: A graphical user interface desktop environment developed and distributed as free software.

GNU: A recursive acronym for "GNU's Not Unix". A Unix-like operating system ultimately developed by the GNU Project focusing on creating a complete Unix-compatible software system composed of free software.

Health information system: A health information system is both software architecture and a discipline at the intersection of information science and healthcare. It deals with the resources, devices and methods required to optimize the acquisition, storage, retrieval, statistical calculation and use of information in health and medicine.

Healthcare public system: The organization of people, institutions and resources to deliver healthcare services to meet the health needs of target populations using public resources.

Information and communication technologies: The physical hardware and software of personal computers and networking, or the use and study of such hardware, software and networks. Also refers to a coherent collection of processes, people and technologies brought together to serve one or multiple (business) purposes.

Information management: The overall process of planning, controlling and exploiting the information resources of an organization to support its operations. This is sometimes referred to as information resources management.

Information system: A combination of information, technology, processes and people brought together to support a given business objective.

Information systems architecture: A formal definition of the business processes and rules, systems structure, technical framework and product technologies for a business or organizational information system.

Information technology: A set of tools, processes, methodologies and associated equipment employed to collect, process and present information.

Innovation: The creation of better or more effective products, processes, services, technologies or ideas that are accepted by markets, governments and society.

Intellectual property rights: A number of distinct types of creations of the mind for which a set of exclusive rights are recognized.

Kamusi Project: An NGO dedicated to producing free resources for African languages.

LAMP stack: LAMP is the acronym for the most common FOSS stack utilizing the GNU/Linux operating system, Apache web server, MySQL database and PHP/Perl/Python programming language.

Linux: An operating system consisting of FOSS components. It is developed with the help of volunteers geographically distributed around the globe.

Linux, Apache, MySQL and PHP: A solution stack of FOSS that forms the principal components to build a viable general-purpose web server.

Linux Terminal Service Project: A Linux thin-client server.

Locale: The set of data needed to configure a device for a particular language and country.

Localization: The process of making software suitable for use in a particular language and region.

Maturity assessment: A systematic process of examining and evaluating the quality of a specific FOSS application to determine whether the software is ready for enterprise use. Existing frameworks for maturity assessment include the Open Source Maturity Model (OSMM), Qualification and Selection of Open Source Software (QSOS) and the Business Readiness Rating (BRR).

Mobile banking: Banking services provided through mobile phones. For example, in Kenya, M-PESA and M-KESHO are famous mobile banking services for money transfer and saving respectively.

mSME: A categorization of businesses as micro, small and medium-sized enterprises (SMEs), typically based on criteria relating to staff headcount or turnover.

One Laptop Per Child: A project aiming at providing one laptop per child in most developing, and some developed, countries.

OpenOffice: A FOSS productivity suite for Windows, Macintosh and GNU/Linux. It includes a word processor (Writer), spreadsheet (Calc), presentations (Impress), database (Base) and graphics (Draw). Forked from OpenOffice in 2010, libreOffice is another productivity suite providing the same functionality.

Open Unified Process: An open source product that packages agile software development principles with best practices and guidelines adapted from the Rational Unified Process (RUP) in a lightweight process framework that preserves many of RUP's essential characteristics of iterative use and case- and scenario-driven development.

Operating system: The central software of a computer, which manages booting, user interface and program launching. Common ones include Microsoft Windows, Macintosh Mac-OS and GNU/Linux, each of which has many versions available.

Patent: A form of IPR that consists of a set of exclusive rights granted by a sovereign state to an inventor or their assignee for a limited period of time in exchange for the public disclosure of an invention.

Peace Corps: A US government programme to send skilled professionals to developing countries for two years with the goals of helping the people of interested countries in meeting their need for trained men and women, helping to promote a better understanding of Americans on the part of the peoples served and helping to promote a better understanding of other peoples on the part of Americans.

Peer-to-peer funding: Funding scheme to provide money directly to a targeted person through websites. "Peer to peer" means the same as "person to person". It is a by-product of internet technologies, especially Web 2.0.

Rural and isolated areas: Areas characterized by being far away from urban centres and having a lack of communication infrastructures (roads, telephone lines, etc.). These areas usually have a low population density and a subsistence economy.

Service learning: A teaching and learning method which combines classroom-based instruction with service provision to the community.

Service-oriented architecture: The policies, practices and frameworks that enable application functionality to be provided and consumed as sets of services published at a granularity relevant to the service consumer. Services can be invoked, published and discovered, and are abstracted away from the implementation site using a single, standards-based form of interface.

SIL International: A non-profit organization whose main purpose is to study, develop and document languages.

Small Business Association of Jamaica: A private non-profit business organization to foster the growth and development of businesses and professional groups and represent the entire small and micro business sector.

Social networking service: An online service to reflect social networks and relations among users. Social networking services include Facebook, MySpace, Twitter, etc.

Software as a service (SaaS): A software delivery method that provides access to software and its functions remotely as a web-based service. It allows organizations to access common business functionality at a cost typically less than paying for equivalent licensed applications. SaaS is one of three common branches of cloud computing.

Statistical Institute of Jamaica: The authorized government agency with responsibility to collect, compile, analyse, abstract and publish statistical information relating to the commercial, industrial, social, economic and general activities and condition of the people of Jamaica.

Sustainable agriculture: The practice of farming using principles of ecology. It is also the study of relationships between organisms and their environment.

Sustainable development: "Development that meets the needs of the present without compromising the ability of future generations to meet their own needs."

Telediagnosis: A diagnosis made at a remote location and based on the evaluation of data transmitted from instruments that monitor the patient via a transfer link to a diagnostic centre.

Telemedicine: The use of medical information exchanged from one site to another via electronic communications to improve patients' health status.

Terminator technology (suicide seeds): Methods to restrict the use of genetically modified plants by causing second-generation seeds to be sterile. Technological products produced by this method.

Thin-client server: A thin-client server allows many computers to connect and run their operating system off one server. This has the advantage of allowing multiple computers with very limited hardware capabilities to run all their programs from a single more powerful computer, and all configuration settings to be controlled from a central account.

Ubuntu: A distribution of the GNU/Linux operating system produced and distributed free of charge by the Canonical company. Ubuntu is originally a Debian-derived Linux distribution.

Unicode: A series of character-encoding standards intended to support the characters used by a large number of the world's languages.

West African Senior School Certificate Examination: A standardized test created by the West African Examinations Council and taken by all students upon completion of secondary school in Ghana, Nigeria, Sierra Leone, Gambia and Liberia.

Web 2.0: A new trend of web services which facilitate user-centred information production and sharing, in contrast to traditional web services in which users are merely passive viewers of websites.

WiFi adapted for long distances: Equivalent to long-range WiFi, systems are based on the WiFi standard with some parameters modified to allow communication over a range up to hundreds of kilometres.

Xubuntu: A distribution of the Linux operating system similar to Ubuntu but with lower hardware requirements. Xubuntu is produced and distributed free of charge by a community of FOSS developers.

Index

Bold refers to glossary definition.

ABET. *See* Accreditation Board for Engineering and Technology (ABET)
AbiWord, 293
Aboriginal groups in Australia, 179
Accreditation Board for Engineering and Technology (ABET), 80, 87
actor-network theory, 10
adaptation of technologies, 94, 270, **321**
Adobe, 167
African Network for Localization (ANLoc), 165, 167–68, 178–80
Agreement on Trade-Related Aspects of Intellectual Property Rights (TRIPS), 27–28, 34, 42
AgriBazaar initiative, 34, 38, 41
agricultural biotechnology, 24–30, 32–33, 35–36, 42–43
Agriculture Department of Malaysia, 34
Agrobacterium tumefaciens gene transfer patent thicket, 35
Ajb'atz' Enlace Quiché [NGO], 84
Algeria, 82–83, 137, 205
Amazon.com's EC2, 231
American Cyanamid, 29
American Telemedicine Association, 266

ANLoc. *See* African Network for Localization (ANLoc)
ANLoc 100 African locales initiative
  African diaspora contacts, 174
  African languages *vs.* English equivalent data fields, 177–78
  Africa's 2,000 languages, 169, 178
  Afrigen software, 168, 171, 175–77, 179
  Afrigen users, list of 294 locales configured for, 171
  Amharic locale and Afrigen software, 166
  Amharic locale data, 167
  ANLoc, first phase of, 168
  ANLoc members, professional networks of, 180
  CLDR dataset revised to accommodate a non-English orientation, 178
  CLDR Survey Tool, 167–68, 178–80
  cyber cafés, 171
  data collection success rate, 176–77
  data collection to build a locale for a language, 169
  English help menu, 167
  Ethnologue, 169–70, 174, 322
  Goethe Institute in Yaoundé, 175
  Goethe Institute of Cameroon, 179–80
  H-Africa academic mailing lists, 180

325

326 INDEX

ANLoc 100 African locales initiative (cont.)
  Kamusi Project, 165, 174, 322
  Kenyan languages completed by the University of Nairobi, 175
  Kwasio language, 171
  L10n project, 165, 167–69
  language localization (L10n), 164, 167–68, 178–79
  locale data for languages throughout the continent, generated, 180
  LocaleGen, 167
  mother-tongue literacy, lack of, 180
  multilingual FOSS project, 168
  School of Computing and Informatics at the University of Nairobi, 174
  social networks to locate project participants, 173–76
  Swahili, 66, 164, 169–70, 172–73
  Tamazight speakers, 175–76
  Tanzania, 120 languages spoken in, 170
  Unicode consortium developed CLDR, 167
  vandalized data, 175
  volunteer recruitment, complications of, 171–73
  W3C internationalization workshop, 166
  Waswahili ethnic group, 169
  written systems for mother tongue language unknown, 171
anti-virus. *See also* computer viruses
  programs, 16, 288, 292–93, 297, 299
  updates, 16
Apache web server, 18, 51, 160, 317
Apple, 160
APToncD disks, 302
Asian Disaster Preparedness Center, 126
assemblage, 10–12, 14, 16–20

Bangladesh, 56, 60, 137
Barcelona School of Informatics of Universitat Politècnica de Catalunya (BarcelonaTech), 76, 80–81, 94
  Institute for Sustainability, 81
  Technology for Everyone (TxT), 81–82
base of the pyramid (BOP), 60–61, **321**
Bayh-Dole Act, 28
Beaumont Hospital (Ireland), 101
Berkeley Software Distribution style of licence, 98

best practices. *See* open source software best practices
β-glucuronidase (GUS) reporter gene, 35
bioinformatics, 26, 42
BioLinux/GPLPG-MTA approach, 34
BioLinux open source, 37
Biological Innovation for Open Society (BiOS), 26, 33–35, 40, 42
BiOsentinels project, 35
biotech
  companies, 29, 33
  crops, 24, 29, 33, 42
  industries, 28, 30–31, 40
  innovation like golden rice, 29
  patents, 29
biotechnological
  innovation, 35
  tools, 33, 35
biotechnologists, 33, 36
biotechnology, 24–26, 34, **321**. *See also* open source biotechnology
  advances, 37
  R&D, 24, 43
  resources and commercialization strategy, 36
  techniques and advances, 37
blogging, 63
blogs, 289
BOP. *See* base of the pyramid (BOP)
Brazil, 50–51, 54, 101, 137, 213, 215, 237
broadband connections, 15
Brundtland Report, 1

Cáceres and Fuenlabrada (Spanish hospitals), 276
Calibre, 144
Cambia. *See* Centre for the Application of Molecular Biology to International Agriculture (Cambia)
Capital for Africa, 61
Casa Guatemala orphanage, 85–86, 89
Catholic University of Peru, 266
  Rural Telecommunication Group, 267
Cauca University in Colombia, 266
CBD. *See* Convention on Biological Diversity (CBD)
CBSE. *See* component-based software engineering (CBSE)
CCD. *See* Cooperation for Development Centre (CCD)
CD-ROM drives, 290–91, 294

cell-phone-based internet, 291
Centre for Public Service Innovation [South Africa], 96
Centre for the Application of Molecular Biology to International Agriculture (Cambia)
  Cambia initiative, 25–26, 35–36
Centro Peruano de Estudios Sociales, 83
CEO. *See* chief executive officer (CEO)
CGIAR. *See* Consultative Group on International Agricultural Research (CGIAR)
Chancay-Huaral irrigation district, 83
chief executive officer (CEO), 110, 113, 216–17, 223, 225
Chile, 101
China, 54, 101, 125, 131, 144
  Integrated Information System for Natural Disaster Mitigation, 131
CLDR. *See* Common Locales Data Repository (CLDR)
Client Satisfaction Survey, 15
cloud computing, 219, 228, 231, 235, 239, **321,** 324
Colombia, 37, 82, 84, 91, 266–67, 272, 279
Common Locales Data Repository (CLDR), 165, 167–68, 171, 178–80
  CLDR 2.0, 168, 171
  CLDR dataset revised to accommodate a non-English orientation, 177–78
  Survey Tool, 167–68, 178–80
component-based software engineering (CBSE), 60–61, 234
Computer System for Meteorological Services (COSMETS), 131
computer viruses, 16–17. *See also* anti-virus
Consortium for Open Source Software in the Public Administration (COSPA), 142, 144, 153
Consultative Group on International Agricultural Research (CGIAR), 32, **321**
  General Challenge Program, 37
Convention on Biological Diversity (CBD), 27–28, 34, 42, **321**
Cooperation for Development Centre (CCD) [Spain], 81, 94
copyleft open source mechanism, 26–27, 36
Cornell University (U.S.), 36
corporate social responsibility (CSR), 60–61

COSMETS. *See* Computer System for Meteorological Services (COSMETS)
COSPA. *See* Consortium for Open Source Software in the Public Administration (COSPA)
Council for Scientific and Industrial Research (CSIR) [South Africa], 96–97, 101, 103–5, 107–8, 118
Creative Commons, 25
  licensing, 279
CRM. *See* customer relationship management (CRM)
crop varieties, 24
crowdsourcing, 20, 68, 158
CSIR. *See* Council for Scientific and Industrial Research (CSIR)
CSR. *See* corporate social responsibility (CSR)
Cuba, 82, 213, 237, 266
customer relationship management (CRM)
  about, 86, 161, 321
  in Jamaican SMEs, 213, 226, 230–31, 234, 236–38
cyber cafés, 171

data mining, 15
Debian-based GNU/Linux operating system, 272
Debian Linux Community, 25
Demola [Finland], 209
Department of Public Service & Administration [South Africa], 205
Department of Science and Technology [South Africa], 96
design science research, 219–21, **321**
Deutsche Gesellschaft für Technische Zusammenarbeit (GTZ), 50–51
developing contexts, 8
development NGOs in Iran
  copyright and international codes on intellectual property, 244
  development NGOs, four criteria for, 245
  Firefox *vs.* Internet Explorer, preference for, 252
  FOSS, advantages and disadvantages of, 246–247, 256
  FOSS, challenge in Iran, 243–44, 258
  FOSS, knowledge of respondents about, 250, 252

development NGOs in Iran (cont.)
  FOSS, percentage use of, 254
  FOSS, use by Iranian NGOs, 243, 249
  FOSS applications for NGOs, 255
  FOSS spirit of a voluntary movement, ethics of collaboration and a philosophy of openness and freedom, 245
  FOSS training workshop, NGOs' willingness to attend, 256
  Iranian laws protect domestic software producers and not foreign software, 244
  Iranians prefer software in their own language, 244
  Linux operating system, six reasons for not using, 252–53
  literature review, 246–48
  NGO networks facilitate FOSS use, 245
  NGOs' activities, fields of respondent, 251
  research methodology, 248–49
  software piracy, widespread, 244
  as stakeholders in sustainable development, 243
  US sanctions and Western software, 243–44
DFSA. See Digital & Free Software Association (DFSA)
diagnostic support tools, 276–78
Diamond v. Chakrabarty case, 28
Digital & Free Software Association (DFSA), 203
disaster management (DM)
  capacity gaps, 130
  case studies, 131–33
  components of, 129
  defined, 125
  information technology and, 127–30
  International Strategy for Disaster Reduction, 128
  life cycle, 128, 135
  piecemeal use of information systems and technologies, 130
  Sahana disaster management system, 132
  sustainable development and natural, 125–26
  sustainable development intervention and, 122
disaster management information systems (DMIS), 129–31, 133–35, 139

disease resistance, 31
Django web platform, 277
DM. See disaster management (DM)
DMIS. See disaster management information systems (DMIS)
Dow Chemical, 28

earthquakes, 135
  in Haiti, 66, 68, 124
  Indian Ocean, 124
  in northern Pakistan, 132
  in Yogjakarta, Indonesia, 132
Eclipse project, 160
e-commerce, 213, 219, 225, 230
Ecuador, 266, 820
e-government, 2
EHAS. See Enlace Hispano Americano de Salud (Hispano American Health Link)
e-health, 2, 266
e-learning, 2, 270
Elective ICT Club, 294
electrocardiograph adapted for rural areas, 277
Engineers without Borders, 266, 270
Enlace Hispano Americano de Salud (Hispano American Health Link) (EHAS), 263, 266–82. See also Peruvian public healthcare system and FOSS
enterprise resource planning (ERP)
  about, 104, 147, 321
  FOSS in Jamaican SMEs, 213, 226, 238
epidemiological information, exchange, 270
epidemiological surveillance systems, 263, 265, 267–68
ERP. See enterprise resource planning (ERP)
Esprit Libre, 203
EST. See expressed sequence tag (EST)
Ethnologue (publication), 169–70, 174, **322**
EU. See European Union (EU)
European Commission on Multilingualism, 171
European Higher Education Area, 82
European Innovation Relay Centres, 161
European Union (EU)
  FOSS adoption processes, 143
  ICT environment survey, 222
  Open Source Observatory, 149

INDEX 329

per capita GDP and Windows XP licence fees, 137
personnel, 20
Public Licence courses, 155
expressed sequence tag (EST), 30

Facebook, 63, 65, 67, 174, 179–80, 289–90
federations
   for infrastructures, 9–12
   learning and FOSS, 14–17
   learning for, 12–14
Fedora-tn, 203
FEMA GIS [United States], 131
FET timetables, 289
Finland FOSS adoption, 185–86, 188, 191, 204–6, 208–9
Finpro, 209
Firefox (web browser), 51, 98, 104, 106, 179, 250–51, 258
First Nations in North America, 179
flash drives, 287, 290, 294, 296–97, 303, 308–10
FLOSSMETRICS, 144, 156
FOSS. *See* free and open source software (FOSS)
FOSS4D. *See* FOSS for development (FOSS4D)
FOSS adoption, 127, 138, 141, 143–45, 147, 154–55, 160, 185–86, 188, **322**
FOSS Bazaar, 25
FOSSFA. *See* Free Software and Open Source Foundation for Africa (FOSSFA)
FOSS for development (FOSS4D). *See also* Information and communication technology (ICT)
   advocacy, purpose of current, 57–58
   collaboration between ordinary people from both Northern and Southern worlds, 70
   earthquake in Haiti and crowdsourcing, 68
   to help the poor improve their lives, 48
   international development, trends in, 60–61
   new development paradigm, challenges facing, 67–69
   new development paradigm, projects as sign of, 66–67
   "peer-to-peer funding," 61
   projects, 51, 58–70

   projects enable local people, 62, 65
   sustainable model for, 68–69
   users are the "have-nots" who do not have enough resources, skill or knowledge, 62
   voluntarism, 48, 68
   Web-community-based FOSS development involving engineers in developing countries working with experienced engineers, 65
FOSS in disaster management
   China's Integrated Information System for Natural Disaster Mitigation, 131
   Computer System for Meteorological Services (COSMETS), 131
   in developing countries, 135–38
   disaster management information systems (DMIS), 129–31, 133–35, 139
   FEMA GIS [United States], 131
   FOSS disaster management system can be readily distributed, localized and customized according to requirements of region or community, 132
   FOSS platform using the LAMP software stack, 132
   four freedoms for users, 126
   GeoCMS24, 132
   GeoCMS system, 133
   global hazards and disaster landscape, 125
   hazard risk analysis and efficient natural DM, supports, 122
   India's disaster management communication, network and information system in Maharashtra, 131
   Indonesia Disaster Management Information System, 131
   in information systems that enhance DM, 127
   innovation in practice of DM, 125
   IT solutions, low-cost, 124
   management information system (MIS), 130
   MapServer application, 133
   proprietary software *vs.*, 126
   sustainable development and, 126–27
   Tikiwiki GeoCMS [Fiji], 132–33
   Vulnerability Atlas of India, 131

330 INDEX

FOSS in Jamaican SMEs
  awareness programme for business owners about the value of ICT adoption, 237
  business applications and key influences in ICT, 227
  cloud computing, 219, 228, 231, 235, 239, 321
  component-based methodologies, hybrid adaptation of agile and, 233–34
  customer relationship management (CRM), 213, 226, 230–31, 234, 236–38
  design science research, survey design, 222–25
  design science research guidelines, 219–21
  design science research methodology, research phases using, 221
  design science research sample characteristics, 224–25
  developing countries, insights and implications for policy and practice in, 235–38
  e-commerce, 213, 219, 225, 230
  enterprise resource planning (ERP), 213, 226, 238
  FOSS, awareness and perceptions of, 229
  FOSS, workshops on, 229–32
  FOSS and office productivity applications, 226
  FOSS awareness and hosted service models, 227–29
  FOSS business applications and internet-based software delivery mechanisms, 239
  FOSS perceived as low cost, unsupported, unfamiliar and risky, 228, 231
  human resource management software, 230
  ICT adoption, determinants of, 228
  ICT enables business expansion or innovation, 217
  ICT enhances economic growth by making other sectors of the economy more efficient which attracts investment, 215
  ICT environment and internet, 225–26
  ICT in business, attitudes towards, 226–27
  ICT literacy challenge, 216
  information system service options, hosted, 230
  micro-enterprises generate 40 per cent of the country's GDP, 213
  Mona School of Business, 222
  mSMEs, low adoption rates by, 213
  mSMEs and IT, 217, 219
  mSMEs in Jamaica, 218
  open source business applications, 233, 235
  open source software adoption, free and, 215–16
  Small Business Association of Jamaica (SBAJ), 223
  SME business case studies, 236–37
  SME FOSS business implementation, ICT artifacts to support, 235
  SME FOSS business solution portfolio, 232–35
  SMEs, determinants of ICT adoption in, 213, 216–17
  SMEs, horizontal and vertical FOSS solutions for, 221
  SMEs, ICT is important driver for development and growth in, 214
  SMEs and e-applications, 213, 217–19
  Statistical Institute of Jamaica, 223
  women-owned businesses in Jamaica, 225
France, 101, 165, 205
free and open source software (FOSS). *See also* Information and communication technology (ICT)
  adaptability to local needs, 138
  adoption, negative and positive factors in, 144–46
  advantages and disadvantages of, 247
  advantages for NGOs, 246, 256
  advantages *vs.* disadvantages of, 281–82
  advocacy, 57–58
  alternative to commercial software, 51
  assemblages address and solve problems which do not have a pure local or global solution, 16
  automated processes *vs.* manual ones, 88
  avoids path dependencies and vendor lock-ins, 19
  awareness and hosted service models, 227–29
  awareness and perceptions of, 229
  benefits are flexibility, security, reliability, performance, high return on investment, reduced TCO and proliferation of innovation, 139

INDEX 331

benefits of collaborative development models do not materialize for the majority of companies and public authorities, 141
Biological Innovation for Open Society (BiOS), 26, 33–35, 40, 42
broadband communications systems tend not to be FOSS solutions, 281
business applications and internet-based software delivery mechanisms, 239
code can be obtained, viewed, changed and redistributed without royalties or other limitations, 136
collaborative and community-driven model of software development and maintenance, 127
copyleft licence, 26
copyright violations, 52
cost, low, 52
cost reduction and broad potential for customization, 247
costs of development and long-term support of solutions developed, 280
Cuba, Venezuela and Brazil have used FOSS as a catalyst for a wider diffusion of ICT, 213, 237
customer relationship management (CRM), 86
developing countries, FOSS benefits are not recognized in, 188
developing countries, 2, 187
disruptive effect of, 88
economic advantages, 53–54
educational software with low hardware requirements, 286
electric power supply is unreliable and limited internet bandwidth, 67
federative attitude as constitutive in designing and implementing FOSS-based information systems, 21
Finland and FOSS adoption, 185–86, 188, 191, 204–6, 208–9
fluidity inscribes a variety of context-bound socio-technical arrangements, 19
FOSS4D projects, 51, 58–70
FOSS *vs.* proprietary software, 64
free to users who are able to understand how to use it, 164
gap between FOSS rationale and reality, 53

global software companies *vs.*, 93
GPL software must be licensed under a GPL compatible licence, 26
HapMap Project for mapping haplotypes of human genome, 26
"humanitarian FOSS" as application of FOSS to alleviate human suffering, 132
ICT4D projects, 280
ICT industry, fosters, 53
ICT literacy is a serious problem, low level, 68
"implementation is the next big thing in IT and business," 136
as important conduit for open access to knowledge and innovation, 215
independence in developing countries, redefines, 138
infrastructure, requires adequate, 87
infrastructures enable processes of experimentation, discovery and invention through trial and error, 20
for international development, 49, 70
in Iran is a major challenge, 243–44
IT development strategies and a broader infrastructure, 20
in Kerala state in India, 13–15, 18–19
key technology to drive and strengthen role (and adoption) of ICT, 185
language customization by people in local communities, 248
for learning, 14–17
learning in the light of the actual and possible role of FOSS, 20–21
learning opportunity, 52
licenses used by free software and open source, 25
Linux scores high on participation in code writing and software modularity, 18
localization (L10n), 52, 164, 167–68, 178–79
local needs, adapts to, 138
local people don't find its strengths attractive, 48
low-cost entry point into the information and internet age, 127
lower cost of ownership and IT innovation, 136–37
for mainstream corporate business solutions, 136

332   INDEX

free and open source software (FOSS) (cont.)
  meaningful only with collaboration of a wide
    community that shares the effort and responsibility, 282
  merits of, 50–53
  minority language, localized for a, 144
  modularized system enables projects to assign complete parts of the system to distributed nodes, 18–19
  multimedia content to schools and, 286
  myths, 2
  new actors in the development field, brings, 70
  new development paradigm, as driver for, 64–66
  new development paradigm, FOSS-enable, 59
  new role of, 58–66
  office productivity applications, 226
  100 Locales Initiative was first effort at FOSS development for multiple languages, 176
  open source licensing, 159–60
  open source programs such as Linux, Apache and BIND, 26
  open source provides a framework for community-driven content and knowledge creation, 187
  open source solutions and government spends less money on buying licences of proprietary software, 187
  participatory design principles which promote learning processes, 11
  perceived as low cost, unsupported, unfamiliar and risky, 228, 231
  pirated versions of proprietary software vs., 257
  projects have the potential to be localized into any language, 179
  promoting local knowledge of, 294–97
  proprietary software is too expensive for many developing countries, 137–38
  proprietary software vs., 92
  relevance to users at local level, 55–57, 70
  replication of development projects in similar settings, 86, 92
  resilient and allows localization of software applications, 127
  role models, lacks, 248
  Sahana disaster management system (Sri Lanka), 67–68, 70, 132, 248
  in schools in developing countries, 286
  security, more, 53
  service learning complements, 87
  socio-technical fragmentation of FOSS-based systems, 21
  software, 291, 294
  software development and distribution model, 186
  software errors can take a long time to get fixed, 88
  spirit of a voluntary movement, ethics of collaboration and a philosophy of openness and freedom, 245
  supplier independence and quicker availability of patches and updates, 247
  sustainable processes for positive change supported by, 74
  technologies and intellectual property rights, 3
  technologies for sustainable development, 3, 317
  technology and business solution, 127
  technology diffusion and adoption, 3
  transcends geographical and cultural boundaries, 2
  Tropical Disease Initiative, 26
  Tunisia, FOSS studies in, 190
  Tunisian software industries, adoption in, 186
  user's skill level, 54–55
  vendor lock-in, prevents, 52
  "viral effect," principle of, 26
  volunteers collaboratively create software for the common good, 48
  Windows XP licence fees, per capita GDP and piracy, 137
  workshops on, 229–32
Free Software and Open Source Foundation for Africa (FOSSFA), 126, 136, 180, 292
  Idlelo conference, 301
Free Software Foundation (FSF), 49
FreeWays, 203
Fundatel (Argentinean foundation), 276

GDP. *See* gross domestic product (GDP)
General Public License (GPL), 25–26, 39, 98, 279

INDEX   333

General Public License for Plant
    Germplasm (GPLPG), 34, 36
gene-scape, 37
Genetech, 29
genetically modified (GM), 28
genetic use restriction technology (GURT),
    30–31
genome, **322**
    human, 26, 37
    Mycobacterium tuberculosis, 38
Genuine Windows licences, 298
GeoCMS system, 133
geographic information system (GIS), 15,
    17, 131, 322
Geo-Info software, 17
Germany, 101, 185
germplasm, 37, **322**
GES. *See* Ghana Education Service
    (GES)
Ghana Education Service (GES), 298,
    300
GIMP, 289, 304
GIS. *See* geographic information system
    (GIS)
global maps, 125
global South, 20, 33, 268
GM. *See* genetically modified (GM)
GNOME, 167, **322**
GNU, 322
GNU General Public License, 98
GNU/Linux
    Debian-based, 272
    open source, 35
    operating system, 16, 35, 138, 272, 274,
        282, **322,** 323–24
    stack, 317
GNU Project, **322**
Goethe Institute in Yaoundé, 175
Goethe Institute of Cameroon, 179–80
    Going Kompyuta project, 179
golden rice, 29, 33
Google, 136
    chat, 290
    Maps, 66
Go Open Source Conference
    (Johannesburg), 102
GPL. *See* General Public License (GPL)
GPLPG. *See* General Public License for
    Plant Germplasm (GPLPG)
grant-back mechanism, 36, 39–40
gross domestic product (GDP), 137–38, 213,
    215

GTZ. *See* Deutsche Gesellschaft fur
    Technische Zusammenarbeit (GTZ)
Guatemala, 82, 84–86, 89, 91, 144. *See also*
    ICT for development (ICT4D)
Guinsaugon landslide [Philippines], 132
GURT. *See* genetic use restriction
    technology (GURT)
GUS reporter system, 36
Gutenberg Project, 289–90, 306, 308, 310

Haiti, 82, 124
    earthquake, 66, 68, 124
Hawaiian Papaya Growers Co-operative,
    36
HC. *See* health centre (HC)
healthcare public system, **322**
health centre (HC), 262–64
health data reporting software, 16
health information system (HIS), 9, 11–12,
    278, 322
health post (HP), 263–64
HF. *See* high frequency (HF)
HF/VHF bands for telemedicine networks,
    272
high frequency (HF), 267
HIS. *See* health information system (HIS)
HP. *See* health post (HP)
HRD module. *See* Human Resource
    Development (HRD module)
Huazhong University (China), 36
Human Resource Development (HRD
    module), 15
human resource management software,
    12–13, 230
human-scale engineering, 82

IBM, 67, 136
ICSU. *See* International Council for Science
    (ICSU)
ICT. *See* information and communication
    technology (ICT)
ICT4D. *See* ICT for development (ICT4D)
ICT for development (ICT4D), 280, 316
    Casa Guatemala orphanage and
        backpackers' hotel project, 85
    collaboration between many actors in
        developing and developed countries,
        75
    criteria frame for ICT access and use,
        78–79
    disruption in communities, potential to
        cause huge, 74

334 INDEX

ICT for development (ICT4D) (cont.)
  engineering students offer time and knowledge to develop the projects, 80
  experience from 50 projects, 74, 82
  farming communities in Peru, 83
  FOSS CRM (customer relationship management), 86
  FOSS vs. proprietary software, 92
  hardware obtained from a "reuse workshop," 81, 86
  ICT environment is lacking making development of software applications difficult, 90
  K'che' language and culture conservation project, 84–85
  means of accelerating development in countries and competitiveness in organizations, 212
  Morocco school, installed Ubuntu and FOSS educational software for, 81
  organizational barriers at local level, 89–90
  political economy of FOSS technologies and, 2
  project life-cycle tasks and responsibilities, 76–77
  projects, assessment framework for, 78
  projects, impact of, 77–79
  projects, lessons learned from, 86–93
  projects as a tools for service learning, 81–82
  projects must empower the community and offer the opportunity to develop, 77
  projects require university to have international partnership, 80
  re-engineering of local social processes by students, 92
  service learning, ICT4D and FOSS, relationship between, 79–80
  service learning as way to integrate community service with instruction and reflection, 75
  service learning might involve additional overhead, 88–89
  social learning in projects, 76
  stakeholders, 74
  students gain a sense of social responsibility and civic awareness, 82
  sustainability projects on social development, 75
  sustainability requires consensus building by all stakeholders, 93
  sustainable development requires consensus building of all stakeholders, 77
  technology acceptance model (TAM), 78
  technology can be a burden rather than a solution, 86
  tool to incorporate positive changes in developing countries, 74
  TxT projects, assessment of, 91
  unified theory of acceptance and use of technology (UTAUT) model, 78
  university academics develop projects in collaboration with students, 75
  UN Western Sahara refugee camps and information system for pharmacy warehouse and for child vaccination programme, 83–84
ict@innovation, 50–51, 56, 205
IDEF0. *See* Integration Definition for Function modelling (IDEF0)
IDRC. *See* International Development Research Centre (IDRC)
IFOSUC. *See* Iran Free/Open Source Software Users Community (IFOSUC)
IICD. *See* International Institute for Communication and Development (IICD)
ImageJ, 277
India, 11, 13, 101, 124, 126, 131, 144
Indian Council of Scientific and Industrial Research, 26
Indian National Natural Disaster Knowledge Network, 131
Indian Ocean earthquake, 124
India's disaster management system in Maharashtra, 131
Indonesia, 37, 131–32
Indonesia Disaster Management Information System, 131
information and communication technology (ICT). *See also* FOSS for development (FOSS4D); free and open source software (FOSS); ICT for development (ICT4D)
  adoption, determinants of, 228

INDEX 335

adoption of open source, studies on the, 185
African languages and, 164
in business, attitudes towards, 226–27
business expansion or innovation, enables, 217
crowdsourcing, 20, 68, 158
developing countries, for economic and social progress in, 185
developing countries lack sustainable local ICT service providers, 185
for economic and social progress in developing countries, 185
economic growth enhanced by ICT by making other sectors of the economy more efficient which attracts investment, 215
enables business expansion or innovation, 217
environment and internet, 225–26
ICT4D 1.0, 61
ICT4D 2.0, 61
in Kerala state in India, 13
literacy challenge, 216
literacy, low level, 68
local users participate as producers in, 70
mobile phones, 60–61, 63–65, 67–68, 70
M-PESA and M-KESHO in Kenya enable poor people to access financial services through mobile phones, 60
open source software and business opportunities for ICT-based companies, 187
peer-to-peer web schemes, 65
Policy and Civil Society Workshop at the UN Economic Commission for Africa, 50
rural telecommunications are a key component of infrastructure development, 50
for sustainable development, 186–87
as tool for development, 48, 61–62
UN reports suggest FOSS is a key technology to strengthen ICT, 187
Ushahidi (website), 66, 70
Web 2.0 tools, 60, 62–67, 70, 136, 316, 324
Web-community-based FOSS development involving engineers in developing countries working with experienced engineers, 65

information infrastructures, 7–8, 10, 12, 15, 20
information system
  architecture, **322**
  defined, **322**
  disaster management information systems (DMIS), 129–31, 133–35, 139
  geographic information system (GIS), 15, 17, 131, 322
  health information system (HIS), 9, 11–12, 278, 322
  management information system (MIS), 130–31 (*See also* disaster management information systems (DMIS))
innovation. *See also* intellectual property (IP)
  biotech, 29
  Centre for Public Service Innovation, 96
  collaborative data sharing and, 41
  cost of patents for, 39
  crowdsourcing and, 68
  defined, **322**
  in disaster management, 125
  European Innovation Relay Centres network of technology transfer centres, 161
  FOSS adaptation to local needs, 138
  FOSS and open access to knowledge and, 215
  FOSS and technological, 70
  FOSS increases flexibility and innovation capabilities, 142
  FOSS solutions and lower cost of ownership and IT innovation, 139
  FOSS solutions and processes foster, 185, 190
  in hardware technology, 63
  home-grown ICT, 101
  ICT-enabled business, 214, 217, 221–22, 226, 239
  ICT for development (ICT4D) area and technology innovation, 49
  in ICTs, 124
  Internet and e-commerce spur, 219
  IP protection as driving force of innovation in life sciences, 28
  IP protection impedes, 25, 32–33, 43
  IP protection on research tools leads to reduced innovations and underused knowledge, 30, 32

336 INDEX

innovation (cont.)
　IP protection restricts research tools which stifles, 43
　IP regimes and non-disclosure of most innovations, 28
　Meraka Institute of the CSIR in South Africa, 103
　multinationals have not contributed to innovation in developing countries, 25
　multinationals neglect innovation to develop orphan crops in poorer countries, 29
　national open innovation models, 207
　open innovation models, establishing, 209
　open source and agricultural, 25–27
　open source biotechnology and biological, 38
　open source communities and, 213
　open source licence policy and, 42
　open source model for, 40
　overlapping rights on research tools among multiple parties keep innovation from poor communities, 40
　patents create less innovation and adversely affect R&D, 30
　"patent thickets" and, 29
　research licence may be blocked from commercial use, 33
　software, 63
　South Africa's National Advisory Council on Innovations, 246
　for sustainable agriculture, FOSS and, 34–38
　terminator technology, 31
　transformative role of IT and evolution in, 19
　Web 2.0 tools and mobile phones, 64
Integrated Information System for Natural Disaster Mitigation [China], 131
Integration Definition for Function modelling (IDEF0), 100
intellectual property (IP). *See also* innovation; Public Intellectual Property Resource for Agriculture (PIPRA)
　adverse effects of patents on innovation, 30
　in agricultural biotechnology affects collaboration and scientific networking between developed and developing countries, 43
　BioForge's free full-text searchable database for IP informatics and analysis, 35
　BiOS open source initiative, 34
　BiOS viral licence and PIPRA's rejection of BiOS licensing terms, 40
　Cambia BiOS initiative for open source for sharing biological innovation, 35
　CBD, TRIPS and UPOV create a friendly IP system encouraging open source for innovative technologies in developing countries, 42
　CBD criticized for not recognizing, 28
　CGIAR General Challenge Program provides common pool of genomic knowledge and research tools, 37
　claims on key inputs and tools used in agricultural biotechnologies, 27
　complex due to several entities represented by different interests, 28
　criticized due to its failure to protect public interests, 32
　as driving force of innovation in life sciences, 28
　golden rice and multiple owners holding overlapping and fragmented IP rights, 29
　GURT to replace IP in developing countries, 32
　as impediment to commercialization of research within academic institutions, 33
　licensing laws and IP systems vary from country to country, 39
　multinational corporate interests are exploiting loopholes in agricultural biotechnology sector IP agreements, 28
　multinational corporate interests restrict access to distribution of seeds protected by, 27
　multinationals such as Monsanto, DuPont, Syngenta and Dow use IP to maximize profit, 28–29
　open source biotechnology for sustainable agricultural development in poorer countries, greater support and promotion required for, 43

open source IP management plan required for agricultural biotechnology, 43
patented technology may be allowed for research but results may not be commercialized, 32
patent is dominant form of IP protection in open source biotechnology, 39
patents create less innovation and adversely affect R&D, 30
plant germplasm, problems in, 34
protection by biotech companies on cash crops (corn, cotton and soybean) through patents, 29
protection by biotech industries of agricultural biotechnology, 30
protection impedes innovation, 25
protection is complex issue due to high costs involved, 38
protection on agricultural inventions, including research tools, 24
protection on research tools leads to reduced innovations and underused knowledge, 30, 32
protection serves corporate interests, 27
Public Intellectual Property Resource for Agriculture (PIPRA), 36
terminator technology targeted at developing countries, 31
threat to the supply of food and fibre to the poor in global South due to access problems to patents in the North, 33
TRIPS, UPOV, the CBD and CGIAR are not adequate to align the current IP system in developing countries, 34
WTO members are obligated under TRIPS agreement to offer IP protection to plant varieties, 28
International Council for Science (ICSU) Regional Office for Africa, 127
International Development Research Centre (IDRC) [Canada], 50, 83, 165, 167
International HapMap Project, 26, 37
International Institute for Communication and Development (IICD), 51, 54
International Open Source Network (IOSN), 50–51, 143

International Strategy for Disaster Reduction, 128
International Telecommunication Union, 63, 143
International Union for the Protection of New Varieties of Plants (UPOV), 27–28, 34, 42
Internet and Multimedia Tunisian Society, 203
internet café, 291, 294, 299, 303
inventory tools, automated software, 157
IOSN. *See* International Open Source Network (IOSN)
IP. *See* intellectual property (IP)
IP telephony, 282
Iran. *See* development NGOs in Iran
Iran Free/Open Source Software Users Community (IFOSUC), 244, 259
IT46 (Swedish social enterprise), 165, 167, 175
IT governance, 13, 130

Jamaica, 213, 217. *See also* FOSS in Jamaican SMEs

Kamusi Project, 165, 174, 322, **322**
K'che' language/culture conservation project, 84–85
Kerala health secretary, 13–14
Kiva (website), 60–61, 63, 67
Klavaro, 292
KTouch, 289, 305

L10n. *See* localization (L10n)
LAMP stack, **322**
Lanka Software Foundation, 132
LibertySoft, 203
Library Linux, 308–9
LibreOffice, 158
Linux (operating system), 51, 98, 103, 105–6, 110, **322**
Linux kernel, 160
Linux Terminal Service Project (LTSP), 293–95, 323
LocaleGen, 167
localization (L10n), 52, 164–68, 178–79, **323**
low bandwidth dial-ups, 15
LTSP. *See* Linux Terminal Service Project (LTSP)

Maemo project from Nokia, 160
Malaysia, 34, 38, 41, 136
Malaysian Institute of Microelectronic Systems, 34
Mampong Technical College of Education (Ghana) (MTCE), 292–94, 296, 299
management information system (MIS), 130–31. *See also* disaster management information systems (DMIS)
management modelling, 15
Maplecroft, 125
map mashups, 63
MapServer application, 133
maturity assessment, 220–21, 231–32, 235, 239, **323**
Mavis Beacon (typing programme), 306
MDG. *See* Millennium Development Goal (MDG)
media sharing, 63
Meego project, 160
micro, small and medium-sized enterprises (mSMEs), 212–13, 217–18, 223, 238, **323**
microfinance, 61
micro-financing, 270
Millennium Development Goal (MDG), 50, 126
Ministry for Foreign Affairs of Finland Commissioned Development Policy Research programme, 185–86
MIS. *See* management information system (MIS)
M-KESHO [Kenya], 60, 63
mobile banking, 63, **323**
mobile phones, 56, 60–61, 63–68, 70, 135, 164, 316
Mona School of Business (University of the West Indies), 222
Monsanto, 28, 32
Morocco, 81–83, 91, 144
Mozambique floods, 124
Mozilla (software), 98, 106, 167
M-PESA [Kenya], 60, 63
mSMEs. *See* micro, small and medium-sized enterprises (mSMEs)
MTCE. *See* Mampong Technical College of Education (Ghana) (MTCE)
Mycobacterium tuberculosis genome sequencing, 38
MySQL, 51, 160, 205

Nagios Core (FOSS product), 274
Nalerigu Senior Secondary School (NASS) [Ghana], 287, 290, 292
National Centre of Retirement and Social Providence, 191
National ICT for Development [Malawi], 50–51
natural disaster
  about, 123–25, 130, 132–33, 138
  causes and effects of, 133
  disaster management, 132
  DM information systems and technologies, 131
  frequency and magnitude of, 125, 138
  hotspots and vulnerable countries, 124
  Indian National Natural Disaster Knowledge Network, 131
  IT systems and resources, lack of, 124
  risk management projects, 125
  risk reduction, 131
  risk reduction and preparedness, 131
natural hazards
  defined, 123
  disaster risk reduction and, 126
  disasters caused by, 135
  FOSS and, 123
  ICT and, 123–24
  identified and classified, 133
  information and capacity gaps about, 130
  mitigation of, 138
  risks, 122
network management system (NMS), 272, 274
NGO. *See* non-governmental organization (NGO)
NMS. *See* network management system (NMS)
non-governmental organizations (NGOs), 8, 11, 20, 67–68, 81–85. *See also* development NGOs in Iran
Norway, 185

ODF. *See* Open Document Format (ODF)
Ohloh, 156
One Laptop Per Child, 54, **323**
OpenDisk, 290
Open Document Format (ODF), 104
OpenLab application, 248
OpenLazlo, 85

INDEX 339

OpenOffice (productivity suite), 18, 51, 64, 98, 104, 106, 160, 167, 258, 289, 292, 303–5, **323**
OpenOffice.org (software), 98
open source biotechnology
  adequate resources must be committed to support, 41
  adoption of, rapid, 42
  advocated for in developing countries, 25
  in agricultural practices, 43
  an alternative distributive model in technological development for agricultural innovation, 27
  benefits and constraints associated with its adoption in developing countries, 43
  collaboration of individuals sharing of discoveries in biological innovation for, 41
  constraints in adopting, 38–40
  farmer compensation for contributing to the growth of plant resources, 42
  FOSS to facilitate introduction and growth of open, 40
  information resource for farming communities, 42
  innovative traits, freely available, 38
  IP-related constraints on access to innovations in agricultural biotech vs., 43
  licensing policies, flexible, 42
  policies and legislation, effective, 41–42
  sustainable agriculture, role to play in, 42–43
  sustainable agriculture with necessary resources, 25
open source business applications, 233, 235
open source GNU/Linux operating system, 35
Open Source Initiative (OSI), 25, 34, 49–50
open source in Tunisia
  action plan for open source, 207
  business organizations, 195, 199, 207
  commercial software, market penetration of, 201
  Computing Centre of the Ministry of Public Health, 194
  development policy, relevance of FOSS to, 193–94
  educational institutions, 202–3, 207
  Finland and FOSS adoption, 185–86, 188, 191, 204–6, 208–9

FOSS, role of company participation in, 196–97
FOSS adoption, factors inhibiting, 202
FOSS and public sector, 194–95
FOSS business models in Tunisian companies, 201
FOSS educational programmes, promoting, 206–7
FOSS in an organization, consequences of using, 200–201
FOSS is inferior because it is free, 195
FOSS stakeholders, 192–93
FOSS studies in Tunisia, 190–92
higher educational institutions, 193, 207
hospitals adopt open source solutions, 194
literature review, 189–90
NGOs and FOSS, 203–4, 207
open source provides a framework for community-driven content and knowledge creation, 187
open-source-related education, 203
open source solutions and government spends less money on buying licences of proprietary software, 187
Professional Master in Open Source Software, 203
research approach: online questions and face-to-face interviews, 188–90
software business organizations, 195
software purchase and licences, central management for, 199
technology parks, private start-ups in, 194
Tunisian electricity and gas company (STEG), 191
Tunisian familiarity with FOSS concept, 192
Tunisian Ministry of Communication Technologies, 190–92, 194, 203
Tunisian national FOSS plan, 190–91, 194
Tunisian Open Source Software Unit, 190, 194, 204
Tunisian software industry and FOSS, 186, 193, 195–96
umbrella organizations, 206
open source software best practices
  automated software inventory tools, 157
  budget allocation, 148
  developing countries and cultural differences, 143–44
  developing countries and infrastructural differences, 143

340 INDEX

open source software best practices (cont.)
  EU Public Licence courses, access to, 155
  expectations from migration or adoption, 147
  fixed and mobile subscribers per head of population, 144
  functional evaluation *vs.* product name, 152–53
  incremental migrations *vs.* "big switch" transitions, 150
  information on similar transitions, seeking advice or searching for, 149–50
  interaction with communities and vendors and online sources, 151
  licences and ancillary conditions, evaluation of, 151–52
  local expert identification and skill improvement, 154–55
  management commitment to open source, 146–47
  management guidelines, 144, 146–53
  Microsoft revenues by partner type *vs.* ecosystem revenues, 149
  policy considerations, 147–58
  review of current software/IT procurement and development procedure, 148–49
  social guidelines, 145, 154–56
  software and hardware affected by the migration process, 157–58
  software packages useful during transition period, 159
  support needs, identify your, 153
  technical guidelines, 145, 155–59
  timetable, realistic, 147
  troubleshooting point, 147–58
  troubleshooting points and overall policy in management guidelines, 153
  Venice University increased work orders from companies with more than 50 employees, 142
open source software (OSS) best practices
  EU study of FOSS and reduced software research and development costs by 36 per cent, 142
  FOSS, local adaptations using the flexibility of, 158
  FOSS, provides background information on, 154
  FOSS adoption, negative and positive factors in, 144–46
  FOSS adoption and use in ICT4D for developing countries, 143
  FOSS and an active development community, 156–57
  FOSS best practices, can significantly lower costs and provide quality IT solutions for SMEs, 142
  FOSS procurement showed cost savings over five years from 20 to 60 per cent, 142
open source software migration
  announce project publicly, 108, 110–10, 116
  change management, 97, 101, 104–5, 115
  communications track, 105, 110–11, 116
  develop migration plan, 108, 110–11, 116
  document lessons learnt, 108, 110, 112, 117
  form project team, 108, 110, 116
  high-level processes, process models from, 116–17
  high-level processes: input and output resources and goals, 110
  high-level process model diagram, 109
  kick-start project, 108, 110, 116
  maintenance track, 110, 112, 117
  open standards promotes support and implementation by multiple vendors, 117
  process models, generic, 114
  Project Vula, 97, 101–8, 118–19
  Project Vula, lessons learnt, 113–18
  research and documentation track, 105–6
  roll-out track, 104–5, 110–11, 117
  support and maintenance, 110, 112–13, 115, 117–18
  technology track, 104, 110–11, 116
  training track, 105, 110–11, 116
open source software (OSS) migration. *See also* organizational open source software (OSS)
  OSS migration process model and PRM extraction, 106–13
  PRMs for organizational OSS migration, 113
OpenSource-tn, 203
OpenTTT, 144, 160, 162, 318
Open Unified Process (OpenUP), 234–35, 239, 319, 323

INDEX   341

OpenUP. *See* Open Unified Process (OpenUP)
operating system (OS)
  Debian-based GNU/Linux operating system, 272
  GNU/Linux, 16, 35, 138, 272, 274, 282, **322,** 323–24
  Linux, 51, 98, 103, 105–6, 110, **322**
  Linux operating system, six reasons for not using, 252–53
  Ubuntu, 289, 292–96, 299–304, 310
  Xubuntu, 293, 324
Organisation for Economic Co-operation and
Development, 8
organizational learning, 18, 20, 75, 92, 119
organizational open source software (OSS). *See also* process reference models (PRMs)
  collaborative development of, 102
  difficulty finding local providers offering adequate support for the technology, 102
  documented steps for migration, lack of adequate, 102
  IT environment, requires ongoing operation and maintenance of, 97
  for lower or free licence costs, easy access to source code, lower total cost of ownership, security, customizability, and stability, 101
  migration projects, 96–97
  migration projects, significant difficulty in planning and implementing, 102
  migrations are complex and require good knowledge of the OSS environment, 101
  produced by a self-organized community comprising developers, users and IT vendors, 98
  Project Vula [South Africa], 97, 101–8, 113–19
  software, driving factors for using, 96
  switching to OSS on Windows, 104
  technical evaluation of, 102
  vendor lock-in, avoidance of, 96
Organization of American States, 123
orphan crops, 29, 33, 37
Orwell High School (United Kingdom), 101
OS. *See* operating system (OS)
OSI. *See* Open Source Initiative (OSI)
OSS. *See* open source software (OSS)

Pakistan, 50, 60, 132
Pan-African Localization Network, 167
Papua New Guinea, indigenous peoples of, 179
patent, **323.** *See also* intellectual property (IP)
  misuse, 39–40
  protection, 28
  thickets, 29–30, 35
patented technology, 32–33, 36
Patent Lens, 35
patient-based data, 15
patient portals, 266
Peace Corps volunteers (PCVs)
  about, 286–87, 291, 299–300, 302, 308–9
  Bourne, Brian (PCV), 303–4
  Dobbe, Grant (Peace Corps volunteer), 293–95, 307
  at Nalerigu Senior High School (NASS), 287
  three months cultural training and two years in a deprived community, 287
Peace Corps volunteers in Ghanaian schools
  AbiWord, 293
  anti-virus programs, 16, 288, 292–93, 297, 299
  APTonCD disks, 302
  blogs, 289
  Bourne, Brian (PCV), 303–4
  CDROM drives, 290
  CD-ROM drives, 290–91, 294
  cell-phone-based internet, 291
  computer labs lacked a single DVD drive, 290
  Dobbe, Grant (PCV), 293–95, 307
  educational syllabi and government policy, 300–301
  Elective ICT Club, 294
  Facebook, 289–90
  FET timetables, 289
  flash drives, 287, 290, 294, 296–97, 303, 308–10
  FOSS, local knowledge of, 294–97
  FOSS and multimedia content to schools, 286
  FOSS educational software with low hardware requirements, 286
  FOSS in schools in developing countries, 286
  FOSS software, 286, 291, 294

Peace Corps volunteers in Ghanaian
    schools (cont.)
Free Software and Open Source
    Foundation for Africa (FOSSFA),
    292
Genuine Windows licences, 298
Ghana Education Service (GES), 298
GIMP, 289, 304
Gutenberg Project, 289–90, 306, 308, 310
hardware and OS installations, 292–94
internet café, 291, 294, 299, 303
internet connections unreliable with slow
    bandwidth, 291
internet connectivity is a key enabler of
    the FOSS movement, 292
Klavaro, 292
KTouch, 289, 305
Library Linux, 308–9
Linux Terminal Service Project (LTSP),
    293–94
Mampong Technical College of
    Education (MTCE), 292–93
Mavis Beacon, 306
MP3 files are not played by Ubuntu, 302
online open source software for Ghana
    survey, 289
OpenDisk, 290
OpenOffice, 289, 292, 303–5
Peace Corps ICT Resource CD with
    FOSS and freeware programs,
    291–92
pirated software, 297, 299–300
pirated Windows XP, 299
platform-neutral policy would free
    schools
    from being locked into expensive
    proprietary software, 300
Qimo for Kids project, 309
RAM restrictions and FOSS, 292–93
SATA drives, 289
software distribution, 290–92
SuperOS, 290, 302
test question bank, 308
timetable software, 307
Tux Paint, 289, 304–6
TuxType, 292
Ubuntu (operating system), 289, 292–96,
    299–304, 310
Ubuntu Club, 296, 299
Ubuntu Customization Kit, 302
Ubuntu forums, online, 295

Ubuntu installation, 303–4
Ubuntu internet forums, 295
Ubuntu LTSP lab, 295
Ubuntu thin-client network, 296
viruses, pirated software and the FOSS
    solution, 297–99
West African Senior School Certificate
    Examination, 300
Where There Is No Doctor (PDF), 291–92
Wikipedia for Schools, 289–90, 306–7,
    310
Windows 7, 298
Windows Vista, 298
Windows XP, 289, 292, 294, 297, 299
Windows XP Genuine Advantage check,
    299
Xubuntu (operating system), 293, 324
Zakaria, Mohammed, 295–96, 299–300
ZenCafe 2.0, 299
peer-to-peer funding, 61, **323**
Peru, 82–83, 90, 264, 266, 272, 277–79. *See
    also* ICT for development (ICT4D)
Peruvian public healthcare system and
    FOSS
diagnostic support tools, 276–78
drug delivery system, 265
EHAS, university research institutions in
    the global South and North
    partnered with, 268
EHAS Foundation (Enlace Hispano
    Americano de Salud (Hispano
    American Health Link)), 263, 266–67
EHAS interventions, evaluation of,
    278–79
EHAS model for improving healthcare,
    267–80
EHAS model for sustainable
    improvement of public healthcare
    services, 269
EHAS technology adapted, 269–70
EHAS VHF station, 271
EHAS website, 279
EHAS WiFi router, 273
e-learning platforms for capacity building,
    270
electrocardiograph adapted for rural
    areas, 277
emergency cases in rural areas,
    management of, 266
epidemiological information, exchange of,
    270

INDEX 343

epidemiological surveillance systems, 263, 265, 267–68
FOSS, costs of development and long-term support of solutions developed, 280
FOSS adaptation of radio technologies, 267
FOSS and open knowledge used throughout process of designing, constructing and maintaining telemedicine networks, 267
FOSS communication technologies and services, 279
FOSS used for network design, simulation and management, 273–74
FOSS used in every aspect of the project, 270, 282
healthcare systems in rural areas of developing countries, 263–65
health centres (HCs), 262–66
health information systems, 278
health posts (HPs), 263–67, 270, 274, 276
HF/VHF bands for telemedicine networks, 272
ICT deployments, 268
incident escalation in management framework, 276
internet access and public switched telephone network, 267
micro-financing local entrepreneurs for maintaining the network, 270
narrowband technologies adapted to data services, 271–72
network simulators like NS-2/NS-3, 274
patient clinical history, 266
primary care communication and access to information needs, 265–66
research and development (R&D), 268
rural e-health, management framework for, 275
Sistema de Interconexión Rural (Rural Interconnection System) [Bolivia], 269
stethoscope, real-time wireless, 276–77
telecommunication network for voice and data connectivity, 270–71
telecommunications networks, 267
telemedical diagnosis and information sharing, 268
telemedicine devices, 281
telemedicine networks, 266–67, 272, 274
telemedicine software and hardware, 276
WiFi adapted for long-distance links, 272–76
pharmaceutical companies, 29, 37
PHI. *See* Programme on Health Information (PHI)
PHI software developer team, 16–17
PIPRA. *See* Public Intellectual Property Resource for Agriculture (PIPRA)
pirated software, 297, 299–300
pirated Windows XP, 299
polymerase chain reaction, 29
Polytechnic University of Madrid, 266
PRM. *See* process reference model (PRM)
process modelling, 99, 107–8
process re-engineering, 99
process reference models (PRMs). *See also* organizational open source software (OSS)
   capture the acquired process knowledge of an organization, 100
   generic process model structures collected in a library, 99
   as generic solutions to improve their business performance, 100
   key generic process models identified, 97
   OSS migration, for organizational, 119
   OSS migration, for planning and executing, 97, 100
   OSS migration for lower or free licence costs, easy access to source code, lower total cost of ownership, security, customizability, and stability, 101
   OSS migration process model and PRM extraction, 106–13
   OSS migration projects, have not been used on, 100
   OSS migrations, for organizational, 113
   reduce risks associated with OSS migrations, 97
   reduce the risks and costs associated with repetitive errors in projects, 99
   represented in various modelling languages and standard notations, 100
   reusable and applicable to other organizations planning OSS migrations, 97
   set of baseline processes that can serve as a starting point for OSS, 118–19

344   INDEX

Programme on Health Information (PHI), 11, 13–15
Project Vula [South Africa], 97, 101–8, 113–19
Public Intellectual Property Resource for Agriculture (PIPRA), 25, 36, 40

Qimo for Kids project, 309
Qualification and Selection of Open Source (QSOS), 152, 156, 323

Rackspace, 231
RadioMobile, 274
radio technologies, 267
RAM restrictions and FOSS, 16, 292–93
Rational Unified Process (RUP), 234, 323
R&D. *See* research and development (R&D)
rDNA (ribosomal DNA), 29
Refugee United (website), 63
remote monitoring of vital signs, 266
remote-sensing images, 130
research and development (R&D), 24, 27, 103, 127, 142, 268
reverse engineering efforts, 16–17
Rey Juan Carlos University, 266
Rhizobium strains (TransBacter system), 35
Rockefeller Foundation, 32
RUP. *See* Rational Unified Process (RUP)
rural and isolated areas, 262–63, 268, **323**

SaaS. *See* software as a service (SaaS)
Sahana disaster management system (Sri Lanka), 67–68, 70, 132, 248
sales order management software, 230
SATA drives, 289
SBAJ. *See* Small Business Association of Jamaica (SBAJ)
SchoolNet Namibia, 248
School of Computing and Informatics at the University of Nairobi, 174
SCO Group of Utah v IBM lawsuit, 39
SecuriNets, 203
seed industry, 27, 37
service learning (SL), 75, 79–82, 87–89, **323**. *See also* ICT for development (ICT4D)
service-oriented architecture, 133, **323**
Sharif University of Technology in Tehran Advanced ICT Research Centre, 244

Sida. *See* Swedish International Development Cooperation (Sida)
SIL International, 169, 324
Sistema de Interconexión Rural (Rural Interconnection System) [Bolivia], 269
Sitecom/Netfilter lawsuit, 39
SL. *See* service learning (SL)
small and medium-sized enterprises (SMEs)
   access to the internet to access to a range of business software and services, 230
   business case studies, 236–37
   e-applications and, 213, 217–19
   FOSS business implementation, ICT artifacts to support, 235
   FOSS business solution portfolio, 232–35
   horizontal and vertical FOSS solutions for, 221
   ICT adoption in, determinants of, 213, 216–17
   ICT is important driver for development and growth in, 214
   IT and survival and competitiveness of, 212
Small Business Association of Jamaica (SBAJ), 223, 324
SMEs. *See* small and medium-sized enterprises (SMEs)
social bookmarking, 63
social media, 316
social networking, 63, **324**
social news, 63
software as a service (SaaS), 126, 197, 206, 228, 231, **324**
software development schemes, top-down, 8, 12
software distribution, 98, 290–92
software migration. *See* open source software migration
Solothurn (Swiss canton), 141
SourceForge.Net, 233
South Africa, 11, 15, 50–51, 96, 318. *See also* Project Vula [South Africa]
South Africa's National Advisory Council on Innovations, 246
South Pacific Applied Geoscience Commission, 132
Spain, 101, 270, 279. *See also* ICT for development (ICT4D)
standard process notation IDEF0, 97

State Information Technology Agency
    [South Africa], 96
Statistical Institute of Jamaica, 223, 324
sterile seed technology, 30
still image transmission, 266
Summer Institute of Linguistics, 169
Sun Microsystems, 136
SuperOS, 290, 302
sustainable agriculture, 24–25, 34, 42–43,
    318, **324**
Swahili, 66, 164, 169–70, 172–73
Swedish International Development
    Cooperation (Sida), 50, 67
Switzerland, 205
Syngenta, 28

Tactical Technology Collective, 291
TAM. *See* technology acceptance model
    (TAM)
TCO. *See* total cost of ownership (TCO)
technology acceptance model (TAM), 78
Technology for Everyone (TxT), 81–82,
    90–91
telecommunications networks, 136, 267
telediagnosis, **324**
tele-education, 281
telehealth, 266
Telematic Department of Cauca University
    in Colombia, 267
telemedicine, 278, 324
    devices, 281
    networks, 266–67, 272, 274
    software and hardware, 276
telephony, 10, 83
terminator technology, 30–32, 318, **324**
"terminator" technology, 30–32
T-GURT. *See* trait-specific genetic use
    restriction technology (T-GURT)
Thailand, 50–51, 101
Thailand ICT master plan, 51
thin-client
    based WAN, 15
    server, **323–24**
    workstations, 232
Tikiwiki GeoCMS [Fiji], 132–33
timetable software, 307
Torvalds, Linus, 7, 35
total cost of ownership (TCO), 54, 101, 137,
    139, 147–48, 318
trait-specific genetic use restriction
    technology (T-GURT), 30–31

transgenic traits, 31–32
TRIPS. *See* Agreement on Trade-Related
    Aspects of Intellectual Property
    Rights (TRIPS)
Tropical Disease Initiative, 37
Tunisia, 185–86, 188–89. *See also* open
    source in Tunisia
Tunisian Ministry of Communication
    Technologies, 190–92, 194, 203
Tunisian Open Source Software Unit, 190,
    194, 204
Tux Paint, 289, 304–6
TuxType, 292
Twitter, 174, 180
TxT. *See* Technology for Everyone (TxT)

Ubuntu
    Club, 296, 299
    Customization Kit, 302
    forums, online, 295
    installation, 303–4
    internet forums, 295
    LTSP lab, 295
    operating system, 81, 289, 292–96,
        299–304, 310, 324
    thin-client network, 296
Ubuntu Linux (computing platform), 103–4,
    112
Ubuntu-tn (club), 203, 296, 299
Ugandan University, 41
UK Office of Government Commerce,
    247
UK SMEs, 212
UN. *See* United Nations (UN)
UN Children's Fund (UNICEF), 60
UN Conference on Trade and Development
    (UNCTAD), 185, 187, 215
UN Development Programme (UNDP),
    50–51, 244
UNICEF. *See* UN Children's Fund
    (UNICEF)
Unicode, 165, 167, **324**
unified theory of acceptance and use of
    technology (UTAUT), 78
United Kingdom, 101
United Nations (UN), 8
    Agenda 21, 1
    Economic Commission for Africa (2002),
        50
    International Open Source Network,
        143

346　INDEX

United Nations (UN) (cont.)
  reports suggests FOSS is a key technology to strengthen ICT, 187
  Research Institute for Social Development Conference on Information Technologies and Social Development, 7
  Western Sahara refugee camps, 83–84
United States (US). *See also* Peace Corps volunteers in Ghanaian schools
  about, 101, 125, 131, 138, 143, 173, 205
  Agency for International Development, 60
  National Science Foundation, 67
Universidad Rey Juan Carlos de Madrid (Spain), 279
UPOV. *See* International Union for the Protection of New Varieties of Plants (UPOV)
Ushahidi (earthquake disaster website), 66, 70
UTAUT. *See* unified theory of acceptance and use of technology (UTAUT)

Validos [Finland], 206
variety-level genetic use restriction technology (V-GURT), 30–32
vendor lock-in, 19, 52, 56, 69, 96, 117, 138, 210
Venezuela, 213, 237
venture capital, 61, 205
very high frequency (VHF), 267, 271–72
V-GURT. *See* variety-level genetic use restriction technology (V-GURT)
VHF. *See* very high frequency (VHF)
VHF/ HF networks, 272
videoconferencing, 266
VMWare virtualization platform, 232
voice over IP (VoIP), 83, 272–73
vTigerCRM (FOSS application), 234, 236–37
Vula project, 97, 101–8
Vulnerability Atlas of India, 131

W3C internationalization workshop, 166
waiting time survey, 15
Water Research Council [South Africa], 96
Web 2.0 tools, 60, 62–67, 70, 136, 316, 324
web-based reporting, 15
web pivot reporter, 15
web portal, 15
West African Senior School Certificate Examination, 300, **324**
Western Sahara, 83–84, 90. *See also* ICT for development (ICT4D)
Where There Is No Doctor (PDF), 291–92
WHO. *See* World Health Organization (WHO)
WiFi over long distances (WiLD), 267, 272–76, 281, **324**
Wikipedia, 125
Wikipedia for Schools, 289–90, 306–7, 310
wikis, 63, 151
WiLD. *See* WiFi over long distances (WiLD)
Windows 7, 298–99
Windows Vista, 298
Windows XP, 289, 292, 294, 297, 299
Windows XP Genuine Advantage check, 299
"wizard" to guide users through all program installations, 16
World Health Organization (WHO), 8
World Trade Organization (WTO), 28, 244, 257
WTO. *See* World Trade Organization (WTO)

Xubuntu (operating system), 293, 324

Yahoo, 167, 249
Youth Science Association Tunisia, 203

Zabbix (FOSS product), 274
ZenCafe 2.0, 299